MAHATMA GANDHI'S

THE STORY OF MY EXPERIMENTS WITH TRUTH

–AN AUTOBIOGRAPHY

Translated from Gujarati
by
MAHADEV DESAI

V&S PUBLISHERS
VALUE & SUBSTANCE

Published by:

V&S PUBLISHERS
VALUE & SUBSTANCE

Head Office
F-2/16, Ansari Road, Daryaganj,
New Delhi-110002 ☎ 23240026, 27, 28
✉ info@vspublishers.com
www.vspublishers.com

Regional Office
5-1-707/1, Brij Bhawan (Beside Central Bank of India Lane) Bank Street, Koti,
Hyderabad - 500 095 ☎ 040-24737290
✉ vspublishershyd@gmail.com

Online Brandstore: amazon.in/vspublishers

Buy Books Online: amazon • Flipkart | **Follow us on:**

ISBN 978-93-579432-9-1
New Edition

Cataloging in Publication Data–DK
Courtesy: D.K. Agencies (P) Ltd. <docinfo@dkagencies.com>
Gandhi, Mahatma, 1869-1948, **author.**
[Satyanā prayogo, athavā, ātmakathā. English]
Mahatma Gandhi's the story of my experiments with truth : an autobiography / translated from Gujarati by Mahadev Desai. – New edition. – pages cm
Translation of: Satyanā prayogo, athavā, Ātmakathā.
Reprint.
ISBN 9789357943291
1. Gandhi, Mahatma, 1869-1948. 2. Statesmen–India–Biography. 3. Nationalists–India–Biography. I. Desai, Mahadev H. (Mahadev Haribhai), 1892-1942, translator. II. Title. III. Title: Story of my experiments with truth.
LCC DS481.G3A3 2022 | DDC 954.035092 23

Printed at : Param Offsetters, Okhla, New Delhi–110020

PUBLISHER'S NOTE

Since the beginning of our operations, we at **V&S Publishers** have been devoted to bringing you the best and widest selections of books across genres. With a standing of over 70 years in Book Publishing and in becoming one of the leading publishers of general trade books in the mass-appeal genre in India with over 1000 titles published across more than 50 categories in 9 languages, we have focused on developing a repertoire of titles that not just seek to inspire our readers to grow and flourish in life, but also spark a love for varied cultures and languages.

With a network of more than 5000 dealers across India and abroad we distribute books across print and digital formats and ensure that any need or lacuna in categories such as literature, children's stories, parenting, popular science, religion and spirituality, self-improvement, etc. is fulfilled. Our success over the last decade can be attributed to the wide acceptability of our books along with their appreciation online on ecommerce platforms.

An extensive market research and editorially driven feedback campaign that ran for over 3 years led us into publishing this unique series of Popular Bestselling Titles in English. We realized that while people were interested and wanted to read these timeless classics, they were often limited by their inability to comprehend difficult old English. Also, the unavailability of high-quality books in the local market An extensive market research and editorially driven feedback campaign that ran for over 3 years led us into publishing this unique series of Popular Bestselling Titles in English. We realized that while people were interested and wanted to read these timeless classics, they were often limited by their inability to comprehend difficult old English. Also, the unavailability of high-quality books in the local market and them getting substituted by cheaper erroneous, often duplicate books was a big challenge for readers especially in India. Owing to our network and quality of book production, we felt we are in the best position to resolve this issue and serve our customers and readers.

V&S Publishers present before you a full range of timeless books in English originally written by Bestselling Authors. These books have been identified and published after a careful consideration of their content and context. Whether it is meditative discourse by ancient philosophers and thinkers; classic tales of love and romance; motivational bestsellers for wealth and success; or masterful thrillers to keep you up through the night, these books and many others have long been considered to be the best in their respective genres. Each of these books has been compiled from its authentic source and rigorously edited to ensure ease of reading.

While there are books from multiple publishers available at lesser prices in market on these topics, what sets us apart from all of them is the quality of production and authenticity in terms of their content and editing. As a special feature, in all books, word meanings have been liberally added on each page for easy understanding especially for younger audience. Exclusive proofreading for error elimination, high class cover and inside designing makes these one of a kind and a must have for readers across demographics and geographies.

We hope these titles and this book here serve to inspire, educate, entertain, and inform you and our readers!

CONTENTS

CHAPTER 1

BIRTH AND PARENTAGE

The Gandhis belong to the Bania caste and seem to have been originally grocers. But for three generations, from my grandfather, they have been Prime Ministers in several Kathiawad States. Uttamchand Gandhi, *alias* Ota Gandhi, my grandfather, must have been a man of principle. State intrigues compelled him to leave Porbandar, where he was Diwan, and to seek refuge[1] in Junagadh. There he saluted the Nawab with the left hand. Someone, noticing the apparent discourtesy, asked for an explanation, which was thus given: 'The right hand is already pledged to Porbandar.'

Ota Gandhi married a second time, having lost his first wife. He had four sons by his first wife and two by his second wife. I do not think that in my childhood I ever felt or knew that these sons of Ota Gandhi were not all of the same mother. The fifth of these six brothers was Karamchand Gandhi, *alias* Kaba Gandhi, and the sixth was Tulsidas Gandhi. Both these brothers were Prime Ministers in Porbandar, one after the other. Kaba Gandhi was my father. He was a member of the Rajasthanik Court. It is now extinct[2], but in those days it was a very influential body for settling disputes between the chiefs and their fellow clansmen. He was for some time Prime Minister in Rajkot and then in Vankaner. He was a pensioner of the Rajkot State when he died.

Kaba Gandhi married four times in succession[3], having lost his wife each time by death. He had two daughters by his first and second marriages. His last wife, Putlibai, bore him a daughter and three sons, I being the youngest.

My father was a lover of his clan, truthful, brave and generous, but short-tempered. To a certain extent he might have been even given to carnal pleasures. For he married for the fourth time when he was over forty. But he was incorruptible[4] and had earned a name for strict impartiality in his family as well as outside. His loyalty to the state was well known. An Assistant Political Agent spoke insultingly of the

1. *refuge: a place or state of safety from danger or trouble*
2. *extinct: no longer in existence*
3. *succession: a number of people or things following one after the other*
4. *incorruptible: not susceptible to corruption, especially by bribery*

Rajkot Thakore Saheb, his chief, and he stood up to the insult. The Agent was angry and asked Kaba Gandhi to apologize. This he refused to do and was therefore kept under detention[1] for a few hours. But when the Agent saw that Kaba Gandhi was adamant, he ordered him to be released.

My father never had any ambition to accumulate[2] riches and left us very little property.

He had no education, save that of experience. At best, he might be said to have read up to the fifth Gujarati standard. Of history and geography he was innocent. But his rich experience of practical affairs stood him in good stead in the solution of the most intricate questions and in managing hundreds of men. Of religious training he had very little, but he had that kind of religious culture which frequent visits to temples and listening to religious discourses make available to many Hindus. In his last days he began reading the Gita at the instance of a learned Brahman friend of the family, and he used to repeat aloud some verses every day at the time of worship.

The outstanding impression my mother has left on my memory is that of saintliness. She was deeply religious. She would not think of taking her meals without her daily prayers. Going to *Haveli* - the Vaishnava temple - was one of her daily duties. As far as my memory can go back, I do not remember her having ever missed the *Chaturmas*[3]. She would take the hardest vows and keep them without flinching. Illness was no excuse for relaxing them. I can recall her once falling ill when she was observing the *Chandrayana*[4] vow, but the illness was not allowed to interrupt the observance. To keep two or three consecutive fasts was nothing to her. Living on one meal a day during *Chaturmas* was a habit with her. Not content with that she fasted every alternate day during one *Chaturmas*. During another *Chaturmas* she vowed not to have food without seeing the sun. We children on those days would stand, staring at the sky, waiting to announce the appearance of the sun to our mother. Everyone knows that at the height of the rainy season the sun often does not condescend to show his face. And I remember days when, at his sudden appearance, we would rush and announce it to her, She would run out to se with her own eyes, but by that time the fugitive[5] sun would be gone, thus depriving[6] her of her meal. "That does not matter," she would say cheerfully, "God

1. *detention: the action or state of detaining or being detained*
2. *accumulate: gather together a number or quantity of*
3. *Chaturmas: literally a period of four months; a vow of fasting and semi fasting during the four months of the rains; the period is a sort of long Lent*
4. *Chandrayana: a sort of fast in which the daily quantity of food is increased or diminished according as the moon waxes or wanes*
5. *fugitive: a person who has escaped from captivity or is in hiding*
6. *depriving: deny a person or place the possession or use of something*

did not want me to eat today." And then she would return to her round of duties.

My mother had strong commonsense. She was well informed about all matters of state, and ladies of the court thought highly of her intelligence. Often I would accompany[1] her, exercising the privilege of childhood, and I still remember many lively discussions she had with the widowed mother of the Thakore Saheb.

Of these parents I was born at Porbandar, otherwise known as Sudamapuri, on the 2nd October, 1869, I passed my childhood in Porbandar. I recollect having been put to school. It was with some difficulty that I got through the multiplication tables. The fact that I recollect[2] nothing more of those days than having learnt, in company with other boys, to call our teacher all kinds of names, would strongly suggest that my intellect must have been sluggish[3], and my memory raw.

1. *accompany: go somewhere with*
2. *recollect: remember*
3. *sluggish: slow moving or inactive*

CHAPTER 2

CHILDHOOD

I must have been about seven when my father left Porbandar for Rajkot to become a member of the Rajasthanik Court. There I was put into a primary school, and I can well recollect those days, including the names and other particulars of the teachers who taught me. As at Porbandar, so here, there is hardly anything to note about my studies. I could have been only a mediocre[1] student. From this school I went to the suburban[2] school and thence to the high school, having already reached my twelfth year. I do not remember having ever told a lie, during this short period, either to my teachers or to my school-mates, I used to be very shy and avoided all company. My books and my lessons were my sole companions[3]. To be at school at the stroke of the hour and to run back home as soon as the school closed-that was my daily habit. I literally ran back, because I could not bear to talk to anybody. I was even afraid lest anyone should poke fun at me.

There is an incident which occurred at the examination during my first year at the high school and which is worth recording. Mr Giles, the educational Inspector, had come on a visit of inspection. He had set us five words to write as a spelling exercise. One of the words was 'Kettle'. I had mis-spelt it. The teacher tried to prompt[4] me with the point of his boot, but I would not be prompted. It was beyond me to see that he wanted me to copy the spelling from my neighbour's slate, for I had thought that the teacher was there to supervise us against copying. The result was that all the boys, except myself, were found to have spelt every word correctly. Only I had been stupid. The teacher tried later to bring this stupidity home to me. but without effect. I never could learn the art of 'copying'.

Yet the incident did not in the least diminish my respect for my teacher. I was by nature, blind to the faults of elders. Later I came to know of many other failings of this teacher, but my regard for him remained the same. For I had learnt to carry out the orders of elders, not to scan their actions.

1. *mediocre: of only moderate or average quality*
2. *suburban: of or characteristic of a suburb*
3. *companions: a person with whom one spends time or travels*
4. *prompt: assist or encourage; supply a forgotten word or line to an actor*

Two other incidents belonging to the same period have always clung to my memory. As a rule I had a distaste for any reading beyond my school books. The daily lessons had to be done, because I disliked being taken to task by my teacher as much as I disliked deceiving[1] him. Therefore I would do the lessons, but often without my mind in them. Thus when even the lessons could not be done properly, there was of course no question of any extra reading. But somehow my eyes fell on a book purchased by my father. It was *Shravana Pitribhakti Nataka* (a play about Sharavana's devotion to his parents). I read it with intense interest. There came to our place about the same time itinerant[2] showmen. One of the pictures I was shown was of Shravana carrying, by means of slings fitted for his shoulders, his blind parents on a pilgrimage[3]. The book and the picture left an indelible impression on my mind. 'Here is an example for you to copy,' I said to myself. The agonized lament[4] of the parents over Shravana's death is still fresh in my memory. The melting tune moved me deeply, and I played it on a concertina which my father had purchased for me.

There was a similar incident connected with another play. Just about this time, I had secured my father's permission to see a play performed by a certain dramatic company. This play-*Harishchandra*-captured my heart. I could never be tired of seeing it. But how often should I be permitted to go? It haunted me and I must have acted *Harishchandra* to myself times without number. 'Why should not all be truthful like Harishchandra?' was the question I asked myself day and night. To follow truth and to go through all the ordeals Harishchandra went through was the one ideal it inspired in me. I literally believed in the story of Harishchandra. The thought of it all often made me weep. My commonsense tells me today that Harishchandra could not have been a historical character. Still both Harishchandra and Shravana are living realities for me, and I am sure I should be moved as before if I were to read those plays again today.

1. *deceiving: deliberately mislead or misrepresent the truth to*
2. *itinerant: traveling from place to place*
3. *pilgrimage: a pilgrim's journey*
4. *lament: expression of grief, sorrow*

CHAPTER 3

CHILD MARRIAGE

Much as I wish that I had not to write this chapter, I know that I shall have to swallow many such bitter[1] draughts in the course of this narrative. And I cannot do otherwise, if I claim to be a worshipper of Truth. It is my painful duty to have to record here my marriage at the age of thirteen. As I see the youngsters of the same age about me who are under my care, and think of my own marriage, I am inclined to pity myself and to congratulate them on having escaped my lot. I can see no moral argument in support of such a preposterously[2] early marriage.

Let the reader make no mistake. I was married, not betrothed[3]. For in Kathiawad there are two distinct rites, betrothal and marriage. Betrothal is a preliminary promise on the part of the parents of the boy and the girl to join them in marriage, and it is not inviolable. The death of the boy entails no widowhood on the girl. It is an agreement purely between the parents, and the children have no concern with it. Often they are not even informed of it. It appears that I was betrothed thrice, though without my knowledge. I was told that two girls chosen for me had died in turn, and therefore I infer that I was betrothed three times. I have a faint recollection, however, that the third betrothal took place in my seventh year. But I do not recollect having been informed about it. In the present chapter I am talking about my marriage, of which I have the clearest recollection.

It will be remembered that we were three brothers. The first was already married. The elders decided to marry my second brother, who was two or three years my senior, a cousin, possibly a year older, and me, all at the same time. In doing so there was no thought of our welfare, much less our wishes. It was purely a question of their own convenience[4] and economy.

Marriage among Hindus is no simple matter. The parents of the bride and the bridegroom often bring themselves to ruin over it. They waste their

1. *bitter: having a sharp, pungent taste or smell; not sweet*
2. *preposterously: utterly absurd or ridiculous*
3. *betrothed: formally engaged to be married*
4. *convenience: freedom from effort or difficulty*

substance, they waste their time. Months are taken up over the preparations in making clothes and ornaments and in preparing budgets for dinners. Each tries to outdo the other in the number and variety of courses to be prepared. Women, whether they have a voice or no, sing themselves hoarse[1], even get ill, and disturb the peace of their neighbours. These in their turn quietly put up with all the turmoil[2] and bustle all the dirt and filth, representing the remains of the feasts, because they know that a time will come when they also will be behaving in the same manner.

It would be better, thought my elders, to have all this bother over at one and the same time. Less expense and greater *eclat*. For money could be freely spent if it had only to be spent once instead of thrice. My father and my uncle were both old, and we were the last children they had to marry. It is likely that they wanted to have the last best time of their lives. In view of all these considerations, a triple wedding was decided upon, and as I have said before, months were taken up in preparation for it.

It was only through these preparations that we got warning of the coming event. I do not think it meant to me anything more than the prospect of good clothes to wear, drum beating, marriage processions, rich dinners and a strange girl to play with. The carnal desire came later. I propose to draw a curtain over my shame, except for a few details worth recording. To these I shall come later. But even they have little to do with the central idea I have kept before me in writing this story.

So my brother and I were both taken to Porbandar from Rajkot. There are some amusing details of the preliminaries[3] to the final drama e.g. smearing our bodies all over with turmeric paste but I must omit them.

My father was a Diwan, but nevertheless a servant, and all the more so because he was in favour with the Thakore Saheb. The latter would not let him go until the last moment. And when he did so, he ordered for my father special stage coaches, reducing the journey by two days. But the fates had willed otherwise. Porbandar is 120 miles from Rajkot, a cart journey of five days. My father did the distance in three, but the coach toppled over in the third stage, and he sustained[4] severe injuries. He arrived bandaged all over. Both his and our interest in the coming event was half destroyed, but the ceremony had to be gone through. For how could the marriage dates be changed? However, I forgot my grief over my father's injuries in the childish amusement of the wedding.

1. *hoarse: (of a voice) rough and harsh*
2. *turmoil: a state of great disturbance, confusion, or uncertainty*
3. *preliminaries: preceding or done in preparation for something fuller or more important*
4. *sustained: suffer*

I was devoted to my parents. But no less was I devoted to the passions that flesh is heir to. I had yet to learn that all happiness and pleasure should be sacrificed in devoted service to my parents. And yet, as though by way of punishment for my desire for pleasures, an incident happened, which has ever since rankled in my mind and which I will relate later. Nishkulanand sings: 'Renunciation[1] of objects, without the renunciation of desires, is short-lived, however hard you may try.' Whenever I sing this song or hear it sung, this bitter untoward[2] incident, rushes to my memory and fills me with shame.

My father put on a brave face in spite of his injuries, and took full part in the wedding. As I think of it, I can even today call before my mind's eye the places where he sat as he went through the different details of the ceremony. Little did I dream then that one day I should severely criticize my father for having married me as a child. Everything on that day seemed to me own right and proper and pleasing. There was also my own eagerness to get married. And as everything that my father did then struck me as beyond reproach[3], the recollection of those things is fresh in my memory. I can picture to myself, even today, how we sat on our wedding dais, how we performed the *Saptapadi*[4] how we, the newly wedded husband and wife, put the sweet *Kansar*[5] into each other's mouth, and how we began to live together. And oh! that first night.Two innocent children all unwittingly hurled themselves into the ocean of life. My brother's wife had thoroughly coached me about my behaviour on the first night. I do not know who had coached my wife. I have never asked her about it, nor am I inclined to do so now. The reader may be sure that we were too nervous to face each other. We were certainly too shy. How was I to talk to her, and what was I to say? The coaching could not carry me far. But no coaching is really necessary in such matters. The impressions of the former birth are potent[6] enough to make all coaching superfluous. We gradually began to know each other, and to speak freely together. We were the same age. but I took no time in assuming the authority of a husband.

1. *renunciation: the action of renouncing*
2. *untoward: unexpected and inappropriate or adverse*
3. *reproach: express to someone one's disapproval of or disappointment in their actions*
4. *Saptapadi: seven steps the Hindu bride and groom walk together, making at the same time promises of mutual fidelity and devotion, after which the marriage becomes irrevocable*
5. *Kansar: a preparation of wheat which the pair partake of together after the completion of the ceremony*
6. *potent: having great power; influence, or effect*

CHAPTER 4

PLAYING THE HUSBAND

About the time of my marriage, little pamphlets costing a pice, or a pie (I now forget how much), used to be issued, in which conjugal love, thrift, child marriages, and other such subjects were discussed. Whenever I came across any of these, I used to go through them cover to cover, and it was a habit with me to forget what I did not like, and to carry out in practice whatever I liked. Lifelong faithfulness to the wife, inculcated[1] in these booklets as the duty of the husband, remained permanently imprinted on my heart. Furthermore, the passion for truth was innate in me, and to be false to her was therefore out of the question. And then there was very little chance of my being faithless at that tender age.

But the lesson of faithfulness had also an untoward[2] effect. 'If I should be pledged to be faithful to my wife, she also should be pledged to be faithful to me,' I said to myself. The thought made me a jealous husband. Her duty was easily converted into my right to exact faithfulness from her, and if it had to be exacted, I should be watchfully tenacious[3] of the right. I had absolutely no reason to suspect my wife's fidelity, but jealousy does not wait for reasons. I must needs be for ever on the look-out regarding her movements, and therefore she could not go anywhere without my permission. This sowed the seeds of a bitter quarrel between us. The restraint was virtually a sort of imprisonment. And Kasturbai was not the girl to brook any such thing. She made it a point to go out whenever and wherever she liked. More restraint on my part resulted in more liberty being taken by her, and in my getting more and more cross. Refusal to speak to one another thus became the order of the day with us, married children. I think it was quite innocent of Kasturbai to have taken those liberties with my restrictions. How could a guileless[4] girl brook any restraint on going to the temple or on going on visits to friends? If I had the right to impose restrictions on her, had not she also similar right? All this is clear to me today. But at that time I had to make good my authority as a husband!

1. *inculcated: to impress upon the mind of another by frequent instruction*
2. *untoward: unexpected and inappropriate or adverse*
3. *tenacious: not readily relinquishing something; keeping a firm hold*
4. *guileless: innocent*

Let not the reader think, however, that ours was a life of unrelieved bitterness. For my severities were all based on love. I wanted to *make* my wife an ideal wife. My ambition was to *make* her live a pure life, learn what I learnt,and identify her life and thought with mine.

I do not know whether Kasturbai had any such ambition. She was illiterate[1]. By nature she was simple, independent, persevering and, with me at least, reticent[2]. She was not impatient of her ignorance and I do not recollect my studies having ever spurred her to go in for a similar adventure. I fancy, therefore, that my ambition was all one-sided. My passion was entirely centred on one woman, and I wanted it to be reciprocated. But even if there were no reciprocity, it could not be all unrelieved misery because there was active love on one side at least.

I must say I was passionately fond of her. Even at school I used to think of her, and the thought of nightfall and our subsequent meeting was ever haunting me. Separation was unbearable. I used to keep her awake till late in the night with my idle talk. If with this devouring passion there had not been in me a burning attachment to duty, I should either have fallen a prey to disease and premature death, or have sunk into a burdensome existence. But the appointed tasks had to be gone through every morning, and lying to anyone was out of the question. It was this last thing that saved me from many a pitfall.

I have already said that Kasturbai was illiterate. I was very anxious to teach her, but lustful love left me no time. For one thing the teaching had to be done against her will, and that too at night. I dared not meet her in the presence of the elders, much less talk to her. Kathiawad had then, and to a certain extent has even today, its own peculiar[3], useless and barbarous[4] *Purdah*. Circumstances were thus unfavourable. I must therefore confess that most of my efforts to instruct Kasturbai in our youth were unsuccessful. And when I awoke from the sleep of lust, I had already launched forth into public life, which did not leave me much spare time. I failed likewise to instruct her through private tutors. As a result Kasturbai can now with difficulty write simple letters and understand simple Gujarati. I am sure that, had my love for her been absolutely untainted with lust, she would be a learned lady today; for I could than have conquered her dislike for studies. I know that nothing is impossible for pure love.

1. *illiterate: unable to read or write*
2. *reticent: not revealing one's thoughts or feelings readily*
3. *peculiar: strange or odd*
4. *barbarous: savagely cruel*

I have mentioned one circumstance that more or less saved me from the disasters of lustful love. There is another worth noting. Numerous examples have convinced me that God ultimately saves him whose motive is pure. Along with the cruel custom of child marriages, Hindu society has another custom which to a certain extent diminishes[1] the evils of the former. Parents do not allow young couples to stay long together. The child-wife spends more than half her time at her father's place. Such was the case with us. That is to say, during the first five years of our married life (from the age of 13 to 18), we could not have lived together longer than an aggregate[2] period of three years. We would hardly have spent six months together, when there would be a call to my wife from her parents. Such calls were very unwelcome in those days, but they saved us both. At the age of eighteen I went to England, and this meant a long and healthy spell of separation. Even after my return from England we hardly stayed together longer than six months. For I had to run up and down between Rajkot and Bombay. Then came the call from South Africa, and that found me already fairly free from the carnal appetite[3].

1. *diminishes: make or become less*
2. *aggregate: a whole formed by combining several disparate elements*
3. *appetite: a natural desire to satisfy a bodily need, especially for food*

CHAPTER 5

AT THE HIGH SCHOOL

I have already said that I was learning at the high school when I was married. We three brothers were learning at the same school. The eldest brother was in a much higher class, and the brother who was married at the same time as I was, only one class ahead of me. Marriage resulted in both of us wasting a year. Indeed the result was even worse for my brother, for he gave up studies altogether. Heaven knows how many youths are in the same plight[1] as he. Only in our present Hindu society do studies and marriage go thus hand in hand.

My studies were continued. I was not regarded as a dunce at the high school. I always enjoyed the affection of my teachers. Certificates of progress and character used to be sent to the parents every year. I never had a bad certificate. In fact I even won prizes after I passed out of the second standard. In the fifth and sixth I obtained scholarships of rupees four and ten respectively, an achievement for which I have to thank good luck more than my merit. For the scholarships were not open to all, but reserved for the best boys amongst those coming from the Sorath Division of Kathiawad. And in those days there could not have been many boys from Sorath in a class of forty to fifty.

My own recollection is that I had not any high regard for my ability. I used to be astonished whenever I won prizes and scholarships. But I very jealously guarded my character. The least little blemish[2] drew tears from my eyes. When I merited, or seemed to the teacher to merit, a rebuke[3], it was unbearable for me. I remember having once received corporal punishment. I did not so much mind the punishment, as the fact that it was considered my desert. I wept piteously[4]. That was when I was in the first or second standard. There was another such incident during the time when I was in the seventh standard. Dorabji Edulji Gimi was the headmaster then. He was popular among boys, as he was a disciplinarian, a man of method and a good teacher. He had made gymnastics and

1. *plight: a dangerous, difficult, or otherwise unfortunate situation*
2. *blemish: a small mark or flaw which spoils the appearance of something*
3. *rebuke: criticize or reprimand sharply*
4. *piteously: deserving or arousing pity*

cricket compulsory for boys of the upper standards. I disliked both. I never took part in any exercise, cricket or football, before they were made compulsory. My shyness was one of the reasons for this aloofness, which I now see was wrong. I then had the false notion that gymnastics had nothing to do with education. Today I know that physical training should have as much place in the curriculum as mental training.

I may mention, however, that I was none the worse for abstaining[1] from exercise. That was because I had read in books about the benefits of long walks in the open air, and having liked the advice, I had formed a habit of taking walks, which has still remained with me. These walks gave me a fairly hardy constitution.

The reason for my dislike for gymnastics was my keen desire to serve as nurse to my father. As soon as the school closed, I would hurry home and begin serving him. Compulsory exercise came directly in the way of this service. I requested Mr. Gimi to exempt me from gymnastics so that I might be free to serve my father. But he would not listen to me. Now it happened that one Saturday, when we had school in the morning, I had to go from home to the school for gymnastics at four o'clock in the afternoon. I had no watch, and the clouds deceived me. Before I reached the school the boys had all left. The next day Mr. Gimi, examining the roll, found me marked absent. Being asked the reason for absence, I told him what had happened. He refused to believe me and ordered me to pay a fine of one or two annas (I cannot now recall how much).

I was convicted of lying! That deeply pained me. How was I to prove my innocence? There was no way. I cried in deep anguish[2]. I saw that a man of truth must also be a man of care. This was the first and last instance of my carelessness in school. I have a faint recollection[3] that I finally succeeded in getting the fine remitted[4]. The exemption from exercise was of course obtained, as my father wrote himself to the headmaster saying that he wanted me at home after school.

But though I was none the worse for having neglected exercise, I am still paying the penalty of another neglect, I do not know whence I got the notion that good handwriting was not a necessary part of education, but I retained it until I went to England. When later, especially in South Africa, I saw the beautiful handwriting of lawyers and young men born and educated in South Africa, I was ashamed of myself and repented of

1. *abstaining: restrain oneself from doing something*
2. *anguish: extreme distress of body or mind*
3. *recollection: the action or faculty of remembering*
4. *remitted: refrain from exacting or inflicting; (theology) pardon a sin*

my neglect. I saw that bad handwriting should be regarded as a sign of an imperfect education. I tried later to improve mine, but it was too late. I could never repair the neglect of my youth. Let every young man and woman be warned by my example, and understand that good handwriting is a necessary part of education. I am now of opinion that children should first be taught the art of drawing before learning how to write. Let the child learn his letters by observation as he does different objects, such as flowers, birds, etc., and let him learn handwriting only after he has learnt to draw objects. He will then write a beautifully formed hand.

Two more reminiscences of my school days are worth recording. I had lost one year because of my marriage, and the teacher wanted me to make good the loss by skipping a class a privilege usually allowed to industrious boys. I therefore had only six months in the third standard and was prompted to the fourth after the examinations which are followed by the summer vacation. English became the medium of instruction in most subjects from the fourth standard. I found myself completely at sea. Geometry was a new subject in which I was not particularly strong, and the English medium made it still more difficult for me. The teacher taught the subject very well, but I could not follow him. Often I would lose heart and think of going back to the third standard, feeling that the packing of two years' studies into a single year was too ambitious. But this would discredit[1] not only me, but also the teacher; because, counting on my industry, he had recommended my promotion. So the fear of the double discredit[1] kept me at my post. When however, with much effort I reached the thirteenth proposition of Euclid, the utter simplicity of the subject was suddenly revealed to me. A subject which only required a pure and simple use of one's reasoning powers could not be difficult. Ever since that time geometry has been both easy and interesting for me.

Samskrit, however, proved a harder task. In geometry there was nothing to memorize, whereas in Samskrit, I thought, everything had to be learnt by heart. This subject also was commenced from the fourth standard. As soon as I entered the sixth I became disheartened. The teacher was a hard taskmaster[2], anxious, as I thought, to force the boys. There was a sort of rivalry[3] going on between the Samskrit and the Persian teachers. The Persian teacher was lenient[4]. The boys used to talk among themselves that Persian was very easy and the Persian teacher very good

1. *discredit: harm the good reputation of; cause to seem false or unreliable*
2. *taskmaster: a person who imposes an onerous workload on someone*
3. *rivalry: competition between people, groups, etc.*
4. *lenient: merciful or tolerant*

and considerate to the students. The 'easiness' tempted me and one day I sat in the Persian class. The Samskrit teacher was grieved. He called me to his side and said: 'How can you forget that you are the son of a Vaishnava father? Won't you learn the language of your own religion? If you have any difficulty, why not come to me? I want to teach you students Samskrit to the best of my ability. As you proceed further, you will find in it things of absorbing interest. You should not lose heart. Come and sit again in the Samskrit class.'

This kindness put me to shame. I could not disregard my teacher's affection. Today I cannot but think with gratitude[1] of Krishnashankar Pandya. For if I had not acquired the little Samskrit that I learnt then, I should have found it difficult to take any interest in our sacred[2] books. In fact I deeply regret that I was not able to acquire a more thorough knowledge of the language, because I have since realized that every Hindu boy and girl should possess sound Samskrit learning.

It is now my opinion that in all Indian curricula of higher education there should be a place for Hindi, Samskrit, Persian, Arabic and English, besides of course the vernacular[3]. This big list need not frighten anyone. If our education were more systematic, and the boys free from the burden of having to learn their subjects through a foreign medium, I am sure learning all these languages would not be an irksome[4] task. but a perfect pleasure. A scientific knowledge of one language makes a knowledge of other languages comparatively easy.

In reality, Hindi, Gujarati and Samskrit may be regarded as one language, and Persian and Arabic also as one. Though Persian belongs to the Aryan, and Arabic to the Semitic family of languages, there is a close relationship between Persian and Arabic, because both claim their full growth through the rise of Islam. Urdu I have not regarded as a distinct language, because it has adopted the Hindi grammar and its vocabulary is mainly Persian and Arabic, and he who would learn good Urdu must learn Persian and Arabic, as one who would learn good Gujarati, Hindi, Bengali, or Marathi must learn Samskrit.

1. *gratitude: thankfulness; appreciation of kindness*
2. *sacred: connected with a deity and so deserving veneration; holy; embodying the doctrines of a religion; sacrosanct*
3. *vernacular: the language or dialect spoken by the ordinary people of a country or region*
4. *irksome: irritating or annoying*

CHAPTER 6

A TRAGEDY

Amongst my few friends at the high school I had, at different times, two who might be called intimate[1]. One of these friendships did not last long, though I never forsook my friend. He forsook me, because I made friends with the other. This latter friendship I regard as a tragedy in my life. It lasted long. I formed it in spirit of a reformer[2].

This companion was originally my elder brother's friend. They were classmates. I knew his weakness, but I regarded him as a faithful friend. My mother, my eldest brother, and my wife warned me that I was in bad company. I was too proud to heed my wife's warning. But I dared not go against the opinion of my mother and my eldest brother. Nevertheless I pleaded with them saying, 'I know he has the weaknesses you attribute to him, but you do not know his virtues. He cannot lead me astray, as my association with him is meant to reform him. For I am sure that if he reforms his ways, he will be a splendid[3] man. I beg you not to be anxious on my account.'

I do not think this satisfied them, but they accepted my explanation and let me go my way.

I have seen since that I had calculated wrongly. A reformer cannot afford to have close intimacy with him whom he seeks to reform. True friendship is an identity of souls rarely to be found in this world. Only between like natures can friendship be altogether worthy and enduring. Friends react on one another. Hence in friendship there is very little scope for reform. I am of opinion that all exclusive intimacies are to be avoided; for man takes in vice far more readily than virtue. And he who would be friends with God must remain alone, or make the whole world his friend. I may be wrong, but my effort to cultivate an intimate friendship proved a failure.

A wave of 'reform' was sweeping[4] over Rajkot at the time when I first came across this friend. He informed me that many of our teachers were

1. *intimate: closely acquainted; familiar*
2. *reformer: a disputant who advocates reform*
3. *splendid: magnificent; very impressive*
4. *sweeping: extending or performed in a long, continuous curve*

secretly taking meat and wine. He also named many well-known people of Rajkot as belonging to the same company. There were also, I was told, some high-school boys among them.

I was surprised and pained. I asked my friend the reason and he explained it thus: 'We are a weak people because we do not eat meat. The English are able to rule over us, because they are meat-eaters. You know how hardy I am, and how great a runner too. It is because I am a meat-eater. Meat-eaters do not have boils or tumours, and even if they sometimes happen to have any, these heal quickly. Our teachers and other distinguished people who eat meat are no fools. They know its virtues. You should do likewise[1]. There is nothing like trying. Try, and see what strength it gives.'

All these pleas on behalf of meat-eating were not advanced at a single sitting. They represent the substance of a long and elaborate argument which my friend was trying to impress upon me from time to time. My elder brother had already fallen. He therefore supported my friend's argument. I certainly looked feeble-bodied by the side of my brother and this friend. They were both hardier, physically stronger, and more daring. This friend's exploits cast a spell over me. He could run long distances and extraordinarily fast. He was an adept[2] in high and long jumping. He could put up with any amount of corporal punishment. He would often display his exploits to me and, as one is always dazzled[3] when he sees in others the qualities that he lacks himself, I was dazzled by this friend's exploits. This was followed by a strong desire to be like him. I could hardly jump or run. Why should not I also be as strong as he?

Moreover, I was a coward. I used to be haunted by the fear of thieves, ghosts, and serpents. I did not dare to stir out of doors at night. Darkness was a terror to me. It was almost impossible for me to sleep in the dark, as I would imagine ghosts coming from one direction, thieves from another and serpents from a third. I could not therefore bear to sleep without a light in the room. How could I disclose my fears to my wife, no child, but already at the threshold[4] of youth, sleeping by my side? I knew that she had more courage than I, and I felt ashamed of myself. She knew no fear of serpents and ghosts. She could go out anywhere in the dark. My friend knew all these weaknesses of mine. He would tell me that he could hold in his hand live serpents, could defy thieves and did not believe in ghosts. And all this was, of course, the result of eating meat.

1. *likewise: also; moreover*
2. *adept: very skilled or proficient*
3. *dazzled: over-whelm with an impressive quality*
4. *threshold: a level or point at which something would start or cease to happen or come into effect*

A doggerel of the Gujarati poet Narmad was in vogue[1] amongst us schoolboys, as follows: Behold the mighty Englishman He rules the Indian small, Because being a meat-eater He is five cubits tall.

All this had its due effect on me. I was beaten. It began to grow on me that meat-eating was good, that it would make me strong and daring, and that, if the whole county took to meat-eating, the English could be overcome.

A day was thereupon fixed for beginning the experiment. It had to be conducted in secret. The Gandhis were Vaishnavas. My parents were particularly staunch[2] Vaishnavas. They would regularly visit the *Haveli*. The family had even its own temples. Jainism was strong in Gujarat, and its influence was felt everywhere and on all occasions. The opposition to and abhorrence[3] of meat-eating that existed in Gujarat among the Jains and Vaishnavas were to be seen nowhere else in India or outside in such strength. These were the traditions in which I was born and bred. And I was extremely devoted to my parents. I knew that the moment they came to know of my having eaten meat, they would be shocked to death. Moreover, my love of truth made me extra cautious. I cannot say that I did not know then that I should have to deceive my parents if I began eating meat. But my mind was bent on the 'reform'. It was not a question of pleasing the palate. I did not know that it had a particularly good relish. I wished to be strong and daring and wanted my countrymen also to be such, so that we might defeat the English and make India free. The word 'Swaraj' I had not yet heard. But I knew what freedom meant. The frenzy of the 'reform' blinded me. And having ensured secrecy, I persuaded[4] myself that mere hiding the deed from parents was no departure from truth.

1. *vogue: the prevailing fashion or style at a particular time*
2. *staunch: very loyal and committed*
3. *abhorrence: detest; hate*
4. *persuaded: cause to do something through reasoning or argument*

CHAPTER 7

A TRAGEDY (*contd.*)

So the day came. It is difficult fully to describe my condition. There were, on the one hand, the zeal for 'reform', and the novelty[1] of making a momentous departure in life. There was, on the other, the shame of hiding like a thief to do this very thing. I cannot say which of the two swayed me more. We went in search of a lonely spot by the river, and there I saw, for the first time in my life - meat. There was baker's bread also. I relished[2] neither. The goat's meat was as tough as leather. I simply could not eat it. I was sick and had to leave off eating.

I had a very bad night afterwards. A horrible night-mare haunted me. Every time I dropped off to sleep it would seem as though a live goat were bleating inside me, and I would jump up full of remorse. But then I would remind myself that meat-eating was a duty and so become more cheerful.

My friend was not a man to give in easily. He now began to cook various delicacies with meat, and dress them neatly. And for dining, no longer was the secluded[3] spot on the river chosen, but a State house, with its dining hall, and tables and chairs, about which my friend had made arrangements in collusion with the chief cook there.

This bait had its effect. I got over my dislike for bread, forswore my compassion for the goats, and became a relisher of meat-dishes, if not of meat itself. This went on for about a year. But not more than half a dozen meat-feasts were enjoyed in all; because the State house was not available every day, and there was the obvious difficulty about frequently preparing expensive savoury[4] meat-dishes. I had no money to pay for this 'reform'. My friend had therefore always to find the wherewithal. I had no knowledge where he found it. But find it he did, because he was bent on turning me into a meat-eater. But even his means must have been limited, and hence these feasts had necessarily to be few and far between.

Whenever I had occasion to indulge in these surreptitious feasts, dinner at home was out of the question. My mother would naturally ask

1. *novelty: the quality of being novel; a new or unfamiliar thing or experience; denoting something intended to be amusing as a result of its originality or unusualness*
2. *relished: enjoy greatly; anticipate with pleasure*
3. *secluded: not seen or visited by many people; sheltered and private*
4. *savoury: salty or spicy rather than sweet*

me to come and take my food and want to know the reason why I did not wish to eat. I would say to her, 'I have no appetite today; there is something wrong with my digestion.' It was not without compunction that I devised these pretexts[1]. I knew I was lying, and lying to my mother. I also knew that, if my mother and father came to know of my having become a meat-eater, they would be deeply shocked. This knowledge was gnawing[2] at my heart.

Therefore I said to myself: 'Though it is essential to eat meat, and also essential to take up food 'reform' in the country, yet deceiving and lying to one's father and mother is worse than not eating meat. In their lifetime, therefore, meat-eating must be out of the question. When they are no more and I have found my freedom, I will eat meat openly, but until that moment arrives I will abstain from it.'

This decision I communicated to my friend, and I have never since gone back to meat. My parents never knew that two of their sons had become meat-eaters.

I abjured meat out of the purity of my desire not to lie to my parents, but I did not abjure the company of my friend. My zeal for reforming[3] him had proved disastrous[4] for me, and all the time I was completely unconscious of the fact.

The same company would have led me into faithlessness to my wife. But I was saved by the skin of my teeth. My friend once took me to a brothel. He sent me in with the necessary instructions. It was all prearranged. The bill had already been paid. I went into the jaws of sin, but God in His infinite mercy protected me against myself. I was almost struck blind and dumb in this den of vice. I sat near the woman on her bed, but I was tongue-tied. She naturally lost patience with me, and showed me the door, with abuses and insults. I then felt as though my manhood had been injured, and wished to sink into the ground for shame. But I have ever since given thanks to God for having saved me. I can recall four more similar incidents in my life, and in most of them my good fortune, rather than any effort on my part, saved me. From a strictly ethical point of view, all these occasions must be regarded as moral lapses; for the carnal desire was there, and it was as good as the act. But from the ordinary point of view, a man who is saved from physically committing sin is regarded as saved. And I was saved only in that sense.

1. *pretexts: an ostensible or false reason used to justify an action*
2. *gnawing: cause persistent anxiety or distress*
3. *reforming: make changes in to relinquish an immoral or criminal lifestyle*
4. *disastrous: highly unsuccessful*

There are some actions from which an escape is a godsend both for the man who escapes and for those about him. Man, as soon as he gets back his consciousness of right, is thankful to the Divine mercy for the escape. As we know that a man often succumbs[1] to temptation[2], however much he say resist it, we also know that Providence often intercedes and saves him in spite of himself. How all this happens, - how far a man is free and how far a creature of circumstances, - how far free-will comes into play and where fate enters on the scene, all this is a mystery and will remain a mystery.

But to go on with the story. Even this was far from opening my eyes to the viciousness of my friend's company. I therefore had many more bitter draughts in store for me, until my eyes were actually opened by an ocular demonstration of some of his lapses quite unexpected by me. But of them later, as we are proceeding chronologically[3].

One thing, however, I must mention now, as it pertains to the same period. One of the reasons of my differences with my wife was undoubtedly the company of this friend. I was both a devoted and a jealous husband, and this friend fanned the flame of my suspicions about my wife. I never could doubt his veracity. And I have never forgiven myself the violence of which I have been guilty in often having pained my wife by acting on his information. Perhaps only a Hindu wife would tolerate these hardships, and that is why I have regarded woman as an incarnation[4] of tolerance. A servant wrongly suspected may throw up his job, a son in the same case may leave his father's roof, and a friend may put an end to the friendship. A wife, if she suspects her husband, will keep quiet, but if her husband suspects her, she is ruined. Where is she to go? A Hindu wife may not seek divorce in a law-court. Law has no remedy for *her*. And I can never forget or forgive myself for a having driven my wife to that desperation.

The canker of suspicion was rooted out only when I understood *Ahimsa*[5] in all its bearings. I saw then the glory of *Brahmacharya*[6] and realized that the wife is not the husband's bondslave, but his companion and his helpmate, and an equal partner in all his joy and sorrows - as free as the husband to choose her own path. Whenever I think of those dark days of doubts and suspicions. I am filled with loathing of my folly and my lustful cruelty, and I deplore my blind devotion to a friend.

1. *succumbs: fail to resist*
2. *temptation: the state or quality of being tempted; a desire to do something; a tempting thing*
3. *chronologically: relating to or arranged according to temporal order*
4. *incarnation: a living embodiment of a deity, spirit, or abstract quality*
5. *Ahimsa: not-hurting, non-violence*
6. *Brahmacharya: conduct that leads one to god; self-restraint, particularly mastery over the sexual organ*

CHAPTER 8

STEALING AND ATONEMENT

I have still to relate some of my failings during this meat-eating period and also previous to it, which date from before my marriage or soon after.

A relative and I became fond of smoking. Not that we saw any good in smoking, or were enamoured[1] of the smell of a cigarette. We simply imagined a sort of pleasure in emitting clouds of smoke from our mouths. My uncle had the habit, and when we saw him smoking, we thought we should copy his example. But we had no money. So we began to pilfer stumps of cigarettes thrown away by my uncle.

The stumps, however, were not always available, and could not emit much smoke either. So we began to steal coppers from the servant's pocket money in order to purchase Indian cigarettes. But the question was where to keep them. We could not of course smoke in the presence of elders. We managed somehow for a few weeks on these stolen coppers. In the meantime we heard that the stalks of a certain plant were porous and could be smoked like cigarettes. We got them and began this kind of smoking.

But we were far from being satisfied with such things as these. Our want of independence[2] began to smart, It was unbearable[3] that we should be unable to do anything without the elders' permission. At last, in sheer disgust, we decided to commit suicide!

But how were we to do it? From where were we to get the poison? We heard that *Dhatura* seeds were an effective poison. Off we went to the jungle in search of these seeds, and got them.

Evening was thought to be the auspicious hour. We went to *Kedarji Mandir,* put ghee in the temple-lamp, had the *Darshan* and then looked for a lonely corner. But our courage failed us. Supposing we were not instantly killed? And what was the good of killing ourselves? Why not rather put up with the lack of independence? But we swallowed two or three seeds nevertheless. We dared not take more. Both of us fought shy of death, and

1. enamoured: be filled with love or admiration for *2. independence: state of being free*
3. unbearable: not able to be endured or tolerated

decided to go to *Ramji Mandir* to compose ourselves, and to dismiss the thought of suicide.

I realized that it was not as easy to commit suicide as to contemplate[1] it. And since then, whenever I have heard of someone threatening to commit suicide, it has had little or on effect on me.

The thought of suicide ultimately resulted in both of us bidding good-bye to the habit of smoking stumps of cigarettes and of stealing the servant's coppers for the purpose of smoking.

Ever since I have been grown up, I have never desired to smoke and have always regarded the habit of smoking as barbarous, dirty and harmful. I have never understood why there is such a rage for smoking throughout the world. I cannot bear to travel in a compartment full of people smoking. I become choked.

But much more serious than this theft was the one I was guilty[2] of a little later. I pilfered the coppers when I was twelve or thirteen, possibly less. The other theft was committed when I was fifteen. In this case I stole a bit of gold out of my meat-eating brother's armlet. This brother had run into a debt of about twenty-five rupees. He had on his arm an armlet of solid gold. It was not difficult to clip a bit out of it.

Well, it was done, and the debt cleared. But this became more than I could bear. I resolved[3] never to steal again. I also made up my mind to confess it to my father. But I did not dare to speak. Not that I was afraid of my father beating me. No I do not recall his ever having beaten any of us. I was afraid of the pain that I should cause him. But I felt that the risk should be taken; that there could not be a cleansing without a confession[4].

I decided at last to write out the confession, to submit it to my father, and ask his forgiveness. I wrote it on a slip of paper and handed it to him myself. In this note not only did I confess my guilt, but I asked adequate punishment for it, and closed with a request to him not to punish himself for my offence. I also pledged[5] myself never to steal in future.

I was trembling as I handed the confession to my father. He was then suffering from a fistula and was confined to bed. His bed was a plain wooden plank. I handed him the note and sat opposite the plank.

He read it through, and pearl-drops trickled down his cheeks, wetting the paper. For a moment he closed his eyes in thought and then tore up the note. He had sat up to read it. He again lay down. I also cried. I could see

1. *contemplate: look at thoughtfully; think about; think profoundly and at length; have as a probable intention*
2. *guilty: culpable of a specified wrongdoing; justly chargeable with a particular fault or error*
3. *resolved: decide firmly on a course of action; take a decision by a formal vote*
4. *confession: admit to a crime wrongdoing; acknowledge reluctantly*
5. *pledged: a solemn promise or undertaking; a promise of a donation to charity*

my father's agony[1]. If I were a painter I could draw a picture of the whole scene today. It is still so vivid in my mind.

Those pearl-drops of love cleansed my heart, and washed my sin away. Only he who has experienced such love can know what it is. As the hymn says: 'Only he Who is smitten with the arrows of love. Knows its power.'

This was, for me, an object-lesson in *Ahimsa*. Then I could read in it nothing more than a father's love, but today I know that it was pure *Ahimsa*. When such *Ahimsa* becomes all-embracing it transforms everything it touches. There is no limit to its power.

This sort of sublime[2] forgiveness was not natural to my father. I had thought that he would be angry, say hard things, and strike his forehead. But he was so wonderfully peaceful, and I believe this was due to my clean confession. A clean confession, combined with a promise never to commit the sin again, when offered before one who has the right to receive it, is the purest type of repentance[3]. I know that my confession made my father feel absolutely safe about me, and increased his affection[4] for me beyond measure.

1. *agony: extreme suffering*
2. *sublime: of such excellence, grandeur, or beauty as to inspire great admiration or awe*
3. *repentance: feel or express sincere regret or remorse*
4. *affection: a feeling of fondness or liking*

CHAPTER 9

MY FATHER'S DEATH AND MY DOUBLE SHAME

The time of which I am now speaking is my sixteenth year. My father, as we have seen, was bed-ridden, suffering from a fistula. My mother, an old servant of the house, and I were his principal attendants. I had the duties of a nurse, which mainly consisted in dressing the wound, giving my father his medicine, and compounding drugs whenever they had to be made up at home, Every night I massaged his legs and retired only when he asked me to do so or after he had fallen asleep. I loved to do this service. I do not remember ever having neglected[1] it. All the time at my disposal, after the performance of the daily duties, was divided between school and attending on my father. I would only go out for an evening walk either when he permitted me or when he was feeling well.

This was also the time when my wife was expecting a baby, - a circumstance[2] which, as I can see today, meant a double shame for me. For one thing I did not restrain myself, as I should have done, whilst I was yet a student. And secondly, this carnal lust got the better of what I regarded as my duty to study, and of what was even a greater duty, my devotion to my parents, Shravana having been my ideal since childhood. Every night whilst my hands were busy massaging my father's legs, my mind was hovering[3] about the bed-room, - and that too at a time when religion, medical science and commonsense alike forbade sexual intercourse. I was always glad to be relieved from my duty, and went straight to the bed-room after doing obeisance[4] to my father.

At the same time my father was getting worse every day. Ayurvedic physicians had tried all their ointments, Hakims their plasters, and local quacks their nostrums. An English surgeon had also used his skill. As the last and only resort he had recommended a surgical operation. But the family physician came in the way. He disapproved of an operation being performed at such an advanced age. The physician was competent and well-known, and his advice prevailed. The operation was abandoned, and various medicines purchased for the purpose were of no account.

1. *neglected: fail to give proper care or attention to; fail to do something*
2. *circumstance: a fact or condition connected with or relevant to an event or action*
3. *hovering: remain in one place in the air*
4. *obeisance: differential respect*

I have an impression that, if the physician had allowed the operation, the wound would have been easily healed. The operation also was to have been performed by a surgeon who was then well known in Bombay. But God had willed otherwise. When death is imminent[1], who can think of the right remedy? My father returned from Bombay with all the paraphernalia[2] of the operation, which were now useless. He despaired of living any longer, He was getting weaker and weaker, until at last he had to be asked to perform the necessary functions in bed. But up to the last he refused to do anything of the kind, always insisting on going through the strain of leaving his bed. The Vaishnavite rules about external cleanliness are so inexorable[3].

Such cleanliness is quite essential no doubt, but Western medical science has taught us that all the functions, including a bath, can be done in bed with the strictest regard to cleanliness, and without the slightest discomfort to the patient, the bed always remaining spotlessly clean. I should regard such cleanliness as quite consistent with Vaishnavism. But my father's insistence[4] on leaving the bed only struck me with wonder then, and I had nothing but admiration for it.

The dreadful night came. My uncle was then in Rajkot. I have a faint recollection that he came to Rajkot having had news that my father was getting worse. The brothers were deeply attached to each other. My uncle would sit near my father's bed the whole day, and would insist on sleeping by his bedside after sending us all to sleep. No one had dreamt that this was to be the fateful night. The danger of course was there.

It was ten-thirty or eleven p.m. I was giving the massage. My uncle offered to relieve me. I was glad and went straight to the bed-room. My wife, poor thing, was fast asleep. But how could she sleep when I was there? I woke her up. In five or six minutes. however, the servant knocked at the door. I started with alarm. 'Get up,' he said, 'Father is very ill.' I knew of course that he was very ill, and so I guessed what 'very ill' meant at that moment. I sprang out of bed. 'What is the matter? Do tell me!' 'Father is no more.' So all was over! I had but to wring my hands. I felt deeply ashamed and miserable. I ran to my father's room. I saw that, if animal passion had not blinded me. I should have been spared the torture of separation from my father during his last moments. I should have been massaging him, and he would have died in my arms. But now

1. *imminent: about to happen*
2. *paraphernalia: miscellaneous articles, especially the equipment needed for a particular activity*
3. *inexorable: impossible to prevent; unrelenting*
4. *insistence: insisting or very demanding*

it was my uncle who had this privilege. He was so deeply devoted to his elder brother that he had earned the honour of doing him the last services! My father had forebodings of the coming event. He had made a sign for pen and paper, and written: 'Prepare for the last rites.' He had then snapped the amulet[1] off his arm and also his gold necklace of *tulasi* beads and flung them aside. A moment after this he was no more.

The shame, to which I have referred in a foregoing chapter, was this of my carnal desire even at the critical hour of my father's death, which demanded wakeful service. It was a blot I have never been able to efface[2] or forget, and I have always thought that, although my devotion to my parents knew no bounds and I would have given up anything for it, yet it was weighed and found unpardonably wanting because my mind was at the same moment in the grip of lust. I have therefore always regarded myself as a lustful, though a faithful, husband. It took me long to get free from the shackles[3] of lust, and I had to pass through many ordeals[4] before I could overcome it.

Before I close this chapter of my double shame. I may mention that the poor mite that was born to my wife scarcely breathed for more than three or four days. Nothing else could be expected. Let all those who are married be warned by my example.

1. *amulet: an ornament or small piece of jewelery thought to give protection against evil or danger*
2. *efface: erase from a surface*
3. *shackles: a pair of fetters connected by a chain, used to fasten a prisoner's wrists or ankles together; restraints or impediments*
4. *ordeals: a prolonged painful or horrific experience*

CHAPTER 10

GLIMPSES OF RELIGION

From my sixth or seventh year up to my sixteenth I was at school, being taught all sorts of things except religion. I may say that I failed to get from the teachers what they could have given me without any effort on their part. And yet I kept on picking up things here and there from my surroundings. The term 'religion' I am using in its broadest sense, meaning thereby self-realization or knowledge of self.

Being born in the Vaishnava faith, I had often to go to the *Haveli*. But it never appealed to me. I did not like its glitter and pomp[1]. Also I heard rumours of immorality being practised there, and lost all interest in it. Hence I could gain nothing from the *Haveli*.

But what I failed to get there I obtained from my nurse, an old servant of the family, whose affection for me I still recall. I have said before that there was in me a fear of ghosts and spirits. Rambha, for that was her name, suggested, as a remedy[2] for this fear, the repetition of *Ramanama*. I had more faith in her than in her remedy, and so at a tender age I began repeating *Ramanama* to cure my fear of ghosts and spirits. This was of course short-lived, but the good seed sown in childhood was not sown in vain. I think it is due to the seed sown by that good woman Rambha that today *Ramanama* is an infallible[3] remedy for me.

Just about this time, a cousin of mine who was a devotee of the *Ramayana* arranged for my second brother and me to learn *Ram Raksha*. We got it by heart, and made it a rule to recite it every morning after the bath. The practice was kept up as long as we were in Porbandar. As soon as we reached Rajkot, it was forgotten. For I had not much belief in it. I recited it partly because of my pride in being able to recite *Ram Raksha* with correct pronunciation[4].

What, however, left a deep impression on me was the reading of the *Ramayana* before my father. During part of his illness my father was in Porbandar. There every evening he used to listen to the *Ramayana*.

1. *pomp: ceremony and splendid display*
2. *remedy: a medicine or treatment for a disease or injury*
3. *infallible: never failing; always effective*
4. *pronunciation: the way in which a word is pronounced*

The reader was a great devotee of Rama, - Ladha Maharaj of Bileshvar. It was said of him that he cured himself of his leprosy not by any medicine, but by applying to the affected parts *bilva* leaves which had been cast away after being offered to the image of Mahadeva in Bileshvar temple, and by the regular repetition of *Ramanama*. His faith it, it was said, had made him whole. This may or may not be true. We at any rate believed the story. And it is a fact that when Ladha Maharaj began his reading of the *Ramayana* his body was entirely free from leprosy[1]. He had a melodious voice. He would sing the *Dohas* (couplets) and *Chopais* (quatrains), and explain them, losing himself in the discourse and carrying his listeners along with him. I must have been thirteen at that time, but I quite remember being enraptured by his reading. That laid the foundation of my deep devotion[2] to the *Ramayana*. Today I regard the *Ramayana* of Tulasidas as the greatest book in all devotional literature.

A few months after this we came to Rajkot. There was no *Ramayana* reading there. The *Bhagavat*, however, used to be read on every *Ekadashi*[3] day. Sometimes I attended the reading, but the reciter was uninspiring. Today I see that the *Bhagavat* is a book which can evoke religious fervour[4]. I have read it in Gujarati with intense interest. But when I heard portions of the original read by Pandit Madan Mohan Malaviya during my twenty-one day's fast, I wished I had heard it in my childhood from such a devotee as he is, so that I could have formed a liking for it at an early age. Impressions formed at that age strike roots deep down into one's nature, and it is my perpetual regret that I was not fortunate enough to hear more good books of this kind read during that period.

In Rajkot, however, I got an early grounding in toleration for all branches of Hinduism and sister religions. For my father and mother would visit the *Haveli* as also Shiva's and Rama's temples, and would take or send us youngsters there. Jain monks also would pay frequent visits to my father, and would even go out of their way to accept food from us-non-Jains. They would have talks with my father on subjects religious and mundane.

He had, besides, Musalman and Parsi friends, who would talk to him about their own faiths, and he would listen to them always with respect, and often with interest. Being his nurse, I often had a chance to be present at these talks. These many things combined to inculcate in me a toleration for all faiths.

1. *leprosy: a contagious bacterial disease that affects the skin, mucous membrane, and nerves, causing discoloration and lumps on the skin and, in severe cases, disfigurement and deformities*
2. *devotion: love, loyalty, or enthusiasm for a person or activity*
3. *Ekadashi: eleventh day of the bright and the dark half of a lunar month*
4. *fervour: intense and passionate feeling*

Only Christianity was at that time an exception[1]. I developed a sort of dislike for it. And for a reason. In those days Christian missionaries used to stand in a corner near the high school and hold forth, pouring abuse on Hindus and their gods. I could not endure this. I must have stood there to hear them once only, but that was enough to dissuade me from repeating the experiment. About the same time, I heard of a well known Hindu having been converted to Christianity. It was the talk of the town that, when he was baptized, he had to eat beef and drink liquor, that he also had to change his clothes, and that thenceforth he began to go about in European costume including a hat. These things got on my nerves. Surely, thought I, a religion that compelled one to eat beef, drink liquor, and change one's own clothes did not deserve the name. I also heard that the new convert had already begun abusing the religion of his ancestors, their customs and their country. All these things created in me a dislike for Christianity.

But the fact that I had learnt to be tolerant[2] to other religions did not mean that I had any living faith in God. I happened, about this time, to come across *Manusmriti*[3] which was amongst my father's collection. The story of the creation and similar things in it did not impress me very much, but on the contrary[4] made me incline somewhat towards atheism[5].

There was a cousin of mine, still alive, for whose intellect I had great regard. To him I turned with my doubts. But he could not resolve them. He sent me away with this answer: 'When you grow up, you will be able to solve these doubts yourself. These questions ought not to be raised at your age.' I was silenced, but was not comforted. Chapters about diet and the like in *Manusmriti* seemed to me to run contrary to daily practice. To my doubts as to this also, I got the same answer.' With intellect more developed and with more reading I shall understand it better', I said to myself.

Manusmriti at any rate did not then teach me *ahimsa*. I have told the story of my meat-eating. *Manusmriti* seemed to support it. I also felt that it was quite moral to kill serpents, bugs and the like. I remember to have killed at that age bugs and such other insects, regarding it as a duty.

But one thing took deep root in me the conviction that morality is the basis of things, and that truth is the substance of all morality. Truth became my sole objective. It began to grow in magnitude every day, and my definition of it also has been ever widening. A Gujarati didactic

1. *exception: a person or thing that is excepted or that does not follow a rule*
2. *tolerant: able to endure specified conditions or treatment*
3. *Manusmriti: laws of manu, a hindu law-giver; they have the sanction of religion*
4. *contrary: opposite in nature, direction, or meaning*
5. *atheism: the theory or belief that god does not exist*

stanza likewise gripped my mind and heart. Its precept-return good for evil-became my guiding principle. It became such a passion[1] with me that I began numerous[2] experiments in it. Here are those (for me) wonderful lines: For a bowl of water give a goodly meal: For a kindly[3] greeting bow thou down with zeal: For a simple penny pay thou back with gold: If thy life be rescued, life do not withhold. Thus the words and actions of the wise regard; Every little service tenfold they reward. But the truly noble[4] know all men as one, And return with gladness good for evil done.

1. *passion: strong and barely controllable emotion; an outburst of such emotion*
2. *numerous: many; consisting of many members*
3. *kindly: in a kind manner*
4. *noble: having fine personal qualities or high moral principles*

CHAPTER 11

PREPARATION FOR ENGLAND

I passed the matriculation examination in 1887. It then used to be held at two centres, Ahmedabad and Bombay. The general poverty of the country naturally led Kathiawad students to prefer the nearer and the cheaper centre. The poverty of my family likewise dictated[1] to me the same choice. This was my first journey from Rajkot to Ahmedabad and that too without a companion[2].

My elders wanted me to pursue my studies at college after the matriculation. There was a college in Bhavnagar as well as in Bombay, and as the former was cheaper, I decided to go there and join the Samaldas College. I went, but found myself entirely at sea. Everything was difficult. I could not follow, let alone taking interest in, the professors' lectures. It was no fault of theirs. The professors in that College were regarded[3] as first-rate. But I was so raw. At the end of the first term, I returned home.

We had in Mavji Dave, who was a shrewd and learned Brahman an old friend and adviser of the family. He had kept up his connection with the family even after my father's death. He happened to visit us during my vacation. In conversation with my mother and elder brother, he inquired about my studies. Learning that I was at Samaldas College, he said: 'The times are changed. And none of you can expect to succeed to your father's *gadi* without having a proper education. Now as this boy is still pursuing[4] his studies, you should all look to him to keep the *gadi*. It will take him four or five years to get his B.A. degree, which will at best qualify him for a sixty rupees' post, not for a Diwanship. If like my son he went in for law, it would take him still longer, by which time there would be a host of lawyers aspiring for a Diwan's post. I would far rather that you sent him to England. My son Kevalram says it is very easy to become a barrister. In three years' time he will return. Also expenses will not exceed[5] four to five thousand rupees. Think of that barrister who has just come back from England. How stylishly he lives! He could get the Diwanship for the

1. *dictated: influence something or make it necessity*
2. *companion: a person with whom one spends time or travels*
3. *regarded: consider in a particular way*
4. *pursuing: seek to attain*
5. *exceed: be greater in number or size than; go beyond what is allowed or stipulated by a set limit, especially of one's authority; surpass*

asking. I would strongly advise you to send Mohandas to England this very year. Kevalram has numerous friends in England. He will give notes of introduction to them, and Mohandas will have an easy time of it there.'

Joshiji that is how we used to call old Mavji Dave turned to me with complete assurance, and asked: 'Would you not rather go to England than study here?' Nothing could have been more welcome to me. I was fighting shy of my difficult studies. So I jumped at the proposal[1] and said that the sooner I was sent the better. It was no easy business to pass examinations quickly. Could I not be sent to qualify for the medical profession?

My brother interrupted me: 'Father never liked it. He had you in mind when he said that we Vaishnavas should have nothing to do with dissection[2] of dead bodies. Father intended you for the bar.'

Joshiji chimed in: 'I am not opposed to the medical profession as was Gandhiji. Our *Shastras* are not against it. But a medical degree will not make a Diwan of you, and I want you to be Diwan, or if possible something better. Only in that way could you take under your protecting care your large family. The times are fast changing and getting harder every day. It is the wisest thing therefore to become a barrister.' Turning to my mother he said: 'Now, I must leave. Pray ponder over what I have said. When I come here next I shall expect to hear of preparations for England. Be sure to let me know if I can assist in any way.'

Joshiji went away, and I began building castles in the air.

My elder brother was greatly exercised in his mind. How was he to find the wherewithal to send me? And was it proper to trust a young man like me to go abroad alone?

My mother was sorely perplexed[3]. She did not like the idea of parting with me. This is how she tried to put me off: 'Uncle,' she said, 'is now the eldest member of the family. He should first be consulted. If he consents we will consider the matter.'

My brother had another idea. He said to me: 'We have a certain claim on the Porbandar State. Mr. Lely is the Administrator. He thinks highly of our family and uncle is in his good books. It is just possible that he might recommend[4] you for some State help for your education in England.'

I liked all this and got ready to start off for Porbandar. There was no railway in those days. It was a five days' bullock-cart journey. I have already

1. *proposal: a plan or suggestion; the action of proposing something*
2. *dissection: the action of methodically cutting up a body or plant to study its internal parts*
3. *perplexed: cause to feel baffled*
4. *recommend: put forward with approval as being suitable for a purpose or role; advise as a course of action; advise to do something*

said that I was a coward. But at that moment my cowardice vanished before the desire to go to England, which completely possessed[1] me. I hired a bullock-cart as far as Dhoraji, and from Dhoraji I took a camel in order to get to Porbandar a day quicker. This was my first camel-ride.

I arrived at last, did obeisance to my uncle, and told him everything. He thought it over and said: 'I am not sure whether it is possible for one to stay in England without prejudice[2] to one's own religion. From all I have heard, I have my doubts. When I meet these big barristers, I see no difference between their life and that of Europeans. They know no scruples[3] regarding food. Cigars are never out of their mouths. They dress as shamelessly as Englishmen. All that would not be in keeping with our family tradition. I am shortly going on a pilgrimage and have not many years to live. At the threshold of death, how dare I give you permission to go to England, to cross the seas? But I will not stand in your way. It is your mother's permission which really matters. If she permits you, then godspeed! Tell her I will not interfere. You will go with my blessings.'

'I could expect nothing more from you,' said I. 'I shall now try to win mother over. But would you not recommend me to Mr. Lely?'

'How can I do that?' said he. 'But he is a good man. You ask for an appointment telling him how you are connected. He will certainly give you one and may even help you.'

I cannot say why my uncle did not give me a note of recommendation. I have a faint idea that he hesitated to co-operate directly in my going to England, which was in his opinion an irreligious act.

I wrote to Mr Lely, who asked me to see him at his residence. He saw me as he was ascending the staircase; and saying curtly, 'Pass your B.A. fist and then see me. No help can be given to you now', he hurried upstairs. I had made elaborate preparations to meet him. I had carefully learnt up a few sentences and had bowed low and saluted him with both hands. But all to no purpose!

I thought of my wife's ornaments[4]. I thought of my elder brother, in whom I had the utmost faith. He was generous to a fault, and he loved me as his own son.

I returned to Rajkot from Porbandar and reported all that had happened. I consulted Joshiji, who of course advised even incurring a debt

1. *possessed: dominate the mind of*
2. *prejudice: preconceived opinion that is not based on reason or actual experience; unjust behavior formed on such a basis*
3. *scruples: a feeling of doubt or hesitation with regard to the morality or propriety of an action*
4. *ornaments: an object designed to add beauty to something; decorative items collectively*

if necessary. I suggested the disposal of my wife's ornaments, which could fetch about two or three thousand rupees. My brother promised to find the money somehow.

My mother, however, was still unwilling[1]. She had begun making minute inquiries. Someone had told her that young men got lost in England. Someone else had said that they took to meat; and yet another that they could not live there without liquor. 'How about all this?' she asked me. I said: 'Will you not trust me? I shall not lie to you. I swear that I shall not touch any of those things. If there were any such danger, would Joshiji let me go?'

'I can trust you,' she said.' But how can I trust you in a distant land? I am dazed and know not what to do. I will ask Becharji Swami.'

Becharji Swami was originally a Modh Bania, but had now become a Jain monk. He too was a family adviser like Joshiji. He came to my help, and said: 'I shall get the boy solemnly to take the three vows, and then he can be allowed to go.' He administered[2] the oath[3] and I vowed not to touch wine, woman and meat. This done, my mother gave her permission.

The high school had a send-off in my honour. It was an uncommon thing for a young man of Rajkot to go to England. I had written out a few words of thanks. But I could scarcely stammer[4] them out. I remember how my head reeled and how my whole frame shook as I stood up to read them.

With the blessings of my elders, I started for Bombay. This was my first journey from Rajkot to Bombay. My brother accompanied me. But there is many a slip, 'twixt the cup and the lip. There were difficulties to be faced in Bombay.

1. *unwilling: not willing*
2. *administered: a solemn promise, often invoking a divine whiteness, as to the truth of something or as a commitment to future action*
3. *oath: attend to the organization or implementation of*
4. *stammer: speak with sudden involuntary pauses and a tendency to repeat the initial letters of words; utter in such a way*

CHAPTER 12
OUTCASTE

With my mother's permission and blessings, I set off exultantly for Bombay, leaving my wife with a baby of a few months. But on arrival there friends told my brother that the Indian Ocean was rough in June and July, and as this was my first voyage, I should not be allowed to sail until November. Someone also reported that a steamer had just been sunk in a gale. This made my brother uneasy[1], and he refused to take the risk of allowing[2] me to sail immediately. Leaving me with a friend in Bombay, he returned to Rajkot to resume his duty. He put the money for my travelling expenses in the keeping of a brother-in-law, and left word with some friends to give me whatever help I might need.

Time hung heavily on my hands in Bombay. I dreamt continually of going to England.

Meanwhile my caste-people were agitated over my going abroad. No Modh Bania had been to England up to now, and if I dared to do so, I ought to be brought to book! A general meeting of the caste was called and I was summoned to appear before it. I went. Now I suddenly managed to muster up courage I do not know. Nothing daunted, and without the slightest hesitation[3], I came before the meeting. The Sheth - the headman of the community who was distantly related to me and had been on very good terms with my father, thus accosted me:

'In the opinion of the caste, your proposal to go to England is not proper. Our religion forbids voyages abroad. We have also heard that it is not possible to live there without compromising[4] out religion. One is obliged to eat and drink with Europeans!'

To which I replied: 'I do not think it is at all against our religion to go to England. I intend going there for further studies. And I have solemnly promised to my mother to abstain from three things you fear most. I am sure the vow will keep me safe.'

1. *uneasy: causing or feeling anxiety; troubled or uncomfortable*
2. *allowing: permit to do something*
3. *hesitation: hesitating; faltering*
4. *compromising: bring into disrepute or danger by indiscreet or reckless behavior revealing an embarrassing or incriminating secret*

'But we tell you,' rejoined the Sheth, 'that it is *not* possible to keep our religion there. You know my relations with your father and you ought to listen to my advice.'

'I know those relations.' said I. 'And you are as an elder to me. But I am helpless in this matter. I cannot alter my resolve to go to England. My father's friend and adviser, who is a learned Brahman, sees no objection[1] to my gong to England, and my mother and brother have also given me their permission.'

'But will you disregard the orders of the caste?'

'I am really helpless. I think the caste should not interfere in the matter.'

This incensed the Sheth. He swore at me. I sat unmoved. So the Sheth pronounced his order: 'This boy shall be treated as an outcaste from today. Whoever helps him or goes to see him off at the dock shall be punishable with a fine of one rupee four annas.'

The order had no effect on me, and I took my leave of the Sheth. But I wondered how my brother would take it. Fortunately he remained firm and wrote to assure me that I had his permission to go, the Sheth's order notwithstanding.

The incident, however, made me more anxious than ever to sail. What would happen if they succeeded in bringing pressure[2] to bear on my brother? Supposing something unforeseen happened? As I was thus worrying over my predicament[3], I heard that a Junagadh vakil was going to England, for being called to the bar, by a boat sailing on the 4th of September. I met the friends to whose care my brother had commended me. They also agreed that I should not let go the opportunity of going in such company. There was no time to be lost. I wired to my brother for permission, which he granted. I asked my brother-in-law to give me the money. But he referred to the order of the Sheth and said that he could not afford to lose caste. I then sought a friend of the family and requested him to accommodate me to the extent of my passage and sundries, and to recover the loan from my brother. The friend was not only good enough to accede to my request, but he cheered me up as well. I was so thankful. With part of the money I at once purchased the passage. Then I had to equip myself for the voyage[4]. There was another friend who had experience in the matter. He got clothes and other things ready. Some

1. *objection: the action of challenging or disagreeing with something; an expression of disapproval or opposition*
2. *pressure: the use of persuasion, intimidation, etc. to make someone do something; a feeling of stressful urgency*
3. *predicament: a difficult situation*
4. *voyage: a long journey involving travel by sea or in space*

of the clothes I liked and some I did not like at all. The necktie, which I delighted in wearing later, I then abhorred. The short jacket I looked upon as immodest[1]. But this dislike was nothing before the desire to go to England, which was uppermost in me. Of provisions[2] also I had enough and to spare for the voyage. A berth was reserved[3] for me by my friends in the same cabin as that of Sjt. Tryambakrai Mazmudar, the Junagadh vakil. They also commended[4] me to him. He was an experienced man of mature age and knew the world. I was yet a stripling of eighteen without any experience of the world. Sjt. Mazmudar told my friends not to worry about me.

I sailed at last from Bombay on the 4th of September.

1. *immodest: not humble, decent, or decorous*
2. *provisions: supplies of food, drink, or requirements, especially for a journey*
3. *reserved: arrange for to be kept for the use of a particular person*
4. *commended: praise formally or officially*

CHAPTER 13

IN LONDON AT LAST

I did not feel at all sea-sick. But as the days passed, I became fidgety[1]. I felt shy even in speaking to the steward[2]. I was quite unaccustomed to talking English, and except for Sjt. Mazmudar all the other passengers in the second saloon[3] were English. I could not speak to them. For I could rarely follow their remarks when they came up to speak to me, and even when I understood I could not reply. I had to frame every sentence in my mind, before I could bring it out. I was innocent of the use of knives and forks and had not the boldness to inquire what dishes on the menu were free of meat, I therefore never took meals at table but always had them in my cabin, and they consisted principally of sweets and fruits which I had brought with me. Sjt. Mazmudar had no difficulty, and he mixed with everybody. He would move about freely on deck, while I hid myself in the cabin the whole day, only venturing up on deck when there were but few people. Sjt. Mazmudar kept pleading with me to associate with the passengers and to talk with them freely. He told me that lawyers should have a long tongue, and related to me his legal experiences. He advised me to take every possible opportunity of talking English, and not to mind making mistakes which were obviously unavoidable[4] with a foreign tongue. But nothing could make me conquer my shyness.

An English passenger, taking kindly to me, drew me into conversation. He was older than I. He asked me what I ate, what I was, where I was going, why I was shy, and so on. He also advised me to come to table. He laughed at my insistence on abjuring meat, and said in a friendly way when we were in the Red Sea: 'It is all very well so far but you will have to revise your decision in the Bay of Biscay. And it is so cold in England that one cannot possibly live there without meat.'

'But I have heard that people *can* live there without eating meat,' I said.

'Rest assured it is a fib,' said he. 'No one, to my knowledge, lives there without being a meat-eater. Don't you see that I am not asking you to take

1. *fidgety: make small movements through nervousness or impatience*
2. *steward: a person who looks after the passengers on a ship or aircraft*
3. *saloon: a public room or building used for a specified purpose*
4. *unavoidable: not able to be avoided or prevented; inevitable*

liquor, though I do so? But I do think you should eat meat, for you cannot live without it.'

'I thank you for your kind advice, but I have solemnly[1] promised to my mother not to touch meat, and therefore I cannot think of taking it. If it be found impossible to get on without it, I will far rather go back to India than eat meat in order to remain there.'

We entered the Bay of Biscay, but I did not begin to feel the need either of meat or liquor. I had been advised to collect certificates of my having abstained from meat, and I asked the English friend to give me one. He gladly gave it and I treasured it for some time. But when I saw later that one could get such a certificate in spite of being a meat-eater, it lost all its charm for me. If my word was not to be trusted, where was the use of possessing a certificate in the matter?

However, we reached Southampton, as far as I remember, on a Saturday. On the boat I had worn a black suit, the white flannel[2] one, which my friends had got me, having been kept especially for wearing when I landed. I had thought that white clothes would suit me better when I stepped ashore, and therefore I did so in white flannels. Those were the last days of September, and I found I was the only person wearing such clothes. I left in charge of an agent of Grindlay and Co. all my kit, including the keys, seeing that many others had done the same and I must follow suit.

I had four notes of introduction: to Dr. P. J. Mehta, to Sjt. Dalpatram Shukla, to Prince Ranjitsinhji and to Dadabhai Naoroji. Someone on board had advised us to put up at the Victoria Hotel in London. Sjt Mazmudar and I accordingly went there. The shame of being the only person in white clothes was already too much for me. And when at the Hotel I was told that I should not get my things from Grindlay's the next day, it being a Sunday, I was exasperated[3].

Dr. Mehta, to whom I had wired from Southampton, called at about eight o'clock the same evening. He gave me a hearty greeting. He smiled at my being in flannels. As we were talking. I casually picked up his top-hat, and trying to see how smooth it was, passed my hand over it the wrong way and disturbed the fur. Dr. Mehta looked somewhat angrily at what I was doing and stopped me. But the mischief had been done. The incident was a warning for the future. This was my first lesson in

1. *solemnly: formal and dignified; a solemn procession*
2. *flannel: a kind of soft-woven woolen or cotton fabric that is slightly milled and raised, men's trousers made of woolen flannel*
3. *exasperated: intensely irritated*

European etiquette, into the details of which Dr. Mehta humorously initiated me. 'Do not touch other people's things,' he said. 'Do not ask questions as we usually do in India on first acquaintance; do not talk loudly; never address people as "sir" whilst speaking to them as we do in India; only servants and subordinates address their masters that way. And so on and so forth. He also told me that it was very expensive to live in a hotel and recommended that I should live with a private family. We deferred consideration of the matter until Monday.

Sjt. Mazmudar and I found the hotel to be a trying affair. It was also very expensive. There was, however, a Sindhi fellow-passenger from Malta who had become friends with Sjt Mazmudar, and as he was not a stranger to London, he offered to find rooms for us. We agreed, and on Monday, as soon as we got our baggage, we paid up our bills and went to the rooms rented for us by the Sindhi friend. I remember my hotel bill came to £3 an amount which shocked me. And I had practically starved[1] in spite of this heavy bill! For I could relish[2] nothing. When I did not like one thing, I asked for another, but had to pay for both just the same. The fact is that all this while I had depended on the provisions which I had brought with me from Bombay.

I was very uneasy even in the new rooms. I would continually think of my home and country. My mother's love always haunted me. At night the tears would stream down my cheeks, and home memories of all sorts made sleep out of the question. It was impossible to share my misery with anyone. And even if I could have done so, where was the use? I knew of nothing that would soothe[3] me. Everything was strange - the people, their ways, and even their dwellings. I was a complete novice[4] in the matter of English etiquette and continually had to be on my guard. There was the additional inconvenience of the vegetarian vow. Even the dishes that I could eat were tasteless and insipid. I thus found myself between Scylla and Charybdis. England I could not bear, but to return to India was not to be thought of. Now that I had come, I must finish the three years, said the inner voice.

1. *starved: very hungry*
2. *relish: great enjoyment; pleasurable anticipation*
3. *soothe: gently calm; reduce pain or discomfort, in; relieve pain*
4. *novice: a person new to and inexperienced in a job or situation*

CHAPTER 14
MY CHOICE

Dr. Mehta went on Monday to the Victoria Hotel expecting[1] to find me there. He discovered that we had left, got our new address, and met me at our rooms. Through sheer folly I had managed to get ringworm on the boat. For washing and bathing we used to have sea-water, in which soap is not soluble. I, however, used soap, taking its use to be a sign of civilization[2], with the result that instead of cleaning the skin it made it greasy. This gave me ringworm. I showed it to Dr. Mehta, who told me to apply acetic acid. I remember how the burning acid made me cry. Dr. Mehta inspected my room and its appointments and shook his head in disapproval[3]. 'This place won't do,' he said. 'We come to England not so much for the purpose of studies as for gaining experience of English life and customs. And for this you need to live with a family. But before you do so, I think you had better serve a period of apprenticeship with -. I will take you there.'

I gratefully accepted the suggestion and removed to the friend's rooms. He was all kindness and attention. He treated me as his own brother, initiated me into English ways and manners, and accustomed me to talking the language. My food, however, became a serious question. I could not relish boiled vegetables cooked without salt or condiments. The landlady was at a loss to know what to prepare for me. We had oatmeal porridge for breakfast, which was fairly filling, but I always starved at lunch and dinner. The friend continually reasoned with me to eat meat, but I always pleaded my vow and then remained silent. Both for luncheon and dinner we had spinach and bread and jam too. I was a good eater and had a capacious stomach; but I was ashamed to ask for more than two or three slices of bread, as it did not seem correct to do so. Added to this, there was no milk either for lunch or dinner. The friend once got disgusted[4] with this state of things, and said: 'Had you been my own brother, I would have sent you packing. What is the value of a vow made before an illiterate mother, and in ignorance of conditions here? It is no vow at all. It would not be regarded

1. *expecting: regard as likely to happen, do, or be the case*
2. *civilization: an advanced stage or system of human social development; the process of achieving this*
3. *disapproval: rejection, not approved*
4. *disgusted: strong revulsion or profound indignation*

as a vow in law. It is pure superstition[1] to stick to such a promise. And I tell you this persistence will not help you to gain anything here. You confess to having eaten and relished meat. You took it where it was absolutely unnecessary, and will not where it is quite essential. What a pity!'

But I was adamant[2].

Day in and day out the friend would argue, but I had an eternal negative to face him with. The more he argued, the more uncompromising I became. Daily I would pray for God's protection and get it. Not that i had any idea of God. It was faith that was at work-faith of which the seed had been sown by the good nurse Rambha.

One day the friend began to read to me Bentham's *Theory of Utility*. I was at my wits' end. The language was too difficult for me to understand. He began to expound it. I said: 'Pray excuse me. These abstruse things are beyond me. I admit it is necessary to eat meat. But I cannot break my vow. I cannot argue about it. I am sure I cannot meet you in argument. But please give me up as foolish or obstinate[3]. I appreciate your love for me and I know you to be my well-wisher. I also know that you are telling me again and again about this because you feel for me. But I am helpless. A vow is a vow. It cannot be broken.'

The friend looked at me in surprise. He closed the book and said: 'All right. I will not argue any more.' I was glad. He never discussed the subject again. But he did not cease to worry about me. He smoked and drank, but he never asked me to do so. In fact he asked me to remain away from both. His one anxiety was lest I should become very weak without meat, and thus be unable to feel at home in England.

That is how I served my apprenticeship for a month. The friend's house was in Richmond, and it was not possible to go to London more than once or twice a week. Dr. Mehta and Sjt. Dalpatram Shukla therefore decided that I should be put with some family. Sjt. Shukla hit upon an Anglo-Indian's house in West Kensington and placed me there. The landlady was a widow. I told her about my vow. The old lady promised to look after me properly, and I took up my residence in her house. Here too I practically had to starve. I had sent for sweets and other eatables from home, but nothing had yet come. Everything was insipid. Every day the old lady asked me whether I liked the food, but what could she do? I was still as shy as ever and dared not ask for more than was put before

1. *superstition: excessively credulous belief in and reverence for the supernatural.a widely held but irrational belief in supernatural influences, especially as bringing good or bad luck*
2. *adamant: refusing to be persuaded or to change one's mind*
3. *obstinate: stubbornly refusingto change one's opinion or chosen course of action*

me. She had two daughters. They insisted on serving me with an extra slice or two of bread. But little did they know that nothing less than a loaf would have filled me.

But I had found my feet now. I had not yet started upon my regular studies. I had just begun reading newspapers, thanks to Sjt. Shukla. In India I had never read a newspaper. But here I succeeded in cultivating a liking for them by regular reading. I always glanced over *The Daily News, The Daily Telegraph, and The Pall Mall Gazette.* This took me hardly an hour. I therefore began to wander[1] about. I launched out in search of a vegetarian restaurant. The landlady had told me that there were such places in the city. I would trot ten or twelve miles each day, go into a cheap restaurant and eat my fill of bread, but would never be satisfied. During these wanderings I once hit on a vegetarian restaurant in Farringdon Street. The sight of it filled me with the same joy that a child feels on getting a thing after its own heart. Before I entered I noticed books for sale exhibited under a glass window near the door. I saw among them Salt's *Plea for Vegetarianism.* This I purchased for a shilling and went straight to the dining room. This was my first hearty meal since my arrival in England. God had come to my aid.

I read Salt's book from cover to cover and was very much impressed by it. From the date of reading this book, I may claim to have become a vegetarian by choice. I blessed the day on which I had taken the vow before my mother. I had all along abstained from meat in the interests of truth and of the vow I had taken, but had wished at the same time that every Indian should be a meat-eater, and had looked forward to being one myself freely and openly some day, and to enlisting[2] others in the cause. The choice was now made in favour of vegetarianism, the spread of which henceforward became my mission.

1. *wander: walk or move in a leisurely, casual, or aimless way*
2. *enlisting: engage a person or their help*

CHAPTER 15

PLAYING THE ENGLISH GENTLEMAN

My faith in vegetarianism grew on me from day to day. Salt's book whetted my appetite for dietetic studies. I went in for all books available on vegetarianism and read them. One of these, Howard Williams' *The Ethics of Diet*, was a 'biographical history of the literature of humane dietetics from the earliest period to the present day.' It tried to make out, that all philosophers and prophets[1] from Pythagoras and Jesus down to those of the present age were vegetarians. Dr. Anna Kingsford's *The Perfect Way in Diet* was also an attractive book. Dr. Allinson's writings on health and hygiene were likewise very helpful. He advocated[2] a curative[3] system based on regulation of the dietary of patients. Himself a vegetarian, he prescribed[4] for his patients also a strictly vegetarian diet. The result of reading all this literature was that dietetic experiments came to take an important place in my life. Health was the principal consideration of these experiments to begin with. But later on religion became the supreme motive.

Meanwhile my friend had not ceased to worry about me. His love for me led him to think that, if I persisted in my objections to meat-eating, I should not only develop a weak constitution, but should remain a duffer, because I should never feel at home in English society. When he came to know that I had begun to interest myself in books on vegetarianism, he was afraid lest these studies should muddle my head; that I should fritter my life away in experiments, forgetting my own work, and become a crank. He therefore made one last effort to reform me. He one day invited me to go to the theatre. Before the play we were to dine together at the Holborn Restaurant, to me a palatial place and the first big restaurant I had been to since leaving the Victoria Hotel. The stay at that hotel had scarcely been a helpful experience, for I had not lived there with my wits about me. The friend had planned to take me to this restaurant evidently imagining that modesty would forbid any questions. And it was a very big company of diners in the midst of which my friend and I sat sharing

1. *prophets: a person who predicts the future; a person who advocates a new belief or theory*
2. *advocated: publicly recommend or support*
3. *curative: able to cure disease*
4. *prescribed: advise and authorize the use of especially in writing*

a table between us. The first course was soup. I wondered what it might be made of, but dared not ask the friend about it. I therefore summoned[1] the waiter. My friend saw the movement and sternly asked across the table what was the matter. With considerable hesitation I told him that I wanted to inquire if the soup was a vegetable soup. 'You are too clumsy for decent society,' he passionately exclaimed 'If you cannot behave yourself, you had better go. Feed in some other restaurant and await me outside.' This delighted[2] me. Out I went. There was a vegetarian restaurant close by, but it was closed. So I went without food that night. I accompanied my friend to the theatre, but he never said a word about the scene I had created. On my part of course there was nothing to say.

That was the last friendly tussle[3] we had. It did not affect our relations in the least. I could see and appreciate the love by which all my friend's efforts were actuated, and my respect for him was all the greater on account of our differences in thought and action.

But I decided that I should put him at ease, that I should assure him that I would be clumsy no more, but try to become polished and make up for my vegetarianism by cultivating other accomplishments which fitted one for polite society. And for this purpose I undertook the all too impossible task of becoming an English gentleman.

The clothes after the Bombay cut that I was wearing were, I thought unsuitable for English society, and I got new ones at the Army and Navy stores. I also went in for a chimney-pot hat costing nineteen shillings an excessive price in those days. Not content with this, I wasted ten pounds on an evening suit made in Bond Street, the centre of fashionable life in London; and got my good and noble-hearted brother to send me a double watch-chain of gold. It was not correct to wear a ready-made tie and I learnt the art of tying one for myself. While in India, the mirror had been a luxury[4] permitted on the days when the family barber gave me a shave. Here I wasted ten minutes every day before a huge mirror, watching myself arranging my tie and parting my hair in the correct fashion. My hair was by no means soft, and every day it meant a regular struggle with the brush to keep it in position. Each time the hat was put on and off, the hand would automatically move towards the head to adjust the hair, not to mention the other civilized habit of the hand every now and then operating for the same purpose when sitting in polished society.

1. *summoned: call people to attend*
2. *delighted: please greatly*
3. *tussle: a vigorous struggle or scuffle*
4. *luxury: the state of great comfort and extravagant living*

As if all this were not enough to make me look the thing, I directed my attention to other details that were supposed to go towards the making of an English gentleman. I was told it was necessary for me to take lessons in dancing, French and elocution. French was not only the language of neighbouring France, but it was the *lingua franca*[1] of the Continent over which I had a desire to travel. I decided to take dancing lessons at a class and paid down £3 as fees for a term. I must have taken about six lessons in three weeks. But it was beyond me To achieve anything like rhythmic[2] motion. I could not follow the piano and hence found it impossible to keep time. What then was I to do? The recluse[3] in the fable kept a cat to keep off the rats, and then a cow to feed the cat with milk, and a man to keep the cow and so on. My ambitions also grew like the family of the recluse. I thought I should learn to play the violin in order to cultivate an ear for Western music. So I invested £3 in a violin and something more in fees. I sought a third teacher to give me lessons in elocution and paid him a preliminary fee of a guinea. He recommended Bell's *Standard Elocutionist* as the text-book, which I purchased. And I began with a speech of Pitt's.

But Mr. Bell rang the bell of alarm in my ear and I awoke.

I had not to spend a lifetime in England, I said to myself. What then was the use of learning elocution? And how could dancing make a gentleman of me? The violin I could learn even in India. I was a student and ought to go on with my studies. I should qualify myself to join the Inns of Court. If my character made a gentleman of me, so much the better. Otherwise I should forego the ambition.

These and similar thoughts possessed me, and I expressed them in a letter which I addressed to the elocution[4] teacher, requesting him to excuse me from further lessons. I had taken only two or three. I wrote a similar letter to the dancing teacher, and went personally to the violin teacher with a request to dispose of the violin for any price it might fetch. She was rather friendly to me, so I told her how I had discovered that I was pursuing a false ideal. She encouraged me in the determination to make a complete change.

This infatuation must have lasted about three months. The punctiliousness in dress persisted for years. But henceforward I became a student.

1. *lingua franca: a language which is used as a common language by people who speak different native languages*
2. *rhythmic: a strong, regular, repeated pattern of movement or sound*
3. *recluse: a person who avoids others and lives a solitary life*
4. *elocution: the skill of clear and expressive speech, especially of distinct pronunciation and articulation; a particular style of speaking*

CHAPTER 16

CHANGES

Let no one imagine that my experiments in dancing and the like marked a stage of indulgence[1] in my life. The reader will have noticed that even then I had my wits about me. That period of infatuation was not unrelieved by a certain amount of self-introspection[2] on my part. I kept account of every farthing I spent, and my expenses were carefully calculated. Every little item such as omnibus fares or postage or a couple of coppers spent on newspapers, would be entered, and the balance struck every evening before going to bed. That habit has stayed with me ever since, and I know that as a result, though I have had to handle public funds amounting to lakhs, I have succeeded in exercising strict economy in their disbursement[3], and instead of outstanding debts have had invariably a surplus balance in respect of all the movements I have led. Let every youth take a leaf out of my book and make it a point to account for everything that comes into and goes out of his pocket, and like me he is sure to be a gainer in the end.

As I kept strict watch over my way of living, I could see that it was necessary to economize. I therefore decided to reduce my expenses by half. My accounts showed numerous items spent on fares. Again my living with a family meant the payment of a regular weekly bill. It also included the courtesy of occasionally taking members of the family out to dinner, and likewise attending parties with them. All this involved heavy items for conveyances, especially as, if the friend was a lady, custom required that the man should pay all the expenses. Also dining out meant extra cost, as no deduction could be made from the regular weekly bill for meals not taken. It seemed to me that all these items could be saved, as likewise the drain on my purse caused through a false sense of propriety[4].

So I decided to take rooms on my own account, instead of living any longer in a family, and also to remove from place to place according to the work I had to do, thus gaining experience at the same time. The rooms were so selected as to enable me to reach the place of business on foot in

1. *indulgence: the action or fact of indulging, a thing that is indulged in; a luxury*
2. *introspection: the examination of one's own thoughts or feelings*
3. *disbursement: pay out money from a fund*
4. *propriety: correctness concerning standards of behavior or morals; the details or rules of conventionally accepted behavior; appropriateness; rightness*

half an hour, and so save fares. Before this I had always taken some kind of conveyance whenever I went anywhere, and had to find extra time for walks. The new arrangement combined walks and economy, as it meant a saving of fares and gave me walks of eight or ten miles a day. It was mainly this habit of long walks that kept me practically free from illness throughout my stay in England and gave me a fairly strong body.

Thus I rented a suite of rooms; one for a sitting room and another for a bedroom. This was the second stage. The third was yet to come.

These changes saved me half the expense. But how was I to utilize[1] the time? I knew that Bar examinations did not require much study, and I therefore did not feel pressed for time. My weak English was a perpetual worry to me. Mr (afterwards Sir Frederic) Lely's words, 'Graduate first and then come to me', still rang in my ears. I should, I thought, not only be called to the Bar, but have some literary degree as well. I inquired about the Oxford and Cambridge University courses, consulted a few friends, and found that, if I elected to go to either of these places, that would mean greater expense and a much longer stay in England than I was prepared for. A friend suggested that, if I really wanted to have the satisfaction of taking a difficult examination, I should pass the London Matriculation. It meant a good deal of labour and much addition to my stock of general knowledge, without any extra expense worth the name. I welcomed the suggestion. But the syllabus frightened me. Latin and a modern language were compulsory[2]! How was I to manage Latin? But the friend entered a strong plea for it: 'Latin is very valuable to lawyers. Knowledge of Latin is very useful in understanding law-books. And one paper in Roman Law is entirely in Latin. Besides a knowledge of Latin means greater command over the English language.' It went home and I decided to learn Latin, no matter how difficult it might be. French I had already begun, so I thought that should be the modern language. I joined a private Matriculation class. Examinations were held every six months and I had only five months at my disposal. It was an almost impossible task for me. But the aspirant[3] after being an English gentleman chose to convert himself into a serious student. I framed my own time-table to the minute; but neither my intelligence nor memory promised to enable me to tackle[4] Latin and French besides other subjects within the given period. The result was that I was ploughed in Latin. I was sorry but did not lose heart. I had

1. *utilize: make practical and effective use of*
2. *compulsory: required by law or a rule; obligatory; involving or exercising compulsion; coercive*
3. *aspirant: aspiring towards a particular achievement or status*
4. *tackle: make determined efforts to deal with a difficult task*

acquired a taste for Latin, also I thought my French would be all the better for another trial and I would select a new subject in the science group. Chemistry which was my subject in science had no attraction for want of experiments, whereas it ought to have been a deeply interesting study. It was one of the compulsory subjects in India and so I had selected it for the London Matriculation. This time, however, I chose Heat and Light instead of Chemistry. It was said to be easy and I found it to be so.

With my preparation for another trial, I made an effort to simplify my life still further. I felt that my way of living did not yet befit the modest means of my family. The thought of my struggling brother, who nobly responded to my regular calls for monetary help, deeply pained me. I saw that most of those who were spending from eight to fifteen pounds monthly had the advantage of scholarships. I had before me examples of much simpler living. I came across a fair number of poor students living more humbly than I. One of them was staying in the slums[1] in a room at two shillings a week and living on two pence worth of cocoa and bread per meal from Lockhart's cheap Cocoa Rooms. It was far from me to think of emulating him, but I felt I could surely have one room instead of two and cook some of my meals at home. That would be a saving of four to five pounds each month. I also came across books on simple living. I gave up the suite[2] of rooms and rented one instead, invested in a stove, and began cooking my breakfast at home. The process scarcely took me more than twenty minutes for there was only oatmeal porridge[3] to cook and water to boil for cocoa[4]. I had lunch out and for dinner bread and cocoa at home. Thus I managed to live on a shilling and three pence a day. This was also a period of intensive[5] study. Plain living saved me plenty of time and I passed my examination.

Let not the reader think that this living made my life by any means a dreary affair. On the contrary the change harmonized[6] my inward and outward life. It was also more in keeping with the means of my family. My life was certainly more truthful and my soul knew no bounds of joy.

1. *slums: a squalid and overcrowded urban area inhabited by very poor people; a house in such a place*
2. *suite: a set of rooms for one person's or family's use or for a particular purpose*
3. *porridge: a dish consisting of oatmeal or another cereal boiled with water or milk*
4. *cocoa: bean-like seeds from which cocoa, cocoa butter, and chocolate are made*
5. *intensive: very through or vigorous*
6. *harmonized: make consistent*

CHAPTER 17

EXPERIMENTS IN DIETETICS

As I searched myself deeper, the necessity for changes both internal and external began to grow on me. As soon as, or even before, I made alterations in my expenses and my way of living, I began to make changes in my diet. I saw that the writers on vegetarianism had examined the question very minutely, attacking it in its religious, scientific, practical and medical aspects. Ethically they had arrived at the conclusion that man's supremacy over the lower animals meant not that the former should prey upon the latter, but that the higher should protect the lower, and that there should be mutual[1] aid between the two as between man and man. They had also brought out the truth that man eats not for enjoyment but to live. And some of them accordingly suggested and effected in their lives abstention[2] not only from flesh-meat but from eggs and milk. Scientifically some had concluded that man's physical structure showed that he was not meant to be a cooking but a frugivorous animal, that he could take only his mother's milk and, as soon as he had teeth, should begin to take solid foods. Medically they had suggested the rejection of all spices and condiments[3]. According to the practical and economic argument they had demonstrated[4] that a vegetarian diet was the least expensive. All these considerations had their effect on me, and I came across vegetarians of all these types in vegetarian restaurants. There was a Vegetarian Society in England with a weekly journal of its own. I subscribed to the weekly, joined the society and very shortly found myself on the Executive Committee. Here I came in contact with those who were regarded as pillars of vegetarianism, and began my own experiments in dietetics.

I stopped taking the sweets and condiments I had got from home. The mind having taken a different turn, the fondness for condiments wore away, and I now relished the boiled spinach which in Richmond tasted insipid, cooked without condiments. Many such experiments taught me that the real seat of taste was not the tongue but the mind.

1. *mutual: experienced or done by each of two or more parties towards the other or others; mutual respect; having the same specified relationship to each other*
2. *abstention: abstinence*
3. *condiments: a substance such as salt that is used to enhance the flavor of food*
4. *demonstrated: clearly show the existence or truth or; give a practical exhibition and explanation of*

The economic consideration was of course constantly before me. There was in those days a body of opinion which regarded tea and coffee as harmful and favoured cocoa. And as I was convinced that one should eat only articles that sustained the body, I gave up tea and coffee as a rule, and substituted cocoa.

There were two divisions in the restaurants I used to visit. One division, which was patronized[1] by fairly well-to-do people, provided any number of courses from which one chose and paid for *a la carte*, each dinner thus costing from one to two shillings. The other division provided six-penny dinners of three courses with a slice of bread. In my days of strict frugality[2] I usually dined in the second division.

There were many minor experiments going on along with the main one; as for example, giving up starchy foods at one time, living on bread and fruit alone at another, and once living on cheese, milk and eggs. This last experiments is worth noting. It lasted not even a fortnight. The reformer who advocated starchless food had spoken highly of eggs and held that eggs were not meat. It was apparent that there was no injury done to living creatures in taking eggs. I was taken in by this plea and took eggs in spite of my vow. But the lapse was momentary[3]. I had no business to put a new interpretation on the vow. The interpretation of my mother who administered the vow was there for me. I knew that her definition of meat included eggs. And as soon as I saw the true import of the vow I gave up eggs and the experiment alike[4].

There is a nice point underlying the argument, and worth noting. I came across three definitions of meat in England. According to the first, meat denoted only the flesh of birds and beasts. Vegetarians who accepted that definition abjured the flesh of birds and beasts, but ate fish, not to mention eggs. According to the second definition, meat meant flesh of all living creatures. So fish was here out of the question, but eggs were allowed. The third definition included under meat the flesh of living beings, as well as all their products, thus covering eggs and milk alike. If I accepted the first definition, I could take not only eggs, but fish also. But I was convinced that my mother's definition was the definition binding on me. If, therefore, I would observe the vow I had taken, I must abjure eggs. I therefore did so. This was a hardship inasmuch as inquiry showed that even in vegetarian restaurants many courses used to contain eggs.

1. *patronized: frequent as a customer*
2. *frugality: sparing or economical as regards money or food*
3. *momentary: brief*
4. *alike: similar*

This meant that unless I knew what was what, I had to go through the awkward process of ascertaining whether a particular course contained eggs or no, for many puddings and cakes were not free from them. But though the revelation of my duty caused this difficulty, it simplified my food. The simplification in its turn brought me annoyance in that I had to give up several dishes I had come to relish. These difficulties were only passing, for the strict observance of the vow produced an inward relish distinctly more healthy, delicate and permanent.

The real ordeal, however, was still to come, and that was in respect of the other vow. But who dare harm whom God protects?

A few observations about the interpretation of vows or pledges may not be out of place here. Interpretation of pledges has been a fruitful[1] source of strife all the world over. No matter how explicit the pledge, people will turn and twist the text to suit their own purposes. They are to be met with among all classes of society, from the rich down to the poor, from the prince down to the peasant. Selfishness turns them blind, and by a use of the ambiguous middle they deceive themselves and seek to deceive the world and God. One golden rule is to accept the interpretation honestly put on the pledge by the party administering it. Another is to accept the interpretation of the weaker party, where there are two interpretations possible. Rejection of these two rules gives rise to strife and iniquity[2], which are rooted in untruthfulness. He who seeks truth alone easily follows the golden rule. He need not seek learned advice for interpretation. My mother's interpretation of meat was, according to the golden rule, the only true one for me, and not the one my wider experience or my pride of better knowledge might have taught me.

My experiments in England were conducted from the point of view of economy and hygiene. The religious aspect[3] of the question was not considered until I went to South Africa where I undertook strenuous experiments which will be narrated later. The seed, however, for all of them was sown in England.

A convert's enthusiasm for his new religion is greater than that of a person who is born in it. Vegetarianism was then a new cult[4] in England, and likewise for me, because, as we have seen, I had gone there a convinced meat-eater, and was intellectually converted to vegetarianism later. Full of the neophyte's zeal for vegetarianism, I decided to start a

1. *fruitful: producing good result; productive*
2. *iniquity: injustice or immoral behavior*
3. *aspect: a particular part or feature; a particular appearance or quality*
4. *cult: a system of religious devotion directed towards a particular figure or object; a relatively small religious group regarded by others as strange or as imposing excessive control over members*

vegetarian club in my locality, Bayswater. I invited Sir Edwin Arnold, who lived there, to be Vice-President. Dr. Oldfield who was Editor of the *The Vegetarian* became President. I myself became the Secretary. The club went well for a while, but came to an end in the course of a few months. For I left the locality, according to my custom of moving from place to place periodically. But this brief and modest experience gave me some little training in organizing and conducting[1] institutions.

1. *conducting: organize and carry out*

CHAPTER 18
SHYNESS MY SHIELD

I was elected to the Executive Committee of the Vegetarian Society, and made it a point to attend every one of its meetings, but I always felt tongue-tied. Dr. Oldfield once said to me, 'You talk to me quite all right, but why is it that you never open your lips at a committee meeting? You are a drone[1].' I appreciated the banter. The bees are ever busy, the drone is a thorough idler[2]. And it was not a little curious that whilst others expressed their opinions at these meetings, I sat quite silent. Not that I never felt tempted to speak. But I was at a loss to know how to express myself. All the rest of the members appeared to me to be better informed than I. Then it often happened that just when I had mustered up courage to speak, a fresh subject would be started. This went on for a long time.

Meantime a serious question came up for discussion. I thought it wrong to be absent, and felt it cowardice[3] to register a silent vote. The discussion arose somewhat in this wise. The President of the Society was Mr. Hills, proprietor of the Thames Iron Works. He was a puritan[4]. It may be said that the existence of the Society depended practically on his financial assistance. Many members of the Committee were more or less his protégés. Dr. Allinson of vegetarian fame was also a member of the Committee. He was an advocate of the then new birth control movement, and preached its methods among the working classes. Mr. Hills regarded these methods as cutting at the root of morals. He thought that the Vegetarian Society had for its object not only dietetic but also moral reform, and that a man of Dr. Allinson's anti-puritanic views should not be allowed to remain in the Society. A motion was therefore brought for his removal. The question deeply interested me. I considered Dr. Allinson's views regarding artificial methods of birth control as dangerous, and I believed that Mr. Hills was entitled, as a puritan, to oppose him. I had also a high regard for Mr. Hills and his generosity. But I thought it was quite improper to exclude a man from a vegetarian society simply because

1. *drone: someone who lives on the efforts and labor of others; a parasite*
2. *idler: a person who idles*
3. *cowardice: displaying a lack of bravery or courage*
4. *puritan: a person with censorious moral beliefs, especially about self-indulgence and sex*

he refused to regard puritan morals as one of the objects of the society. Mr. Hills' view regarding the exclusion of anti-puritans from the Society was personal to himself, and it had nothing to do with the declared object of the Society, which was simply the promotion of vegetarianism and not of any system of morality[1]. I therefore held that any vegetarian could be a member of the Society irrespective of his views on other morals.

There were in the Committee others also who shared my view, but I felt myself personally called upon to express my own. How to do it was the question. I had not the courage to speak and I therefore decided to set down my thoughts in writing. I went to the meeting with the document in my pocket. So far as I recollect, I did not find myself equal even to reading it, and the President had it read by someone else. Dr. Allinson lost the day. Thus in the very first battle of the kind I found myself siding with the losing party. But I had comfort in the thought that the cause was right. I have a faint recollection that, after this incident, I resigned from the Committee.

This shyness I retained[2] throughout my stay in England. Even when I paid a social call the presence of half a dozen or more people would strike[3] me dumb.

I once went to Ventnor with Sjt. Mazmudar. We stayed there with a vegetarian family. Mr. Howard, the author of *The Ethics of Diet*, was also staying at the same watering-place. We met him, and he invited us to speak at a meeting for the promotion of vegetarianism. I had ascertained[4] that it was not considered incorrect to read one's speech. I knew that many did so to express themselves coherently and briefly. To speak *ex tempore* would have been out of the question for me. I had therefore written down my speech. I stood up to read it, but could not. My vision became blurred and I trembled, though the speech hardly covered a sheet of foolscap. Sjt. Mazmudar had to read it for me. His own speech was of course excellent and was received with applause. I was ashamed of myself and sad at heart for my incapacity.

My last effort to make a public speech in England was on the eve of my departure for home. But this time too I only succeeded in making myself ridiculous. I invited my vegetarian friends to dinner in the Holborn Restaurant referred to in these chapters. 'A vegetarian dinner could be had,' I said to myself, 'in vegetarian restaurants as a matter of course.

1. *morality: principles concerning the distinction between right and wrong or good and bad behavior; a system of values and moral principles*
2. *retained: continue to have; keep possession of; not abolish, discard, or alter*
3. *strike: a sudden attack, typically a military one*
4. *ascertained: find out for certain*

But why should it not be possible in a non-vegetarian restaurant too?' And I arranged with the manager of the Holborn Restaurant to provide a strictly vegetarian meal. The vegetarians hailed the new experiment with delight. All dinners are meant for enjoyment, but the West has developed the thing into an art. They are celebrated with great *éclat*[1], music and speeches. And the little dinner party that I gave was also not unaccompanied by some such display. Speeches, therefore, there had to be. When my turn for speaking came, I stood up to make a speech. I had with great care thought out one which would consist of a very few sentences. But I could not proceed[2] beyond the first sentence. I had read of Addison that he began his maiden[3] speech in the House of Commons, repeating 'I conceive' three times, and when he could proceed no further, a wag stood up and said, 'The gentleman conceived thrice but brought forth nothing.' I had thought of making a humorous speech taking this anecdote[4] as the text. I therefore began with it and stuck there. My memory entirely failed me and in attempting a humorous speech I made myself ridiculous. I thank you, gentlemen, for having kindly responded to my invitation,' I said abruptly, and sat down.

It was only in South Africa that I got over this shyness, though I never completely overcame it. It was impossible for me to speak *impromptu.* I hesitated whenever I had to face strange audiences and avoided making a speech whenever I could. Even today I do not think I could or would even be inclined to keep a meeting of friends engaged in idle talk.

I must say that, beyond occasionally exposing me to laughter, my constitutional shyness has been no disadvantage whatever. In fact I can see that, on the contrary, it has been all to my advantage. My hesitancy in speech, which was once an annoyance, is now a pleasure. Its greatest benefit has been that it has taught me the economy of words. I have naturally formed the habit of restraining my thoughts. And I can now give myself the certificate that a thoughtless word hardly ever escapes my tongue or pen. I do not recollect ever having had to regret anything in my speech or writing. I have thus been spared many a mishap and waste of time. Experience has taught me that silence is part of the spiritual discipline of a votary of truth. Proneness to exaggerate, to suppress or modify the truth, wittingly or unwittingly, is a natural weakness of man and silence is necessary in order to surmount it. A man of few words will

1. *éclat: a strong and dazzling effect*
2. *proceed: move forward*
3. *maiden: being or involving the first attempt or act of its kind*
4. *anecdote: a short entertaining story about a real incident or person; an account regarded as unreliable or as being hearsay*

rarely be thoughtless in his speech; he will measure every word. We find so many people impatient to talk. There is no chairman of a meeting who is not pestered[1] with notes for permission to speak. And whenever the permission is given the speaker generally exceeds the time-limit, asks for more time, and keeps on talking without permission. All this talking can hardly be said to be of my benefit to the world. It is so much waste of time. My shyness has been in reality my shield and buckler[2]. It has allowed me to grow. It has helped me in my discernment of truth.

1. *pestered: trouble or annoy with persistent requests or interruptions*
2. *buckler: a small round shield held by a handle or worn on the forearm*

CHAPTER 19

THE CANKER OF UNTRUTH

There were comparatively few Indian students in England forty years ago. It was a practice with them to affect the bachelor even though they might be married. School or college students in England are all bachelors, studies being regarded as incompatible[1] with married life. We had that tradition in the good old days, a student then being invariably[2] known as a *brahmachari*. But in these days we have child-marriages, a thing practically unknown in England. Indian youths in England, therefore, felt ashamed to confess that they were married. There was also another reason for dissembling[3], namely that in the event of the fact being known it would be impossible for the young men to go about or flirt with the young girls of the family in which they lived. The flirting was more or less innocent. Parents even encouraged it; and that sort of association between young men and young women may even be a necessity there, in view of the fact that every young man has to choose his mate. If, however, Indian youths on arrival in England indulge in these relations, quite natural to English youths, the result is likely to be disastrous, as has often been found. I saw that our youths had succumbed to the temptation and chosen a life of untruth for the sake of companionships which, however innocent in the case of English youths, were for them undesirable. I too caught the contagion[4]. I did not hesitate to pass myself off as a bachelor though I was married and the father of a son. But I was none the happier for being a dissembler. Only my reserve and my reticence saved me from going into deeper waters. If I did not talk, no girl would think it worth her while to enter into conversation with me or to go out with me.

My cowardice was on a par with my reserve. It was customary in families like the one in which I was staying at Ventnor for the daughter of the landlady to take out guests for a walk. My landlady's daughter took me one day to the lovely hills round Ventnor. I was no slow walker, but my companion walked even faster, dragging me after her and chattering

1. *incompatible: not able to exist or be used together; unable to live together harmoniously*
2. *invariably: never changing*
3. *dissembling: hide or disguise one's true motives or feelings*
4. *contagion: the communication of disease form one person to another by close contact; a disease spread in such a way*

away all the while. I responded to her chatter sometimes with a whispered 'yes' or 'no', or at the most 'yes, how beautiful!' She was flying like a bird whilst I was wondering when I should get back home. We thus reached the top of a hill. How to get down again was the question. In spite of her high-heeled boots this sprightly[1] young lady of twenty-five darted[2] down the hill like an arrow. I was shamefacedly struggling to get down. She stood at the foot smiling and cheering me and offering to come and drag me. How could I be so chicken hearted? With the greatest difficulty, and crawling at intervals, I somehow managed to scramble[3] to the bottom. She loudly laughed 'bravo[4]' and shamed me all the more, as well she might.

But I could not escape scatheless everywhere. For God wanted to rid me of the canker of untruth. I once went to Brighton, another watering-place like Ventnor. This was before the Ventnor visit. I met there at a hotel an old widow of moderate means. This was my first year in England. The courses on the *menu* were all described in French, which I did not understand. I sat at the same table as the old lady. She saw that I was a stranger and puzzled, and immediately came to my aid. 'You seem to be a stranger,' she said, 'and look perplexed. Why have you not ordered anything?' I was spelling through the *menu* and preparing to ascertain the ingredients of the courses from the waiter, when the good lady thus intervened. I thanked her, and explaining my difficulty told her that I was at a loss to know which of the courses were vegetarian as I did not understand French.

'Let me help you,' she said. 'I shall explain the card to you and show you what you may eat.' I gratefully availed myself of her help. This was the beginning of an acquaintance that ripened into friendship and was kept up all through my stay in England and long after. She gave me her London address and invited me to dine at her house every Sunday. On special occasions also she would invite me, help me to conquer my bashfulness and introduce me to young ladies and draw me into conversation with them. Particularly marked out for these conversations was a young lady who stayed with her, and often we would be left entirely alone together.

I found all this very trying at first. I could not start a conversation nor could I indulge in any jokes. But she put me in the way. I began to learn; and in course of time looked forward to every Sunday and came to like the conversations with the young friend.

1. *sprightly: lively; energetic*
2. *darted: move suddenly or rapidly*
3. *scramble: move or make one's way quickly and awkwardly, typically by using one's hands as well as one's feet*
4. *bravo: used to express approval for a performer*

The old lady went on spreading her net wider every day. She felt interested in our meetings. Possibly she had her own plans about us.

I was in a quandary. 'How I wished I had told the good lady that I was married!' I said to myself. 'She would then have not thought of an engagement between us. It is, however, never too late to mend. If I declare the truth, I might yet be saved more misery.' With these thoughts in my mind, I wrote a letter to her somewhat to this effect:

'Ever since we met at Brighton you have been kind to me. You have taken care of me even as a mother of her son. You also think that I should get married and with that view you have been introducing me to young ladies. Rather than allow matters to go further, I must confess to you that I have been unworthy of your affection. I should have told you when I began my visits to you that I was married. I knew that Indian students in England dissembled the fact of their marriage and I followed suit. I now see that I should not have done so. I must also add that I was married while yet a boy, and am the father of a son. I am pained that I should have kept this knowledge from you so long. But I am glad God has now given me the courage to speak out the truth. Will you forgive me? I assure you I have taken no improper liberties with the young lady you were good enough to introduce to me. I knew my limits. You, not knowing that I was married, naturally desired[1] that we should be engaged. In order that things should not go beyond the present stage, I must tell you the truth.

'If on receipt of this, you feel that I have been unworthy of your hospitality[2], I assure you I shall not take it amiss. You have laid me under an everlasting debt of gratitude by your kindness and solicitude[3]. If, after this, you do not reject me but continue to regard me as worthy of your hospitality, which I will spare no pains to deserve, I shall naturally be happy and count it a further token of your kindness.'

Let the reader know that I could not have written such a letter in a moment. I must have drafted and redrafted it many times over. But it lifted a burden that was weighing me down. Almost by return post came her reply somewhat as follows:

'I have your frank letter. We were both very glad and had a hearty laugh over it. The untruth you say you have been guilty of is pardonable[4]. But it is well that you have acquainted us with the real state of things. My

1. *desired: a strong feeling of wanting to have something or wishing for something to happen*
2. *hospitality: the friendly and generous reception and entertainment of guests or strangers*
3. *solicitude: care or concern*
4. *pardonable: the action of forgiving or being forgiven for an error of offence*

invitation still stands and we shall certainly expect you next Sunday and look forward to hearing all about your child-marriage and to the pleasure of laughing at your expense. Need I assure you that our friendship is not in the least affected by this incident?'

I thus purged[1] myself of the canker of untruth, and I never thenceforward hesitated to talk of my married state wherever necessary.

1. purged: rid of an unwanted feeling or condition

CHAPTER 20

ACQUAINTANCE WITH RELIGIONS

Towards the end of my second year in England I came across two Theosophists, brothers, and both unmarried. They talked to me about the *Gita*. They were reading Sir Edwin Arnold's translation *The Song Celestial* and they invited me to read the original with them. I felt ashamed, as I had read the divine[1] poem neither in Samskrit nor in Gujarati. I was constrained to tell them that I had not read the *Gita*, but that I would gladly read it with them, and that though my knowledge of Samskrit was meagre[2], still I hoped to be able to understand the original to the extent of telling where the translation failed to bring out the meaning. I began reading the *Gita* with them. The verses in the second chapter - If one Ponders on objects of the sense, there springs Attraction; from attraction grows desire, Desire flames to fierce passion, passion breeds Recklessness[3]; then the memory all betrayed Lets noble purpose go, and saps the mind, Till purpose, mind, and man are all undone. made a deep impression[4] on my mind, and they still ring in my ears. The book struck me as one of priceless worth. The impression has ever since been growing on me with the result that I regard it today as the book *par excellence* for the knowledge of Truth. It has afforded me invaluable help in my moments of gloom. I have read almost all the English translations of it, and I regard Sir Edwin Arnold's as the best. He has been faithful to the text, and yet it does not read like a translation. Though I read the *Gita* with these friends, I cannot pretend to have studied it then. It was only after some years that it became a book of daily reading.

The brothers also recommended *The Light of Asia* by Sir Edwin Arnold, whom I knew till then as the author only of *The Song Celestial*, and I read it with even greater interest than I did the *Bhagavadgita*. Once I had begun it I could not leave off. They also took me on one occasion to the Blavatsky Lodge and introduced me to Madame Blavatsky and Mrs. Besant. The latter had just then joined the Theosophical Society, and I was following with great interest the controversy about her conversion.

1. *divine: of from or like god or a god; devoted to god; sacred*
2. *meagre: lacking in quantity or quality*
3. *recklessness: without thought or care for the consequences of an action*
4. *impression: an idea, feeling, oropinion; an effect produced or someone*

The friends advised me to join the Society, but I politely declined saying, 'With my meagre knowledge of my own religion I do not want to belong to any religious body.' I recall having read, at the brothers' instance, Madame Blavatsky's *Key to Theosophy*. This book stimulated in me the desire to read books on Hinduism, and disabused[1] me of the notion fostered by the missionaries that Hinduism was rife[2] with superstition.

About the same time I met a good Christian from Manchester in a vegetarian boarding house. He talked to me about Christianity. I narrated to him my Rajkot recollections. He was pained to hear them. He said, 'I am a vegetarian. I do not drink. Many Christians are meat-eaters and drink, no doubt; but neither meat-eating nor drinking is enjoined by Scripture. Do please read the Bible.' I accepted his advice, and he got me a copy. I have a faint recollection that he himself used to sell copies of the Bible, and I purchased from him an edition containing maps, concordance, and other aids. I began reading it, but I could not possibly read through the Old Testament. I read the book of Genesis, and the chapters that followed invariably sent me to sleep. But just for the sake of being able to say that I had read it, I plodded[3] through the other books with much difficulty and without the least interest or understanding. I disliked reading the book of Numbers.

But the New Testament produced a different impression, especially the Sermon[4] on the Mount which went straight to my heart. I compared it with the *Gita*. The verses, 'But I say unto you, that ye resist not evil: but whosoever shall smite thee on thy right cheek, turn to him the other also. And if any man take away thy coat let him have thy cloke too,' delighted me beyond measure and put me in mind of Shamal Bhatt's 'For a bowl of water, give a goodly meal' etc. My young mind tried to unify the teaching of the *Gita, the Light of Asia* and the Sermon on the Mount. That renunciation was the highest form of religion appealed to me greatly.

This reading whetted my appetite for studying the lives of other religious teachers. A friend recommended Carlyle's *Heroes and Hero-Worship*. I read the chapter on the Hero as a prophet and learnt of the Prophet's greatness and bravery and austere living.

Beyond this acquaintance with religion I could not go at the moment, as reading for the examination left me scarcely any time for outside subjects. But I took mental note of the fact that I should read more religious books and acquaint myself with all the principal religions.

1. *disabused: persuade that an idea or belief is mistaken*
2. *rife: wide spread*
3. *plodded: work slowly and perseveringly at a dull task*
4. *sermon: a talk on a religious or moral subject, especially one given during a church service and based on a passage from the Bible*

And how could I help knowing something of atheism too? Every Indian knew Bradlaugh's name and his so-called atheism. I read some book about it, the name of which I forget. It had no effect on me, for I had already crossed the Sahara of atheism. Mrs. Besant who was then very much in the limelight, had turned to theism from atheism, and that fact also strengthened my aversion to atheism. I had read her book *How I became a Theosophist*.

It was about this time that Bradlaugh died. He was buried in the Working Cemetery. I attended the funeral, as I believe every Indian residing[1] in London did. A few clergymen also were present to do him the last honours. On our way back from the funeral we had to wait at the station for our train. A champion atheist from the crowd heckled one of these clergymen. 'Well sir, you believe in the existence of God?'

'I do,' said the good man in a low tone.

'You also agree that the circumference[2] of the Earth is 28,000 miles, don't you?' said the atheist with a smile of self-assurance. 'Indeed.' 'Pray tell me then the size of your God and where he may be?'

'Well, if we but knew, He resides in the hearts of us both.'

'Now, now, don't take me to be a child,' said the champion with a triumphant look at us.

The clergyman assumed a humble[3] silence. This talk still further increased my prejudice against atheism.

1. *residing: have one's permanent home in a particular place*
2. *circumference: the enclosing boundary of a circle*
3. *humble: having or showing a modest or low estimate of one's importance*

CHAPTER 21

NIRBAL KE BAL RAM[1]

Though I had acquired a nodding acquaintance[2] with Hinduism and other religions of the world, I should have known that it would not be enough to save me in my trails. Of the thing that sustains him through trials man has no inkling[3], much less knowledge, at the time. If an unbeliever, he will attribute his safety to chance. If a believer, he will say God saved him. He will conclude, as well he may, that his religious study or spiritual discipline was at the back of the state of grace within him. But in the hour of his deliverance he does not know whether his spiritual discipline or something else saves. Who that has prided himself on his spiritual strength has not seen it humbled to the dust? A knowledge of religion, as distinguished from experience, seems but chaff[4] in such moments of trial.

It was in England that I first discovered the futility of mere religious knowledge. How I was saved on previous occasions is more than I can say, for I was very young then; but now I was twenty and had gained some experience as husband and father.

During the last year, as far as I can remember, of my stay in England, that is in 1890, there was a Vegetarian Conference at Portsmouth to which an Indian friend and I were invited. Portsmouth is a sea-port with a large naval population. It has many houses with women of ill fame, women not actually prostitutes, but at the same time, not very scrupulous[5] about their morals. We were put up in one of these houses. Needles to say, the Reception Committee did not know anything about it. It would have been difficult in a town like Portsmouth to find out which were good lodgings and which were bad for occasional travelers like us.

We returned from the Conference in the evening. After dinner we sat down to play a rubber of bridge, in which our landlady joined, as is customary in England even in respectable households. Every player indulges in innocent jokes as a matter of course, but here my companion and our hostess began to make indecent ones as well. I did not know that

1. *nirbal ke bal Ram: refrain of Surdas' famous hymn, 'he is the help of the helpless, the strength of the weak*
2. *acquaintance: know personally*
3. *inkling: a slight suspicion; a hint*
4. *chaff: the husks of grain or other seed separated by winnowing or threshing; chopped hay and straw used as fodder*
5. *scrupulous: very concerned to avoid doing wrong*

my friend was an adept in the art. It captured me and I also joined in. Just when I was about to go beyond the limit, leaving the cards and the game to themselves. God through the good companion uttered the blessed warning: 'Whence this devil in you, my boy? Be off, quick!'

I was ashamed. I took the warning and expressed within myself gratefulness to my friend. Remembering the vow I had taken before my mother, I fled from the scene. To my room I went quaking[1], trembling, and with beating heart, like a quarry escaped from its pursuer.

I recall this as the first occasion on which a woman, other than my wife, moved me to lust. I passed that night sleeplessly, all kinds of thoughts assailing me. Should I leave this house? Should I run away from the place? Where was I? What would happen to me if I had not my wits about me? I decided to act thenceforth with great caution[2]; not to leave the house, but somehow leave Portsmouth. The Conference was not to go on for more than two days, and I remember I left Portsmouth the next evening, my companion staying there some time longer.

I did not then know the essence[3] of religion or of God, and how He works in us. Only vaguely I understood that God had saved me on that occasion. On all occasions of trial He has saved me. I know that the phrase 'God saved me' has a deeper meaning for me today, and still I feel that I have not yet grasped its entire meaning. Only richer experience can help me to a fuller understanding. But in all my trials of a spiritual nature, as a lawyer, in conducting institutions, and in politics I can say that God saved me. When every hope is gone. 'When helpers fail and comforts flee[4],' I find that help arrives somehow, from I know not where. Supplication, worship, prayer are no superstition; they are acts more real than the acts of eating, drinking, sitting or walking. It is no exaggeration to say that they alone are real, all else is unreal.

Such worship or prayer is no flight of eloquence; it is no lip-homage. It springs from the heart. If, therefore, we achieve that purity of the heart when it is 'emptied of all but love', if we keep all the chords in proper tune, they 'trembling pass in music out of sight'. Prayer needs no speech. It is in itself independent of any sensuous effort. I have not the slightest doubt that prayer is an unfailing means of cleansing the heart of passions. But it must be combined with the utmost humility.

1. *quaking: shaking or trembling*
2. *caution: care taken to avoid danger or mistakes*
3. *essence: the intrinsic nature of something the quality which determines something's character; (philosophy) a property or group of properties of something without which it would not exist or be what it is*
4. *flee: run away*

CHAPTER 22

NARAYAN HEMCHANDRA

Just about this time Narayan Hemchandra came to England. I had heard of him as a writer. We met at the house of Miss Manning of the National Indian Association. Miss Manning knew that I could not make myself sociable[1]. When I went to her place I used to sit tongue-tied, never speaking except when spoken to. She introduced me to Narayan Hemchandra. He did not know English. His dress was queer[2] a clumsy pair of trousers, a wrinkled, dirty, brown coat after the Parsi fashion, no necktie or collar, and a tasseled woolen cap. He grew a long beard.

He was lightly built and short of stature[3]. His round face was scarred[4] with small-pox, and had a nose which was neither pointed nor blunt. With his hand he was constantly turning over his beard.

Such a queer-looking and queerly dressed person was bound to be singled out in fashionable society.

'I have heard a good deal about you,' I said to him. 'I have also read some of your writings. I should be very pleased if you were kind enough to come to my place.'

Narayan Hemchandra had a rather hoarse voice. With a smile on his face he replied?' 'Yes, where do you stay?' 'In Store Street.' 'Then we are neighbours. I want to learn English. Will you teach me?' 'I shall be happy to teach you anything I can, and will try my best. If you like, I will go to your place.'

'Oh, no. I shall come to you. I shall also bring with me a Translation Exercise Book.' So we made an appointment. Soon we were close friends.

Narayan Hemchandra was innocent of grammar. 'Horse' was a verb with him and 'run' a noun I remember many such funny instances. But he was not to be baffled by his ignorance. My little knowledge of grammar could make no impression on him. Certainly he never regarded his ignorance of grammar as a matter for shame.

With perfect nonchalance he he said: 'I have never been to school like you. 'I have never felt the need of grammar in expressing my thoughts.

1. *sociable: engaging readily with other people; marked by friendliness*
2. *queer: strange; odd*
3. *scarred: a mark left on the skin or within body tissue after the healing of a wound or burn*
4. *stature: a person's natural height when standing*

Well, do you know Bengali? I know it. I have travelled in Bengal. It is I who have given Maharshi Devendranath Tagore's works to the Gujarati speaking world. And I wish to translate into Gujarati the treasures of many other languages. I always content myself with bringing out the spirit. Others, with their better knowledge, may be able to do more in future. But I am quite satisfied with what I have achieved without the help of grammar. I know Marathi, Hindi, Bengali, and now I have begun to know English. What I want is a copious vocabulary. And do you think my ambition ends here? No fear. I want to go to France and learn French. I am told that language has an extensive[1] literature. I shall go to Germany also, if possible, and there learn German.' And thus he would talk on unceasingly. He had a boundless ambition for learning languages and for foreign travel.

'Then you will go to America also?'

'Certainly. How can I return to India without having seen the New World?'

'But where will you find the money?'

'What do I need money for? I am not a fashionable fellow like you. The minimum amount of food and the minimum amount of clothing suffice[2] for me. And for this what little I get out of my books and from my friends is enough. I always travel third class. While going to America also I shall travel on deck.'

Narayan Hemchandra's simplicity was all his own, and his frankness was on a par with it. Of pride he had not the slightest trace, excepting, of course, a rather undue[3] regard for his own capacity as a writer.

We met daily. There was a considerable amount of similarity between our thoughts and actions. Both of us were vegetarians. We would often have our lunch together. This was the time when I lived on 17s. a week and cooked for myself. Sometimes when I would go to his room, and sometimes he would come to mine. I cooked in the English style. Nothing but Indian style would satisfy him. He would not do without *dal*. I would make soup of carrots etc., and he would pity me for my taste. Once he somehow hunted out *mung*[4] cooked it and brought it to my place. I ate it with delight. This led on to a regular system of exchange between us. I would take my delicacies[5] to him and he would bring his to me.

1. *extensive: covering a large area; large in amount or scale*
2. *suffice: be enough or adequate; meet the needs of*
3. *undue: unwarranted or inappropriate; become excessive or disproportionate*
4. *mung: an Indian pulse*
5. *delicacies: gourmet food*

Cardinal Manning's name was then on every lip. The dock labourers' strike had come to an early termination owing to the efforts of John Burns and Cardinal Manning. I told Narayan Hemchandra of Disraeli's tribute[1] to the Cardinal's simplicity. 'Then I must see the sage,' said he.

'He is a big man. How do you expect to meet him?'

'Why? I know how. I must get you to write to him in my name. Tell him I am an author and that I want to congratulate him personally on his humanitarian work, and also say that I shall have to take you as interpreter[2] as I do not know English.'

I wrote a letter to that effect. In two or three days came Cardinal Manning's card in reply giving us an appointment. So we both called on the Cardinal. I put on the usual visiting suit. Narayan Hemchandra was the same as ever, in the same coat and the same trousers. I tried to make fun of this, but he laughed me out and said:

'You civilized fellows are all cowards. Great men never look at a person's exterior[3]. They think of his heart.'

We entered the Cardinal's mansion. As soon as we were seated, a thin, tall, old gentleman made his appearance, and shook hands with us. Narayan Hemchandra thus gave his greetings:

'I do not want to take up your time. I had heard a lot about you and I felt I should come and thank you for the good work you have done for the strikers. It has been my custom to visit the sages of the world and that is why I have put you to this trouble.'

This was of course my translation of that he spoke in Gujarati.

'I am glad you have come. I hope your stay in London will agree with you and that you will get in touch with people here. God bless you.'

With these words the Cardinal stood up and said good-bye.

Once Narayan Hemchandra came to my place in a shirt and *dhoti*. The good landlady opened the door, came running to me in a fright this was a new landlady who did not know Narayan Hemchandra and said: 'A sort of a madcap wants to see you.' I went to the door and to my surprise found Narayan Hemchandra. I was shocked. His face, however, showed nothing but his usual smile.

'But did not the children in the street rag you?'

'Well, they ran after me, but I did not mind them and they were quiet.'

1. *tribute: an act, statement, or gift that is intended to show gratitude, respect, or admiration; something resulting from and indicating the worth if something else*
2. *interpreter: a person who interprets foreign speech orally*
3. *exterior: the outer surface or structure of something*

Narayan Hemchandra went to Paris after a few months' stay in London. He began studying French and also translating French books. I knew enough French to revise[1] his translation, so he gave it to me to read. It was not a translation, it was the substance.

Finally he carried out his determination to visit America. It was with great difficulty that he succeeded in securing a duck ticket. While in the United States he was prosecuted[2] for 'being indecently dressed', as he once went out in a shirt and *dhoti*. I have a recollection that he was discharged.

1. *revise: examine and improve or amend something, especially written matter*
2. *prosecuted: institute legal proceedings against, institute legal proceedings in respect of a claim or focused or sued in a lawsuit*

CHAPTER 23

THE GREAT EXHIBITION

There was a great Exhibition at Paris in 1890. I had read about its elaborate preparations, and I also had a keen desire to see Paris. So I thought I had better combine two things in one and go there at this juncture[1]. A particular attraction of the Exhibition was the Eiffel Tower, constructed entirely of iron, and nearly 1,000 feet high. There were of course many other things of interest, but the Tower was the chief one, inasmuch as it had been supposed till then that a structure of that height could not safely stand.

I had heard of a vegetarian restaurant in Paris. I engaged a room there and stayed seven days. I managed everything very economically, both the journey to Paris and the sight-seeing there. This I did mostly on foot and with the help of a map of Paris, as also a map of and guide to the Exhibition. These were enough to direct one to the main streets and chief places of interest.

I remember nothing of the Exhibition excepting its magnitude and variety. I have fair recollection of the Eiffel Tower as I ascended it twice or thrice. There was a restaurant on the first platform, and just for the satisfaction of being able to say that I had had my lunch at a great height, I threw away seven shillings on it.

The ancient churches of Paris are still in my memory. Their grandeur[2] and their peacefulness are unforgettable. The wonderful construction of Notre Dame and the elaborate decoration of the interior with its beautiful sculptures cannot be forgotten. I felt then that those who expended millions on such divine cathedrals could not but have the love of God in their hearts.

I had read a lot about the fashions and frivolity[3] of Paris. These were in evidence in every street, but the churches stood noticeably apart from these scenes. A man would forget the outside noise and bustle as soon as he entered one of these churches. His manner would change, he would behave with dignity and reverence[4] as he passed someone kneeling before

1. *juncture: a place where things join*
2. *grandeur: splendor and impressiveness; high rank or social importance*
3. *frivolity: light hardheartedness, foolishness*
4. *reverence: deep respect*

the image of the Virgin. The feeling I had then has since been growing on me, that all this kneeling and prayer could not be mere superstition; the devout souls kneeling before the Virgin could not be worshipping mere marble. They were fired with genuine devotion[1] and they worshipped not stone, but the divinity of which it was symbolic. I have an impression that I felt then that by this worship they were not detracting from, but increasing, the glory of God.

I must say a word about the Eiffel Tower. I do not know what purpose it serves today. But I then heard it greatly disparaged[2] as well as praised. I remember that Tolstoy was the chief among those who disparaged it. He said that the Eiffel Tower was a monument[3] of man's folly, not of his wisdom. Tobacco, he argued, was the worst of all intoxicants[4], inasmuch as a man addicted to it was tempted to commit crimes which a drunkard never dared to do; liquor made a man mad, but tobacco clouded his intellect and made him build castles in the air. The Eiffel Tower was one of the creations of a man under such influence. There is no art about the Eiffel Tower. In no way can it be said to have contributed to the real beauty of the Exhibition. Men flocked to see it and ascended it as it was a novelty and of unique dimensions. It was the toy of the Exhibition. So long as we are children we are attracted by toys, and the Tower was a good demonstration of the fact that we are all children attracted by trinkets. That may be claimed to be the purpose served by the Eiffel Tower.

1. *devotion: love, loyalty, or enthusiasm for a person or activity*
2. *disparaged: represent as being of little worth; scorn*
3. *monument: a statue, building, or other structure erected to commemorate a notable person or event*
4. *intoxicants: an intoxicating substance*

CHAPTER 24

'CALLED'-BUT THEN?

I have deferred saying anything up to now about the purpose for which I went to England, viz. being called to the bar. It is time to advert[1] to it briefly.

There were two conditions which had to be fulfilled before a student was formally called to the bar: 'keeping terms,' twelve terms equivalent to about three years; and passing examinations. 'Keeping terms' meant eating one's terms, i.e. attending at least six out of about twenty four dinners in a term. Eating did not mean actually partaking[2] of the dinner, it meant reporting oneself at the fixed hours and remaining present throughout the dinner. Usually of course every one ate and drank the good commons and choice wines provided. A dinner cost from two and six to three and six, that is from two to three rupees. This was considered moderate[3], inasmuch as one had to pay that same amount for wines alone if one dined at a hotel. To us in India it is a matter for surprise, if we are not 'civilized', that the cost of drink should exceed the cost of food. The first revelation gave me a great shock, and I wondered how people had the heart to throw away so much money on drink. Later I came to understand. I often ate nothing at these dinners, for the things that I might eat were only bread, boiled potato and cabbage. In the beginning I did not eat these, as I did not like them; and later, when I began to relish them, I also gained the courage to ask for other dishes.

The dinner provided for the benchers used to be better than that for the students. A Parsi student, who was also a vegetarian, and I applied, in the interests of vegetarianism, for the vegetarian courses which were served to the benchers. The application was granted, and we began to get fruits and other vegetables from the benchers' table.

Two bottles of wine were allowed to each group of four, and as I did not touch them, I was ever in demand to form a quarter, so that three might empty two bottles. And there was a 'grand night' in each term when extra

1. *advert: (formal) refer to*
2. *partaking: take part in an activity or event*
3. *moderate: average in amount, intensity, or degree*

wines, like champagne, in addition to port and sherry were served. I was therefore specially requested to attend and was in great demand on that 'grand night'.

I could not see then, nor have I seen since, how these dinners qualified the students better for the bar. There was once a time when only a few students used to attend these dinners and thus there were opportunities for talks between them and the benchers, and speeches were also made. These occasions helped to give them knowledge of the world with a sort of polish and refinement, and also improved their power of speaking. No such thing was possible in my time, as the benchers had a table all to themselves. The institution had gradually lost all its meaning but conservative[1] England retained it nevertheless.

The curriculum of study was easy, barristers being humorously[2] known as 'dinner barristers'. Everyone knew that the examinations had practically no value. In my time there were two, one in Roman Law and the other in Common Law. There were regular text-books prescribed for these examinations which could be taken in compartments, but scarcely any one read them. I have known many to pass the Roman Law examination by scrambling through notes on Roman Law in a couple of weeks, and the Common Law examination by reading notes on the subject in two or three months. Question papers were easy and examiners were generous. The percentage of passes in the Roman Law examination used to be 95 to 99 and of those in the final examination 75 or even more. There was thus little fear of being plucked, and examinations were held not once but four times in the year. They could not be felt as a difficulty.

But I succeeded in turning them into one. I felt that I should read all the text-books. It was a fraud, I thought, not to read these books. I invested much money in them. I decided to read Roman Law in Latin. The Latin which I had acquired in the London Matriculation stood me in good stead. And all this reading was not without its value later on in South Africa, where Roman Dutch is the common law. The reading of Justinian, therefore, helped me a great deal in understanding the South African law.

It took me nine months of fairly hard labour to read through the Common Law of England. For Broom's *Common Law*, a big but interesting volume, took up a good deal of time. Snell's *Equity* was full of interest, but

1. *conservative: averse to change or innovation and holding traditional values*
2. *humorously: causing amusement*

a bit hard to understand. White and Tudor's *Leading Cases*, from which certain cases were prescribed, was full of interest and instruction. I read also with interest Williams' and Edwards' *Real Property*, and Goodeve's *Personal Property*. Williams' book read like a novel. The one book I remember to have read, on my return to India, with the same unflagging interest, was Mayne's *Hindu Law*. But it is out of place to talk here of Indian law books.

I passed my examinations, was called to the bar on the 10th of June 1891, and enrolled in the High Court on the 11th. On the 12th sailed for home.

But notwithstanding my study there was no end to my helplessness and fear. I did not feel myself qualified to practise law.

But a separate chapter is needed to describe this helplessness of mine.

CHAPTER 25

MY HELPLESSNESS

It was easy to be called, but it was difficult to practise at the bar. I had read the laws, but not learnt how to practise law. I had read with interest 'Legal Maxims', but did not know how to apply them in my profession. '*Sic utere tuo ut alienum non laedas*' (Use your property in such a way as not to damage that of others) was one of them, but I was at a loss to know how one could employ this maxim for the benefit of one's client. I had read all the leading cases on this maxim, but they gave me no confidence in the application of it in the practice of law.

Besides, I had learnt nothing at all of Indian law. I had not the slightest idea of Hindu and Mahomedan Law. I had not even learnt how to draft[1] a plaint, and felt completely at sea. I had heard of Sir Pherozeshah Mehta as one who roared like a lion in law courts. How, I wondered, could he have learnt the art in England? It was out of the question for me ever to acquire his legal acumen[2], but I had serious misgivings[3] as to whether I should be able even to earn a living by the profession.

I was torn with these doubts and anxieties whilst I was studying law. I confided my difficulties to some of my friends. One of them suggested that I should seek Dadabhai Naoroji's advice. I have already said that, when I went to England, I possessed a note of introduction to Dadabhai. I availed myself of it very late. I thought I had no right to trouble such a great man for an interview. Whenever an address by him was announced, I would attend it, listen to him from a corner of the hall, and go away after having feasted my eyes and ears. In order to come in close touch with the students he had founded an association, I used to attend its meetings, and rejoiced at Dadabhai's solicitude[4] for the students, and the latter's respect for him. In course of time I mustered up courage to present to him the note of introduction. He said: 'You can come and have my advice whenever you like.' But I never availed myself of his offer. I thought it wrong to trouble him without the most pressing necessity. Therefore

1. *draft: a preliminary version of a piece of writing; a plan or sketch*
2. *acumen: the ability to make good judgments and take quick decisions*
2. *misgivings: a feeling of doubt of apprehension about something*
4. *solicitude: care or concern*

I dared not venture to accept my friend's advice to submit my difficulties to Dadabhai at that time. I forget now whether it was the same friend or someone else who recommended me to meet Mr. Frederick Pincutt. He was a Conservative, but his affection for Indian students was pure and unselfish. Many students sought his advice and I also applied to him for an appointment, which he granted. I can never forget that interview. He greeted me as a friend. He laughed away my pessimism[1]. 'Do you think,' he said, 'that everyone must be a Pherozeshah Mehta? Pherozeshahs and Badruddins are rare. Rest assured it takes no unusual skill to be an ordinary lawyer. Common honesty and industry are enough to enable him to make a living. All cases are not complicated. Well, let me know the extent of your general reading.'

When I acquainted him with my little stock of reading, he was, as I could see, rather disappointed. But it was only for a moment. Soon his face beamed[2] with a pleasing smile and he said, 'I understand your trouble. Your general reading is meagre. You have no knowledge of the world, *a sine qua non* for a vakil. You have not even read the history of India. A vakil should know human nature. He should be able to read a man's character from his face. And every Indian ought to know Indian history. This has no connection with the practice of law, but you ought[3] to have that knowledge. I see that you have not even read Kaye's and Malleson's history of the Mutiny of 1857. Get hold of that at once and also read two more books to understand human nature.' These were Lavator's and Shemmelpennick's books on physiognomy.

I was extremely grateful to this venerable friend. In his presence I found all my fear gone, but as soon as I left him I began to worry again. 'To know a man from his face' was the question that haunted me, as I thought of the two books on my way home. The next day I purchased Lavator's book. Shemmelpennick's was not available at the shop. I read Lavator's book and found it more difficult than Snell's *Equity*, and scarcely interesting. I studied Shakespeare's physiognomy, but did not acquire the knack of finding out the Shakespeares walking up and down the streets of London.

Lavator's book did not add to my knowledge. Mr. Pincutt's advice did me very little direct service, but his kindliness stood me in good stead[4]. His smiling open face stayed in my memory, and I trusted his advice that

1. *pessimism: lack of hope or confidence in the future*
2. *beamed: smile radiantly*
3. *ought: used to indicate duty or correctness; used to indicate a desirable or expected state; used to give or ask advice*
4. *stead: the place or role that someone or something should have or fill: appointed in his stead*

Pherozeshah Mehta's acumen[1], memory and ability were not essential to the making of a successful lawyer; honesty and industry were enough. And as I had a fair share of these last I felt somewhat reassured.

I could not read Kaye and Malleson's volumes in England, but I did so in South Africa as I had made a point of reading them at the first opportunity.

Thus with just a little leaven of hope mixed with my despair, I landed at Bombay from S.S. *Assam*. The sea was rough in the harbour, and I had to reach the quay in a launch.

1. *acumen: the ability to make good judgements and take quick decisions*

CHAPTER 26

RAYCHANDBHAI

I said in the last chapter that the sea was rough in Bombay harbour, not an unusual thing in the Arabian Sea in June and July. It had been choppy all the way from Aden. Almost every passenger was sick; I alone was in perfect form, staying on deck to see the stormy surge[1], and enjoying the splash of the waves. At breakfast there would be just one or two people besides myself, eating their oatmeal porridge from plates carefully held in their laps, lest the porridge itself find its place there.

The outer storm was to me a symbol of the inner. But even as the former left me unperturbed, I think I can say the same thing about the latter. There was the trouble with the caste that was to confront me. I have already adverted to my helplessness in starting on my profession. And then, as I was a reformer. I was taxing myself as to how best to begin certain reforms. But there was even more in store for me than I knew.

My elder brother had come to meet me at the dock. He had already made the acquaintance of Dr. Mehta and his elder brother and as Dr. Mehta insisted on putting me up at his house, we went there. Thus the acquaintance begun in England continued in India and ripened into a permanent friendship between the two families.

I was pining to see my mother. I did not know that she was no more in the flesh to receive me back into her bosom. The sad news was now given me, and I underwent the usual ablution[2]. My brother had kept me ignorant[3] of her death, which took place whilst I was still in England. He wanted to spare me the blow in a foreign land. The news, however, was none the less a severe[4] shock to me. But I must not dwell upon it. My grief was even greater than over my father's death. Most of my cherished hopes were shattered. But I remember that I did not give myself up to any wild expression of grief. I could even check the tears, and took to life just as though nothing had happened.

Dr. Mehta introduced me to several friends, one of them being his brother Shri Revashankar Jagjivan, with whom there grew up a lifelong

1. *surge: a sudden powerful forward or upward movement; tidal surges*
2. *ablution: the ritual of washing of a priest's hands or of sacred vessels*
3. *ignorant: lacking knowledge or awareness in general, uninformed about or unaware of a specific subject or fact*
4. *severe: very great; intense*

friendship. But the introduction that I need particularly take note of was the one to the poet Raychand or Rajchandra, the son-in-law of an elder brother of Dr. Mehta, and partner of the firm of jewellers conducted in the name of Revashankar Jagjivan. He was not above twenty-five then, but my first meeting with him convinced me that he was a man of great character and learning. He was also known as *Shatavadhani* (one having the faculty of remembering or attending to a hundred things simultaneously[1]), and Dr. Mehta recommended me to see some of his memory feats. I exhausted my vocabulary of all the European tongues I knew, and asked the poet to repeat the words, He did so in the precise order in which I had given them. I envied his gift without, however, coming under its spell. The thing that did cast its spell over me I came to know afterwards. This was his wide knowledge of the scriptures[2], his spotless character, and his burning passion for self-realization. I saw later that this last was the only thing for which he lived. The following lines of Muktanand were always on his lips and engraved[3] on the tablets of his heart:

'I shall think myself blessed only when I see Him in every one of my daily acts; Verily He is the thread, Which supports Muktanand's life.'

Raychandbhai's commercial transactions[4] covered hundreds of thousands. He was a connoisseur of pearls and diamonds. No knotty business problem was too difficult for him. But all these things were not the centre round which his life revolved. That centre was the passion to see God face to face. Amongst the things on his business table there were invariably to be found some religious book and his diary. The moment he finished his business he opened the religious book or the diary. Much of his published writings is a reproduction from this diary. The man who, immediately on finishing his talk about weighty business transaction, began to write about the hidden things of the spirit could evidently not be a businessman at all, but a real seeker after Truth. And I saw him thus absorbed in godly pursuits in the midst of business, not once or twice, but very often. I never saw him lose his state of equipoise. There was no business or other selfish tie that bound him to me, and yet I enjoyed the closest association with him. I was but a briefless barrister then, and yet whenever I saw him he would engage me in conversation of a seriously religious nature. Though I was then groping and could not be said to have any serious interest in religious discussion, still I found his talk of

1. *simultaneously: occurring, operating, or done at the same time*
2. *scriptures: the sacred writings Christianity contained in the Bible; the sacred writings of another religion*
3. *engraved: cut or carve a text or design on a hard surface; cut or carve a text or design on; cut a design as lines on a metal plate for printing*
4. *transactions: an instance of buying or selling; the action of conducting business*

absorbing interest. I have since met many a religious leader or teacher. I have tried to meet the heads of various faiths, and I must say that no one else has ever made on me the impression that Raychandbhai did. His words went straight home to me. His intellect compelled as great a regard from me as his moral earnestness[1], and deep down in me was the conviction that he would never willingly lead me astray and would always confide to me his innermost thoughts. In my moments of spiritual crisis, therefore, he was my refuge.

And yet in spite of this regard for him I could not enthrone[2] him in my heart as my Guru. The throne has remained vacant and my search still continues.

I believe in the Hindu theory of Guru and his importance in spiritual realization. I think there is a great deal of truth in the doctrine[3] that true knowledge is impossible without a Guru. An imperfect teacher may be tolerable in mundane matters, but not in spiritual matters. Only a perfect *gnani*[4] deserves to be enthroned as Guru. There must, therefore, be ceaseless[5] striving after perfection. For one gets the Guru that one deserves. Infinite striving after perfection is one's right. It is its own reward. The rest is in the hands of God.

Thus, though I could not place Raychandbhai on the throne of my heart as Guru, we shall see he was, on many occasions, my guide and helper. Three moderns have left a deep impress on my life, and captivated me: Raychandbhai by his living contact; Tolstoy by his book, The Kingdom of God is Within You; and Ruskin by his *Unto this Last*. But of these more in their proper place.

1. *earnestness: intensely serious*
2. *enthrone: install a monarch or bishop on a throne with due ceremony; treat with honor and respect*
3. *doctrine: a set of beliefs or principles held and taught by a church, political party, or other group*
4. *gnani: a knowing one; a seer*
5. *ceaseless: constant and unending*

CHAPTER 27

HOW I BEGAN LIFE

My elder brother had built high hopes on me. The desire for wealth and name and fame was great in him. He had a big heart, generous to a fault. This, combined with his simple nature, had attracted to him many friends, and through them he expected to get me briefs. He had also assumed that I should have a swinging practice and had, in that expectation, allowed the household expenses to become top-heavy. He had also left no stone unturned in preparing the field for my practice.

The storm in my caste over my foreign voyage was still brewing. It had divided the caste into two camps, one of which immediately re-admitted me, while the other was bent on keeping me out. To please the former my brother took me to Nasik before going to Rajkot, gave me a bath in the sacred river and, on reaching Rajkot. gave a caste dinner. I did not like all this. But my brother's love for me was boundless, and my devotion to him was in proportion[1] to it, and so I mechanically acted as he wished, taking his will to be law. The trouble about re-admission to the caste was thus practically over.

I never tried to seek admission to the section that had refused it. Nor did I feel even mental resentment[2] against any of the headmen of that section. Some of these regarded me with dislike, but I scrupulously avoided hurting their feelings. I fully respected the caste regulations about ex-communication. According to these, none of my relations, including my father-in-law and mother-in-law, and even my sister and brother-in-law, could entertain me; and I would not so much as drink water at their houses. They were prepared secretly to evade the prohibition[3], but it went against the grain with me to do a thing in secret that I would not do in public.

The result of my scrupulous conduct was that I never had occasion to be troubled by the caste; nay, I have experienced nothing but affection and generosity from the general body of the section that still regards me

1. *proportion: a part, share, or number considered in relation to a whole; the ratio of one thing to another; the correct or pleasing relation of things or between the parts of a whole*
2. *resentment: bitterness; indignation*
3. *prohibition: formally forbidden by law, rules, etc.*

as ex-communicated. They have even helped me in my work, without ever expecting me to do anything for the caste. It is my conviction that all these good things are due to my non-resistance. Had I agitated[1] for being admitted to the caste, had I attempted to divide it into more camps, had I provoked the castemen, they would surely have retaliated[2], and instead of steering clear of the storm, I should on arrival from England, have found myself in a whirlpool of agitation, and perhaps a party to dissimulation[3].

My relations with my wife were still not as I desired. Even my stay in England had not cured me of jealousy. I continued my squeamishness and suspiciousness in respect of every little thing, and hence all my cherished desires remained unfulfilled. I had decided that my wife should learn reading and writing and that I should help her in her studies, but my lust came in the way and she had to suffer for my own shortcoming. Once I went the length of sending her away to her father's house, and consented to receive her back only after I had made her thoroughly miserable. I saw later that all this was pure folly on my part.

I had planned reform in the education of children, My brother had children, and my own child which I had left at home when I went to England was now a boy of nearly four. It was my desire to teach these little ones physical exercise and make them hardy, and also to give them the benefit of my personal guidance. In this I had my brother's support and I succeeded in my efforts more or less. I very much liked the company of children, and the habit of playing and joking with them has stayed with me till today. I have ever since thought that I should make a good teacher of children.

The necessity for food 'reform' was obvious. Tea and coffee had already found their place in the house. My brother had thought it fit to keep some sort of English atmosphere ready for me on my return, and to that end, crockery and such other things, which used to be kept in the house only for special occasions, were now in general use. My 'reforms' put the finishing touch. I introduced oatmeal porridge, and cocoa was to replace tea and coffee. But in truth it became an addition to tea and coffee. Boots and shoes were already there. I completed the Europeanization by adding the European dress.

1. *agitated: campaign to arouse public concern about an issue*
2. *retaliated: make an attack or assault in return for a similar attack*
3. *dissimulation: hide or disguise one's thoughts or feelings*

Expenses thus went up. New things were added every day. We had succeeded in tying a white elephant at our door. But how was the wherewithal to be found? To start practice in Rajkot would have meant sure ridicule. I had hardly the knowledge of a qualified vakil and yet I expected to be paid ten times his fees! No client would be fool enough to engage me. And even if such a one was to be found, should I add arrogance[1] and fraud to my ignorance, and increase the burden of debt I owed to the world?

Friends advised me to go to Bombay for some time in order to gain experience of the High Court, to study Indian law and to try to get what briefs I could. I took up the suggestion and went.

In Bombay I started a household with a cook as incompetent[2] as myself. He was a Brahman. I did not treat him as a servant but as a member of the household. He would pour water over himself but never wash. His *dhoti* was dirty, as also his sacred thread, and he was completely innocent of the scriptures. But how was I to get a better cook?

'Well, Ravishankar,' (for that was his name), I would ask him, 'you may not know cooking, but surely you must know your *sandhya* (daily worship), etc.

'*Sandhya*, sir! the plough is our *sandhya* and the spade our daily ritual. That is the type of Brahman I am. I must live on your mercy. Otherwise agriculture is of course there for me.'

So I had to be Ravishankar's teacher. Time I had enough. I began to do half the cooking myself and introduced the English experiments in vegetarian cookery. I invested in a stove, and with Ravishankar began to run the kitchen. I had no scruples about inter-dining, Ravishankar too came to have none, and so we went on merrily together. There was only one obstacle[3]. Ravishankar had sworn to remain dirty and to keep the food unclean!

But it was impossible for me to get along in Bombay for more than four or five months, there being no income to square with the ever-increasing expenditure.

This was how I began life. I found the barrister's profession a bad job-much show and little knowledge. I felt a crushing sense of my responsibility.

1. *arrogance: overbearing pride evidenced by a superior manner toward inferiors*
2. *incompetent: a person's in ability to do something successfully*
3. *obstacle: a thing that blocks one's way or hinders progress*

CHAPTER 28

THE FIRST CASE

While in Bombay, I began, on the one hand, my study of Indian law and, on the other, my experiments in dietetics in which Virchand Gandhi, a friend, joined me. My brother, for his part, was trying his best to get me briefs.

The study of Indian law was a tedious[1] business. The Civil Procedure Code I could in no way get on with. Not so however, with the Evidence Act. Virchand Gandhi was reading for the solicitor's examination and would tell me all sorts of stories about barristers and vakils. 'Sir Pherozeshah's ability,' he would say, 'lies in his profound[2] knowledge of law. He has the Evidence Act by heart and knows all the cases on the thirty-second section. Badruddin Tyabji's wonderful power of argument inspires the judges with awe.'

The stories of stalwarts such as these would unnerve me.

'It is not unusual,' he would add, 'for a barrister to vegetate for five or seven years. That's why I have signed the articles for solicitorship. You should count yourself lucky if you can paddle your own canoe[3] in three years' time.'

Expenses were mounting up every month. To have a barister's board outside the house, whilst still preparing for the barrister's profession inside, was a thing to which I could not reconcile[4] myself. Hence I could not give undivided attention to my studies. I developed some liking for the Evidence Act and read Mayne's *Hindu Law* with deep interest, but I had not the courage to conduct a case. I was helpless beyond words, even as the bride come fresh to her father-in-law's house!

About this time, I took up the case of one Mamibai. It was a 'small cause.' 'You will have to pay some commission to the tout,' I was told. I emphatically declined.

'But even that great criminal lawyer Mr. So-and-So, who makes three to four thousand a month, pays commission!'

1. *tedious: too long, slow, or dull*
2. *profound: very great or intense: profound social changes; severe*
3. *canoe: a narrow keel-less boat with pointed ends propelled with a paddle*
4. *reconcile: restore friendly relations between, settle a quarrel*

'I do not need to emulate[1] him,' I rejoined. 'I should be content with Rs. 300 a month. Father did not get more.'

'But those days are gone. Expenses in Bombay have gone up frightfully[2]. You must be business-like.'

I was adamant. I gave no commission, but got Mamibai's case all the same. It was an easy case. I charged Rs. 30 for my fees. The case was not likely to last longer than a day.

This was my *début* in the Small Causes Court. I appeared for the defendant and had thus to cross-examine the plaintiff's[2] witnesses. I stood up, but my heart sank into my boots. My head was reeling and I felt as though the whole court was doing likewise. I could think of no question to ask. The judge must have laughed, and the vakils no doubt enjoyed the spectacle. But I was past seeing anything. I sat down and told the agent that I could not conduct the case, that he had better engage Patel and have the fee back from me. Mr. Patel was duly engaged for Rs. 51. To him, of course, the case was child's play.

I hastened from the Court, not knowing whether my client[4] won or lost her case, but I was ashamed of myself, and decided not to take up any more cases until I had courage enough to conduct them. Indeed I did not go to Court again until I went to South Africa. There was no virtue in my decision. I had simply made a virtue of necessity. There would be no one so foolish as to entrust his case to me, only to lose it!

But there was another case in store for me at Bombay. It was a memorial to be drafted. A poor Mussalman's land was confiscated in Porbandar. He approached me as the worthy son of a worthy father. His case appeared to be weak, but I consented to draft a memorial for him, the cost of printing to be borne by him. I drafted it and read it out to friends. They approved of it, and that to some extent made me feel confident that I was qualified enough to draft a memorial, as indeed I really was.

My business could flourish if I drafted memorials without any fees. But that would being no grist to the mill. So I thought I might take up a teacher's job. My knowledge of English was good enough, and I should have loved to teach English to Matriculation boys in some school. In this way I could have met part at least of the expenses. I came across an advertisement in the papers: 'Wanted, an English teacher to teach one

1. *emulate: attempt to much or surpass, typically by imitation*
2. *frightfully: very unpleasantly, seriously, or shockingly*
3. *plaintiff: a person who brings a case against another in a court of law*
4. *client: a person using the services of a professional person or organization*

hour daily. Salary Rs 75.' The advertisement was from a famous high school. I applied for the post and was called for an interview. I went there in high spirits, but when the principal found that I was not a graduate, he regretfully refused me.

'But I have passed the London Matriculation with Latin as my second language.'

'True but we want a graduate.'

There was no help for it. I wrung my hands in despair. My brother also felt much worried. We both came to the conclusion that it was no use spending more time in Bombay. I should settle in Rajkot where my brother, himself a petty pleader, could give me some work in the shape of drafting applications and memorials. And then as there was already a household at Rajkot, the breaking up of the one at Bombay meant a considerable saving. I liked the suggestion. My little establishment was thus closed after a stay of six months in Bombay.

I used to attend High Court daily whilst in Bombay, but I cannot say that I learnt anything there. I had not sufficient knowledge to learn much. Often I could not follow the cases and dozed[1] off. There were others also who kept me company in this, and thus lightened my load of shame. After a time, I even lost the sense of shame, as I learnt to think that it was fashionable to doze in the High Court.

If the present generation has also its briefless barristers like me in Bombay, I would commend them a little practical precept about living. Although I lived in Girgaum I hardly ever took a carriage or a tram-car. I had made it a rule to walk to the High Court. It took me quite forty-five minutes, and of course I invariably returned home on foot. I had inured myself to the heat of the sun. This walk to and from the Court saved a fair amount of money, and when many of my friends in Bombay used to fall ill, I do not remember having once had an illness. Even when I began to earn money, I kept up the practice of walking to and from the office, and I am still reaping the benefits of that practice.

1. *dozed: sleep lightly*

CHAPTER 29

THE FIRST SHOCK

Disappointed, I left Bombay and went to Rajkot where I set up my own office. Here I got along moderately well. Drafting applications and memorials brought me in, on an average, Rs 300 a month. For this work I had to thank influence rather than my own ability, for my brother's partner had a settled practice. All applications etc. which were, really or to his mind of an important character, he sent to big barristers. To my lot fell the applications to be drafted on behalf of his poor clients.

I must confess that here I had to compromise the principle of giving no commission, which in Bombay I had so scrupulously observed. I was told that conditions in the two cases were different; that whilst in Bombay commissions had to be paid to touts, here they had to be paid to vakils who briefed you; and that here as in Bombay all barristers, without exception, paid a percentage of their fees as commission. The argument of my brother was, for me, unanswerable. 'You see,' said he, 'that I am in partnership with another vakil. I shall always be inclined to make over to you all our cases with which you can possibly deal, and if you refuse to pay a commission to my partner, you are sure to embarrass me. As you and I have a joint establishment, your fee comes to our common purse, and I automatically get a share. But what about my partner? Supposing he gave the same case to some other barrister he would certainly get his commission from him.' I was taken in by this plea, and felt that, if I was to practise as a barrister, I could not press my principle regarding commissions in such cases. That is how I argued with myself, or to put it bluntly, how I deceived myself. Let me add, however, that I do not remember ever to have given commission in respect of any other case.

Though I thus began to make both ends meet, I got the first shock of my life about this time. I had heard what a British officer was like, but up to now had never been face to face with one.

My brother had been secretary and adviser to the late Ranasaheb of Porbandar before he was installed on his *gadi*[1] and hanging over his head

1. *gadi: throne*

at this time was the charge of having given wrong advice when in that office. The matter had gone to the Political Agent who was prejudiced against my brother. Now I had known this officer when in England, and he may be said to have been fairly friendly to me. My brother thought that I should avail[1] myself of the friendship and, putting in a good word on his behalf, try to disabuse the Political Agent of his prejudice. I did not at all like this idea. I should not, I thought, try to take advantage of a trifling acquaintance in England. If my brother was really at fault, what use was my recommendation? If he was innocent, he should submit a petition in the proper course and, confident of his innocence, face the result. My brother did not relish this advice. 'You do not know Kathiawad, he said, and you have yet to know the world. Only influence counts here. It is not proper for you, a brother, to shirk your duty, when you can clearly put in a good word about me to an officer you know.'

I could not refuse him, so I went to the officer much against my will. I knew I had no right to approach him and was fully conscious that I was compromising my self-respect. But I sought an appointment and got it. I reminded him of the old acquaintance, but I immediately saw that Kathiawad was different from England; that an officer on leave was not the same as an officer on duty. The political Agent owned the acquaintance, but the reminder seemed to stiffen[2] him. 'Surely you have not come here to abuse that acquaintance, have you?' appeared to be the meaning of that stiffness, and seemed to be written on his brow. Nevertheless I opened my case. The *sahib* was impatient. 'Your brother is an intriguer. I want to hear nothing more from you. I have no time. If your brother has anything to say, let him apply through the proper channel. The answer was enough, was perhaps deserved. But selfishness is blind. I went on with my story. The *sahib* got up and said: 'You must go now.'

'But please hear me out,' said I. That made him more angry. He called his peon and ordered him to show me the door. I was still hesitating when the peon came in, placed his hands on my shoulders and put me out of the room.

The *sahib* went away as also the peon, and I departed, fretting and fuming. I at once wrote out and sent over a note to this effect: 'You have insulted me. You have assaulted me through your peon. If you make no amends, I shall have to proceed against you.'

1. *avail: use or take advantage of*

2. *stiffen: make or become stiff*

Quick came the answer through his sowar:

'You were rude to me. I asked you to go and you would not. I had no option but to order my peon to show you the door. Even after he asked you to leave the office, you did not do so. He therefore had to use just enough force to send you out. You are at liberty to proceed as you wish.'

With this answer in my pocket, I came home crest fallen, and told my brother all that had happened. He was grieved, but was at a loss as to how to console me. He spoke to his vakil friends. For I did not know how to proceed against the *sahib*. Sir Pherozeshah Mehta happened to be in Rajkot at this time, having come down from Bombay for some case. But how could a junior barrister like me dare to see him? So I sent him the papers of my case, through the vakil who had engaged him, and begged for his advice. 'Tell Gandhi,' he said, 'such things are the common experience of many vakils and barristers. He is still fresh from England, and hot-blooded. He does not know British officers. If he would earn something and have an easy time here, let him tear up the note and pocket the insult. He will gain nothing by proceeding against the *sahib*, and on the contrary will very likely ruin himself. Tell him he has yet to know life.'

The advice was as bitter as poison[1] to me, but I had to swallow it. I pocketed the insult, but also profited by it, 'Never again shall I place myself in such a false position, never again shall I try to exploit friendship in this way,' said I to myself, and since then I have never been guilty of a breach of that determination. This shock changed the course of my life.

1. *poison: a substance that causes death or harm when introduced into or aborted by a living organism*

CHAPTER 30

PREPARING FOR SOUTH AFRICA

I was no doubt at fault in having gone to that officer. But his impatience and overbearing anger were out of all proportion to my mistake. It did not warrant expulsion. I can scarcely have taken up more than five minutes of his time. But he simply could not endure my talking. He could have politely asked me to go, but power had intoxicated him to an inordinate extent. Later I came to know that patience was not one of the virtues of this officer. It was usual for him to insult his visitors. The slightest unpleasantness was sure to put the *sahib* out.

Now most of my work would naturally be in his court. It was beyond me to conciliate him. I had no desire to curry favour with him, Indeed, having once threatened to proceed against him, I did not like to remain silent.

Meanwhile I began to learn something of the petty politics of the country. Kathiawad, being a conglomeration[1] of small states, naturally had its rich crop of politicals. Petty intrigues between states, and intrigues of officers for power were the order of the day. Princes were always at the mercy of others and ready to lend their ears to sycophants. Even the *sahib's* peon had to be cajoled, and the *sahib's shirastedar* was more than his master, as he was his eyes, his ears and his interpreter. The *shirastedar's* will was law, and his income was always reputed to be more than the *sahib's*. This may have been an exaggeration, but he certainly lived beyond his salary.

This atmosphere appeared to me to be poisonous, and how to remain unscathed was a perpetual problem for me.

I was thoroughly depressed and my brother clearly saw it. We both felt that, if I could secure some job, I should be free from this atmosphere of intrigue. But without intrigue a ministership or judgeship was out of the question. And the quarrel with the *sahib* stood in the way of my practice.

Probandar was then under administration, and I had some work there in the shape of securing more powers for the prince. Also I had to

1. *conglomeration: something consisting of a number of different and distinct things; a large corporation formed by the merging of separate firms*

see the Administrator in respect of the heavy *vighoti* (land rent) exacted from the Mers. This officer, though an Indian, was, I found, one better than the *sahib* in arrogance. He was able, but the ryots appeared to me to be none the better off for his ability. I succeeded in securing a few more powers for the Rana, but hardly any relief for the Mers. It struck me that their cause was not even carefully gone into.

So even in this mission I was comparatively disappointed. I thought justice was not done to my clients, but I had not the means to secure it. At the most I could have appealed to the Political Agent or to the Governor who would have dismissed the appeal saying, 'We decline to interfere.'

If there had been any rule or regulation governing such decisions, it would have been something, but here the *sahib's* will was law.

I was exasperated.

In the meantime a Meman firm from Porbandar wrote to my brother making the following offer: 'We have business in South Africa. Ours is a big firm, and we have a big case there in the Court, our claim being £40,000. It has been going on for a long time. We have engaged the services of the best vakils and barristers. If you sent your brother there, he would be useful to us and also to himself. He would be able to instruct our counsel better than ourselves. And he would have the advantage of seeing a new part of the world, and of making new acquaintances.'

My brother discussed the proposition[1] with me. I could not clearly make out whether I had simply to instruct the counsel or to appear in court. But I was tempted.

My brother introduced me to the late Sheth Abdul Karim Jhaveri a partner of Dada Abdulla & Co; the firm in question. 'It won't be a difficult job' the Sheth assured me. 'We have big Europeans as our friends, whose acquaintance you will make. You can be useful to us our shop. Much of our correspondence is in English and you can help us with that too. You will, of course, be our guest and hence will have no expense whatever.'

'How long do you require my services?' I asked. 'And what will be the payment?'

'Not more than a year. We will pay you a first class return fare and a sum of £105, all found.'

1. *proposition: a proposed scheme or plan*

This was hardly going there as a barrister. It was going as a servant of the firm. But I wanted somehow to leave India. There was also the tempting opportunity of seeing a new country, and of having new experience. Also I could send £105 to my brother and help in the expenses of the household. I closed with the offer without any haggling, and got ready to go to South Africa.

CHAPTER 31

ARRIVAL IN NATAL

When starting for South Africa I did not feel the wrench of separation which I had experienced when leaving for England. My mother was now no more. I had gained some knowledge of the world and of travel abroad, and going from Rajkot to Bombay was no unusual affair.

This time I only felt the pang of parting with my wife. Another baby had been born to us since my return from England. Our love could not yet be called free from lust, but it was getting gradually purer. Since my return from Europe, we had lived very little together; and as I had now become her teacher, however indifferent[1], and helped her to make certain reforms, we both felt the necessity of being more together, if only to continue the reforms. But the attraction of South Africa rendered the separation bearable. 'We are bound to meet again in a year,' I said to her, by way of consolation, and left Rajkot for Bombay.

Here I was to get my passage through the agent of Dada Abdulla and Co. But no berth was available on the boat, and if I did not sail then, I should be stranded in Bombay. 'We have tried our best,' said the agent, 'to secure a first class passage, but in vain unless you are prepared to go on deck[2]. Your meals can be arranged for in the saloon.' Those were the days of my first class traveling, and how could a barrister travel as a deck passenger? So I refused the offer. I suspected the agent's veracity, for I could not believe that a first class passage was not available. With the agent's consent I set about securing it myself. I went on board the boat and met the chief officer. He said to me quite frankly, 'We do not usually have such a rush. But as the Governor-General of Mozambique is going by this boat, all the berths are engaged.'

'Could you not possibly squeeze me in?' I asked. He surveyed me from top to toe and smiled. 'There is just one way,' he said. 'There is an extra berth in my cabin, which is usually not available for passengers. But I am prepared to give it to you.' I thanked him and got the agent to

1. *indifferent: having no particular interest or sympathy; unconcerned*
2. *deck: a floor of a ship, especially the upper, open level*

purchase the passage. In April 1893 I set forth full of zest to try my luck in South Africa.

The first port of call was Lamu which we reached in about thirteen days. The Captain and I had become great friends by this time. He was fond of playing chess, but as he was quite a novice, he wanted one still more of a beginner for his partner, and so he invited me. I had heard a lot about the game but had never tried my hand at it. Players used to say that this was a game in which there was plenty of scope for the exercise of one's intelligence. The Captain offered to give me lessons, and he found me a good pupil as I had unlimited patience. Every time I was the loser, and that made him all the more eager to teach me. I liked the game, but never carried my liking beyond the boat or my knowledge beyond the moves of the pieces.

At Lamu the ship remained at anchor for some three to four hours, and I landed to see the port. The Captain had also gone ashore, but he had warned me that the harbour was treacherous[1] and that I should return in good time.

It was a very small place. I went to the Post Office and was delighted to see the Indian clerks there, and had a talk with them. I also saw the Africans and tried to acquaint myself with their ways of life which interested me very much. This took up some time.

There were some deck passengers with whom I had made acquaintance, and who had landed with a view to cooking their food on shore and having a quiet meal. I now found them preparing to return to the steamer, so we all got into the same boat. The tide was high in the harbour and our boat had more than its proper load. The high current was so strong that it was impossible to hold the boat to the ladder of the steamer. It would just touch the ladder and be drawn away again by the current. The first whistle to start had already gone. I was worried. The Captain was witnessing our plight[2] from the bridge. He ordered the steamer to wait an extra five minutes. There was another boat near the ship which a friend hired for me for ten rupees. This boat picked me up from the overloaded one. The ladder had already been raised. I had therefore to be drawn up by means of a rope and the steamer started immediately. The other passengers were left behind. I now appreciated the Captain's warning.

1. *treacherous: having hidden or unpredictable dangers*
2. *plight: a dangerous, difficult, or otherwise unfortunate situation*

After Lamu the next port was Mombasa and then Zanzibar. The halt[1] here was a long one eight or ten days and we then changed to another boat.

The Captain liked me much but the liking took an undesirable turn. He invited an English friend and me to accompany him on an outing, and we all went ashore in his boat. I had not the least notion of what the outing meant. And little did the Captain know what an ignoramus[2] I was in such matters. We were taken to some Negro women's quarters by a tout. We were each shown into a room. I simply stood there dumb with shame. Heaven only knows what the poor woman must have thought of me. When the Captain called me I came out just as I had gone in. He saw my innocence. At first I felt very much ashamed, but as I could not think of the thing except with horror, the sense of shame wore away, and I thanked God that the sight of the woman had no moved me in the least. I was disgusted at my weakness and pitied myself for not having had the courage to refuse to go into the room.

This in my life was the third trial of its kind. Many a youth, innocent at first, must have been drawn into sin by a false sense of shame. I could claim no credit for having come out unscathed. I could have credit if I had refused to enter that room. I must entirely thank the All-merciful for having saved me. The incident increased my faith in God and taught me, to a certain extent, to cast off false shame.

As we had to remain in this port for a week. I took rooms in the town and saw good deal by wandering about the neighbourhood. Only Malabar can give any idea of the luxuriant vegetation of Zanzibar. I was amazed at the gigantic trees and the size of the fruits.

The next call was at Mozambique and thence we reached Natal towards the close of May.

1. halt: bring or come to an abrupt stop

2. ignoramus: an ignorant or stupid person

CHAPTER 32

SOME EXPERIENCES

The port of Natal is Durban also known as Port Natal. Abdulla Sheth was there to receive me. As the ship arrived at the quay and I watched the people coming on board to meet their friends, I observed that the Indians were not held in much respect. I could not fail to notice a sort of snobbishness[1] about the manner in which those who knew Abdulla Sheth behaved towards him, and it stung me. Abdulla Sheth had got used to it. Those who looked at me did so with a certain amount of curiosity. My dress marked me out from other Indians. I had a frock-coat and a turban, an imitation of the Bengal *pugree.*

I was taken to the firm's quarters and shown into the room set apart for me, next to Abdulla Sheth's. He did not understand me. I could not understand him. He read the papers his brother had sent through me, and felt more puzzled[2]. He thought his brother had sent him a white elephant. My style of dress and living struck him as being expensive like that of the Europeans. There was no particular work then which could be given me. Their case was going on in the Transvaal. There was no meaning in sending me there immediately. And how far could he trust my ability and honesty? He would not be in Pretoria to watch me. The defendants were in Pretoria, and for aught he knew they might bring undue[3] influence to bear on me. And if work in connection with the case in question was not to be entrusted to me, what work could I be given to do, as all other work could be done much better by his clerks? The clerks could be brought to book, if they did wrong. Could I be, if I also happened to err? So if no work in connection with the case could be given me, I should have to be kept for nothing.

Abdulla Sheth was practically unlettered, but he had a rich fund of experience. He had an acute intellect and was conscious of it. By practice he had picked up just sufficient English for conversational purposes, but that served him for carrying on all his business, whether it was dealing

1. *snobbishness: a person who has an exaggerated respect for high social position or wealth and who looks down on those regarded as socially inferior; a person with a similar respect for tastes considered superior in a particular area: a wine snob*
2. *puzzled: confusing or difficult to understand*
3. *undue: unwarranted or inappropriate because excessive or disproportionate*

with Bank Managers and European merchants or explaining his case to his counsel. The Indians held him in very high esteem. His firm was then the biggest, or at any rate one of the biggest, of the Indian firms. With all these advantages he had one disadvantage he was by nature suspicious[1].

He was proud of Islam and loved to discourse on Islamic philosophy. Though he did not know Arabic, his acquaintance with the Holy Koran and Islamic literature in general was fairly good. Illustrations he had in plenty, always ready at hand. Contact with him gave me a fair amount of practical knowledge of Islam. When we came closer to each other, we had long discussions on religious topics.

On the second or third day of my arrival, he took me to see the Durban court. There he introduced me to several people and seated me next to his attorney. The Magistrate kept staring at me and finally asked me to take off my turban[2]. This I refused to do and left the court.

So here too there was fighting in store for me.

Abdulla Sheth explained to me why some Indians were required to take off their turbans. Those wearing the Musalman costume might, he said, keep their turbans on, but the other Indians on entering a court had to take theirs off as a rule.

I must enter into some details to make this nice distinction intelligible. In the course of these two or three days I could see that the Indians were divided into different groups. One was that of Musalman merchants, who would call themselves 'Arabs.' Another was that of Hindu, and yet another of Parsi, clerks. The Hindu clerks were neither here nor there, unless they cast in their lot with the 'Arab[3].' The Parsi clerks would call themselves Persians. These three classes had some social relations with one another. But by far the largest class was that composed of Tamil, Telugu and North Indian indentured[4] and freed labourers. The indentured labourers were those who went to natal on an agreement to serve for five years, and came to be known there as *girmitiyas* from girmit, which was the corrupt form of the English word 'agreement'. The other three classes had none but business relations with this class. Englishmen called them' coolies' and as the majority of Indians belonged to the labouring class, all Indians were called 'coolies,' or *'samis'*. *'sami'* is a Tamil suffix occurring after many Tamil names, and it is nothing else than the Samskrit *Swami*, meaning a master. Whenever, therefore, an Indian resented being addressed as

1. *suspicious: showing a cautious distrust of something or someone*
2. *turban: a man's headdress, consisting of a long length of material wound round a cap or the head, worn especially by muslims and sikhs*
3. *Arab: a member of a semitic people inhabiting much of the middle east and north Africa*
4. *indentured: historical a contract by which a person agreed to work for a set period for a colonial landowner in exchange for passage to the colony*

a *'sami'* and had enough wit in him, he would try to return the compliment in this wise: 'You may call me *sami*, but you forget that *sami* means a master. I am not your master!' Some Englishmen would wince at this, while others would get angry, swear at the Indian and, if there was a chance, would even belabour him; for *sami* to him was nothing better than a term of contempt. To interpret it to mean a master amounted to an insult!

I was hence known as a 'coolie barrister.' The merchants were known as 'coolie merchants.' The original meaning of the word 'coolie' was thus forgotten, and it became a common appellation[1] for all Indians. The Musalman merchant would resent this and say: 'I am not a coolie, I am an Arab,' or 'I am a merchant,' and the Englishman, if courteous, would apologize to him.

The question of wearing the turban had a great importance in this state of things, Being obliged[2] to take off one's Indian turban would be pocketing an insult. So I thought I had better bid good-bye to the Indian turban and begin wearing an English hat, which would save me from the insult and the unpleasant controversy[3].

But Abdulla Sheth disapproved of the idea. He said, 'If you do anything of the kind, it will have a very bad effect. You will compromise those insisting on wearing Indian turbans. And an Indian turban sits well on your head. If you wear an English hat, you will pass for a waiter.'

There was practical wisdom, patriotism[4] and a little bit of narrowness in this advice. The wisdom was apparent, and he would not have insisted on the Indian turban except out of patriotism; the slighting reference to the waiter betrayed a kind of narrowness. Amongst the indentured Indians there were three classes Hindus, Musalmans and Christians. The last were the children of indentured Indians who became converts to Christanity. Even in 1893 their number was large. They wore the English costume, and the majority of them earned their living by service as waiters in hotels. Abdulla Sheth's criticism of the English hat was with reference to this class. It was considered degrading to serve as a waiter in a hotel. The belief persists even today among many.

On the whole I liked Abdulla Sheth's advice. I wrote to the press about the incident and defended the wearing of my turban in the court. The question was very much discussed in the papers, which described

1. *appellation: a name or title*
2. *obliged: compel legally or morally*
3. *controversy: disagreement, typically when prolonged and public*
4. *patriotism: filled with sense of nationalism*

me as an 'unwelcome visitor.' Thus the incident gave me an unexpected advertisement in South Africa within a few days of my arrival there. Some supported me while others severely criticized my temerity[1].

My turban stayed with me practically until the end of my stay in South Africa. When and why I left off wearing any head-dress at all in South Africa, we shall see later.

1. *temerity: excessive confidence or boldness; audacity*

CHAPTER 33

ON THE WAY TO PRETORIA

I soon came in contact with the Christian Indians living in Durban. The Court Interpreter, Mr. Paul, was a Roman Catholic. I made his acquaintance, as also that of the late Mr. Subhan Godfrey, then a teacher under the Protestant Mission, and father of James Godfery, who, as a member of the South African Deputation, visited India in 1924. I likewise met the late Parsi Rustomji and the late Adamji Miyakhan about the same time. All these friends, who up to then had never met one another except on business, came ultimately into close contact, as we shall see later.

Whilst I was thus widening the circle of my acquaintance[1], the firm received a letter from their lawyer saying that preparations should be made for the case, and that Abdulla Sheth should go to Pretoria himself or send a representative.

Abdulla Sheth gave me this letter to read, and asked me if I would go to Pretoria. 'I can only say after I have understood the case from you,' said I. 'At present I am at a loss to know what I have to do there.' He thereupon asked his clerks to explain the case to me.

As I began to study the case, I felt as though I ought to begin from the A B C of the subject. During the few days I had had at Zanzibar, I had been to the court to see the work there. A Parsi lawyer was examining a witness and asking him questions regarding credit and debit entries in account books. It was all Greek to me. Book-keeping I had learnt neither at school nor during my stay in England. And the case for which I had come to South Africa was mainly about accounts. Only one who knew accounts could understand and explain it. The clerk went on talking about this debited and that credited, and I felt more and more confused. I did not know what a P. Note meant. I failed to find the word in the dictionary. I revealed my ignorance to the clerk, and I learnt from him that a P. Note meant a promisory note[2]. I purchased a book on book-keeping and studied it. That gave me some confidence. I understood

1. *acquaintance: a person one knows slightly, but who is not a close friend*

2. *promisory note: a signed document containing a written promise to pay a stated sum to a specified person or the bearer at a specified date or on demand*

the case. I saw that Abdulla Sheth, who did not know how to keep accounts, had so much practical knowledge that he could quickly solve intricacies[1] of book-keeping. I told him that I was prepared to go to Pretoria.

'Where will you put up?' asked the Sheth. 'Wherever you want me to,' said I. 'Then I shall write to our lawyer. He will arrange for your lodgings. I shall also write to my Meman friends there, but I would not advise you to stay with them. The other party has great influence in Pretoria. Should any one of them manage to read our private correspondence, it might do us much harm. The more you avoid familiarity with them, the better for us.'

'I shall stay where your lawyer puts me up, or I shall find out independent lodgings. Pray don't worry. Not a soul shall know anything that is confidential between us. But I do intend cultivating the acquaintance of the other party. I should like to be friends with them. I would try, if possible, to settle the case out of court. After all Tyeb Sheth is a relative of yours.'

Sheth Tyeb Haji Khan Muhammad was a near relative of Abdulla Sheth.

The mention of a probable settlement somewhat startled the Sheth, I could see. But I had already been six or seven days in Durban, and we now knew and understood each other. I was no longer a 'white elephant.' So he said:

'Y...es, I see. There would be nothing better than a settlement out of court. But we are all relatives and know one another very well indeed. Tyeb Sheth is not a man to consent to a settlement easily. With the slightest unwariness on our part, he would screw all sorts of things out of us, and do us down in the end. So please think twice before you do anything.'

'Don't be anxious about that,' said I. 'I need not talk to Tyeb Sheth, or for that matter to anyone else, about the case. I would only suggest to him to come to an understanding, and so save a lot of unnecessary[2] litigation[3].'

On the seventh or eighth day after my arrival, I left Durban. A first class seat was booked for me. It was usual there to pay five shillings extra, if one needed a bedding. Abdulla Sheth insisted that I should book one bedding but, out of obstinacy and pride and with a view to saving five shillings, I declined. Abdulla Sheth warned me. 'Look, now,' said he, 'this is

1. *intricacies: details*

2. *unnecessary: not necessary; more than is necessary*

3. *litigation: the process of taking legal action*

a different country from India. Thank God, we have enough and to spare. Please do not stint yourself in anything that you may need.'

I thanked him and asked him not to be anxious.

The train reached Maritzburg, the capital of Natal, at about 9 p.m. Beddings used to be provided at this station. A railway servant came and asked me if I wanted one. 'No,' said I, 'I have one with me.' He went away. But a passenger came next, and looked me up and down. He saw that I was a 'coloured' man. This disturbed[1] him. Out he went and came in again with one or two officials. They all kept quiet, when another official came to me and said, 'Come along, you must go to the van compartment.'

'But I have a first class ticket,' said I.

'That doesn't matter,' rejoined the other. 'I tell you, you must go to the van compartment.'

'I tell you, I was permitted to travel in this compartment at Durban, and I insist on going on in it.'

'No, you won't,' said the official. 'You must leave this compartment, or else I shall have to call a police constable to push you out.'

'Yes, you may. I refuse to get out voluntarily.'

The constable came. He took me by the hand and pushed me out. My luggage was also taken out. I refused to go to the other compartment and the train steamed away. I went and sat in the waiting room, keeping my hand-bag with me, and leaving the other luggage where it was. The railway authorities had taken charge of it.

It was winter, and winter in the higher regions of South Africa is severely cold. Maritzburg being at a high altitude, the cold was extremely bitter. My over-coat was in my luggage, but I did not dare to ask for it lest I should be insulted again, so I sat and shivered. There was no light in the room. A passenger came in at about midnight and possibly wanted to talk to me. But I was in no mood to talk.

I began to think of my duty. Should I fight for my rights or go back to India, or should I go on to Pretoria without minding the insults, and return to India after finishing the case? It would be cowardice[2] to run back to India without fulfilling my obligation. The hardship to which I was subjected was superficial only a symptom of the deep disease of colour prejudice. I should try, if possible, to root out the disease and suffer

1. *disturbed: upset; unsettled*

2. *cowardice: lack of bravery*

hardships in the process. Redress[1] for wrongs I should seek only to the extent that would be necessary for the removal of the colour prejudice.

So I decided to take the next available train to Pretoria.

The following morning I sent a long telegram to the General Manager of the Railway and also informed Abdulla Sheth, who immediately met the General Manager. The Manager justified the conduct of the railway authorities, but informed him that he had already instructed the Station Master to see that I reached my destination safely. Abdulla Sheth wired to the Indian merchants in Maritzburg and to friends in other places to meet me and look after me. The merchants came to see me at the station and tried to comfort me by narrating their own hardships and explaining that what had happened to me was nothing unusual. They also said that Indians traveling first or second class had to expect trouble from railway officials and white passengers. The day was thus spent in listening to these tales of woe. The evening train arrived. There was a reserved berth for me. I now purchased at Maritzburg the bedding ticket I had refused to book at Durban.

The train took me to Charlestown.

1. *redress: remedy or set right (an undesirable or unfair situation)*

CHAPTER 34
MORE HARDSHIPS

The train reached Charlestown in the morning. There was no railway, in those days, between Charlestown and Johannesburg, but only a stagecoach, which halted at Standerton for the night *en route*[1]. I possessed a ticket for the coach, which was not cancelled by the break of the journey at Maritzburg for a day; besides, Abdulla Sheth had sent a wire to the coach agent at Charlestown.

But the agent only needed a pretext[2] for putting me off, and so, when he discovered me to be a stranger, he said, 'Your ticket is cancelled.' I gave him the proper reply. The reason at the back of his mind was not want of accommodation, but quite another. Passengers had to be accommodated inside the coach, but as I was regarded as a 'coolie' and looked a stranger, it would be proper, thought the 'leader', as the white man in charge of the coach was called, not to seat me with the white passengers. There were seats on either side of the coachbox. The leader sat on one of these as a rule. Today he sat inside and gave me his seat. I knew it was sheer[3] injustice and an insult, but I thought it better to pocket it, I could not have forced myself inside, and if I had raised a protest, the coach would have gone off without me. This would have meant the loss of another day, and Heaven only knows what would have happened the next day. So, much as I fretted[4] within myself, I prudently sat next the coachman.

At about three o'clock the coach reached Pardekoph. Now the leader desired to sit where I was seated, as he wanted to smoke and possibly to have some fresh air. So he took a piece of dirty sack-cloth from the driver, spread it on the footboard and, addressing me said, '*Sami*, you sit on this, I want to sit near the driver,.' The insult was more than I could bear. In fear and trembling I said to him, 'It was you who seated me here, though I should have been accommodated inside. I put up with the insult. Now that you want to sit outside and smoke, you would have me sit at your feet. I will not do so, but I am prepared to sit inside.'

As I was struggling through these sentences, the man came down upon me and began heavily to box my ears. He seized me by the arm and

1. *en route: on the way to somewhere*
2. *pretext: an ostensible or false reason used to justify an action*
3. *sheer: nothing other than; unmitigated: sheer hard work*
4. *fretted: anxious or irritated*

tried to drag me down. I clung[1] to the brass rails of the coachbox and was determined to keep my hold even at the risk of breaking my wrist bones. The passengers were witnessing the scene - the man swearing at me, dragging and belabouring me, and I remaining still. He was strong and I was weak. Some of the passengers were moved to pity[2] and exclaimed: 'Man, let him alone. Don't beat him. He is not to blame. He is right. If he can't stay there, let him come and sit with us.' 'No fear,' cried the man, but he seemed somewhat crestfallen and stopped beating me. He let go my arm, swore at me a little more, and asking the Hottentot servant who was sitting on the other side of the coachbox to sit on the footboard, took the seat so vacated[3].

The passengers took their seats and, the whistle given, the coach rattled away. My heart was beating fast within my breast, and I was wondering whether I should ever reach my destination alive. The man cast an angry look at me now and then and, pointing his finger at me, growled: 'Take care, let me once get to Standerton and I shall show you what I do.' I sat speechless and prayed to God to help me.

After dark we reached Standerton and I heaved a sigh of relief on seeing some Indian faces. As soon as I got down, these friends said: 'We are hereto receive you and take you to Isa Sheth's shop. We have had a telegram[4] from Dada Abdulla.' I was very glad, and we went to Sheth Isa Haji Sumar's shop. The Sheth and his clerks gathered round me. I told them all that I had gone through. They were very sorry to hear it and comforted me by relating to me their own bitter experiences.

I wanted to inform the agent of the Coach Company of the whole affair. So I wrote him a letter, narrating everything that had happened, and drawing his attention to the threat his man had held out. I also asked for an assurance that he would accommodate me with the other passengers inside the coach when we started the next morning. To which the agent replied to this effect: 'From Standerton we have a bigger coach with different men in charge. The man complained of will not be there tomorrow, and you will have a seat with the other passengers.' This somewhat relieved me. I had, of course, no intention of proceeding against the man who had assaulted me, and so the chapter of the assault closed there.

In the morning Isa Sheth's man took me to the coach, I got a good seat and reached Johannesburg quite safely that night.

1. *clung: hold on tightly to; adhere or stick to*
2. *pity: the feeling of sorrow and compassion caused by the sufferings of others*
3. *vacated: leave a place; give up a position or job*
4. *telegram: a message sent by telegraphand delivered in written or printed form, used in the uk only for international messages since 1981*

Standerton is a small village and Johannesburg a big city. Abdulla Sheth had wired to Johannesburg also, and given me the name and address of Muhammad Kasam Kamruddin's firm there. Their man had come to receive me at the stage, but neither did I see him nor did he recognize me. So I decided to go to a hotel. I knew the names of several. Taking a cab I asked to be driven to the Grand National Hotel. I saw the Manager and asked for a room. He eyed me for a moment, and politely saying, 'I am very sorry, we are full up', bade me good-bye. So I asked the cabman to drive to Muhammad Kasam Kamruddin's shop. Here I found Abdul Gani Sheth expecting me, and he gave me a cordial greeting. He had a hearty laugh over the story of my experience at the hotel. 'How ever did you expect to be admitted to a hotel?' he said.

'Why not?' I asked.

'You will come to know after you have stayed here a few days,' said he. 'Only we can live in a land like this, because, for making money, we do not mind pocketing insults, and here we are.' With this he narrated to me the story of the hardships[1] of Indians in South Africa.

Of Sheth Abdul Gani we shall know more as we proceed.

He said: 'This country is not for men like you. Look now, you have to go to Pretoria tomorrow. You will have to travel third class. Conditions in the Transvaal are worse than in Natal. First and second class tickets are never issued to Indians.'

'You cannot have made persistent[2] efforts in this direction.'

'We have sent representations, but I confess our own men too do not want as a rule to travel first or second.

I sent for the railway regulations and read them. There was a loophole. The language of the old Transvaal enactments was not very exact or precise; that of the railway regulations was even less so.

I said to the Sheth: 'I wish to go first class, and if I cannot, I shall prefer to take a cab to Pretoria, a matter of only thirty-seven miles.'

Sheth Abdul Gani drew my attention to the extra time and money this would mean, but agreed to my proposal to travel first, and accordingly we sent a note to the Station Master. I mentioned in my note that I was a barrister and that I always travelled first. I also stated in the letter that I needed to reach Pretoria as early as possible, that as there was no time to await his reply I would receive it in person at the station, and that I should expect to get a first class ticket. There was of course a purpose

1. *hardships: severe suffering*

2. *persistent: continuing to exist or occur over a prolonged period*

behind asking for the reply in person. I thought that if the Station master gave a written reply, he would certainly say 'No', especially because he would have his own notion of a 'collie' barrister. I would therefore appear before him in faultless English dress, talk to him and possibly persuade him to issue a first class ticket. So I went to the station in a frock[1]-coat and necktie, placed a sovereign[2] for my fare on the counter and asked for a first class ticket.

'You sent me that note?' he asked.

'That is so. I shall be much obliged if you will give me a ticket. I must reach Pretoria today.'

He smiled and, moved to pity, said: 'I am not a Transvaaler. I am a Hollander. I appreciate your feelings, and you have my sympathy. I do want to give you a ticket on one condition, however, that, if the guard should ask you to shift to the third class, you will not involve me in the affair, by which I mean that you should not proceed against the railway company. I wish you a safe journey. I can see you are a gentleman.'

With these words he booked the ticket. I thanked him and gave him the necessary assurance.

Sheth Abdul Gani had come to see me off at the station. The incident gave him an agreeable surprise, but he warned me saying: 'I shall be thankful if you reach Pretoria all right. I am afraid the guard will not leave you in peace in the first class and even if he does, the passengers will not.'

I took my seat in a first class compartment and the train started. At Germiston the guard came to examine the tickets. He was angry to find me there, and signaled to me with his finger to go to the third class. I showed him my first class ticket. 'That doesn't matter,' said he, 'remove to the third class.'

There was only one English passenger in the compartment. He took the guard to task. 'What do you mean by troubling the gentleman?' he said. 'Don't you see he has a first class ticket? I do not mind in the least his travelling with me.' Addressing me, he said, 'You should make yourself comfortable where you are.'

The guard muttered; If you want to travel with a coolie, what do I care?' and went away.

At about eight o'clock in the evening the train reached Pretoria.

1. *frock: a loose outer garment, in particular a long gown with flowing sleeves worn by monks, priests, or clergy*

2. *sovereign: a former [british] gold coin worth one pound sterling, now only minted for commemorative purpose*

CHAPTER 35

FIRST DAY IN PRETORIA

I had expected someone on behalf of Dada Abdulla's attorney to meet me at Pretoria station. I knew that no Indian would be there to receive me, since I had particularly promised not to put up at an Indian house. But the attorney had sent no one. I understood later that, as I had arrived on a Sunday, he could not have sent anyone without inconvenience. I was perplexed, and wondered where to go, as I feared that no hotel would accept me.

Pretoria station in 1893 was quite different from what it was in 1914. The lights were burning dimly. The travellers were few. I let all the other passengers go and thought that, as soon as the ticket collector was fairly free, I would hand him my ticket and ask him if he could direct me to some small hotel or any other such place where I might go; otherwise I would spend the night at the station. I must confess I shrank from asking him even this, for I was afraid of being insulted.

The station became clear of all passengers. I gave my ticket to the ticket collector and began my inquiries. He replied to me courteously, but I saw that he could not be of any considerable help. But an American Negro who was standing near by broke into the conversation.

'I see,' said he, 'that you are an utter[1] stranger here, without any friends. If you will come with me, I will take you to a small hotel, of which the proprietor is an American who is very well known to me. I think he will accept you.'

I had my own doubts about the offer, but I thanked him and accepted his suggestion. He took me to Johnson's Family Hotel. He drew Mr. Johnson aside to speak to him, and the latter agreed to accommodate me for the night, on condition that I should have my dinner served in my room.

'I assure you,' said he, 'that I have no colour prejudice. But I have only European custom, and, if I allowed you to eat in the dining-room, my guests might be offended[2] and even go away.'

1. *utter: complete; absolute: utter amazement*
2. *offended: cause to feel hurt or resentful*

'Thank you,' said I, 'even for accommodating me for the night. I am now more or less acquainted with the conditions here, and I understand your difficulty. I do not mind your serving the dinner in my room. I hope to be able to make some other arrangement tomorrow.'

I was shown into a room, where I now sat waiting for the dinner and musing, as I was quite alone. There were not many guests in the hotel, and I had expected the waiter to come very shortly with the dinner. Instead Mr. Johnston appeared. He said: I was ashamed of having asked you to have your dinner here. So I spoke to the other guests about you, and asked them if they would mind your having your dinner in the dining-room. They said they had no objection, and that they did not mind your staying here as long as you liked. Please, therefore, come to the dining-room, if you will, and stay here as long as you wish.'

I thanked him again, went to the dining-room and had a hearty dinner.

Next morning I called on the attorney, Mr. A. W. Baker. Abdulla Sheth had given me some description of him, so his cordial[1] reception did not surprise me. He received me very warmly and made kind inquiries. I explained all about myself. Thereupon he said: 'We have no work for you here as barrister, for we have engaged the best counsel. The case is a prolonged and complicated one, so I shall take your assistance only to the extent of getting necessary information. And of course you will make communication with my client easy for me, as I shall now ask for all the information I want from him through you. That is certainly an advantage, I have not yet found rooms for you. I thought I had better do so after having seen you. There is a fearful amount of colour prejudice here, and therefore it is not easy to find lodgings for such as you. But I know a poor woman. She is the wife of a baker. I think she will take you and thus add to her income at the same time. Come, let us go to her place.'

So he took me to her house. He spoke with her privately about me, and she agreed to accept me as a boarder at 35 shilling a week.

Mr. Baker, besides being an attorney, was a staunch[2] lay preacher, He is still alive and now engaged purely in missionary work, having given up the legal profession. He is quite well-to-do. He still corresponds with me. In his letters he always dwells on the same theme. He upholds the excellence of Christianity from various points of view, and contends that

1. *cordial: warm and friendly*

2. *staunch: very loyal and committed*

it is impossible to find eternal[1] peace, unless one accepts Jesus as the only son of God and the Saviour of mankind.

During the very first interview Mr. Baker ascertained[2] my religious views. I said to him: 'I am a Hindu by birth. And yet I do not know much of Hinduism, and I know less of other religions. In fact I do not know where I am, and what is and what should be my belief. I intend to make a careful study of my own religion and, as far as I can, of other religions as well.'

Mr. Baker was glad to hear all this, and said: 'I am one of the directors of the South Africa General Mission. I have built a church at my own expense, and deliver sermons[3] in it regularly. I am free from colour prejudice. I have some co-workers, and we meet at one o'clock every day for a few minutes and pray for peace and light. I shall be glad if you will join us there. I shall introduce you to my co-workers who will be happy to meet you, and I dare say you will also like their company. I shall give you, besides some religious books to read, though of course the book of books is the Holy Bible, which I would specially recommend to you.'

I thanked Mr. Baker and agreed to attend the one o'clock prayers as regularly as possible.

'So I shall expect you here tomorrow at one o'clock, and we shall go together to pray,' added Mr. Baker, and we said good-bye.

I had little time for reflection just yet.

I went to Mr. Johnston, paid the bill and removed to the new lodgings, where I had my lunch. The landlady was good woman. She had cooked a vegetarian meal for me. It was not long before I made myself quite at home with the family.

I next went to see the friend to whom Dada Abdulla had given me a note. From him I learnt more about the hardships of Indians in South Africa. He insisted that I should stay with him. I thanked him, and told him that I had already made arrangements. He urged me not to hesitate to ask for anything I needed.

It was now dark. I returned home, had my dinner, went to my room and lay there absorbed in deep thought. There was not any immediate work for me. I informed Abdulla Sheth of it. What, I thought, can be the meaning of Mr. Baker's interest in me? What shall I gain from his religious

1. *eternal: lasting or existing forever; without end*
2. *ascertained: find (something) out for certain; make sure of*
3. *sermons: talks on a religious or moral subject*

co-workers? How far should I undertake the study of Christianity? How was I to obtain literature about Hinduism? And how was I to understand Christianity in its proper perspective[1] without thoroughly knowing my own religion? I could come to only one conclusion: I should make a dispassionate study of all that came to me, and deal with Mr. Baker's group as God might guide me; I should not think of embracing another religion before I had fully understood my own.

Thus musing[2] I fell asleep.

1. *perspective: a view or prospect*

2. *musing: characterized by reflection or deep thought*

CHAPTER 36

CHRISTIAN CONTACTS

The next day at one o'clock I went to Mr. Baker's prayer-meeting. There I was introduced to Miss Harris, Miss Gabb, Mr. Coates and others. Everyone kneeled[1] down to pray, and I followed suit. The prayers were supplications to God for various things, according to each person's desire. Thus the usual forms were for the day to be passed peacefully, or for God to open the doors of the heart.

A prayer was now added for my welfare: 'Lord, show the path to the new brother who has come amongst us, Give him, Lord, the peace that Thou hast given us. May the Lord Jesus who has saved us save him too. We ask all this in the name of Jesus.' There was no singing of hymns[2] or other music at these meetings. After the supplication[3] for something special every day, we dispersed, each going to his lunch, that being the hour for it. The prayer did not take more than five minutes.

The Misses Harris and Gabb were both elderly maiden ladies. Mr. Coates was a Quaker. The two ladies lived together, and they gave me a standing invitation to four o'clock tea at their house every Sunday.

When we met on Sundays, I used to give Mr. Coates my religious diary for the week, and discuss with him the books I had read and the impression they had left on me. The ladies used to narrate their sweet experiences and talk about the peace they had found.

Mr. Coates was a frank-hearted staunch[4] young man. We went out for walks together, and he also took me to other Christian friends.

As we came closer to each other, he began to give me books of his own choice, until my shelf was filled with them. He loaded me with books, as it were. In pure faith I consented to read all those books, and as I went on reading them we discussed them.

I read a number of such books in 1893. I do not remember the names of them all, but they included the *Commentary* of Dr. Parker of the City Temple, Pearson's *Many Infallible Proofs* and Butler's *Analogy*. Parts

1. *kneeled: sit with one or both knees on the ground*
2. *hymns: a religious song of praise, typically a christian song in praise of god*
3. *supplication: a prayer or request to god*
4. *staunch: firm believer, very loyal*

of these were unintelligible[1] to me. I liked some things in them, while I did not like others. *Many Infallible*[2] *Proofs* were proofs in support of the religion of the Bible, as the author understood it. The book had no effect on me. Parker's *Commentary* was morally stimulating[3], but it could not be of any help to one who had no faith in the prevalent Christian beliefs. Butler's *Analogy* struck me to be a very profound and difficult book, which should be read four or five times to be understood properly. It seemed to me to be written with a view to converting atheists to theism. The arguments advanced in it regarding the existence of God were unnecessary for me, as I had then passed the stage of unbelief; but the arguments in proof of Jesus being the only incarnation of God and the Mediator between God and man left me unmoved[4].

But Mr. Coates was not the man easily to accept defeat. He had great affection for me. He saw, round my neck, the *Vaishnava* necklace of Tulasi-beads. He thought it to be superstition and was pained by it. 'This superstition does not become you. Come, let me break the necklace.'

'No, you will not. It is a sacred gift from my mother.' 'But do you believe in it?'

'I do not know its mysterious significance. I do not think I should come to harm if I did not wear it. But I cannot, without sufficient reason, give up a necklace that she put round my neck out of love and in the conviction that it would be conducive to my welfare. When, with the passage of time, it wears away and breaks of its own accord. I shall have no desire to get a new one. But this necklace cannot be broken.'

Mr. Coates could not appreciate my argument, as he had no regard for my religion. He was looking forward to delivering me from the abyss of ignorance. He wanted to convince me that, no matter whether there was some truth in other religions, salvation was impossible for me unless I accepted Christianity which represented the truth, and that my sins would not be washed away except by the intercession of Jesus, and that all good works were useless.

Just as he introduced me to several books, he introduced me to several friends whom he regarded as staunch Christians. One of these introductions was to a family which belonged to the Plymouth Brethren, a Christian sect.

1. *unintelligible: not understandable*
2. *infallible: incapable of making mistakes or being wrong*
3. *stimulating: sparking interest or enthusiasm*
4. *unmoved: emotionally unaffected*

Many of the contacts for which Mr. Coates was responsible were good. Most struck me as being God fearing. But during my contact with this family, one of the Plymouth Brethren confronted me with an argument for which I was not prepared:

'You cannot understand the beauty of our religion. From what you say it appears that you must be brooding[1] over your transgressions[2] every moment of your life, always mending them and atoning for them. How can this ceaseless cycle of action bring you redemption[3]? You can never have peace. You admit that we are all sinners. Now look at the perfection of our belief. Our attempts at improvement and atonement are futile. And yet redemption we must have. How can we bear the burden of sin? We can but throw it on Jesus. He is the only sinless Son of God. It is His word that those who believe in Him shall have everlasting life. Therein lies God's infinite mercy. And as we believe in the atonement[4] of Jesus, our own sins do not bind us. Sin we must, It is impossible to live in this world sinless. And therefore Jesus suffered and atoned for all the sins of mankind.

Only he who accepts His great redemption can have eternal peace. Think what a life of restlessness is yours, and what a promise of peace we have.'

The argument utterly failed to convince me. I humbly replied:

'If this be the Christianity acknowledged by all Christians, I cannot accept it. I do not seek redemption from the consequences of my sin. I seek to be redeemed from sin itself, or rather from the very thought of sin. Until I have attained that end, I shall be content to be restless.'

To which the Plymouth Brother rejoined: I assure you, your attempt is fruitless. Think again over what I have said.'

And the Brother proved as good as his word. he knowingly committed transgressions, and showed me that he was undisturbed by the thought of them.

But I already knew before meeting with these friends that all Christians did not believe in such a theory of atonement. Mr. Coates himself walked in the fear of God, His heart was pure, and he believed in the possibility of self-purification. The two ladies also shared this belief. Some of the books that came into my hands were full of devotion, So,

1. *brooding: think deeply about something that makes one unhappy*
2. *transgressions: go beyond the limits set by a moral principle, standard, law, etc.*
3. *redemption: the action of redeeming someone or something, or of being redeemed*
4. *atonement: making amends for a wrongful action*

although Mr. Coates was very much disturbed by this latest experience of mine. I was able to reassure him and tell him that the distorted[1] belief of a Plymouth Brother could not prejudice me against Christianity.

My difficulties lay elsewhere. They were with regard to the Bible and its accepted interpretation[2].

1. *distorted: pull or twist out of shape*
2. *interpretation: explanation*

CHAPTER 37

SEEKING TOUCH WITH INDIANS

Before writing further about Christian contacts, I must record other experiences of the same period.

Sheth Tyeb Haji Khan Muhammad had in Pretoria the same position as was enjoyed by Dada Abdulla in Natal. There was no public movement that could be conducted without him. I made his acquaintance the very first week and told him of my intention to get in touch with every Indian in Pretoria. I expressed a desire to study the conditions of Indians there, and asked for his help in my work, which he gladly agreed to give.

My first step was to call a meeting of all the Indians in Pretoria and to present to them a picture of their condition in the Transvaal. The meeting was held at the house of Sheth Haji Muhammad Haji Joosab, to whom I had a letter of introduction. It was principally attended by Meman merchants, though there was a sprinkling of Hindus as well. The Hindu population in Pretoria was, as a matter of fact, very small.

My speech at this meeting may be said to have been the first public speech in my life. I went fairly prepared with my subject, which was about observing truthfulness in business. I had always heard the merchants[1] say that truth was not possible in business. I did not think so then, nor do I now. Even today there are merchant friends who contend that truth is inconsistent with business. Business, they say, is a very practical affair, and truth a matter of religion; and they argue that practical affairs are one thing, while religion is quite another. Pure truth, they hold, is out of the question in business, one can speak it only so far as is suitable. I strongly contested the position in my speech and awakened the merchants to a sense of their duty, which was two-fold. Their responsibility to be truthful was all the greater in a foreign land, because the conduct of a few Indians was the measure of that of the millions of their fellow-countrymen.

I had found our people's habits to be insanitary[2], as compared with those of the Englishmen around them, and drew their attention to it.

1. *merchants: traders*

2. *insanitary: unclean and dangerous to health*

I laid stress on the necessity of forgetting all distinctions such as Hindus, Musalmans, Parsis, Christians, Gujaratis, Madrasis, Punjabis, Sindhis, Kachchhis, Surtis and so on.

I suggested, in conclusion, the formation of an association to make representations to the authorities concerned in respect of the hardships of the Indian settlers, and offered to place at its disposal as much of my time and service as was possible.

I saw that I made a considerable impression on the meeting.

My speech was followed by discussion. Some offered to supply me with facts. I felt encouraged. I saw that very few amongst my audience knew English. As I felt that knowledge of English would be useful in that country, advised those who had leisure to learn English. I told them that it was possible to learn a language even at an advanced age, and cited cases of people who had done so. I undertook, besides, to teach a class, if one was started or personally to instruct individuals desiring to learn the language.

The class was not started, but three young men expressed their readiness[1] to learn at their convenience, and on condition that I went to their places to teach them. Of these, two were Musalmans one of them a barber and the other a clerk and the third was a Hindu, a petty[2] shopkeeper. I agreed to suit them all. I had no misgivings regarding my capacity to teach. My pupils[3] might become tired, but not I. Sometimes it happened that I would go to their places only to find them engaged in their business. But I did not lose patience. None of the three desired a deep study of English, but two may be said to have made fairly good progress in about eight months. Two learnt enough to keep accounts and write ordinary business letters. The barber's ambition was confined to acquiring just enough English for dealing with his customers. As a result of their studies, two of the pupils were equipped for making a fair income.

I was satisfied with the result of the meeting. It was decided to hold such meetings, as far as I remember, once a week or, maybe, once a month. These were held more or less regularly, and on these occasions there was a free exchange of ideas. The result was that there was now in Pretoria no Indian I did not know, or whose condition I was not acquainted with. This prompted me in turn to make the acquaintance of the British Agent in Pretoria, Mr. Jacobus de Wet. He had sympathy for the Indians, but he

1. *readiness: willingness to do something*
2. *petty: mean; small minded*
3. *pupils: a person who is taught by another, especially a schoolchild; [british] a trainee barrister*

had very little influence. However, he agreed to help us as best he could, and invited me to meet him whenever I wished.

I now communicated with the railway authorities and told them that, even under their own regulations, the disabilities about travelling under which the Indians laboured could not be justified. I got a letter in reply to the effect that first and second class tickets would be issued to Indians who were properly dressed. This was far from giving adequate[1] relief, as it rested with the station master to decide who was 'properly dressed.'

The British Agent showed me some papers dealing with Indian affairs. Tyeb Sheth had also given me similar papers. I learnt from them how cruelly the Indians were hounded[2] out from the Orange Free State.

In short, my stay in Pretoria enabled me to make a deep study of the social, economic and political condition of the Indians in the Transvaal and the Orange Free State. I had no idea that this study was to be of invaluable service to me in the future. For I had thought of returning home by the end of the year, or even earlier, if the case was finished before the year was out.

But God disposed otherwise.

1. *adequate: satisfactory or acceptable*

2. *hounded: harassed or chased*

CHAPTER 38

WHAT IT IS TO BE A 'COOLIE'

It would be out of place here to describe fully the condition of Indians in the Transvaal and the Orange Free State. I would suggest that those who wish to have a full idea of it may turn to my *History of Satyagraha in South Africa*. It is, however, necessary to give here a brief outline[1].

In the Orange Free State the Indians were deprived of all their rights by a special law enacted in 1888 or even earlier. If they chose to stay there, they could do so only to serve as waiters in hotels or to pursue some other such menial[2] calling. The traders were driven away with a nominal[3] compensation. They made representations and petitions, but in vain.

A very stringent[4] enactment was passed in the Transvaal in 1885. It was slightly amended in 1886, and it was provided under the amended law that all Indians should pay a poll tax of £3 as fee for entry into the Transvaal. They might not own land except in locations set apart for them, and in practice even that was not to be ownership. They had no franchise. All this was under the special law for Asiatics, to whom the laws for the coloured people were also applied. Under these latter, Indians might not walk on public footpaths, and might not move out of doors after 9 p.m. without a permit. The enforcement of this last regulation was elastic so far as the Indians were concerned. Those who passed as 'Arabs' were, as a matter of favour, exempted from it. The exemption thus naturally depended on the sweet will of the police.

I had to experience the effect of both these regulations. I often went out at night for a walk with Mr. Coates, and we rarely got back home much before ten o'clock. What if the police arrested me? Mr. Coates was more concerned about this than I. He had to issue passes to his Negro servants. But how could he give one to me? Only a master might issue a permit to a servant. If I had wanted one, and even if Mr. Coates had been ready to give it, he could not have done so, for it would have been fraud.

1. *outline: a general plan showing essential features but no detail; the main features of something*
2. *menial: requiring little skill and lacking prestige; domestic*
3. *nominal: existing in name only; relating to or consisting of names*
4. *stringent: strict, precise, and exacting*

So Mr. Coates or some friend of his took me to the State Attorney, Dr. Krause. We turned out to be barristers of the same Inn. The fact that I needed a pass to enable me to be out of doors after 9 p.m. was too much for him. He expressed sympathy for me. Instead of ordering for me a pass, he gave me a letter authorizing[1] me to be out of doors at all hours without police interference. I always kept this letter on me whenever I went out. The fact that I never had to make use of it was a mere[2] accident.

Dr. Krause invited me to his place, and we may be said to have become friends. I occasionally called on him, and it was through him that I was introduced to his more famous brother, who was public Prosecutor in Johannesburg. During the Boer War he was court-martialled for conspiring[3] to murder an English officer, and was sentenced to imprisonment for seven years. He was also disbarred[4] by the Benchers. On the termination of hostilities he was released and being honourably readmitted to the Transvaal bar, resumed practice.

These connections were useful to me later on in my public life, and simplified much of my work.

The consequences of the regulation regarding the use of footpaths were rather serious for me. I always went out for a walk through President Street to an open plain. President Kruger's house was in this street a very modest, unostentatious building, without a garden, and not distinguishable from other houses in its neighbourhood. The houses of many of the millionaires in Pretoria were far more pretentious, and were surrounded by gardens. Indeed President Kruger's simplicity was proverbial. Only the presence of a police patrol before the house indicated that it belonged to some official. I nearly always went along the footpath past this patrol without the slightest hitch or hindrance.

Now the man on duty used to be changed from time to time. Once one of these men, without giving me the slightest warning, without even asking me to leave the footpath, pushed and kicked me into the street. I was dismayed. Before I could question him as to his behaviour, Mr. Coates, who happened to be passing the spot on horseback, hailed me and said:

'Gandhi, I have seen everything. I shall gladly be your witness in court if you proceed against the man. I am very sorry you have been so rudely assaulted.'

1. *authorizing: give official permission for or approval to*
2. *mere: that is solely or nomore or better than what is specified: mere mortals*
3. *conspiring: a secret plan by a group to do something unlawful or harmful*
4. *disbarred: expelled from the bar*

'You need not be sorry,' I said. 'What does the poor man know? All coloured people are the same to him. He no doubt treats Negroes just as he has treated me. I have made it a rule not go to court in respect of any personal grievance. So I do not intend to proceed against him.'

'That is just like you,' said Mr. Coates, but do think it over again. We must teach such men a lesson.' He then spoke to the policeman and reprimanded him. I could not follow their talk, as it was in Dutch, the policeman being a Boer. But he apologized to me, for which there was no need. I had already forgiven him.

But I never again went through this street. There would be other men coming in this man's place and, ignorant of the incident, they would behave likewise. Why should I unnecessarily court another kick? I therefore selected a different walk.

The incident deepened my feeling for the Indian settlers. I discussed with them the advisability[1] of making a test case, if it were found necessary to do so, after having seen the British Agent in the matter of these regulations[2].

I thus made an intimate study of the hard condition of the Indian settlers, not only by reading and hearing about it, but by personal experience. I saw that South Africa was no country for a self-respecting Indian, and my mind became more and more occupied with the question as to how this state of thing might be improved.

But my principal duty for the moment was to attend to the case of Dada Abdulla.

1. *advisability: the quality of being advisable*

2. *regulations: a rule or directive made and maintained by an authority; in accordance with regulations; [informal] of a familiar or predictable type*

CHAPTER 39

PREPARATION FOR THE CASE

The year's stay in Pretoria was a most valuable experience in my life. Here it was that I had opportunities of learning public work and acquired some measure of my capacity for it. Here it was that the religious spirit within me became a living force, and here too I acquired a true knowledge of legal practice. Here I learnt the things that a junior barrister learns in a senior barrister's chamber, and here I also gained confidence that I should not after all fail as a lawyer. It was likewise here that I learnt the secret of success as a lawyer.

Dada Abdulla's was no small case. The suit was for £40,000. Arising out of business transactions, it was full of intricacies of accounts. Part of the claim was based on promissory[1] notes, and part on the specific performance of promise to deliver promissory notes. The defence was that the promissory notes were fraudulently taken and lacked sufficient consideration. There were numerous points of fact and law in this intricate case.

Both parties had engaged the best attorneys and counsel. I thus had a fine opportunity of studying their work. The preparation of the plaintiff's case for the attorney and the sorting of facts in support of his case had been entrusted[2] to me. It was an education to see how much the attorney accepted, and how much he rejected from my preparation, as also to see how much use the counsel made of the brief prepared by the attorney. I saw that this preparation for the case would give me a fair measure of my powers of comprehension and my capacity for marshalling[3] evidence[4].

I took the keenest interest in the case. Indeed I threw myself into it. I read all the papers pertaining to the transactions. My client was a man of great ability and reposed absolute confidence in me, and this rendered my work easy. I made a fair study of book-keeping. My capacity for translation was improved by having to translate the correspondence, which was for the most part in Gujarati.

1. *promissory: implying a promise or assurance*
2. *entrusted: assign a responsibility to; put into someone's care*
3. *marshalling: arrange or organize*
4. *evidence: information indicating whether a belief or proposition is true or valid; [law] information used to establish facts in a legal investigation or admissible as testimony in a [law] court; signs; indications*

Although, as I have said before, I took a keen interest in religious communion and in public work and always gave some of my time to them, they were not then my primary interest. The preparation of the case was my primary interest. Reading of law and looking up law cases, when necessary, had always a prior[1] claim on my time. As a result, I acquired such a grasp of the facts of the case as perhaps was not possessed even by the parties themselves, inasmuch as I had with me the papers of both the parties.

I recalled the late Mr. Pincutt's advice - facts are three-fourths of the law. At a later date it was amply borne out by that famous barrister of South Africa, the late Mr. Leonard. In a certain case in my charge I saw that, though justice was on the side of my client, the law seemed to be against him. In despair I approached Mr. Leonard for help. He also felt that the facts of the case were very strong. He exclaimed, 'Gandhi, I have learnt one thing, and it is this, that if we take care of the facts of a case, the law will take care of itself. Let us dive deeper into the facts of this case.' With these words he asked me to study the case further and then see him again. On a re-examination of the facts I saw them in an entirely new light, and I also hit upon an old South African case bearing on the point. I was delighted and went to Mr. Leonard and told him everything. 'Right,' he said, 'we shall win the case. Only we must bear in mind which of the judges takes it.'

When I was making preparation for Dada Abdulla's case, I had not fully realized this paramount[2] importance of facts. Facts mean truth, and once we adhere to truth, the law comes to our aid naturally. I saw that the facts of Dada Abdulla's case made it very strong indeed, and that the law was bound to be on his side. But I also saw that the litigation, if it were persisted in, would ruin the plaintiff and the defendant, who were relatives and both belonged to the same city. No one knew how long the case might go on. Should it be allowed to continue to be fought out in court, it might go on indefinitely[3] and to no advantage of either party. Both, therefore, desired an immediate termination of the case, if possible.

I approached Tyeb Sheth and requested and advised him to go to arbitration. I recommended him to see his counsel. I suggested to him that if an arbitrator commanding the confidence of both parties could appointed, the case would be quickly finished. The lawyers' fees were so

1. *prior: existing or coming before in time, order or importance*
2. *paramount: more important than anything else; supreme*
3. *indefinitely: lasting for an unknown or unstated length of time*

rapidly mounting up that they were enough to devour all the resources of the clients, big merchants as they were. The case occupied so much of their attention that they had no time left for any other work. In the meantime mutual ill-will was steadily increasing. I became disgusted with the profession. As lawyers the counsel on both sides were bound to rake[1] up points of law in support of their own clients. I also saw for the first time that the winning party never recovers all the costs incurred. Under the Court Fees Regulation there was a fixed scale of costs to be allowed as between party and party, the actual costs as between attorney and client being very much higher. This was more than I could bear. I felt that my duty was to befriend both parties and bring them together. I strained every nerve to bring about a compromise. At last Tyeb Sheth agreed. An arbitrator was appointed, the case was argued before him, and Dada Abdulla won.

But that did not satisfy me. If my client were to seek immediate execution of the award, it would be impossible for Tyeb Sheth to meet the whole of the awarded amount, and there was an unwritten law among the Porbandar Memans living in South Africa that death should be preferred to bankruptcy. It was impossible for Tyeb Sheth to pay down the whole sum of about £37,000 and costs. He meant to pay not a pie less than the amount, and he did not want to be declared bankrupt. There was only one way. Dada Abdulla should allow him to pay in moderate installments. He was equal to the occasion, and granted Tyeb Sheth installments spread over a very long period. It was more difficult for me to secure this concession of payment by installments than to get the parties to agree to arbitration. But both were happy over the result, and both rose in the public estimation. My joy was boundless. I had learnt the true practice of law. I had learnt to find out the better side of human nature and to enter men's hearts. I realized that the true function of a lawyer was to unite parties riven[2] asunder[3]. The lesson was so indelibly[4] burnt into me that a large part of my time during the twenty years of my practice as a lawyer was occupied in bringing about private compromises of hundreds of cases. I lost nothing thereby - not even money, certainly not my soul.

1. *rake: gather quickly or with ease*
2. *riven: violently divided*
3. *asunder: [archaic or poetic – literary] apart*
4. *indelibly: that cannot be removed forgotten*

CHAPTER 40

RELIGIOUS FERMENT

It is now time to turn again to my experiences with Christian friends.

Mr. Baker was getting anxious about my future. He took me to the Wellington Convention. The Protestant Christians organize such gatherings every few years for religious enlightenment[1] or, in other words, self-purification. One may call this religious restoration or revival. The Wellington Convention was of this type. The chairman was the famous divine of the place, the Rev. Andrew Murray. Mr. Baker had hoped that the atmosphere of religious exaltation[2] at the Convention, and the enthusiasm and earnestness of the people attending it, would inevitably lead me to embrace Christianity.

But his final hope was the efficacy of prayer. He had an abiding faith in prayer. It was his firm conviction that God could not but listen to prayer fervently offered. He would cite the instances of men like George Muller of Bristol, who depended entirely on prayer even for his temporal needs. I listened to his discourse on the efficacy[3] of prayer with unbiased[4] attention, and assured him that nothing could prevent me from embracing Christianity, should I feel the call. I had no hesitation in giving him this assurance, as I had long since taught myself to follow the inner voice. I delighted in submitting to it. To act against it would be difficult and painful to me.

So we went to Wellington. Mr. Baker was hard put to it in having a 'coloured man' like me for his companion. He had to suffer inconveniences on many occasions entirely on account of me. We had to break the journey on the way, as one of the days happened to be a Sunday, and Mr. Baker and his party would not travel on the Sabbath. Though the manager of the station hotel agreed to take me in after much altercation, he absolutely refused to admit me to the dining-room. Mr. Baker was not the man to give way easily. He stood by the rights of the guests of a hotel. But I could see his difficulty. At Wellington also I stayed with Mr. Baker. In spite of

1. *enlightenment: give greater knowledge and understanding to; give spiritual insight to*
2. *exaltation: great happiness*
3. *efficacy: ability to produce results*
4. *unbiased: fair and impartial*

his best efforts to conceal the little inconveniences that he was put to, I could see them all.

This Convention was an assemblage of devout Christians. I was delighted at their faith. I met the Rev. Murray. I saw that many were praying for me. I liked some of their hymns, they were very sweet.

The Convention lasted for three days. I could understand and appreciate the devoutness of those who attended it. But I saw no reason for changing my belief my religion. It was impossible for me to believe that I could go to heaven or attain salvation only by becoming a Christian. When I frankly said so to some good Christian friends, they were shocked. But there was no help for it.

My difficulties lay deeper. It was more than I could believe that Jesus was the only incarnate son of God, and that only he who believed in Him would have everlasting life. If God could have sons, all of us were His sons. If Jesus was like God, or God Himself, then all men were like God and could be God Himself. My reason was not ready to believe literally that Jesus by his death and by his blood redeemed[1] the sins of the world. Metaphorically there might be some truth in it. Again, according to Christianity only human beings had souls, and not other living beings, for whom death meant complete extinction; while I held a contrary[2] belief. I could accept Jesus as a martyr[3], an embodiment of sacrifice, and a divine teacher, but not as the most perfect man ever born. His death on the Cross was a great example to the world, but that there was anything like a mysterious or miraculous virtue in it my heart could not accept. The pious lives of Christians did not give me anything that the lives of men of other faiths had failed to give. I had seen in other lives just the same reformation that I had heard of among Christians. Philosophically there was nothing extraordinary in Christian principles. From the point of view of sacrifice, it seemed to me that the Hindus greatly surpassed[4] the Christians. It was impossible for me to regard Christianity as a perfect religion or the greatest of all religions.

I shared this mental churning with my Christian friends whenever there was an opportunity, but their answers could not satisfy me.

Thus if I could not accept Christianity either as a perfect, or the greatest religion, neither was I then convinced of Hinduism being such. Hindu defects were pressingly visible to me. If untouchability could be a part of Hinduism, it could but be a rotten part or an excrescence.

1. *redeemed: compensate for the faults or bad aspects of; make up for one's poor past performance or behavior; save from sin, error, or evil*
2. *contrary: opposite in nature, direction, or meaning*
3. *martyr: a person who is killed because of their religious or other beliefs*
4. *surpassed: be greater or better than; incomparable or outstanding*

I could not understand the *raison d'etre*[1] of a multitude of sects and castes. What was the meaning of saying that the Vedas were the inspired Word of God? If they were inspired, why not also the Bible and the Koran?

As Christian friends were endeavouring[2] to convert me, even so were Musalman friends. Abdulla Sheth had kept on inducing me to study Islam, and of course he had always something to say regarding its beauty.

I expressed my difficulties in a letter to Raychandbhai. I also corresponded with other religious authorities in India and received answers from them. Raychandbhai's letter somewhat pacified[3] me. He asked me to be patient and to study Hinduism more deeply. One of his sentences was to this effect: 'On a dispassionate view of the question I am convinced that no other religion has the subtle and profound[4] thought of Hinduism, its vision of the soul, or its charity.'

I purchased Sale's translation of the Koran and began reading it. I also obtained other books on Islam. I communicated with Christian friends in England. One of them introduced me to Edward Maitland, with whom I opened correspondence. He sent me *The Perfect Way*, a book he had written in collaboration with Anna Kingsford. The book was a repudiation of the current Christian belief. He also sent me another book, *The New Interpretation of the Bible*. I liked both. They seemed to support Hinduism. Tolstoy's *The Kingdom of God is Within You* overwhelmed me. It left an abiding impression on me. Before the independent thinking, profound morality, and the truthfulness of this book, all the books given me by Mr. Coates seemed to pale into insignificance.

My studies thus carried me in a direction unthought of by the Christian friends. My correspondence with Edward Maitland was fairly prolonged, and that with Raychandbhai continued until his death. I read some of the books he sent me. These included *Panchikaran, Maniratnamala, Mumukshu Prakaran of Yogavasishtha, Haribhadra Suri's Shaddarshana Samuchchaya* and others.

Though I took a path my Christian friends had not intended for me, I have remained for ever indebted to them for the religious quest that they awakened in me. I shall always cherish the memory of their contact. The years that followed had more, not less, of such sweet and sacred contacts in store for me.

1. *raison d'etre: justification for the existence*
2. *endeavouring: try hard to do or achieve something*
3. *pacified: remove agitation and bring peace*
4. *profound: very great or intense; profound social changes; severe*

CHAPTER 41

MAN PROPOSES, GOD DISPOSES

The case having been concluded, I had no reason for staying in Pretoria. So I went back to Durban and began to make preparations for my return home. But Abdulla Sheth was not the man to let me sail without a send-off. He gave a farewell[1] party in my honour at Sydenham.

It was proposed to spend the whole day there. Whilst I was turning over the sheets of some of the newspapers I found there, I chanced to see a paragraph in a corner of one of them under the caption 'Indian Franchise[2]'. It was with reference to the bill then before the House of Legislature, which sought to deprive the Indians of their right to elect members of the Natal Legislative Assembly. I was ignorant of the bill, and so were the rest of the guests who had assembled there.

I inquired of Abdulla Sheth about it. He said: 'What can we understand in these matters? We can only understand things that affect our trade. As you know all our trade in the Orange Free State has been swept away. We agitated about it, but in vain. We are after all lame men, being unlettered. We generally take in newspapers simply to ascertain[3] the daily market rates, etc. What can we know of legislation[4]? Our eyes and ears are the European attorneys here.'

'But,' said I, 'there are so many young Indians born and educated here, Do they not help you?'

'They!' exclaimed Abdulla Sheth in despair. 'They never care to come to us, and to tell you the truth, we care less to recognize them. Being Christians, they are under the thumb of the white clergymen, who in their turn are subject to the Government.'

This opened my eyes. I felt that this class should be claimed as our own. Was this the meaning of Christianity? Did they cease to be Indians because they had become Christians?

But I was on the point of returning home and hesitated to express what was passing through my mind in this matter. I simply said to

1. *farewell: good wishes expressed during a parting*
2. *franchise: an authorization granted by a government or company to an individual or group enabling them to carry out specified commercial activities, a business or service granted such authorization, leaguer to own a sports team, (north american) [informal] a team granted such authorization*
3. *ascertain: find out for certain*
4. *legislation: making and enacting laws*

Abdulla Sheth: 'This bill, if it passes into law, will make our lot extremely difficult. It is the first nail into our coffin[1]. It strikes at the root of our self-respect.'

'It may,' echoed Sheth Abdulla. 'I will tell you the genesis of the franchise question. We knew nothing about it. But Mr. Escombe, one of our best attorneys, whom you know, put the idea into our heads. It happened thus. He is a great fighter, and there being no love lost between, him and the Wharf Engineer, he feared that the Engineer might deprive him of his votes and defeat him at the election. So he acquainted us with our position, and at his instance we all registered ourselves as voters, and voted for him. You will now see how the franchise has not for us the value that you attach to it. But we understand what you say. Well, then, what is your advice?'

The other guests were listening to this conversation with attention. One of them said: 'Shall I tell you what should be done? You cancel your passage by this boat, stay here a month longer, and we will fight as you direct us.'

All the others chimed in: 'Indeed, indeed. Abdulla Sheth, you must detain Gandhibhai.'

The Sheth was a shrewd man. He said: 'I may not detain him now. Or rather, you have as much right as I to do so. But you are quite right. Let us all persuade him to stay on. But you should remember that he is a barrister. What about his fees?'

The mention of fees pained me, and I broke in: 'Abdulla Sheth, fees are out of the question. There can be no fees for public work. I can stay, if at all, as a servant. And as you know, I am not acquainted with all these friends. But if you believe that they will co-operate[2], I am prepared to stay a month longer. There is one thing, however. Though you need not pay me anything, work of the nature we contemplate[3] cannot be done without some funds to start with. Thus we may have to send telegrams, we may have to print some literature, some touring may have to be done, the local attorneys may have to be consulted, and as I am ignorant of your laws, I may need some law-books for reference. All this cannot be done without money. And it is clear that one man is not enough for this work. Many must come forward to help him.'

1. *coffin: a long, narrow box in which a dead body is buried or cremated*
2. *co-operate: work jointly towards the same end; assist someone or comply with their requests*
3. *contemplate: look at thoughtfully; think about; think profoundly and at length; have as a probable intention*

And a chorus of voices was heard: 'Allah is great and merciful. Money will come in. Men there are, as many as you may need. You please consent to stay, and all will be well.'

The farewell party was thus turned into a working committee. I suggested finishing dinner etc. quickly and getting back home. I worked out in my own mind an outline of the campaign. I ascertained the names of those who were on the list of voters, and made up my mind to stay on for a month.

Thus God laid the foundations of my life in South Africa and sowed[1] the seed of the fight for national self-respect.

1. *sowed: plant by scattering it on or in the earth; plant with seed*

CHAPTER 42

SETTLED IN NATAL

Sheth Haji Muhammad Haji Dada was regarded as the foremost leader of the Indian community in Natal in 1893. Financially Sheth Abdulla Haji Adam was the chief among them, but he and others always gave the first place to Sheth Haji Muhammad in public affairs. A meeting was therefore, held under his presidentship at the house of Abdulla Sheth, at which it was resolved to offer opposition to the Franchise Bill.

Volunteers were enrolled. Natal-born Indians, that is, mostly Christian Indian youths, had been invited to attend this meeting Mr. Paul, the Durban court interpreter, and Mr. Subhan Godfrey, headmaster of a mission school, were present, and it was they who were responsible for bringing together at the meeting a good number of Christian youths. All these enrolled themselves as volunteers.

Many of the local merchants were of course enrolled, noteworthy among them Sheths Dawud Muhammad, Muhammad Kasam Kamruddin, Adamji Miyakhan, A. Kolandavellu Pillai, C. Lachhiram, Rangasami Padiachi, and Amod Jiva. Parsi Rustomji was of course there. From among the clerks were Messrs Manekji, Joshi, Narsinhram and others, employees of Dada Abdulla and Co. and other big firms. They were all agreeably surprised to find themselves taking a share in public work. To be invited thus to take part was a new experience in their lives. In face of the calamity that had overtaken the community, all distinctions such as high and low, small and great, master and servant[1], Hindus, Musalmans, Parsis, Christians, Gujaratis, Madrasis, Sindhis, etc., were forgotten. All were alike the children and servants of the motherland.

The bill had already passed, or was about to pass, its second reading. In the speeches on the occasion the fact that Indians had expressed no opposition the stringent bill was urged[2] as proof[3] of their unfitness[4] for the franchise.

I explained the situation to the meeting. The first thing we did was to despatch a telegram to the Speaker of the Assembly requesting him to

1. *servant: a person employed to perform duties for others, especially in a house on domestic duties or as a personal attendant; a person employed in the service of a government; a devoted and helpful follower or supporter*
2. *urged: strongly recommend; encourage to move more quickly*
3. *proof: evidence establishing a fact or the truth of a statement*
4. *unfitness: unsuitable or inadequate for something*

postpone further discussion of the bill. A similar telegram was sent to the premier, Sir John Robinson, and another to Mr. Escombe, as a friend of Dada Abdulla's. The Speaker promptly replied that discussion of the bill would be postponed for two days. This gladdened our hearts.

The petition to be presented to the Legislative Assembly was drawn up. Three copies had to be prepared and one extra was needed for the press. It was also proposed to obtain as many signatures to it as possible, and all this work had to be done in the course of a night. The volunteers with a knowledge of English and several others sat up the whole night. Mr. Arthur, an old man, who was known for his calligraphy[1], wrote the principal copy. The rest were written by others to someone's dictation. Five copies were thus got ready simultaneously. Merchant volunteers went out in their own carriages, or carriages whose hire they had paid, to obtain signatures to the petition. This was accomplished in quick time and the petition was despatched. The newspapers published it with favourable comments. It likewise created an impression on the Assembly. It was discussed in the House. Partisans of the bill offered a defence, an admittedly lame one, in reply to the arguments advanced in the petition. The bill, however, was passed.

We all knew that this was a foregone conclusion, but the agitation had infused new life into the community and had brought home to them the conviction that the community was one and indivisible[2], and that it was as much their duty to fight for its political rights as for its trading rights.

Lord Ripon was at this time Secretary of State for the Colonies. It was decided to submit to him a monster petition. This was no small task and could not be done in a day. Volunteers were enlisted, and all did their due share of the work.

I took considerable pains over drawing up this petition[3]. I read all the literature available on the subject. My argument centred round a principle and on expedience. I argued that we had a right to the franchise in Natal, as we had a kind of franchise in India. I urged that it was expedient to retain it, as the Indian population capable of using the franchise was very small.

Ten thousand signatures were obtained in the course of a fortnight[4]. To secure this number of signatures from the whole of the province was no light task, especially when we consider that the men were perfect

1. *calligraphy: decorative handwriting or handwritten lettering, the art of producing this*
2. *indivisible: unable to be divided or separated*
3. *petition: a formal written request, typically signed by many people, appealing to authority in respect of a cause; an appeal or request*
4. *fortnight: (chiefly british) a period of two weeks; [informal] two weeks from that day*

strangers to the work. Specially competent volunteers had to be selected for the work, as it had been decided not to take a single signature without the signatory fully understanding the petition. The villages were scattered at long distances. The work could be done promptly only if a number of workers put their whole heart into it. And this they did. All carried out their allotted[1] task with enthusiasm. But as I am writing these lines, figures of Sheth Dawud Muhammad, Rustomji, Adamji Miyakhan, and Amod Jiva rise clearly before my mind. They brought in the largest number of signatures. Dawud Sheth kept going about in his carriage the whole day. And it was all a labour of love, not one of them asking for even his out-of-pocket expenses. Dada Abdulla's house became at once a caravanserai and a public office. A number of educated fiends who helped me and many others had their food there. Thus every helper was put to considerable expense.

The petition was at last submitted. A thousand copies had been printed for circulation[2] and distribution. It acquainted the Indian public for the first time with conditions in Natal. I sent copies to all the newspapers and publicists I knew.

The Times of India, in a leading article on the petition, strongly supported the Indian demands. Copies were sent to journals and publicists in England representing different parties. The London *Times* supported our claims, and we began to entertain hopes of the bill being vetoed.

It was now impossible for me to leave Natal. The Indian friends surrounded me on all sides and importuned me to remain there permanently. I expressed my difficulties. I had made up my mind not to stay at public expense. I felt it necessary to set up an independent household[3]. I thought that the house should be good and situated in a good locality. I also had the idea that I could not add to the credit of the community, unless I lived in a style usual for barristers. And it seemed to me to be impossible to run such a household with anything less than 300 a year. I therefore decided that I could stay only if the members of the community guaranteed[4] legal work to the extent of that minimum, and I communicated my decision to them.

'But,' said they, 'we should like you to draw that amount for public work, and we can easily collect it. Of course this is apart from the fees you must charge for private legal work.'

1. *allotted: apportioned or assigned*
2. *circulation: movement to and fro or around something; the continuous motion by while blood travels through the body*
3. *household: a house and its occupants regarded as a unit*
4. *guaranteed: a formal assurance*

'No, I could not thus charge you for public work,' said I. 'The work would not involve the exercise on my part of much skill as barrister. My work would be mainly to make you all work. And how could I charge you for that? And then I should have to appeal to you frequently for funds for the work, and if I were to draw my maintenance from you, I should find myself at a disadvantage in making an appeal for large amounts, and we should ultimately find ourselves at a standstill[1]. Besides I want the community to find more than 300 annually for public work.'

'But we have now known you for some time, and are sure you would not draw anything you do not need. And if we wanted you to stay here, should we not find your expenses?'

'It is your love and present enthusiasm that make you talk like this. How can we be sure that this love and enthusiasm will endure[2] for ever? And as your friend and servant, I should occasionally have to say hard things to you. Heaven only knows whether I should then retain your affection. But the fact is that I must not accept any salary for public work. It is enough for me that you should all agree to entrust me with your legal work. Even that may be hard for you. For one thing I am not a white barrister. How can I be sure that the court will respond to me? Nor can I be sure how I shall fare as a lawyer. So even in giving me retainers you may be running some risk. I should regard even the fact of your giving them to me as the reward of my public work.'

The upshot[3] of this discussion was that about twenty merchants gave me retainers for one year for their legal work. Besides this, Dada Abdulla purchased me the necessary furniture in lieu of a purse he had intended to give me on my departure,

Thus I settled in Natal.

1. *standstill: a situation or condition without movement or activity*
2. *endure: remain in existence*
3. *upshot: the eventual outcome or conclusion*

CHAPTER 43

NATAL INDIAN CONGRESS

Practice as a lawyer was and remained for me a subordinate occupation. It was necessary that I should concentrate on public work to justify my stay in Natal. The despatch of the petition regarding the disfranchising bill was not sufficient[1] in itself. Sustained agitation was essential for making an impression on the Secretary of State for the Colonies. For this purpose it was thought necessary to bring into being a permanent organization. So I consulted Sheth Abdulla and other friends, and we all decided to have a public organization of a permanent character.

To find out a name to be given to the new organization perplexed me sorely. It was not to identify itself with any particular party. The name 'Congress', I knew, was in bad odour with the Conservatives in England, and yet the Congress was the very life of India. I wanted to popularize it in Natal. It savoured of cowardice to hesitate to adopt the name. Therefore, with full explanation of my reasons, I recommended that the organization should be called the Natal Indian Congress, and on the 22nd May the Natal Indian Congress came into being.

Dada Abdulla's spacious[2] room was packed to the full on that day. The Congress received the enthusiastic approval of all present. Its constitution was simple, the subscription was heavy. Only he who paid five shillings monthly could be a member. The well-to-do classes were persuaded to subscribe as much as they could. Abdulla Sheth headed the list with £2 per month. Two other friends also put down the same. I thought I should not stint my subscription, and put down a pound per month. This was for me no small amount. But I thought that I would not be beyond my means, if I was to pay my way. And God helped me. We thus got a considerable number of members who subscribed £1 per month. The number of those who put down 10s. was even larger. Besides this, there were donations which were gratefully[3] accepted.

Experience showed that no one paid his subscription for the mere asking. It was impossible to call frequently on members outside Durban.

1. *sufficient: enough; adequate*
2. *spacious: having plenty of space*
3. *gratefully: feeling or showing gratitude*

The enthusiasm of one moment seemed to wear away the next. Even the members in Durban had to be considerably dunned before they would pay in their subscriptions.

The task of collecting subscriptions lay with me. I being the secretary. And we came to a stage when I had to keep my clerk engaged all day long in the work of collection. The man got tired of the job, and I felt that, if the situation was to be improved, the subscriptions should be made payable annually and not monthly, and that too strictly in advance. So I called a meeting of the Congress. Everyone welcomed the proposal for making the subscription annual instead of monthly and for fixing the minimum at £3. Thus the work of collection was considerably facilitated[1].

I had learnt at the outset not to carry on public work with borrowed money. One could rely on people's promises in most matters except in respect of money. I had never found people quick to pay the amounts they had undertaken[2] to subscribe, and the Natal Indians were no exception to the rule. As, therefore, no work was done unless there were funds on hand, the Natal Indian Congress has never been in debt[3].

My co-workers evinced extraordinary enthusiasm in canvassing members. It was work which interested them and was at the same time an invaluable experience. Large numbers of people gladly came forward with cash subscriptions. Work in the distant villages of the interior was rather difficult. People did not know the nature of public work. And yet we had invitations to visit far away places, leading merchants of every place extending their hospitality[4].

On one occasion during this tour the situation was rather difficult. We expected our host to contribute £6, but he refused to give anything more than £3. If we had accepted that amount from him, others would have followed suit, and our collections would have been spoiled. It was a late hour of the night, and we were all hungry. But how could we dine without having first obtained the amount we were bent on getting? All persuasion was useless. The host seemed to be adamant[5]. Other merchants in the town reasoned with him, and we all sat up throughout the night, he as well as we determined not to budge one inch. Most of my co-workers were burning with rage, but they contained themselves. At last, when day was already breaking, the host yielded, paid down £6 and feasted us. This happened at Tongaat, but the repercussion of the

1. *facilitated: make easy or easier*
2. *undertaken: commit oneself to and begin an enterprise or responsibility; take on*
3. *debt: money or services owed or due*
4. *hospitality: the friendly and generous reception and entertainment of guests or strangers*
5. *adamant: refusing to be persuaded or to change one's mind*

incident was felt as far as Stanger on the North Coast and Charlestown in the interior. It also hastened our work of collection.

But collecting funds was not the only thing to do. In fact I had long learnt the principle of never having more money at one's disposal than necessary.

Meetings used to be held once a month or even once a week if required. Minutes of the proceedings[1] of the preceding[2] meeting would be read, and all sorts of questions would be discussed. People had no experience of taking part in public discussion or of speaking briefly and to the point. Everyone hesitated to stand up to speak. I explained to them the rules of procedure at meetings and they respected them. They realized that it was an education for them, and many who had never been accustomed to speaking before an audience soon acquired the habit of thinking and speaking publicly about matters of public interest.

Knowing that in public work minor expenses at times absorbed large accounts, I had decided not to have even the receipt books printed in the beginning. I had a cyclostyle[3] machine in my office, on which I took copies of receipts and reports. Such things I began to get printed only when the Congress coffers were full, and when the number of members and work had increased. Such economy is essential for every organization, and yet I know that it is not always exercised. That is why I have thought it proper to enter into these little details of the beginnings of a small but growing organization.

People never cared to have receipts for the amounts they paid, but we always insisted on the receipts being given. Every pie was thus clearly accounted for, and I dare say the account books for the year 1894 can be found intact even today in the records of Natal Indian Congress. Carefully kept accounts are a *sine qua non* for any organization. Without them it falls into disrepute[4]. Without properly kept accounts it is impossible to maintain truth in its pristine purity.

Another feature of the Congress was service of colonial-born educated Indians. The colonial-born Indian Educational Association was founded under the auspices of the Congress. The members consisted mostly of these educated youths. They had to pay a nominal subscription. The Association served to ventilate their needs and grievances, to stimulate thought amongst them, to bring them into touch with Indian merchants

1. *preceding: come or go before in time, order, or position; preface something with*
2. *proceedings: an event or a series of activities with a set procedure*
3. *cyclostyle: an early device for duplicating handwriting, in which a pen with a small toothed wheel makes a stencil in a sheet of waxed paper*
4. *disrepute: the state of being discredited*

and also to afford them scope for service of the community. It was a sort of debating society. The members met regularly and spoke or read papers on different subjects. A small library was also opened in connection with the Association.

The third feature of the Congress was propaganda. This consisted in acquainting the English in South Africa and England and people in India with the real state of things in Natal. With that end in view I wrote two pamphlets[1]. The first was *An Appeal to Every Briton in South Africa*. It contained a statement, supported by evidence, of the general condition of Natal Indians. The other was entitled *The Indian Franchise An Appeal*. It contained a brief history of the Indian franchise in Natal with facts and figures. I had devoted considerable labour and study to the preparation of these pamphlets, and the result was quite commensurate with the trouble taken. They were widely circulated.

All this activity resulted in winning the Indians numerous friends in South Africa and in obtaining the active sympathy of all parties in India. It also opened out and placed before the South African Indians a definite line of action.

1. *pamphlets: a small booklet or leaflet containing information or arguments about a single subject*

CHAPTER 44
COLOUR BAR

The symbol of a Court of justice is pair of scales held evenly by an impartial and blind but sagacious woman. Fate has purposely made her blind, in order that she may not judge a person from his exterior but from his intrinsic worth. But the Law Society of Natal set out to persuade the Supreme Court to act in contravention of this principle and to belie[1] its symbol.

I applied for admission as an advocate of the Supreme Court. I held a certificate of admission from the Bombay High Court. The English certificate I had to deposit with the Bombay High Court when I was enrolled there. It was necessary to attach two certificates of character to the application for admission, and thinking that these would carry more weight if given by Europeans, I secured them from two well-known European merchants whom I knew through Sheth Abdulla. The application had to be presented through a member of the bar, and as a rule the Attorney General presented such applications without fees. Mr. Escombe, who, as we have seen, was legal adviser to Messrs. Dada Abdulla & Co, was the Attorney General. I called on him, and he willingly consented to present my application.

The Law Society now sprang a surprise on me by serving me with a notice opposing my application for admission. One of their objections was that the original English certificate was not attached to my application. But the main objection was that, when the regulations regarding admission of advocates were made, the possibility of a coloured man applying could not have been contemplated. Natal owed its growth to European enterprise, and therefore it was necessary that the European element should predominate[2] in the bar. If coloured people were admitted, they might gradually outnumber the Europeans, and the bulwark[3] of their protection would break down.

The Law Society had engaged a distinguished lawyer to support their opposition. As he too was connected with Dada Abdulla & Co,

1. *belie: fail to give a true notion of*

2. *predominate: be the strongest or main element; have or exert control or power*

3. *bulwark: a defensive wall*

he sent me word through Sheth Abdulla to go and see him. He talked with me quite frankly, and inquired about my antecedents, which I gave. Then he said:

'I have nothing to say against you. I was only afraid lest you should be some colonial-born adventurer. And the fact that your application was unaccompanied by the original certificate supported my suspicion. There have been men who have made use of diplomas which did not belong to them. The certificates of character from European traders you have submitted have no value for me. What do they know about you? What can be the extent of their acquaintance with you?

'But,' said I, 'everyone here is a stranger to me. Even Sheth Abdulla first came to know me here.'

'But then you say he belongs to the same place as you? It your father was Prime Minister there, Sheth Abdulla is bound to know your family. If you were to produce his affidavit, I should have absolutely no objection. I would then gladly communicate to the Law Society my inability to oppose your application.'

This talk enraged me, but I restrained my feelings. 'If I had attached Dada Abdulla's certificate.' said I to myself, 'it would have been rejected, and they would have asked for Europeans' certificates. And what has my admission as advocate to do with my birth and my antecedents[1]? How could my birth, whether humble or objectionable, be used against me?' But I contained myself and quietly replied:

'Though I do not admit that the Law Society has any authority to require all these details, I am quite prepared to present the affidavit[2] you desire.'

Sheth Abdulla's affidavit was prepared and duly submitted to the counsel for the Law Society. He said he was satisfied. But not so the Law Society. it opposed my application before the Supreme Court, which ruled out the opposition without even calling upon Mr. Escombe to reply. The Chief justice said in effect:

'The objection that the applicant has not attached the original certificate has no substance. If he has made a false affifavit, he can be prosecuted, and his name can then be struck off the roll, if he is proved guilty. The law makes no distinction between white and coloured people. The court has therefore no authority to prevent Mr. Gandhi from being

1. *antecedents: a person's ancestors and social background*

2. *affidavit: a written statement confirmed by oath or affirmation, for use as evidence in court*

enrolled as an advocate. We admit his application. Mr. Gandhi, you can now take the oath.'

I stood up and took the oath before the Registar. As soon as I was sworn in, the Chief Justice, addressing me, said:

'You must now take off your turban, Mr. Gandhi. you must submit to the rules of the court with regard to the dress to be worn by practising barristers.'

I saw my limitations. The turban that I had insisted on wearing in the District Magistrate's Court I took off in obedience to the order of the Supreme Court. Not that, if I had resisted the order, the resistance could not have been justified. But I wanted to reserve my strength for fighting bigger battles. I should not exhaust my skill as a fighter in insisting on retaining my turban. It was worthy of a better cause.

Sheth Abdulla and other friends did not like my submission (or was it weakness?). They felt that I should have stood by my right to wear the turban while practising in the Court. I tried to reason with them. I tried to press home to them the truth of the maxim, 'When at Rome do as the Romans do.' 'It would be right,' I said, 'to refuse to obey, if in India an English officer or judge ordered you to take off your turban; but as an officer of the court, it would have ill become me to disregard a custom of the court in the province of Natal.'

I pacified the friends somewhat with these and similar arguments, but I do not think I convinced them completely, in this instance, of the applicability of the principle of looking at a thing from a different standpoint[1] in different circumstances. But all my life through, the very insistence on truth has taught me to appreciate the beauty of compromise. I saw in later life that this spirit was an essential part of Satyagraha. It has often meant endangering my life and incurring[2] the displeasure of friends. But truth is hard as adamant and tender as a blossom[3].

The opposition of the Law Society gave me another advertisement in South Africa. Most of the newspapers condemned the opposition and accused the Law Society of jealousy. The advertisement, to some extent, simplified my work.

1. *standpoint: the position form which a scene or an object is viewed*
2. *incurring: become subject to as a result of one's actions*
3. *blossom: a flower or a mass of flowers on a tree or bush; the state or period of flowering*

CHAPTER 45
BALASUNDARAM

The heart's earnest and pure desire is always fulfilled. In my own experience I have often seen this rule verified[1]. Service of the poor has been my heart's desire, and it has always thrown me amongst the poor and enabled me to identify myself with them.

Although the members of the Natal Indian Congress included the colonial-born Indians and the clerical class, the unskilled wage-earners, the indentured labourers were still outside its pale. The Congress was not yet theirs. They could not afford to belong to it by paying the subscription and becoming its members. The Congress could win their attachment only by serving them. An opportunity[2] offered itself when neither the Congress nor I was really ready for it. I had put in scarcely[3] three or four months' practice, and the Congress also was still in its infancy[4], when a Tamil man in tattered clothes, head-gear in hand, two front teeth broken and his mouth bleeding, stood before me trembling and weeping. He had been heavily belaboured by his master. I learnt all about him from my clerk, who was a Tamilian. Balasundaram - as that was the visitor's name - was serving his indenture under a well-known European resident of Durban. The master, getting angry with him, had lost self-control, and had beaten Balasundaram severely, breaking two of his teeth.

I sent him to a doctor. In those days only white doctors were available. I wanted a certificate from the doctor about the nature of the injury Balasundaram had sustained. I secured the certificate, and straightway took the injured man to the magistrate, to whom I submitted his affidavit. The magistrate was indignant when he read it, and issued a summons against the employer.

It was far from my desire to get the employer punished. I simply wanted Balasundaram to be released from him. I read the law about indentured labour. If an ordinary servant left service without giving notice, he was liable to be sued by his master in a civil court. With the

1. *verified: anything that can be substantiated, proved correct or otherwise*
2. *opportunity: a favorable time or set of circumstances for doing something*
3. *scarcely: of a resource insufficient for the demand*
4. *infancy: denoting something in an early stage of development*

indentured labourer the case was entirely different. He was liable, in similar circumstances, to be proceeded against in a criminal court and to be imprisoned on conviction. That is why Sir William Hunter called the indenture system almost as bad as slavery. Like the slave the indentured labourer was the property of his master.

There were only two ways of releasing Balasundaram: either by getting the Protector of Indentured Labourers to cancel his indenture or transfer him to someone else, or by getting Balasundaram's employer to release him. I called on the latter and said to him: 'I do not want to proceed against you and get you punished. I think you realize that you have severely beaten the man. I shall be satisfied if you will transfer[1] the indenture to someone else.' To this he readily agreed. I next saw the Protector. He also agreed, on condition that I found a new employer.

So I went off in search of an employer. He had to be a European, as no Indians could employ indentured labour. At that time I knew very few Europeans. I met one of them. He very kindly agreed to take on Balasundaram. I gratefully acknowledged his kindness[2]. The magistrate convicted Balasundaram's employer, and recorded that he had undertaken to transfer the indenture to someone else.

Balasundaram's case reached the ears of every indentured labourer, and I came to be regarded as their friend. I hailed this connection with delight. A regular stream of indentured labourers began to pour into my office, and I got the best opportunity of learning their joys and sorrows.

The echoes of Balasundaram's case were heard in far off Madras. Labourers from different parts of the province[3], who went to Natal on indenture, came to know of this case through their indentured brethren.

There was nothing extraordinary in the case itself, but the fact that there was someone in Natal to espouse their cause and publicly work for them gave the indentured labourer a joyful[4] surprise and inspired him with hope.

I have said that Balasundaram entered my office, head-gear in hand. There was a peculiar pathos about the circumstance which also showed our humiliation. I have already narrated the incident when I was asked to take off my turban. A practice had been forced upon every indentured labourer and every Indian stranger to take off his head-gear when visiting a European, whether the head-gear were a cap, turban or

1. *transfer: move from one place to another*
2. *kindness: the quality of being kind*
3. *province: a principal administrative division of a country or empire*
4. *joyful: feeling or causing joy*

a scarf wrapped round the head. A salute even with both hands was not sufficient. Balasundaram thought that he should follow the practice even with me. This was the first case in my experience. I felt humiliated and asked him to tie up his scarf. He did so, not without a certain hesitation, but I could perceive[1] the pleasure on his face.

It has always been a mystery to me how men can feel themselves honoured by the humiliation of their fellow beings.

1. *perceive: become aware or conscious of*

CHAPTER 46

THE £3 TAX

Balasundaram's case brought me into touch with the indentured Indians. What impelled me, however, to make a deep study of their condition was the campaign for bringing them under special heavy taxation.

In the same year, 1894, the Natal Government sought to impose an annual tax of £25 on the indentured Indians. The proposal astonished me. I put the matter before the Congress for discussion, and it was immediately resolved to organize the necessary opposition.

At the outset I must explain briefly the genesis of the tax.

About the year 1860 the Europeans in Natal, finding that there was considerable scope for sugar-cane cultivation, felt themselves in need of labour. Without outside labour the cultivation of cane and the manufacture of sugar were impossible, as the Natal Zulus were not suited to this form of work. The Natal Government therefore corresponded with the Indian Government, and secured their permission to recruit[1] Indian labour. These recruits were to sign an indenture to work in Natal for five years, and at the end of the term they were to be at liberty to settle there and to have full rights of ownership of land. Those were the inducements[2] held out to them, for the whites then had looked forward to improving their agriculture by the industry of the Indian labourers after the term of their indentures had expired.

But the Indians gave more than had been expected of them. They grew large quantities of vegetables. They introduced a number of Indian varieties and made it possible to grow the local varieties[3] cheaper. They also introduced the mango. Nor did their enterprise stop at agriculture. They entered trade. They purchased land for building, and many raised themselves from the status of labourers to that of owners of land and houses. Merchants from India followed them and settled there for trade. The late Sheth Abubakar Amod was first among them. He soon built up an extensive[4] business.

1. *recruit: enroll as a member or worker in an organization*
2. *inducements: succeed in persuading or leading to do something*
3. *varieties: a number of things of the same general class that are distinct in character or quality*
4. *extensive: covering a large area; large in amount or scale*

The white traders were alarmed. When they first welcomed the Indian labourers, they had not reckoned[1] with their business skill. They might be tolerated as independent agriculturists, but their competition in trade could not be brooked.

This sowed the seed of the antagonism to Indians. Many other factors contributed to its growth. Our different ways of living, our simplicity, our contentment with small gains, our indifference to the laws of hygiene and sanitation, our slowness in keeping our surroundings clean and tidy, and our stinginess in keeping our houses in good repair all these, combined with the difference in religion, contributed to fan the flame of antagonism[2]. Through legislation this antagonism found its expression in the disfranchising bill and the bill to impose a tax on the indentured Indians. Independent of legislation a number of pinpricks[3] had already been started.

The first suggestion was that the Indian labourers should be forcibly repatriated[4], so that the term of their indentures might expire in India. The Government of India was not likely to accept the suggestion. Another proposal was therefore made to the effect that

1. the indentured labourer should return to India on the expiry of his indenture; or that
2. he should sign a fresh indenture every two years, an increment being given at each renewal; and that
3. in the case of his refusal to return to India or renew the indenture he should pay an annual tax of £25.

A deputation composed of Sir Henry Binns and Mr. Mason was sent to India to get the proposal approved by the Government there. The Viceroy at that time was Lord Elgin. He disapproved of the £25 tax, but agreed to a poll tax of £3. I thought then, as I do even now, that this was a serious blunder on the part of the Viceroy. In giving his approval he had in no way thought of the interests of India. It was no part of his duty thus to accommodate the Natal Europeans. In the course of three or four years an indentured labourer with his wife and each male child over 16 and female child over 13 came under the impost. To levy a yearly tax of £12 from a family of four husband, wife and two children when the average income of the husband was never more than 14s. a month, was atrocious and unknown anywhere else in the world.

1. *reckoned: take into account*
2. *antagonism: active hostility or opposition*
3. *pinpricks: a very small dot or amount*
4. *repatriated: send back to their own country*

We organized a fierce campaign against this tax. If the Natal Indian Congress had remained silent on the subject, the Viceroy might have approved of even the £25 tax. The reduction from £25 to £3 was probably due solely to the Congress agitation. But I may be mistaken in thinking so. It may be possible that the Indian Government had disapproved of the £25 tax from the beginning and reduced it to £3, irrespective of the opposition from the Congress. In any case it was a breach[1] of trust on the part of the Indian Government. As trustee[2] of the welfare of India, the Viceroy ought never to have approved of this inhuman tax.

The Congress could not regard it as any great achievement to have succeeded in getting the tax reduced from £25 to £3. The regret was still there that it had not completely safeguarded[3] the interests of the indentured Indians. It ever remained its determination to get the tax remitted[4], but it was twenty years before the determination was realized. And when it was realized, it came as a result of the labours of not only the Natal Indians but of all the Indians in South Africa. The breach of faith with the late Mr. Gokhale became the occasion of the final campaign, in which the indentured Indians took their full share, some of them losing their lives as a result of the firing that was resorted to, and over ten thousand suffering imprisonment.

But truth triumphed in the end. The sufferings of the Indians were the expression of that truth. Yet it would not have triumphed except for unflinching faith, great patience and incessant effort. Had the community given up the struggle, had the Congress abandoned the campaign and submitted to the tax as inevitable, the hated impost would have continued to be levied from the indentured Indians until this day, to the eternal shame of the Indians in South Africa and of the whole of India.

1. *breach: an act of breaking a law, agreement, or code of conduct*
2. *trustee: an individual or member of a board given powers of administration of property in trust with a legal obligation to administer it solely for the purposes specified*
3. *safeguarded: a measure taken to protect or prevent something*
4. *remitted: refrain from exacting or inflicting; [theology] pardon a sin*

CHAPTER 47

COMPARATIVE STUDY OF RELIGIONS

I found myself entirely absorbed in the service of the community, the reason behind it was my desire for self-realization. I had made the religion of service my own, as I felt that God could be realized only through service. And service for me was the service of India, because it came to me without my seeking, because I had an aptitude for it. I had gone to South Africa for travel, for finding an escape from Kathiawad intrigues and for gaining my own livelihood. But as I have said, I found myself in search of God and striving for self-realization.

Christian friends had whetted my appetite[1] for knowledge, which had become almost insatiable[2], and they would not leave me in peace, even if I desired to be indifferent. In Durban Mr. Spencer Walton, the head of the South Africa General Mission, found me out. I became almost a member of his family. At the back of this acquaintance was of course my contact with Christians in Pretoria. Mr. Walton had a manner all his own. I do not recollect his ever having invited me to embrace Christianity. But he placed his life as an open book before me, and let me watch all his movements. Mrs. Walton was a very gentle and talented woman. I liked the attitude of this couple. We knew the fundamental differences between us. Any amount of discussion could not efface[3] them. Yet even differences prove helpful, where there are tolerance[4], charity and truth. I liked Mr. and Mrs. Walton's humility, perseverance and devotion to work, and we met very frequently.

This friendship kept alive my interest in religion. It was impossible now to get the leisure that I used to have in Pretoria for my religious studies. But what little time I could spare I turned to good account. My religious correspondence continued. Raychandbhai was guiding me. Some friend sent me Narmadashanker's book *Dharma Vichar*. Its preface proved very helpful. I had heard about the Bohemian way in which the poet had lived, and a description in the preface of the revolution effected

1. *appetite: a natural desire to satisfy a bodily need, especially for food*
2. *insatiable: difficult to satisfy*
3. *efface: erase from a surface*
4. *tolerance: the ability, willingness, or capacity to tolerate something*

in his life by his religious studies captivated[1] me. I came to like the book, and read it from cover to cover with attention. I read with interest Max Muller's book, *India What Can It Teach Us?* and the translation of the *Upanishads* published by the Theosophical Society. All this enhanced my regard for Hinduism, and its beauties began to grow upon me. It did not, however, prejudice me against other religions. I read Washington Irving's *Life of Mahomet and His Successors*[2] and Carlyle's panegyric on the Prophet[3]. These books raised Muhammad in my estimation. I also read a book called *The Sayings of Zarathustra.*

Thus I gained more knowledge of the different religions. The study stimulated my self-introspection and fostered in me the habit of putting into practice whatever appealed to me in my studies. Thus I began some of the Yogic practices, as well as I could understand them from a reading of the Hindu books. But I could not get on very far, and decided to follow them with the help of some expert when I returned to India. The desire has never been fulfilled.

I made too an intensive study of Tolstoy's books. *The Gospels in Brief, What to Do?* and other books made a deep impression on me. I began to realize more and more the infinite possibilities of universal[4] love.

About the same time I came in contact with another Christian family. At their suggestion I attended the Wesleyan church every Sunday. For these days I also had their standing invitation to dinner. The church did not make a favourable impression on me. The sermons seemed to be uninspiring. The congregation did not strike me as being particularly religious. They were not an assembly of devout souls; they appeared rather to be worldly-minded people, going to church for recreation and in conformity to custom. Here, at times, I would involuntarily doze. I was ashamed, but some of my neighbours, who were in no better case, lightened the shame. I could not go on long like this, and soon gave up attending the service.

My connection with the family I used to visit every Sunday was abruptly broken. In fact it may be said that I was warned to visit it no more. It happened thus. My hostess was a good and simple woman, but somewhat narrow-minded. We always discussed religious subjects. I was then re-reading Arnold's *Light of Asia*. Once we began to compare the life of Jesus with that of Buddha. 'Look at Gautama's compassion!' said I.

1. *captivated: attract and hold the interest and attention of; charm*
2. *successors: a person or thing that succeeds another*
3. *Prophet: an inspired teacher or proclaimed of the will of god; Muhammad*
4. *universal: of, affecting, or done by all people or things in the world or in a particular group*

'It was not confined to mankind, it was extended to all living beings. Does not one's heart overflow with love to think of the lamb joyously perched on his shoulders? One fails to notice this love for all living beings in the life of Jesus.' The comparison pained the good lady. I could understand her feelings. I cut the matter short, and we went to the dining room. Her son, a cherub[1] aged scarcely five, was also with us. I am happiest when in the midst of children, and this youngster and I had long been friends. I spoke derisively of the piece of meat on his plate and in high praise of the apple on mine. The innocent boy was carried away and joined in my praise of the fruit.

But the mother? she was dismayed.

I was warned. I checked myself and changed the subject. The following week I visited the family as usual, but not without trepidation[2]. I did not see that I should stop going there, I did not think it proper either. But the good lady made my way easy.

'Mr. Gandhi,' she said, 'please don't take it ill if I feel obliged to tell you that my boy is none the better for your company. Every day he hesitates to eat meat and asks for fruit, reminding me of your argument. This is too much. If he gives up meat, he is bound to get weak, if not ill. How could I bear it? Your discussion should henceforth be only with us elders. They are sure to react badly on children.'

'Mrs---,' I replied, 'I am sorry. I can understand your feelings as a parent, for I too have children. We can very easily end this unpleasant[3] state of things. What I eat and omit to eat is bound to have a greater effect on the child than what I say. The best way, therefore, is for me to stop these visits. That certainly need not affect our friendship.'

'I thank you,' she said with evident relief.

1. *cherub: a sweet innocent baby*
2. *trepidation: a feeling of fear or agitation about something that may happen*
3. *unpleasant: not pleasant; disagreeable*

CHAPTER 48

AS A HOUSEHOLDER

To set up a household was no new experience for me. But the establishment in Natal was different from the ones that I had had in Bombay and London. This time part of the expense was solely for the sake of prestige[1]. I thought it necessary to have a household in keeping with my position as an Indian barrister in Natal and as a representative. So I had a nice little house in a prominent[2] locality. It was also suitably furnished[3]. Food was simple, but as I used to invite English friends and Indian co-workers, the housekeeping bills were always fairly high.

A good servant is essential in every household. But I have never known how to keep anyone as a servant.

I had a friend as companion and help, and a cook who had become a member of the family. I also had office clerks boarding and lodging with me.

I think I had a fair amount of success in this experiment, but it was not without its modicum of the bitter experiences of life.

The companion was very clever and, I thought, faithful to me. But in this I was deceived. He became jealous of an office clerk who was staying with me, and wove such a tangled web that I suspected the clerk. This clerical friend had a temper of his own. Immediately he saw that he had been the object of my suspicion, he left both the house and the office. I was pained. I felt that perhaps I had been unjust to him, and my conscience always stung me.

In the meanwhile, the cook needed a few days leave, or for some other cause was away. It was necessary to procure another during his absence. Of this new man I learnt later that he was a perfect scamp[4]. But for me he proved a godsend. Within two or three days of his arrival, he discovered certain irregularities that were going on under my roof without my knowledge, and he made up his mind to warn me. I had the reputation of being a credulous but straight man. The discovery was to him,

1. *prestige: widespread respect and admiration attracted through a perception of high achievements or quality*
2. *prominent: important; famous*
3. *furnished: provide with furniture and fitting*
4. *scamp: a mischievous person, especially a child*

therefore, all the more shocking. Every day at one o'clock I used to go home from office for lunch. At about twelve o'clock one day the cook came panting[1] to the office, and said, 'Please come home at once. There is a surprise for you.'

'Now, what is this?' I asked. 'You must tell me what it is. How can I leave the office at this hour to go and see it?'

'You will regret it, if you don't come. That is all I can say.'

I felt an appeal in his persistence[2]. I went home accompanied by a clerk and the cook who walked ahead of us. He took me straight to the upper floor, pointed at my companion's room, and said, 'Open this door and see for yourself.'

I saw it all. I knocked at the door. No reply! I knocked heavily so as to make the very walls shake. The door was opened. I saw a prostitute[3] inside. I asked her to leave the house, never to return.

To the companion I said, 'From this moment I cease[4] to have anything to do with you. I have been thoroughly deceived and have made a fool of myself. That is how you have requited my trust in you?'

Instead of coming to his senses, he threatened to expose me.

'I have nothing to conceal,' said I, 'Expose whatever I may have done. But you must leave me this moment.'

This made him worse. There was no help for it. So I said to the clerk standing downstairs: 'Please go and inform the police superintendent, with my compliments, that a person living with me has misbehaved himself. I do not want to keep him in my house, but he refuses to leave. I shall be much obliged if police help can be sent me.'

This showed him that I was in earnest. His guilt unnerved him. He apologized to me, entreated me not to inform the police, and agreed to leave the house immediately, which he did.

The incident came as a timely warning in my life. Only now could I see clearly how thoroughly I had been beguiled by this evil genius. In harbouring him I had chosen a bad means for a good end. I had expected to 'gather figs of thistles' I had known that the companion was a bad character, and yet I believed in his faithfulness to me. In the attempt to reform him I was near ruining myself. I had disregarded the warning of kind friends. Infatuation had completely blinded me.

1. *panting: breathe with short, quick breaths, typically from exertion or excitement*
2. *persistence: continue firmly or obstinately in an opinion or a course of action in spite of difficulty or opposition*
3. *prostitute: a person, typically a woman, who engages in sexual activity for payment*
4. *cease: come or bring to an end; stop*

But for the new cook I should never have discovered the truth and being under the influence of the companion, I should probably have been unable to lead the life of detachment that I then began. I should always have been wasting time on him. He had the power to keep me in the dark and to mislead[1] me.

But God came to the rescue[2] as before. My intentions were pure, and so I was saved in spite of my mistakes, and this early experience thoroughly forewarned me for the future.

The cook had been almost a messenger sent from Heaven. He did not know cooking, and as a cook he could not have remained at my place. But no one else could have opened my eyes. This was not the first time, as I subsequently[3] learnt, that the woman had been brought into my house. She had come often before, but no one had the courage of this cook. For everyone knew how blindly I trusted the companion. The cook had, as it were, been sent to me just to do this service, for he begged leave of me that very moment.

'I cannot stay in your house,' he said. 'You are so easily misled. This is no place for me.'

I let him go.

I soon discovered that the man who had poisoned my ears against the clerk was no other than this companion, I tried very hard to make amends[4] to the clerk for the injustice I had done him. It has, however, been my eternal regret that I could never satisfy him fully. Howsoever you may repair it, a rift is a rift.

1. *mislead: cause to have a wrong impression about someone or something*
2. *rescue: save from a dangerous or distressing situation*
3. *subsequently: after a particular thing has happened*
4. *amends: make minor improvements to*

CHAPTER 49

HOMEWARD

By now I had been three years in South Africa. I had got to know the people and they had got to know me. In 1896 I asked permission to go home for six months, for I saw that I was in for a long stay there. I had established a fairly good practice, and could see that people felt the need of my presence. So I made up my mind to go home, fetch my wife and children, and then return and settle out there. I also saw that, if I went home, I might be able to do there some public work by educating public opinion and creating more interest in the Indians of South Africa. The £3 tax[1] was an open sore. There could be no peace[2] until it was abolished.

But who was to take charge of the Congress work and Education Society in my absence? I could think of two men Adamji Miyakhan and Parsi Rustomji. There were many workers now available from the commercial class. But the foremost among those who could fulfill the duties of the secretary by regular work, and who also commanded the regard of the Indian community, were these two. The secretary certainly needed a working knowledge of English. I recommended the late Adamji Miyakhan's name to the Congress, and it approved of his appointment as secretary. Experience showed that the choice was a very happy one. Adamji Miyakhan satisfied all with his perseverance[3], liberality, amiability[4] and courtesy, and proved to every one that the secretary's work did not require a man with a barrister's degree or high English education.

About the middle of 1896 I sailed for home in the *s.s. Pongola* which was bound for Calcutta.

There were very few passengers on board. Among them were two English officers, with whom I came in close contact. With one of them I used to play chess for an hour daily. The ship's doctor gave me a *Tamil Self-Teacher* which I began to study. My experience in Natal had shown me that I should acquire a knowledge of Urdu to get into closer contact with the Musalmans, and of Tamil to get into closer touch with the Madras Indians.

1. *tax: a compulsory contribution to state revenue, levied by the government on personal income and business profits or added to the cost of some goods, services, and transactions*
2. *peace: freedom from disturbance, tranquility*
3. *perseverance: continue in a course of action in spite of difficulty or with little or no indication of success*
4. *amiability: friendly and pleasant in manner*

At the request of the English friend, who read Urdu with me, I found out a good Urdu Munshi from among the deck passengers, and we made excellent progress in our studies. The officer had a better memory than I. He would never forget a word after once he had seen it; I often found it difficult to decipher Urdu letters. I brought more perseverance to bear, but could never overtake the officer.

With Tamil I made fair progress. There was no help available, but the *Tamil Self-Teacher* was a well-written book, and I did not feel in need of much outside help.

I had hoped to continue these studies even after reaching India, but it was impossible. Most of my reading since 1893 has been done in jail. I did make some progress in Tamil and Urdu, in jails - Tamil in South African jails, and Urdu in Yeravda jail. But I never learnt to speak Tamil, and the little I could do by way of reading is now rusting away for want of practice.

I still feel what a handicap this ignorance of Tamil or Telugu has been. The affection that the Dravidians in South Africa showered on me has remained a cherished memory. Whenever I see a Tamil or Telugu friend, I cannot but recall the faith, perseverance and selfless[1] sacrifice of many of his compatriots in South Africa. And they were mostly illiterate, the men no less than the women. The fight in South Africa was for such, and it was fought by illiterate soldiers; it was for the poor, and the poor took their full share in it. Ignorance of their language, however, was never a handicap to me in stealing the hearts of these simple and good countrymen. They spoke broken Hindustani or broken English, and we found no difficulty in getting on with our work. But I wanted to requite their affection by learning Tamil and Telugu. In Tamil as I have said, I made some little progress, but in Telugu, which I tried to learn in India, I did not get beyond the alphabet. I fear now I can never learn these languages, and am therefore hoping that the Dravidians will learn Hindustani. The non-English-speaking among them in South Africa do speak Hindi or Hindustani, however indifferently. It is only the English-speaking ones who will not learn it, as though a knowledge of English were an obstacle to learning our own languages.

But I have digressed[2]. Let me finish the narrative of my voyage. I have to introduce to my readers the captain of the s.s. *Poongola*. We had become friends. The good captain was a Plymouth Brother. Our talks were more about spiritual subjects than nautical[3]. He drew a line between

1. *selfless: concerned more with the needs and wished of others than with one's own*
2. *digressed: leave the main subject temporarily in speech or writing*
3. *nautical: of or concerning sailors or navigation; maritime*

morality and faith. The teaching of the Bible was to him child's play. Its beauty lay in its simplicity. Let all, men, women and children, he would say, have faith in Jesus and his sacrifice, and their sins were sure to be redeemed. This friend revived[1] my memory of the Plymouth Brother of Pretoria. The religion that imposed any moral restrictions was to him no good. My vegetarian food had been the occasion of the whole of this discussion. Why should I not eat meat, or for that matter beef? Had not God created all the lower animals for the enjoyment of mankind as, for instance, He had created the vegetable kingdom? These questions inevitably drew us into religious discussion.

We could not convince each other. I was confirmed in my opinion that religion and morality[2] were synonymous[3]. The captain had no doubt about the correctness of his opposite conviction[4].

At the end of twenty-four days the pleasant voyage came to a close, and admiring the beauty of the Hooghly, I landed at Calcutta. The same day I took the train for Bombay.

1. *revived: an instance of something becoming popular, active, or important again; a reawakening of religious fervor, especially by means of evangelistic meetings*
2. *morality: principles concerning the distinction between right and wrong or good and bad behavior; a system of values and moral principles*
3. *synonymous: having the same meaning as another word or phrase in the same language; closely associated with something; his name was synonymous with victory*
4. *conviction: a firmly held belief or opinion; the quality of showing that one is firmly convinced of something*

CHAPTER 50

IN INDIA

On my way to Bombay the train stopped at Allahabad for forty-five minutes. I decided to utilize the interval for a drive through the town. I also had to purchase some medicine at a chemist's shop. The chemist was half asleep, and took an unconscionable time in dispensing[1] the medicine, with the result that when I reached the station, the train had just started. The station master had kindly detained the train one minute for my sake, but not seeing me coming, had carefully ordered my luggage to be taken out of the train.

I took a room at Kellner's, and decided to start work there and then. I had heard a good deal about *The Pioneer* published from Allahabad, and I had understood it to be an opponent of Indian aspirations. I have an impression that Mr. Chesney Jr. was the editor at that time. I wanted to secure the help of every party, so I wrote a note to Mr. Chesney, telling him how I had missed the train, and asking for an appointment so as to enable me to leave the next day. He immediately gave me one, at which I was very happy especially when I found that he gave me a patient hearing. He promised to notice in his paper anything that I might write, but added that he could not promise to endorse[2] all the Indian demands, inasmuch as he was bound to understand and give due weight to the viewpoint of the Colonials as well.

'It is enough,' I said, 'that you should study the question and discuss it in your paper. I ask and desire nothing but the barest justice that is due to us.'

The rest of the day was spent in having a look round admiring the magnificent confluence of the three rivers, the *Triveni*, and planning the work before me.

This unexpected interview with the editor of *The Pioneer* laid the foundation of the series of incidents which ultimately led to my being lynched[3] in Natal.

1. *dispensing: supply according to a doctor's prescription*
2. *endorse: declare one's public approval of*
3. *lynched: kill for an alleged offence without a legal trial, especially by hanging*

I went straight to Rajkot without halting at Bombay and began to make preparations for writing a pamphlet on the situation in South Africa. The writing and publication of the pamphlet took about a month. It had a green cover and came to be known afterwards as the Green Pamphlet. In it I drew a purposely subdued picture of the conditions of Indians in South Africa. The language I used was more moderate than that of the two pamphlets which I have referred to before, as I knew that things heard of from a distance appear bigger than they are.

Ten thousand copies were printed and sent to all the papers and leaders of every party in India. *The Pioneer* was the first to notice it editorially. A summary[1] of the article was cabled by Reuter to England, and a summary of that summary was cabled to Natal by Reuter's London office. This cable[2] was not longer than three lines in print. It was a miniature, but exaggerated, edition of the picture I had drawn of the treatment accorded[3] to the Indians in Natal, and it was not in my words. We shall see later on the effect this had in Natal. In the meanwhile every paper of note commented at length on the question.

To get these pamphlets ready for posting was no small matter. It would have been expensive too, if I had employed paid help for preparing wrappers etc. But I hit upon a much simpler plan. I gathered together all the children in my locality and asked them to volunteer two or three hours' labour of a morning, when they had no school. This they willingly agreed to do. I promised to bless them and give them, as a reward[4], used postage stamps which I had collected. They got through the work in no time. That was my first experiment of having little children as volunteers. Two of those little friends are my co-workers today.

Plague broke out in Bombay about this time, and there was panic all around. There was fear of an outbreak in Rajkot. As I felt that I could be of some help in the sanitation department, I offered my services to the State. They were accepted, and I was put on the committee which was appointed to look into the question. I laid especial emphasis on the cleanliness of latrines, and the committee decided to inspect these in every street. The poor people had no objection to their latrines being inspected, and what is more, they carried out the improvements suggested to them. But when we went to inspect the houses of the upper ten, some of them even refused us admission, not to talk of listening

1. *summary: a brief statement of the main points of something*
2. *cable: a cablegram*
3. *accorded: give or grant someone*
4. *reward: a thing given in recognition of service, effort, or achievement; a fair return for good or bad behavior; a sum offered for the detection of a criminal, the restoration, of lost property, etc.*

to our suggestions. It was our common experience that the latrines of the rich were more unclean. They were dark and stinking[1] and reeking[2] with filth[3] and worms. The improvements we suggested were quite simple, e.g., to have buckets for excrement instead of allowing it to drop on the ground; to see that urine also was collected in buckets, instead of allowing it to soak into the ground, and to demolish the partitions between the outer walls the latrines, so as to give the latrines more light and air and the enable the scavenger to clean them properly. The upper classes raised numerous objections to this last improvement, and in most cases it was not carried out.

The committee had to inspect untouchables' quarters also. Only one member of the committee was ready to accompany me there. To the rest it was something preposterous to visit those quarters, still more so to inspect their latrines. But for me those quarters were an agreeable surprise. That was the first visit in my life to such a locality. The men and women there were surprised to see us. I asked them to let us inspect their latrines.

'Latrines for us!' they exclaimed in astonishment. 'We go and perform our functions out in the open. Latrines are for you big people.'

'Well, then, you won't mind if we inspect your houses?' I asked.

'You are perfectly welcome, sir. You may see every nook and corner of our houses. Ours are no houses, they are holes.'

I went in and was delighted to see that the insides were as clean as the outsides. The entrances were well swept, the floors were beautifully smeared[4] with cow-dung, and the few pots and pans were clean and shining. There was no fear of an outbreak in those quarters.

In the upper class quarters we came across a latrine which I cannot help describing in some detail. Every room had its gutter, which was used both for water and urine, which meant that the whole house would stink. But one of the houses had a storeyed bedroom with a gutter which was being used both as a urinal and a latrine. The gutter had a pipe discending to the ground floor. It was not possible to stand the foul smell in this room. How the occupant could sleep there I leave the readers to imagine.

The committee also visited the Vaishnava *Haveli*. The priest in charge of the *Haveli* was very friendly with my family. So he agreed to let us

1. *stinking: have a strong unpleasant smell; fill a place with such a smell*
2. *reeking: have a foul smell*
3. *filth: disgusting dirt*
4. *smeared: coat or mark with a greasy or sticky substance*

inspect everything and suggest whatever improvements we liked. There was a part of the *Haveli* premises that he himself had never seen. It was the place where refuse and leaves used as dinner-plates used to be thrown over the wall. It was the haunt of crows and kites. The latrines were of course dirty. I was not long enough in Rajkot to see how many of our suggestions the priest[1] carried out.

It pained me to see so much uncleanliness about a place of worship. One would expect a careful observance of the rules of sanitation and hygiene in a place which is regarded as holy. The authors of the Smritis, as I knew even then, have laid the greatest emphasis on cleanliness both inward and outward.

1. *priest: an ordained minister of the catholic, orthodox's or anglican church, authorized to perform certain rise and administer certain sacraments; a person who performs ceremonies in a non-christian religion*

CHAPTER 51

TWO PASSIONS

Hardly ever have I known anybody to cherish such loyalty as I did to the British Constitution. I can see now that my love of truth was at the root of this loyalty. It has never been possible for me to simulate[1] loyalty or, for that matter, any other virtue. The National Anthem used to be sung at every meeting that I attended in Natal. I then felt that I must also join in the singing. Not that I was unaware[2] of the defects in British rule, but I thought it was on the whole acceptable. In those days I believed that British rule was on the whole beneficial to the ruled.

The colour prejudice that I saw in South Africa was, I thought, quite contrary[3] to British traditions, and I believed that it was only temporary and local. I therefore vied with Englishmen in loyalty to the throne. With careful perseverance I learnt the tune of the 'National Anthem' and joined in the singing whenever it was sung. Whenever there was an occasion for the expression of loyalty without fuss or ostentation, I readily took part in it.

Never in my life did I exploit this loyalty, never did I seek to gain a selfish end by its means. It was for me more in the nature of an obligation[4], and I rendered it without expecting a reward.

Preparations were going on for the celebration of Queen Victoria's Diamond Jubilee when I reached India. I was invited to join the committee appointed for the purpose in Rajkot. I accepted the offer, but had a suspicion that the celebrations would be largely a matter of show. I discovered much humbug about them and was considerably pained. I began to ask myself whether I should remain on the committee or not, but ultimately decided to rest content with doing my part of the business.

One of the proposals was to plant trees. I saw that many did it merely for show and for pleasing the officials. I tried to plead with them that tree-planting was not compulsory, but merely a suggestion. It should be done seriously or not at all. I have an impression that they laughed at my

1. *simulate: imitate or reproduce the appearance, character, or conditions of*
2. *unaware: having no knowledge of a situation or fact*
3. *contrary: opposite in nature, direction, or meaning*
4. *obligation: compulsory; having binding force*

ideas. I remember that I was in earnest when I planted the tree allotted to me and that I carefully watered and tended it.

I likewise taught the National Anthem to the children of my family. I recollect having taught it to students of the local Training College, but I forget whether it was on the occasion of the jubilee[1] or of King Edward VII's coronation[2] as Emperor of India. Later on the text began to jar on me. As my conception of *Ahimsa* went on maturing[3], I became more vigilant about my thought and speech. The lines in the Anthem: 'Scatter her enemies, And make them fall; Confound their politics, Frustrate their knavish[4] tricks.' particularly jarred upon my sentiment of *Ahimsa*. I shared my feelings with Dr. Booth who agreed that it ill became a believer in *Ahimsa* to sing those lines. How could we assume that the so-called 'enemies' were 'knavish'? And because they were enemies, were they bound to be in the wrong? From God we could only ask for justice. Dr. Booth entirely endorsed my sentiments, and composed a new anthem for his congregation. But of Dr. Booth more later.

Like loyalty an aptitude for nursing was also deeply rooted in my nature. I was fond of nursing people, whether friends or strangers.

Whilst busy in Rajkot with the pamphlet on South Africa, I had an occasion to pay a flying visit to Bombay. It was my intention to educate public opinion in cities on this question by organizing meetings, and Bombay was the first city I chose. First of all I met Justice Ranade, who listened to me with attention, and advised me to meet Sir Pherozeshah Mehta. Justice Badruddin Tyabji, whom I met next, also gave the same advice. 'Justice Ranade and I can guide you but little,' he said. 'You know our position. We cannot take an active part in public affairs, but our sympathies are with you. The man who can effectively guide you is Sir Pherozeshah Mehta.'

I certainly wanted to see Sir Pherozeshah Mehta, but the fact that these senior men advised me to act according to his advice gave me a better idea of the immense influence that Sir Pherozeshah had on the public. In due course I met him. I was prepared to be awed by his presence. I had heard of the popular titles that he had earned, and knew that I was to see the 'Lion of Bombay', the 'Uncrowned King of the Presidency.' But the king did not overpower me. He met me, as a loving father would meet his grown up son. Our meeting took place at his chamber. He was surrounded by a

1. *jubilee: a special anniversary, especially one celebrating twenty-five or fifty years of something*
2. *coronation: the ceremony of crowning a sovereign for a sovereigns' consort*
3. *maturing: the state, fact, or period of being mature*
4. *knavish: an act of dishonesty*

circle of friends and followers. Amongst them were Mr. D. E. Wacha and Mr. Cama, to whom I was introduced. I had already heard of Mr. Wacha. He was regarded as the right-hand man of Sir Pherozeshah, and Sjt. Virchand Gandhi had described him to me as a great statistician. Mr. Wacha said, 'Gandhi, we must meet again.'

These introductions could scarcely have taken two minutes. Sir Pherozeshah carefully listened to me. I told him that I had seen Justices Ranade and Tyabji. 'Gandhi,' said he, 'I see that I must help you. I must call a public meeting here.' With this he turned to Mr. Munshi, the secretary, and told him to fix up the date of the meeting. The date was settled, and he bade me good-bye, asking me to see him again on the day previous to the meeting. The interview removed my fears, and I went home delighted.

During this stay in Bombay I called on my brother-in-law, who was staying there and lying ill. He was not a man of means, and my sister(his wife) was not equal to nursing him. The illness was serious, and I offered to take him to Rajkot. He agreed, and so I returned home with my sister and her husband. The illness was much more prolonged[1] than I had expected. I put my brother-in-law in my room and remained with him night and day. I was obliged to keep awake part of the night and had to get through some of my South African work whilst[2] I was nursing him. Ultimately, however, the patient died, but it was a great consolation[3] to me that I had had an opportunity to nurse him during his last days.

My aptitude for nursing gradually developed into a passion, so much so that it often led me to neglect my work, and on occasions I engaged not only my wife but the whole household in such service.

Such service can have no meaning unless one takes pleasure in it. When it is done for show or for fear of public opinion, it stunts the man and crushes his spirit. Service which is rendered without joy helps neither the servant nor the served. But all other pleasures and possessions pale into nothingness before service which is rendered in a spirit of joy.

1. *prolonged: extend the duration of*
2. *whilst: while*
3. *consolation: comfort received by someone after a loss or disappointment; a source of such comfort*

CHAPTER 52

THE BOMBAY MEETING

On the very day after my brother-in-law's death I had to go to Bombay for the public meeting. There had hardly been time for me to think out my speech. I was feeling exhausted after days and nights of anxious vigil, and my voice had become husky[1]. However, I went to Bombay trusting entirely to God. I had never dreamt of writing out my speech.

In accordance with Sir Pherozeshah's instructions I reported myself at his office at 5 P. M. on the eve[2] of the meeting.

'Is your speech ready, Gandhi?' he asked.

'No sir,' said I, trembling with fear, 'I think of speaking *ex tempore*.'

'That will not do in Bombay. Reporting here is bad, and if we would benefit by this meeting, you should write out your speech, and it should be printed before daybreak tomorrow. I hope you can manage this?'

I felt rather nervous, but I said I would try.

'Then, tell me, what time should Mr. Munshi come to you for the manuscript?' 'Eleven o'clock tonight,' said I.

On going to the meeting the next day, I saw the wisdom of Sir Pherozeshah's advice. The meeting was held in the hall of the Sir Cowasji Jehangir Institute. I had heard that when Sir Pherozeshah Mehta addressed meetings the hall was always chiefly. Chiefly by the students intent on hearing him, leaving not an inch of room. This was the first meeting of the kind in my experience. I saw that my voice could reach only a few. I was trembling[3] as I began to read my speech. Sir Pherozeshah cheered me up continually by asking me to speak louder and still louder. I have a feeling that, far from encouraging me, it made my voice sink lower and lower.

My old friend Sjt. Keshavrao Deshpande came to my rescue. I handed my speech to him. His was just the proper voice. But the audience refused[4] to listen. The hall rang with the cries of 'Wacha,' 'Wacha.' So Mr. Wacha stood up and read the speech, with wonderful results. The audience

1. *husky: sounding low-pitched and slightly hoarse*
2. *eve: the day or period of time immediately before an event or occasion; the evening or day before a religious festival*
3. *trembling: shake involuntarily, typically as a result of anxiety, excitement, or frailty; be in a state of extreme apprehension; shake or quiver slightly*
4. *refused: indicate unwillingness; indicate unwillingness to accept or grant something offered or requested; decline to jump a fence or other obstacle*

became perfectly quiet, and listened to the speech to the end, punctuating it with applause and cries of 'shame' where necessary. This gladdened my heart.

Sir Pherozeshah liked the speech. I was supremely happy.

The meeting won me the active sympathy of Sjt. Deshpande and a Parsi friend, whose name I hesitate to mention, as he is a high-placed Government official today. Both expressed their resolve to accompany me to South Africa. Mr. C. M. Cursetji, who was then Small Causes Court Judge, however, moved the Parsi friend from his resolve as he had plotted[1] his marriage. He had to choose between marriage and going to South Africa, and he chose the former. But Parsi Rustomji made amends for the broken resolve, and a number of Parsi sisters are now making amends for the lady who helped in the breach by dedicating themselves to khadi work. I have therefore gladly forgiven that couple, Sjt. Deshpande had no temptations of marriage, but he too could not come. Today he is himself doing enough reparation for the broken pledge[2]. On my way back to South Africa I met one of the Tyabjis at Zanzibar. He also promised to come and help me, but never came. Mr. Abbas Tyabji is atoning[3] for that offence. Thus none of my three attempts to induce[4] barristers to go to South Africa bore any fruit.

In this connection I remember Mr. Pestonji Padshah. I had been on friendly terms with him ever since my stay in England. I first met him in a vegetarian restaurant in London. I knew of his brother Mr. Barjorji Padshah by his reputation as a 'crank'. I had never met him, but friends said that he was eccentric. Out of pity for the horses he would not ride in tram-cars, he refused to take degrees in spite of a prodigious memory, he had developed an independent spirit, and he was a vegetarian, though a Parsi. Pestonji had not quite this reputation, but he was famous for his erudition even in London. The common factor between us, however, was vegetarianism, and not scholarship in which it was beyond my power to approach him.

I found him out again in Bombay. He was Protonotary in the High Court. When I met him he was engaged on his contribution to a Higher Gujarati Dictonary. There was not a friend I had not approached for help in my South African work. Pestonji Padshah, however, not only refused to aid me, but even advised me not to return to South Africa.

1. *plotted: a plan made in secret by a group of people to do something illegal or harmful*
2. *pledge: a solemn promise or undertaking; a promise of a donation to charity; a solemn undertaking to abstain from alcohol*
3. *atoning: make amends or reparation for*
4. *induce: succeed in persuading or leading to do something*

'It is impossible to help you,' he said. 'But I tell you I do not like even *your* going to South Africa. Is there lack of work in our country? Look, now, there is not a little to do for our language. I have to find out scientific words. But this is only one branch[1] of the work. Think of the poverty of the land. Our people in South Africa are no doubt in difficulty, but I do not want a man like you to be sacrificed for that work. Let us win self-government here, and we shall automatically help our countrymen there. I know I cannot prevail upon you, but I will not encourage anyone of your type to throw in his lot with you.'

I did not like this advice, but it increased my regard for Mr. Pestonji Padshah. I was struck with his love for the country and for the mother tongue. The incident brought us closer to each other. I could understand his point of view. But far from giving up my work in South Africa, I became firmer in my resolve. A patriot cannot afford to ignore any branch of service to the motherland. And for me the text of the Gita was clear and emphatic: 'Finally, this is better, that one do His own task as he may, even though he fail, Than take tasks not his own, though they seem good. To die performing duty is no ill; But who seeks other roads shall wander still.'

1. branch: a division of a large organization

CHAPTER 53

POONA AND MADRAS

Sir Pherozeshah had made my way easy. So from Bombay I went to Poona. Here there were two parties. I wanted the help of people of every shade[1] of opinion. First I met Lokamanya Tilak. He said:

'You are quite right in seeking the help of all parties. There can be no difference of opinion on the South African question. But you must have a non-party man for your president. Meet Professor Bhandarkar. He has been taking no part of late in any public movement. But this question might possibly draw him out. See him and let me know what he says. I want to help you to the fullest extent. Of course you will meet me whenever you like. I am at your disposal.'

This was my first meeting with the Lokamanya. It revealed to me the secret of his unique popularity.

Next I met Gokhale. I found him on the Fergusson College grounds. He gave me an affectionate welcome, and his manner immediately won my heart. With him too this was my first meeting, and yet it seemed as though we were renewing[2] an old friendship. Sir Pherozeshah had seemed to me like the Himalaya, the Lokamanya like the ocean. But Gokhale was as the Ganges. One could have a refreshing bath in the holy river. The Himalaya was unscaleable, and one could not easily launch forth on the sea, but the Ganges invited one to its bosom. It was a joy to be on it with a boat and an oar. Gokhale closely examined me, as a schoolmaster would examine a candidate seeking admission to a school. He told me whom to approach and how to approach them. He asked to have a look at my speech. He showed me over the college, assured me that he was always at my disposal, asked me to let him know the result of the interview with Dr. Bhandarkar, and sent me away exultantly happy. In the sphere of politics the place that Gokhale occupied in my heart during his lifetime[3] and occupies even now was and is absolutely unique.

Dr. Bhandarkar received me with the warmth of a father. It was noon when I called on him. The very fact that I was busy seeing people at that

1. *shade: a slightly differing variety; all shades of opinion*
2. *renewing: resume or re-establish after an interruption*
3. *lifetime: the duration of a person's life; the duration of a thing or its usefulness*

hour appealed greatly to this indefatigable savant, and my insistence on a non-party man for the president of the meeting had his ready approval, which was expressed in the spontaneous[1] exclamation, 'That's it,' 'That's it.'

After he had heard me out he said: 'Anyone will tell you that I do not take part in politics. But I cannot refuse you. Your case is so strong and your industry[2] is so admirable that I cannot decline to take part in your meeting. You did well in consulting Tilak and Gokhale. Please tell them that I shall be glad to preside over the meeting to be held under the joint auspices of the two Sabhas. You need not have the time of the meeting from me, Any time that suits them will suit me.' With this he bade me good-bye with congratulations and blessings.

Without any ado this erudite and selfless band of workers in Poona held a meeting in an unostentatious little place, and sent me away rejoicing[3] and more confident of my mission.

I next proceeded to Madras. It was wild with enthusiasm. The Balasundaram incident made a profound[4] impression on the meeting. My speech was printed and was, for me, fairly long. But the audience listened to every word with attention. At the close of the meeting there was a regular run on the 'Green Pamphlet.' I brought out a second and revised edition of 10,000 copies. They sold like hot cakes, but I saw that it was not necessary to print such a large number. In my enthusiasm I had overcalculated the demand. It was the English-speaking public to which my speech had been addressed, and in Madras that class alone could not take the whole ten thousand.

The greatest help here came to me from the late Sjt. G. Parameshvaran Pillay, the editor of *The Madras Standard*. He had made a careful study of the question, and he often invited me to his office and gave me guidance. Sjt. G. Subrahmaniam of *The Hindu* and Dr. Subrahmaniam also were very sympathetic. But Sjt. G. Parameshvaran Pillay placed the columns of *The Madras Standard* entirely at my disposal, and I freely availed myself of the offer. The meeting in Pachaiappa's Hall, so far as I can recollect, was with Dr. Subrahmaniam in the chair.

The affection showered on me by most of the friends I met and their enthusiasm for the cause were so great that, in spite of my having to communicate with them in English, I felt myself entirely at home. What barrier is there that love cannot break?

1. *spontaneous: performed or occurring as a result of an unpremeditated inner impulse and without external stimulus; occurring without apparent external cause; instinctive or involuntary*
2. *industry: hard work*
3. *rejoicing: feel or show great joy [archaic] cause joy to*
4. *profound: very great or intense; profound social changes; severe*

CHAPTER 54

'RETURN SOON'

From Madras I proceeded to Calcutta where I found myself hemmed by difficulties. I knew no one there. So I took a room in the Great Eastern Hotel. Here I became acquainted with Mr. Ellerthorpe, a representative of *The Daily Telegraph*. He invited me to the Bengal Club, where he was staying. He did not then realize that an Indian could not be taken to the drawing-room of the club. Having discovered the restriction, he took me to his room. He expressed his sorrow regarding this prejudice of the local Englishmen and apologized to me for not having been able to take me to the drawing-room.

I had of course to see Surendranath Banerji, the 'Idol of Bengal'. When I met him, he was surrounded by a number of friends. He said: 'I am afraid people will not take interest in your work. As you know, our difficulties here are by no means few. But you must try as best you can. You will have to enlist the sympathy of Maharajas. Mind, you meet the representatives of the British Indian Association. You should meet Raja Sir Pyarimohan Mukarji and Maharaja Tagore. Both are liberal-minded and take a fair share in public work.'

I met these gentlemen, but without success. Both gave me a cold reception and said it was no easy thing to call a public in Calcutta, and if anything could be done, it would practically all depend on Surendranath Banerji.

I saw that my task was becoming more and more difficult. I called at the office of The *Amrita Bazar Patrika*. The gentleman whom I met there took me to be a wandering Jew. *The Bangabasi* went even one better. The editor kept me waiting for an hour. He had evidently many interviewers, but he would not so much as look at me, even when he had disposed of the rest. On my venturing to broach[1] my subject after the long wait, he said: 'Don't you see our hands are full? There is no end to the number of visitors like you. You had better go. I am not disposed to listen to you.'

1. *broach: raise for discussion*

For a moment I felt offended, but I quickly understood the editor's position. I had heard of the fame of *The Bangabasi*. I could see that there was a regular stream of visitors there. And they were all people acquainted with him. His paper had no lack of topics to discuss, and South Africa was hardly known at that time.

However serious a grievance may be in the eyes of the man who suffers from it, he will be but one of the numerous people invading the editor's office, each with a grievance of his own. How is the editor to meet them all? Moreover, the aggrieved party imagines that the editor is a power in the land. Only he knows that his powers can hardly travel beyond the threshold[1] of his office. But I was not discouraged. I kept on seeing editors of other papers. As usual I met the Anglo-Indian editors also. *The Statesman* and *The Englishman* realized the importance of the question. I gave them long interviews, and they published them in full.

Mr. Saunders, editor of *The Englishman*, claimed me as his own. He placed his office and paper at my disposal. He even allowed me the liberty of making whatever changes I liked in the leading article he had written on the situation, the proof of which he sent me in advance. It is no exaggeration[2] to say that a friendship grew up between us. He promised to render me all the help he could, carried out the promise to the letter, and kept on his correspondence with me until the time when he was seriously ill.

Throughout my life I have had the privilege of many such friendships, which have sprung up quite unexpectedly. What Mr. Saunders liked in me was my freedom from exaggeration and my devotion to truth. He subjected me to a searching cross-examination before he began to sympathize with my cause, and he saw that I had spared neither will nor pains to place before him an impartial statement of the case even of the white man in South Africa and also to appreciate it.

My experience has shown me that we win justice quickest by rendering justice to the other party.

The unexpected help of Mr. Saunders had begun to encourage me to think that I might succeed after all in holding a public meeting in Calcutta, when I received the following cable from Durban: 'Parliament opens January. Return soon.'

So I addressed a letter to the press, in which I explained why I had to leave Calcutta so abruptly[3], and set off for Bombay. Before starting

1. *threshold: a strip of wood or stone forming the bottom of a doorway and crossed in entering a house or room*
2. *exaggeration: represent as being larger or better than it really is; enlarged or altered beyond normal proportions*
3. *abruptly: sudden and unexpected*

I wired to the Bombay agent of Dada Abdulla & Co, to arrange for my passage by the first possible boat to South Africa. Dada Abdulla had just then purchased the steamship *Courland* and insisted on my travelling on that boat, offering to take me and my family free of charge. I gratefully accepted the offer, and in the beginning of December set sail a second time for South Africa, now with my wife and two sons and the only son of my widowed sister. Another steamship *Naderi* also sailed for Durban at the same time. The agents of the Company were Dada Abdulla & Co. The total number of passengers these boats carried must have been about eight hundred, half of whom were bound for the Transvaal.

CHAPTER 55

RUMBLINGS OF THE STORM

This was my first voyage with my wife and children. I have often observed in the course of this narrative that, on account of child marriages amongst middle class Hindus, the husband will be literate whilst the wife remains practically unlettered. A wide gulf[1] thus separates them, and the husband has to become his wife's teacher. So I had to think out the details of the dress to be adopted by my wife and children, the food they were to eat, and the manners which would be suited to their new surroundings. Some of the recollections of those days are amusing to look back upon.

A Hindu wife regards implicit obedience to her husband as the highest religion. A Hindu husband regards himself as lord and master of his wife who must ever dance attendance upon him.

I believed, at the time of which I am writing, that in order to look civilized, our dress and manners had as far as possible to approximate[2] to the European standard. Because I thought only thus could we have some influence, and without influence it would not be possible to serve the community.

I therefore determined the style of dress for my wife and children. How could I like them to be known as Kathiawad Banias? The Parsis used then to be regarded as the most civilized people amongst Indians, and so, when the complete European style seemed to be unsuited, we adopted the Parsi style. Accordingly my wife wore the Parsi *sari*, and the boys the Parsi coat and trousers. Of course no one could be without shoes and stockings. It was long before my wife and children could get used to them. The shoes cramped their feet and the stockings stank with perspiration. The toes often got sore, I always had my answers ready to all these objections[3]. But I have an impression that it was not so much the answers as the force of authority that carried conviction. They agreed to the changes in dress as there was no alternative. In the same spirit and with even more reluctance they adopted the use of knives and forks.

1. *gulf: a deep ravine, chasm, or abyss*
2. *approximate: come close in quality or quantity*
3. *objections: the action of challenging or disagreeing with something; an expression of disapproval or opposition*

When my infatuation for these signs of civilization wore away, they gave up the knives and forks. After having become long accustomed to the new style, it was perhaps no less irksome[1] for me to return to the original mode. But I can see today that we feel all the freer and lighter for having cast off the tinsel[2] of 'civilization.'

On board the same steamer with us were some relatives and acquaintances. These and other deck passengers I frequently met, because, the boat belonging to my client's friends, I was free to move about anywhere and every where I liked.

Since the steamer was making straight for Natal, without calling at intermediate[3] ports, our voyage was of only eighteen days. But as though to warn us of the coming real storm on land, a terrible gale overtook us, whilst we were only four days from Natal. December is a summer month of monsoon in the southern hemisphere, and gales, great and small, are, therefore, quite common in the southern seas at that season. The gale in which we were caught was so violent and prolonged that the passengers became alarmed. It was a solemn scene. All became one in face of the common danger. They forgot their differences and began to think of the one and only God - Musalmans, Hindus, Christians and all. Some took various vows. The captain also joined the passengers in their prayers. He assured them that, though the storm was not without danger, he had had experience of many worse ones, and explained to them that a well-built ship could stand almost any weather. But they were inconsolable. Every minute were heard sounds and crashes which foreboded breaches and leaks. The ship rocked and rolled to such an extent that it seemed as though she would capsize at any moment. It was out of the question for anyone to remain on deck. 'His will be done' was the only cry on every lip. So far as I can recollect, we must have been in this plight for about twenty-four hours. At last the sky cleared, the sun made its appearance, and the captain said that the storm had blown over. People's faces beamed with gladness, and with the disappearance of danger disappeared also the name of God from their lips, Eating and drinking, singing and merry-making again became the order of the day. The fear of death was gone, and the momentary mood of earnest prayer gave place to *maya*[4]. There were of course the usual *namaz*[5] and the prayers, yet they had none of the solemnity[6] of that dread hour.

1. *irksome: irritating annoying*
2. *tinsel: a form of decoration consisting of thin strips of shiny metal foil attached to a length of thread*
3. *intermediate: coming between two things in time, place, character, etc.*
4. *maya: the famous word in Hindu philosophy which is nearly untranslatable, but has been frequently translated in english as 'delusion', 'illusion'*
5. *namaz: the prayer prescribed by the koran*
6. *solemnity: the state of quality of being solemn*

But the storm had made me one with the passengers. I had little fear of the storm, for I had had experience of similar ones. I am a good sailor and do not get sea-sick. So I could fearlessly move amongst the passengers, bringing them comfort and good cheer, and conveying to them hourly reports of the captain. The friendship I thus formed stood me, as we shall see, in very good stead[1].

The ship cast anchor[2] in the port of Durban on the 18th or 19th of December. *The Naderi* also reached the same day. But the real storm was still to come.

1. *stead: the place or role that someone or something should have or fill*
2. *anchor: a heavy object used to moor a ship to the sea bottom, typically having a metal shank with a pair of curved, barbed flukes; the brakes of a car*

CHAPTER 56

THE STORM

We have seen that the two ships cast anchor in the port of Durban on or about the 18th of December. No passengers are allowed to land at any of the South African ports before being subjected to a thorough medical examination. If the ship has any passenger suffering from a contagious disease, she has to undergo[1] a period of quarantine. As there had been plague in Bombay when we met sail, we feared that we might have to go through a brief quarantine. Before the examination every ship has to fly a yellow flag, which is lowered only when the doctor has certified[2] her to be healthy. Relatives and friends of passengers are allowed to come on board only after the yellow flag has been lowered.

Accordingly our ship was flying the yellow flag,when the doctor came and examined us. He ordered a five days quarantine because, in his opinion, plague[3] germs took twenty-three days at the most to develop. Our ship was therefore ordered to be put in quarantine until the twenty-third day of our sailing from Bombay. But this quarantine order had more than health reasons behind it.

The white residents of Durban had been agitating for our repatriation, and the agitation was one of the reasons for the order. Dada Abdulla and Co. kept us regularly informed about the daily happenings in the town. The whites were holding monster meetings every day. They were addressing all kinds of threats and at times offering even inducements to Dada Abdulla and Co. They were ready to indemnify[4] the Company if both the ships should be sent back. But Dada Abdulla and Co. were not the people to be afraid of threats. Sheth Abdul Karim Haji Adam was then the managing partner of the firm. He was determined to moor the ships at the wharf and disembark the passengers at any cost. He was daily sending me detailed letters. Fortunately the Sjt. Mansukhlal Naazar was then in Durban having gone there to meet me. He was capable and fearless and guided the Indian community. Their advocate Mr. Laughton

1. *undergo: experience or be subjected to something unpleasant or arduous*
2. *certified: formally attest or confirm*
3. *plague: a contagious bacterial disease characterized by fever and delirium, typically with the formation of bosons and sometimes infection of the lungs*
4. *indemnify: compensate in respect of harm or loss*

was an equally fearless man. He condemned the conduct of the white residents and advised the community, not merely as their paid advocate, but also as their true friend.

Thus Durban had become the scene of an unequal[1] duel. On one side there was a handful of poor Indians and a few of their English friends, and on the other were ranged the white men, strong in arms, in numbers, in education and in wealth. They had also the backing of the State, for the Natal Government openly helped them. Mr. Harry Escombe, who was the most influential of the members of the Cabinet, openly took part in their meetings.

The real object of the quarantine was thus to coerce[2] the passengers into returning to India by somehow intimidating them or the Agent Company. For now threats began to be addressed to us also: 'If you do not go back, you will surely be pushed into the sea. But if you consent to return, you may even get your passage money back.' I constantly moved amongst my fellow-passengers cheering them up. I also sent messages of comfort to the passengers of the s.s. *Naderi*. All of them kept calm and courageous.

We arranged all sorts of games on the ship for the entertainment of the passengers. On Christmas Day the captain invited the saloon passengers to dinner. The principal among these were my family and I. In the speeches after dinner I spoke on Western civilization. I knew that this was not an occasion for a serious speech. But mine could not be otherwise. I took part in the merriment, but my heart was in the combat that was going on in Durban. For I was the real target. There were two charges against me:

1. that whilst in India I had indulged in unmerited condemnation of the Natal whites;
2. that with a view to swamping Natal with Indians I had specially brought the two shiploads of passengers to settle there.

I was conscious of my responsibility. I knew that Dada Abdulla and Co. had incurred grave risks on my account, the lives of the passengers were in danger, and by bringing my family with me I had put them likewise in jeopardy.

But I was absolutely innocent. I had induced no one to go to Natal. I did not know the passengers when they embarked. And with the

1. *unequal: not equal in quantity, size, or value; not fair, evenly balanced, or having equal advantage*
2. *coerce: persuade to do something by using force or threats*

exception of a couple of relatives, I did not know the name and address of even one of the hundreds of passengers on board. Neither had I said, whilst in India, a word about the whites in Natal that I had not already said in Natal itself. And I had ample evidence in support of all that I had said.

I therefore deplored the civilization of which the Natal whites were the fruit, and which they represented and championed. This civilization had all along been on my mind, and I therefore offered my views concerning it in my speech before that little meeting. The captain and other friends gave me a patient hearing, and received my speech in the spirit in which it was made. I do not know that it in any way affected the course of their lives, but afterwards I had long talks with the captain and other officers regarding the civilization of the West. I had in my speech described Western civilization as being, unlike the Eastern, predominantly[1] based on force. The questioners pinned me to my faith, and one of them the captain, so far as I can recollect said to me:

'Supposing the whites carry out their threats, how will you stand by your principle of non-violence?' To which I replied: 'I hope God will give me the courage and the sense to forgive them and to refrain from bringing them to law. I have no anger against them. I am only sorry for their ignorance and their narrowness. I know that they sincerely believe that what they are doing today is right and proper. I have no reason therefore to be angry with them.'

The questioner smiled, possibly distrustfully[2].

Thus the days dragged on their weary length. When the quarantine would terminate was still uncertain. The Quarantine Officer said that the matter had passed out of his hands and that, as soon as he had orders from the Government, he would permit us to land.

At last ultimatums[3] were served on the passengers and me. We were asked to submit, if we would escape with our lives. In our reply the passengers and I both maintained our right to land at Port Natal, and intimated our determination to enter Natal at any risk.

At the end of twenty-three days the ships were permitted to enter the harbour, and orders permitting the passengers to land were passed.

1. *predominantly: present as the strongest or main element; having or exerting the greatest control or power*
2. *distrustfully: have little trust in; regard with suspicion*
3. *ultimatums: a final demand or statement of terms, the rejection of which will result in retaliation or breakdown in relations*

CHAPTER 57

THE TEST

So the ships were brought into the dock and the passengers began to go ashore[1]. But Mr. Escombe had sent word to the captain that, as the whites were highly enraged against me and my life was in danger, my family and I should be advised to land at dusk, when the port superintendent Mr. Tatum would escort[2] us home. The captain communicated the message to me. and I agreed to act accordingly. But scarcely half an hour after this, Mr. Laughton came to the captain. He said: 'I would like to take Mr. Gandhi with me, should he have no objection. As the legal adviser of the Agent Company I tell you that you are not bound to carry out the message you have received from Mr. Escombe.' After this he came to me and said somewhat to this effect: 'If you are not afraid, I suggest that Mrs. Gandhi and the children should drive to Mr. Rustomji's house, whilst you and I follow them on foot. I do not at all like the idea of your entering the city like a thief[3] in the night. I do not think there is any fear of anyone hurting you. Everything is quiet now. The whites have all dispersed. But in any case I am convinced that you ought not to enter the city stealthily.' I readily agreed. My wife and children drove safely to Mr. Rustomji's place. With the captain's permission I went ashore with Mr. Laughton. Mr Rustomji's house was about two miles from the dock.

As soon as we landed, some youngsters recognized me and shouted 'Gandhi, Gandhi.' About half a dozen men rushed to the spot and joined in the shouting. Mr. Laughton feared that the crowd might swell and hailed a rickshaw. I had never liked the idea of being in a rickshaw. This was to be my first experience. But the youngsters would not let me get into it. They frightened the rickshaw boy out of his life, and he took to his heels. As we went ahead, the crowd continued to swell, until it became impossible to proceed further. They first caught hold of Mr. Laughton and separated us. Then they pelted[4] me with stones, brickbats and rotten eggs. Someone snatched away my turban, whilst others began to batter

1. *ashore: to or on the shore or land from the direction of the sea; on land as opposed to at sea*
2. *escort: a person or vehicle or group of these accompanying another to provide protection or as a mark of rank*
3. *thief: a person who steals another person's belongings*
4. *pelted: hurl missiles at*

and kick me. I fainted and caught hold of the front railings of a house and stood there to get my breath. But it was impossible. They came upon me boxing and battering. The wife of the police superintendent, who knew me, happened to be passing by. The brave lady came up, opened her parasol though there was no sun then, and stood between the crowd and me. This checked the fury of the mob, as it was difficult for them to deliver blows on me without harming Mrs. Alexander.

Meanwhile an Indian youth who witnessed the incident had run to the police station. The police superintendent Mr. Alexander sent a posse of men to ring me round and escort me safely to my destination. They arrived in time. The police station lay on our way. As we reached there, the superintendent asked me to take refuge in the station, but I gratefully declined the offer, 'They are sure to quiet down when they realize their mistake,' I said. 'I have trust in their sense of fairness.' Escorted by the police, I arrived without further harm at Mr. Rustomji's place. I had bruises[1] all over, but no abrasions except in one place. Dr. Dadibarjor, the ship's doctor, who was on the spot, rendered the best possible help.

There was quiet inside, but outside the whites surrounded the house. Night was coming on, and the yelling crowd was shouting, 'We must have Gandhi.' The quick-sighted police superintendent was already there trying to keep the crowds under control, not by threats, but by humouring them. But he was not entirely free from anxiety. He sent me a message to this effect: 'If you would save your friend's house and property and also your family, you should escape from the house in disguise, as I suggest.'

Thus on one and the same day I was faced with two contradictory positions. When danger to life had been no more than imaginary, Mr. Laughton advised me to launch forth openly. I accepted the advice. When the danger was quite real, another friend gave me the contrary advice, and I accepted that too. Who can say whether I did so because I saw that my life was in jeopardy[2], or because I did not want to put my friend's life and property or the lives of my wife and children in danger? Who can say for certain that I was right both when I faced the crowd in the first instance bravely, as it was said, and when I escaped from it in disguise[3]?

It is idle to adjudicate upon the right and wrong of incidents that have already happened. It is useful to understand them and, if possible,

1. *bruises: an injury appearing as an area of discolored skin on the body, caused by a blow or impact rupturing underlying blood vessels*
2. *jeopardy: danger of loss, harm, or failure*
3. *disguise: alter the appearance, sound, taste, or smell of so as to conceal the identity; conceal the nature or existence of a feeling or situation*

to learn a lesson from them for the future. It is difficult to say for certain how a particular man would act in a particular set of circumstances. We can also see that judging a man from his outward act is no more than a doubtful inference[1], inasmuch as it is not based on sufficient data.

Be that as it may, the preparations for escape made me forget my injuries. As suggested by the superintendent, I put on an Indian constable's uniform and wore on my head a Madrasi scarf, wrapped round a plate to serve as a helmet. Two detectives accompanied me, one of them disguised as an Indian merchant and with his face painted to resemble that of an Indian. I forget the disguise of the other. We reached a neighbouring shop by a by-lane and, making our way through the gunny[2] bags piled in the godown, escaped by the gate of the shop and threaded our way through the crowd to a carriage that had been kept for me at the end of the street. In this we drove off to the same police station where Mr. Alexander had offered me refuge a short time before, and I thanked him and the detective officers.

Whilst I had been thus effecting my escape Mr. Alexander had kept the crowd amused by singing the tune: 'Hang old Gandhi On the sour apple tree.' When he was informed of my safe arrival at the police station, he thus broke the news to the crowd: 'Well, your victim had made good his escape through a neighbouring shop. You had better go home now.' Some of them were angry, others laughed, some refused to believe the story.

'Well then,' said the superintendent, 'If you do not believe me, you may appoint one or two representatives, whom I am ready to take inside the house, If they succeed in finding out Gandhi, I will gladly deliver him to you. But if they fail, you must disperse. I am sure that you have no intention of destroying Mr. Rustomji's house or of harming Mr. Gandhi's wife and children.'

The crowed sent their representatives to search the house. They soon returned with disappointing news, and the crowd broke up at last, most of them admiring the superintendent's tactful handling of the situation, and a few fretting and fuming.

The late Mr. Chamberlain, who was then Secretary of State for the Colonies, cabled asking the Natal Government to prosecute my assailants. Mr. Escombe sent for me, expressed his regret for the injuries I had

1. *inference: a conclusion reached on the basis of evidence and reasoning*
2. *gunny: coarse sacking, typically made of jute fiber*

sustained, and said: 'Believe me, I cannot feel happy over the least little injury done to your person. You had a right to accept Mr. Laughton's advice and to face the worst, but I am sure that, if you had considered my suggestion favourably, these sad occurrences would not have happened. If you can identify the assailants, I am prepared to arrest and prosecute them. Mr. Chamberlain also desires me to do so.'

To which I gave the following reply:

'I do not want to prosecute anyone. It is possible that I may be able to identify one or two of them, but what is the use of getting them punished? Besides, I do not hold the assailants[1] to blame. They were given to understand that I had made exaggerated statements in India about the whites in Natal and calumniated them. If they believed these reports, it is no wonder that they were enraged. The leaders and, if you will permit me to say so, you are to blame. You could have guided the people properly, but you also believed Reuter and assumed that I must have indulged in exaggeration. I do not want to bring anyone to book. I am sure that, when the truth becomes known, they will be sorry for their conduct.'

'Would you mind giving me this in writing?' said Mr. Escombe. 'Because I shall have to cable to Mr. Chamberlain to that effect. I do not want you to make any statement in haste[2]. You may, if you like, consult Mr. Laughton and your other friends, before you come to a final decision. I may confess, however, that, if you waive the right of bringing your assailants to book, you will considerably help me in restoring quiet, besides enhancing your own reputation.'

'Thank you,' said I. 'I need not consult anyone. I had made my decision in the matter before I came to you. It is my conviction that I should not prosecute the assailants, and I am prepared this moment to reduce my decision to writing.'

With this I gave him the necessary statement.

1. assailants: make a concerned or violent attack on

2. haste: excessive speed or urgency of action

CHAPTER 58

THE CALM AFTER THE STORM

I had not yet left the police station, when, after two days, I was taken to see Mr.Escombe. Two constables were sent to protect me, though no such precaution was then needed.

On the day of landing, as soon as the yellow flag was lowered, a representative of *The Natal Advertiser* had come to interview me. He had asked me a number of questions, and in reply I had been able to refute everyone of the charges that had been leveled against me. Thanks to Sir Pherozeshah Mehta, I had delivered only written speeches in India, and I had copies of them all, as well as of my other writings. I had given the interviewer all this literature and showed him that in India I had said nothing which I had not already said in South Africa in stronger language. I had also shown him that I had had no hand in bringing the passengers of the *Courland* and *Naderi* to South Africa. Many of them were old residents, and most of them, far from wanting to stay in Natal, meant to go to the Transvaal. In those days the Transvaal offered better prospects than Natal to those coming in search of wealth, and most Indians, therefore, preferred to go there. This interview and my refusal to prosecute the assailants produced such a profound impression that the Europeans of Durban were ashamed of their conduct. The press declared me to be innocent and condemned the mob. Thus the lynching ultimately proved to be a blessing for me, that is, for the cause. It enhanced the prestige of the Indian community in South Africa and made my work easier. In three or four days I went to my house, and it was not long before I settled down again. The incident added also to my professional practice. But if it enhanced the prestige of the community, it also fanned the flame of prejudice against it. As soon as it was proved that the Indian could put up a manly fight, he came to be regarded as a danger. Two bills were introduced in the Natal Legislative Assembly, one of them calculated to affect the Indian trader adversely[1], and the other to impose a stringent[2] restriction on Indian immigration. Fortunately the

1. *adversely: harmful; unfavorable*

2. *stringent: strict, precise, and exacting*

fight for the franchise had resulted in a decision to the effect that no enactment might be passed against the Indians as such, that is say, that the law should make no distinctions of colour or race. The language of the bills above mentioned made them applicable to all, but their object undoubtedly was to impose[1] further restrictions on the Indian residents of Natal. The bills considerably increased my public work and made the community more alive then ever to their sense of duty. They were translated into Indian languages and fully explained, so as to bring home to the community their subtle[2] implications[3]. We appealed to the Colonial Secretary, but he refused to interfere and the bills became law. Public work now began to absorb[4] most of my time. Sjt. Mansukhlal Naazar, who, as I have said, was already in Durban, came to stay with me, and as he gave his time to public work, he lightened my burden to some extent. Sheth Adamji Miyakhan had, in my absence, discharged his duty with great credit. He had increased the membership and added about £1,000 to the coffers of the Natal Indian Congress. The awakening caused by the bills and the demonstration against the passengers I turned to good account by making an appeal for membership and funds, which now amounted to £5,000. My desire was to secure for the Congress a permanent fund, so that it might procure property of its own and then carry on its work out of the rent of the property. This was my first experience of managing a public institution. I placed my proposal before my co-workers, and they welcomed it. The property that was purchased was leased out and the rent was enough to meet the current expenses of the Congress. The property was vested in a strong body of trustees and is still there today, but it has become the source of much internecine quarrelling with the result that the rent of the property now accumulates in the court. This sad situation developed after my departure from South Africa, but my idea of having permanent funds for public institutions underwent a change long before this difference arose. And now after considerable experience with the many public institutions which I have managed, it has become my firm conviction that it is not good to run public institutions on permanent funds. A permanent fund carries in itself the seed of the moral fall of the institution. A public institution means an institution conducted with the approval, and from the funds, of the public. When such an institution ceases to have public support, it forfeits its right to exist. Institutions maintained on permanent funds

1. *impose: force to be accepted, undertaken, or complied with*
2. *subtle: so delicate or precise as to be difficult to analyze or describe; a subtle distinction; capable of making fine distinctions; delicately complex and understated; subtle lighting*
3. *implications: the implicit conclusion that can be drawn from something; a likely consequence*
4. *absorb: soak up (liquid or another substance)*

are often found to ignore public opinion, and are frequently responsible for acts contrary to it. In our country we experience this at every step. Some of the so-called religious trusts have ceased to render any accounts. The trustees have become the owners and are responsible to none. I have no doubt that the ideal is for public institutions to live, like nature, from day to day. The institution that fails to win public support has no right to exist as such. The subscriptions that an institution annually receives are a test of its popularity and the honesty of its management[1]; and I am of opinion that every institution should submit to that test. But let no one misunderstand me. My remarks do not apply to the bodies which cannot, by their very nature, be conducted without permanent buildings. What I mean to say is that the current expenditure should be found from subscriptions voluntarily received from year to year. These views were confirmed during the days of the Satyagraha in South Africa. That magnificent campaign extending over six years was carried on without permanent funds, though lakhs of rupees were necessary for it. I can recollect times when I did not know what would happen the next day if no subscriptions came in. But I shall not anticipate future events. The reader will find the opinion expressed above amply borne[2] out in the coming narrative.

1. *management: the people managing an organization*
2. *borne: past participle of bear*

CHAPTER 59

EDUCATION OF CHILDREN

When I landed at Durban in January 1897, I had three children with me, my sister's son ten years old, and my own sons nine and five years of age. Where was I to educate them?

I could have sent them to the schools for European children, but only as a matter of favour and exception. No other Indian children were allowed to attend them. For these there were schools established by Christian missions, but I was not prepared to send my children there, as I did not like the education imparted[1] in those schools. For one thing, the medium of instruction would be only English, or perhaps incorrect Tamil or Hindi; this too could only have been arranged with difficulty. I could not possibly put up with this and other disadvantages. In the meantime I was making my own attempt to teach them. But that was at best irregular, and I could not get hold of a suitable Gujarati teacher.

I was at my wits' end. I advertised for an English teacher who should teach the children under my direction. Some regular instruction was to be given them by this teacher, and for the rest they should be satisfied with what little I could give them irregularly. So I engaged an English governess at £7 a month. This went on for some time, but not to my satisfaction. The boys acquired some knowledge of Gujarati through my conversation and intercourse with them, which was strictly in the mother-tongue. I was loath[2] to send them back to India, for I believed even then that young children should not be separated from their parents. The education that children naturally imbibe in a well-ordered household is impossible to obtain in hostels[3]. I therefore kept my children with me. I did send my nephew and elder son to be educated at residential schools in India for a few months, but I soon had to recall them. Later, the eldest son, long after he had come of age, broke away from me, and went to India to join a high school in Ahmedabad. I have an impression that the nephew[4] was satisfied with what I could give him.

1. *imparted: communicate; bestow a quality*
2. *loath: reluctant; unwilling*
3. *hostels: an establishment which provides cheap food and lodging for a specific group of people*
4. *nephew: a son of one's brother or sister, or of one's brother-in-law or sister-in-law*

Unfortunately he died in the prime of youth after a brief illness. The other three of my sons have never been at a public school, though they did get some regular schooling in an improvised[1] school which I started for the children of Satyagrahi parents in South Africa.

These experiments were all inadequate. I could not devote to the children all the time I had wanted to give them. My inability to give them enough attention and other unavoidable causes prevented me from providing them with the literary education I had desired, and all my sons have had complaints to make against me in this matter. Whenever they come across an M.A. or a B.A., or even a matriculate, they seem to feel the handicap of a want of school education.

Nevertheless I am of opinion that, if I had insisted on their being educated somehow at public schools, they would have been deprived of the training that can be had only at the school of experience, or from constant contact with the parents. I should never have been free, as I am today, from anxiety on their score, and the artificial[2] education that they could have had in England or South Africa, torn from me, would never have taught them the simplicity and the spirit of service that they show in their lives today, while their artificial ways of living might have been a serious handicap in my public work. Therefore, though I have not been able to give them a literary education either to their or to my satisfaction, I am not quite sure, as I look back on my past years, that I have not done my duty by them to the best of my capacity. Nor do I regret not having sent them to public schools. I have always felt that the undesirable traits I see today in my eldest son are an echo of my own undisciplined and unformulated early life. I regard that time as a period of half-baked knowledge and indulgence. It coincided with the most impressionable years of my eldest son, and naturally he has refused to regard it as my time of indulgence and inexperience. He has on the contrary believed that that was the brightest period of my life, and the changes, effected later, have been due to delusion[3] miscalled enlightenment. And well he might. Why should he not think that my earlier years represented a period of awakening, and the later years of radical[4] change, years of delusion and egotism? Often have I been confronted with various posers from friends : What harm had there been, if I had given my boys an academical education? What right had I thus to clip their wings? Why

1. *improvised: created spontaneously*
2. *artificial: made as a copy of something natural*
3. *delusion: an idiosyncratic belief or impression that is not in accordance with a generally accepted reality*
4. *radical: of, relating to, or affecting the fundamental nature of something; innovative or progressive*

should I have come in the way of their taking degrees and choosing their own careers?

I do not think that there is much point in these questions. I have come in contact with numerous students. I have tried myself or through others to impose my educational ‘fads[1]’ on other children too and have seen the results thereof. There are within my knowledge a number of young men today contemporaneous[2] with my sons. I do not think that man to man they are any better that my sons, or that my sons have much to learn from them.

But the ultimate result of my experiments is in the womb of the future. My object in discussing this subject here is that a student of the history of civilization may have some measure of the difference between disciplined home education and school education, and also the effect produced on children through changes introduced by parents in their lives. The purpose of this chapter is also to show the lengths to which a votary of truth is driven by his experiments with truth, as so of to show the votary of liberty how many are the sacrifices demanded by that stern goddess. Had I been without a sense of self-respect[3] and satisfied myself with having for my children the education that other children could not get, I should have deprived them of the object-lesson in liberty and self-respect that I gave them at the cost of the literary training. And where a choice has to be made between liberty and learning, who will not say that the former has to be preferred a thousand times to the latter?

The youths whom I called out in 1920 from those citadels[4] of slavery – their schools and colleges – and whom I advised that it was far better to remain unlettered and break stones for the sake of liberty than to go in for a literary education in the chains of slaves will probably be able now to trace my advice to its source.

1. *fads: a craze*
2. *contemporaneous: existing at or occurring in the same period of time*
3. *self-respect: pride and confidence in oneself*
4. *citadels: a fortress protecting or dominating a city*

CHAPTER 60

SPIRIT OF SERVICE

My profession progressed satisfactorily, but that was far from satisfying me. The question of further simplifying my life and of doing some concrete act of service to my fellowmen had been constantly agitating me, when a leper came to my door. I had not the heart to dismiss him with a meal. So I offered him shelter, dressed his wounds, and began to look after him. But I could not go on like that indefinitely. I could not afford, I lacked the will to keep him always with me. So I sent him to the government hospital for indentured labourers.

But I was still ill at ease. I longed for some humanitarian work of a permanent nature. Dr. Booth was the head of the St. Aidan's Mission. He was a kind-hearted man and treated his patients free. Thanks to a Parsi Rustomji's charities, it was possible to open a small charitable hospital under Dr. Booth's charge. I felt strongly inclined to serve as a nurse in this hospital. The work of dispensing medicines took from one to two hours daily, and I made up my mind to find time from my office-work, so as to be able to fill the place of a compounder in the dispensary attached to the hospital. Most of my professional work was chamber work, conveyancing and arbitration[1]. I of course used to have a few cases in the magistrate's court, but most of them were of a non-controversial character, and Mr. Khan, who had followed me to South Africa and was then living with me, undertook to take them if I was absent. So I found time to serve in the small hospital. This meant two hours every morning, including the time taken in going to and from the hospital. This work brought me some peace. It consisted in ascertaining the patient's complaints, laying the facts before the doctor and dispensing the prescriptions. It brought me in close touch with suffering Indians, most of them indentured Tamil, Telugu or North Indian men.

The experience stood me in good stead, when during the Boer War I offered my services for nursing the sick and wounded soldiers.

1. *arbitration: act between parties with a view to reconciling differences*

The question of the rearing of children had been ever before me. I had two sons born in South Africa, and my service in the hospital was useful in solving the question of their upbringing. My independent spirit was a constant source of trial. My wife and I had decided to have the best medical aid at the time of her delivery, but if the doctor and the nurse were to leave us in the lurch at the right moment, what was I to do? Then the nurse had to be an Indian. And the difficulty of getting a trained Indian nurse in South Africa can be easily imagined from the similar difficulty in India. So I studied the things necessary for safe labour[1]. I read Dr. Tribhuvandas' book, *Ma-ne Shikhaman* - Advice to a mother - and I nursed both my children according to the instructions given in the book, tempered here and there by experiences as I had gained elsewhere. The services of a nurse were utilized-not for more than two months each time-chiefly for helping my wife and not for taking care of the babies, which I did myself.

The birth of the last child put me to the severest test. The travail[2] came on suddenly. The doctor was not immediately available, and some time was lost in fetching the midwife. Even if she had been on the spot, she could not have helped delivery. I had to see through the safe delivery of the baby. My careful study of the subject in Dr. Tribhuvandas' work was of inestimable[3] help. I was not nervous.

I am convinced that for the proper upbringing of children the parents ought to have a general knowledge of the care and nursing of babies. At every step I have seen the advantages of my careful study of the subject. My children would not have enjoyed the general health that they do today, had I not studied the subject and turned my knowledge to account. We labour under a sort of superstition that a child has nothing to learn during the first five years of its life. On the contrary the fact is that the child never learns in after life what it does in its first five years. The education of the child begins with conception. The physical and mental states of the parents at the moment of conception are reproduced[4] in the baby. Then during the period of pregnancy it continues to be affected by the mother's moods, desires and temperament, as also by her ways of life. After birth the child imitates the parents, and for a considerable number of years entirely depends on them for its growth.

The couple who realize these things will never have sexual union for the fulfillment of their lust, but only when they desire issue. I think it is

1. *labour: the process of childbirth from the start of uterine contractions to delivery*
2. *travail: painful or laborious effort; labor pains*
3. *inestimable: not able to be measured; very great*
4. *reproduced: produce a copy or representation of; create something in a different medium or context that is very similar to*

the height of ignorance to believe that the sexual act is an independent function necessary like sleeping or eating. The world depends for its existence on the act of generation, and as the world is the play-ground of God and a reflection of His glory, the act of generation should be controlled for the ordered growth of the world. He who realizes this will control his lust at any cost, equip himself with the knowledge necessary for the physical, mental and spiritual well-being of his progeny[1], and give the benefit of that knowledge to posterity[2].

1. *progeny: offspring*

2. *posterity: all future generation*

CHAPTER 61

BRAHMACHARYA - I

We now reach the stage in this story when I began seriously to think of taking the *brahmacharya* vow. I had been wedded to a monogamous ideal ever since my marriage, faithfulness to my wife being part of the love of truth. But it was in South Africa that I came to realize the importance of observing *brahmacharya* even with respect to my wife. I cannot definitely say what circumstance or what book it was, that set my thoughts in that direction, but I have a recollection that the predominant factor was the influence of Raychandbhai, of whom I have already written, I can still recall a conversation that I had with him. On one occasion I spoke to him in high praise of Mrs. Gladstone's devotion to her husband. I had read some where that Mrs. Gladstone insisted on preparing tea for Mr. Gladstone even in the House of Commons, and that this had become a rule in the life of this illustrious[1] couple, whose actions were governed by regularity. I spoke of this to the poet, and incidentally eulogized[2] conjugal love. 'Which of the two do you prize more,' asked Raychandbhai, 'the love of Mrs. Gladstone for her husband as his wife, or her devoted service irrespective of her relation to Mr. Gladstone? Supposing she had been his sister, or his devoted servant, and ministered to him with the same attention, what would you have said? Do we not have instances of such devoted sisters or servants? Supposing you had found the same loving devotion in a male servant, would you have been pleased in the same way as in Mrs. Gladstone's case? Just examine the viewpoint suggested by me.'

Raychandbhai was himself married. I have an impression that at the moment his words sounded harsh, but they gripped me irresistibly. The devotion of a servant was, I felt, a thousand times more praiseworthy than that of a wife to her husband. There was nothing surprising in the wife's devotion to her husband, as there was an indissoluble[3] bond between them. The devotion was perfectly natural. But it required. a

1. *illustrious: well known and admired for past achievements*
2. *eulogized: a speech or piece of writing that praises someone highly*
3. *indissoluble: lasting unable to be destroyed*

special effort to cultivate equal devotion between master and servant. The poet's point of view began gradually to grow upon me. What then, I asked myself, should be my relation with my wife? Did my faithfulness consist in making my wife the instrument of my lust? So long as I was the slave of lust, my faithfulness was worth nothing. To be fair to my wife, I must say that she was never the temptress. It was therefore the easiest thing for me to take the vow of *brahmacharya,* if only I willed it. It was my weak will or lustful attachment that was the obstacle. Even after my conscience had been roused[1] in the matter, I failed twice. I failed because the motive that actuated the effort was none the highest. My main object was to escape having more children. Whilst in England I had read something about contraceptives[2]. I have already referred to Dr. Allinson's birth control propaganda in the chapter on Vegetarianism. If it had some temporary effect on me, Mr. Hill's opposition to those methods and his advocacy of internal efforts as opposed to outward means, in a word, of self-control, had a far greater effect, which in due time came to be abiding. Seeing, therefore, that I did not desire more children I began to strive after self-control. There was endless difficulty in the task. We began to sleep in separate beds. I decided to retire to bed only after the day's work had left me completely exhausted. All these efforts did not seem to bear much fruit, but when I look back upon the past, I feel that the final resolution was the cumulative effect of those unsuccessful strivings.

The final resolution could only be made as late as 1906. Satyagraha had not then been started. I had not the least notion[3] of its coming. I was practising in Johannesburg at the time of the Zulu 'Rebellion' in Natal, which came soon after the Boer War. I felt that I must offer my services to the Natal Government on that occasion. The offer was accepted, as we shall see in another chapter. But the work set me furiously thinking in the direction of self-control, and according to my wont I discussed my thoughts with my co-workers, It became my conviction that procreation and the consequent care of children were inconsistent with public service. I had to break up my household at Johannesburg to be able to serve during the 'Rebellion'. Within one month of offering my services, I had to give up the house I had so carefully furnished. I took my wife and children to Phoenix and led the Indian ambulance corps[4] attached to the Natal forces. During the difficult marches that had then to be

1. *roused: bring out of sleep; awaken; cease to sleep; wake up*
2. *contraceptives: the use of artificial methods or other techniques to prevent pregnancy*
3. *notion: a concept or belief; a vague awareness or understanding*
4. *corps: a main subdivision of an army in the field, consisting of two or more divisions; a branch of an army assigned to a particular kind of work; a body of people engaged in a particular activity*

performed, the idea flashed upon me that if I wanted to devote myself to the service of the community in this manner, I must relinquish the desire for children and wealth and live the life of a *vanaprastha* - of one retired from household cares. The 'Rebellion' did not occupy me for more than six weeks, but this brief period proved to be a very important epoch in my life. The importance of vows grew upon me more clearly than ever before. I realized that a vow, far from closing the door to real freedom, opened it. Up to this time I had not met with success because the will had been lacking, because I had had no faith in myself, no faith in the grace of God, and therefore, my mind had been tossed on the boisterous[1] sea of doubt. I realized that in refusing to take a vow man was drawn into temptation, and that to be bound by a vow was like a passage from libertinism[2] to a real monogamous marriage. 'I believe in effort, I do not want to bind myself with vows,' is the mentality of weakness and betrays a subtle desire for the thing to be avoided. Or where can be the difficulty in making a final decision? I vow to flee from the serpent[3] which I know will bite me, I do not simply make an effort to flee from him. I know that mere effort may mean certain death. Mere effort means ignorance of the certain fact that the serpent is bound to kill me. The fact, therefore, that I could rest content with an effort only, means that I have not yet clearly realized the necessity of definite action.'But supposing my views are changed in the future, how can I bind myself by a vow? 'Such a doubt often deters us. But that doubt also betrays a lack of clear perception that a particular thing must be renounced. That is why Nishkulanand has sung:

'Renunciation without aversion is not lasting.'

Where therefore the desire is gone, a vow of renunciation is the natural and inevitable fruit.

1. *boisterous: wild or stormy*
2. *libertinism: a person who is freely indulgent in sensual pleasures*
3. *serpent: a large snake; a dragon or other mythical snake-like reptile; a biblical name for satan; a sly or treacherous person*

CHAPTER 62

BRAHM ACHARYA – II

After full discussion and mature deliberation I took the vow in 1906. I had not shared my thoughts with my wife until then, but only consulted[1] her at the time of taking the vow. She had no objection. But I had great difficulty in making the final resolve. I had not the necessary strength. How was I to control my passions? The elimination of carnal relationship with one's wife seemed then a strange thing. But I launched forth with faith in the sustaining power of God. As I look back upon the twenty years of the vow, I am filled with pleasure and wonderment. The more or less successful practice of self-control had been going on since 1901. But the freedom and joy that came to me after taking the vow had never been experienced before 1906. Before the vow I had been open to being overcome by temptation at any moment. Now the vow was a sure shield against temptation. The great potentiality of *brahmacharya* daily became more an more patent to me. The vow was taken when I was in Phoenix. As soon as I was free from ambulance work, I went to Phoenix, whence I had to return to Johannesburg. In about a month of my returning there, the foundation of Satyagraha was laid. As though unknown to me, the *brahmacharya* vow had been preparing me for it. Satyagraha had not been a preconceived[2] plan. It came on spontaneously, without my having willed it. But I could see that all my previous steps had led up to that goal. I had cut down my heavy household expenses at Johannesburg and gone to Phoenix to take, as it were, the *brahmacharya* vow.

The knowledge that a perfect observance of *brahmacharya* means realization of *brahman*, I did not owe to a study of the Shastras. It slowly grew upon me with experience. The shastric texts on the subject I read only later in life. Every day of the vow has taken me nearer the knowledge that in *brahmacharya* lies the protection of the body, the mind and the soul. For *brahmacharya* was now no process of hard penance[3], it was a matter of consolation and joy. Every day revealed a fresh beauty in it.

1. *consulted: seek information or advice from someone, especially an expert or professional; seek permission or approval from; engaged in the business of giving advice to other in the same field; a consulting engineer*
2. *preconceived: formed prior to having evidence for its truth or usefulness*
3. *penance: voluntary self-punishment as an open expression of repentance for wrongdoing*

But if it was a matter of ever-increasing joy, let no one believe that it was an easy thing for me. Even when I am past fifty-six years, I realize how hard a thing it is. Every day I realize more and more that it is like walking on the sword's[1] edge, and I see every moment the necessity for eternal vigilance.

Control of the palate is the first essential in the observance of the vow. I found that complete control of the palate made the observance very easy, and so I now pursued my dietetic experiments not merely from the vegetarian's but also from the *brahmachari's* point of view. As the result of these experiments I saw that the *brahmachari's* food should be limited, simple, spiceless, and, if possible, uncooked.

Six years of experiment have showed me that the *brahmachari's* ideal food is fresh fruit and nuts. The immunity[2] from passion that I enjoyed when I lived on this food was unknown to me after I changed that diet. *Brahmacharya* needed no effort on my part in South Africa when I lived on fruits and nuts alone. It has been a matter of very great effort ever since I began to take milk. How I had to go back to milk from a fruit diet will be considered in its proper place. It is enough to observe here that I have not the least doubt that milk diet makes the *brahmacharya* vow difficult to observe. Let no one deduce from this that all *brahmacharis* must give up milk. The effect on *brahmacharya* of different kinds of food can be determined only after numerous[3] experiments. I have yet to find a fruit substitute for milk which is an equally good muscle-builder and easily digestible. The doctors, *vaidyas* and *hakims* have alike failed to enlighten me. Therefore, though I know milk to be partly a stimulant, I cannot, for the time being, advise anyone to give it up.

As an external aid to *brahmacharya*, fasting is as necessary as selection and restriction in diet. So overpowering are the senses that they can be kept under control only when they are completely hedged in on all sides, from above and from beneath. It is common knowledge that they are powerless without food, and so fasting undertaken with a view to control of the senses is, I have no doubt, very helpful. With some, fasting is of no avail, because assuming that mechanical fasting alone will make them immune, they keep their bodies without food, but feast their minds upon all sorts of delicacies, thinking all the while what they will eat and what they will drink after the fast terminates. Such fasting

1. *sword: a weapon with a long metal blade and a hilt with a hand-guard, used for thrusting or striking and often worn as part of ceremonial dress; military power, violence*
2. *immunity: protection or exemption from something, especially an obligation or penalty*
3. *numerous: many; consisting of many members*

helps them in controlling neither palate nor lust. Fasting is useful, when mind co-operates with starving body, that is to say, when it cultivates a distaste for the objects that are denied to the body. Mind is at the root of all sensuality[1]. Fasting therefore, has a limited use, for a fasting man may continue to be swayed[2] by passion. But it may be said that extinction of the sexual passion is as a rule impossible without fasting, which may be said to be indispensable for the observance of *brahmacharya*. Many aspirants after *brahmacharya* fail, because in the use of their other senses they want to carry on like those who are not *brahmacharis*. Their effort is, therefore, identical with the effort to experience the bracing cold of winter in the scorching summer months. There should be a clear line between the life of a *brahmachari* and of one who is not. The resemblance that there is between the two is only apparent. The distinction ought to be clear as daylight. Both use their eyesight, but whereas the *brahmachari* uses it to see the glories of God, the other uses it to see the frivolity around him. Both use their ears, but whereas the one hears nothing but praises of God, the other feasts his ears upon ribaldry. Both often keep late hours, but whereas the one devotes them to prayer, the other fritters them away in wild and wasteful mirth[3]. Both feed the inner man, but the one only to keep the temple of God in good repair, while the other gorges himself and makes the sacred vessel a stinking gutter. Thus both live as the poles apart, and the distance between them will grow and not diminish with the passage of time.

Brahmacharya means control of the senses in thought, word and deed. Every day I have been realizing more and more the necessity for restraints of the kind I have detailed above. There is no limit to the possibilities of renunciation even as there is none to those of *brahamacharya*. Such *brahamacharya* is impossible of attainment by limited effort. For many it must remain only as an ideal. An aspirant after *brahamacharya* will always be conscious of his shortcomings, will seek out the passions lingering in the innermost recesses of his heart and will incessantly strive to get rid of them. So long as thought is not under complete control of the will, *brahamacharya* in its fullness is absent. Involuntary thought is an affection of the mind, and curbing of thought, therefore, means curbing of the mind which is even more difficult to curb than the wind. Nevertheless the existence of God within makes even control of the mind

1. *sensuality: of or relating to the physical senses, especially as a source of pleasure*
2. *swayed: cause to change in opinion, action, etc.; influence*
3. *mirth: amusement; laughter*

possible. Let no one think that it is impossible because it is difficult. It is the highest goal, and it is no wonder that the highest effort should be necessary to attain it.

But it was after coming to India that I realized that such *brahmacharya* was impossible to attain by mere human effort. Until then I had been labouring under the delusion that fruit diet alone would enable me to eradicate all passions, and I had flattered myself with the belief that I had nothing more to do.

But I must not anticipate the chapter of my struggles. Meanwhile let me make it clear that those who desire to observe *brahmacharya* with a view to realizing God need not despair, provided their faith in God is equal to their confidence in their own effort.

The Bhagavad Gita, 2-59.

'The sense-objects turn away from an abstemious[1] soul, leaving the relish behind. The relish also disappears with the realization of the Highest.' Therefore His name and His grace are the last resources of the aspirant after *moksha*. This truth came to me only after my return to India.

1. *abstemious: not self-indulgent, especially as regards eating and drinking*

CHAPTER 63

SIMPLE LIFE

I had started on a life of ease and comfort, but the experiment was short-lived. Although I had furnished the house with care, yet it failed to have any hold on me. So no sooner had I launched forth on that life, than I began to cut down expenses. The washerman's bill was heavy, and as he was besides by no means noted for his punctuality[1], even two to three dozen shirts and collars proved insufficient for me. Collars had to be changed daily and shirts, if not daily, at least every alternate day. This meant a double expense, which appeared to me unnecessary. So I equipped myself with a washing outfit to save it. I bought a book on washing, studied the art and taught it also to my wife. This no doubt added to my work, but its novelty[2] made it a pleasure.

I shall never forget the first collar that I washed myself. I had used more starch[3] than necessary, the iron had not been made hot enough, and for fear of burning the collar I had not pressed it sufficiently. The result was that, though the collar was fairly stiff, the superfluous[4] starch continually dropped off it. I went to court with the collar on, thus inviting the ridicule of brother barristers, but even in those days I could be impervious to ridicule.

'Well,' said I, 'this is my first experiment at washing my own collars and hence the loose starch. But it does not trouble me, and then there is the advantage of providing you with so much fun.'

'But surely there is no lack of laundries here?' asked a friend.

'The laundry bill is very heavy,' said I. 'The charge for washing a collar is almost as much as its price, and even then there is the eternal dependence on the washerman. I prefer by far to wash my things myself.'

But I could not make my friends appreciate the beauty of self-help. In course of time I became an expert washerman so far as my own work went, and my washing was by no means inferior to laundry washing. My collars were no less stiff or shiny than others.

1. *punctuality: happening or doing something at the appointed time*
2. *novelty: the quality of being novel; a new or unfamiliar thing or experience; denoting something intended to be amusing as a result of its originality or unusualness*
3. *starch: powder or spray made from this substance, used to stiffen fabric*
4. *superfluous: unnecessary, especially through being more than enough*

When Gokhale came to South Africa, he had with him a scarf which was a gift from Mahadeo Govind Ranade. He treasured the memento with the utmost[1] care and used it only on special occasions. One such occasion was the banquet[2] given in his honour by the Johannesburg Indians.

The scarf was creased[3] and needed ironing. It was not possible to send it to the laundry and get it back in time. I offered to try my art.

'I can trust to your capacity as a lawyer, but not as a washerman,' said Gokhale; 'What if you should soil it? Do you know what it means to me?'

With this he narrated, with much joy, the story of the gift. I still insisted, guaranteed good work, got his permission to iron it, and won his certificate. After that I did not mind if the rest of the world refused me its certificate.

In the same way, as I freed myself from slavery to the washerman, I threw off dependence on the barber. All people who go to England learn there at least the art of shaving, but none, to my knowledge, learn to cut their own hair. I had to learn that too. I once went to an English hair-cutter in Pretoria. He contemptuously refused to cut my hair. I certainly felt hurt, but immediately purchased a pair of clippers and cut my hair before the mirror. I succeeded more or less in cutting the front hair, but I spoiled the back. The friends in the court shook with laughter.

'What's wrong with your hair, Gandhi? Rats have been at it?' 'No. The white barber would not condescend to touch my black hair,' said I, 'so I preferred to cut it myself, no matter how badly.'

The reply did not surprise the friends.

The barber was not at fault in having refused to cut my hair. There was every chance of his losing his custom, if he should serve black men. We do not allow our barbers to serve our untouchable brethren. I got the reward of this in South Africa, not once, but many times, and the conviction that it was the punishment for our own sins saved me from becoming angry.

The extreme forms in which my passion for self-help and simplicity ultimately expressed itself will be described in their proper place. The seed had been long sown. It only needed watering to take root, to flower and to fructify, and the watering came in due course.

1. *utmost: most extreme; greatest*
2. *banquet: an elaborate and formal meal for many people*
3. *creased: smooth with an iron*

CHAPTER 64

THE BOER WAR

I must skip many other experiences of the period between 1897 and 1899 and come straight to the Boer War.

When the war was declared, my personal sympathies were all with the Boers, but I believed then that I had yet no right, in such cases, to enforce my individual convictions. I have minutely dealt with the inner struggle regarding this in my history of the Satyagraha in South Africa, and I must not repeat the argument here. I invite the curious to turn to those pages. Suffice it to say that my loyalty to the British rule drove me to participation with the British in that war. I felt that, if I demanded rights as a British citizen, it was also my duty, as such, to participate in the defence of the British Empire. I held then that India could achieve her complete emancipation[1] only within and through the British Empire. So I collected together as many comrades[2] as possible, and with very great difficulty got their services accepted as an ambulance corps.

The average Englishman believed that the Indian was a coward, incapable of taking risks or looking beyond his immediate self-interest. Many English friends, therefore, threw cold water on my plan. But Dr. Booth supported it whole-heartedly. He trained us in ambulance work. We secured medical certificates of fitness for service. Mr. Laughton and the late Mr. Escombe enthusiastically supported the plan, and we applied at last for service at the front. The Government thankfully acknowledged our application, but said that our services were not then needed.

I would not rest satisfied, however with this refusal. Through the introduction of Dr. Booth, I called on the Bishop of Natal. There were many Christian Indians in our corps. The Bishop was delighted with my proposal and promised to help us in getting our services accepted. Time too was working with us. The Boer had shown more pluck[3], determination and bravery than had been expected; and our services were ultimately needed. Our corps was 1,100 strong, with nearly 40 leaders,

1. *emancipation: set free, especially from legal, social, or political restrictions; free from slavery [law] set free from the authority of its father or parents*
2. *comrades: a companion who shares one's activities or is a fellow member of an organization*
3. *pluck: spirited and determined courage*

About three hundred were free Indians, and the rest indentured. Dr. Booth was also with us, The corps acquitted itself well. Though our work was to be outside the firing line, and though we had the protection of the Red Cross, we were asked at a critical moment to serve within the firing line. The reservation had not been of our seeking. The authorities did not want us to be within the range of fire. The situation, however, was changed after the repulse at Spion Kop, and General Buller sent the message that, though we were not bound to take the risk, Government would be thankful if we would do so and fetch the wounded from the field. We had no hesitation, and so the action at Spion Kop found us working within the firing line. During these days we had to march from twenty to twenty-five miles a day, bearing the wounded on stretchers. Amongst the wounded we had the honour of carrying soldiers like General Woodgate.

The corps was disbanded[1] after six weeks' service. After the reverses at Spion Kop and Vaalkranz, the British Commander-in-Chief abandoned the attempt to relieve Ladysmith and other places by summary[2] procedure, and decided to proceed slowly, awaiting reinforcements from England and India.

Our humble work was at the moment much applauded[3], and the Indians' prestige was enhanced. The newspapers published laudatory[4] rhymes with the refrain, 'We are sons of Empire after all.'

General Buller mentioned with appreciation the work of the corps in his despatch, and the leaders were awarded the War Medal.

The Indian community became better organized. I got into closer touch with the indentured Indians. There came a greater awakening amongst them, and the feeling that Hindus, Musalmans, Christians, Tamilians, Gujaratis and Sindhis were all Indians and children of the same motherland took deep root amongst them. Everyone believed that the Indians' grievances were now sure to be redressed. At the moment the white man's attitude seemed to be distinctly changed. The relations formed with the whites during the war were of the sweetest. We had come in contact with thousands of tommies. They were friendly with us and thankful for being there to serve them. I cannot forbear from recording a sweet reminiscence of how human nature shows itself at its best in moments of trial. We were marching towards Chievely Camp

1. *disbanded: break up or cause to break up*
2. *summary: dispensing with needless details or formalities*
3. *applauded: show approval by clapping; praise or approve of*
4. *laudatory: expressing praise and commendation*

where Lieutenant Roberts, the son of Lord Roberts, had received a mortal wound. Our corps had the honour of carrying the body from the field. It was a sultry[1] day – the day of our march. Everyone was thirsting for water. There was a tiny brook on the way where we could slake[2] our thirst. But who was to drink first? We had proposed to come in after the tommies had finished. But they would not begin first and urged us to do so, and for a while a pleasant competition went on for giving precedence to one another.

1. *sultry: hot and humid*
2. *slake: quench; satisfy*

CHAPTER 65

SANITARY REFORM AND FAMINE RELIEF

It has always been impossible for me to reconcile myself to any one member of the body politic remaining out of use. I have always been loath to hide or connive[1] at the. weak points of the community or to press for its rights without having purged it of its blemishes[2]. Therefore, ever since my settlement in Natal, I had been endeavouring[3] to clear the community of a charge that had been leveled against it, not without a certain amount of truth. The charge had often been made that the Indian was slovenly[4] in his habits and did not keep his house and surroundings clean. The principal men of the community had, therefore, already begun to put their houses in order, but house-to-house inspection was undertaken only when plague was reported to be imminent in Durban. This was done after consulting, and gaining the approval of, the city fathers, who had desired our co-operation. Our co-operation made work easier for them and at the same time lessened our hardships. For whenever there is an outbreak of epidemics, the executive, as a general rule, get impatient, take excessive measures and behave to such as may have incurred their displeasure with a heavy hand. The community saved itself from this oppression by voluntarily taking sanitary measures.

But I had some bitter experiences. I saw that I could not so easily count on the help of the community in getting it to do its own duty, as I could in claiming for it rights. At some places I met with insults, at others with polite indifference. It was too much for people to bestir themselves to keep their surroundings clean. To expect them to find money for the work was out of the question. These experiences taught me, better than ever before, that without infinite patience it was impossible to get the people to do any work. It is the reformer who is anxious for the reform, and not society, from which he should expect nothing better than opposition, abhorrence and even mortal persecution. Why may not society regard as retrogression what the reformer holds dear as life itself?

1. *connive: secretly allow a wrongdoing; conspire*
2. *blemishes: a small mark or flaw which spoils the appearance of something*
3. *endeavouring: try hard to do or achieve something*
4. *slovenly: untidy and dirty*

Nevertheless the result of this agitation was that the Indian community learnt to recognize more or less the necessity for keeping their houses and environments clean. I gained the esteem of the authorities. They saw that, though I had made it my business to ventilate grievances and press for rights, I was no less keen and insistent upon self-purification[1].

There was one thing, however, which still remained to be done, namely, the awakening in the Indian settler of a sense of duty to the motherland. India was poor, the Indian settler went to South Africa in search of wealth, and he was bound to contribute part of his earnings for the benefit of his countrymen in the hour of their adversity. This the settler did during the terrible famines of 1897 and 1899. They contributed handsomely for famine relief, and more so in 1899 than in 1897. We had appealed to Englishmen also for funds, and they had responded well. Even the indentured Indians gave their share to the contribution, and the system inaugurated[2] at the time of these famines has been continued ever since, and we know that Indians in South Africa never fail to send handsome contributions to India in times of national calamity[3].

Thus service of the Indians in South Africa ever revealed to me new implications of Truth at every stage. Truth is like a vast tree, which yields more and more fruit, the more you nurture it. The deeper the search in the mine of Truth the richer the discovery of the gems buried there, in the shape of openings for an ever greater variety of service.

1. *purification: remove contaminants from*
2. *inaugurated: beginning of a system, policy, thing*
3. *calamity: an event causing great and often sudden damage or distress*

CHAPTER 66

RETURN TO INDIA

On my relief from war-duty I felt that my work was no longer in South Africa but in India. Not that there was nothing to be done in South Africa, but I was afraid that my main business might become merely money-making. Friends at home were also pressing me to return, and I felt that I should be of more service in India. And for the work in South Africa, there were, of course, Messrs Khan and Mansukhlal Naazar. So I requested my co-workers to relieve me. After very great difficulty my request was conditionally accepted, the condition being that I should be ready to go back to South Africa if, within a year, the community should need me. I thought it was a difficult condition but the love that bound me to the community made me accept it. 'The Lord has bound me With the cotton-thread of love, I am His bondslave,' sang Mirabai. And for me, too, the cotton-thread of love that bound me to the community was too strong to break. The voice of the people is the voice of God, and here the voice of friends was too real to be rejected. I accepted the condition and got their permission to go.

At this time I was intimately connected only with Natal. The Natal Indians bathed me with the nectar[1] of love. Farewell meetings were arranged at every place, and costly gifts were presented to me.

Gifts had been bestowed[2] on me before when I returned to India in 1899, but this time the farewell was overwhelming. The gifts of course included things in gold and silver, but there were articles of costly diamond as well.

What right had I to accept all these gifts? Accepting them, how could I persuade myself that I was serving the community without remuneration? All the gifts, excepting a few from my clients, were purely for my service to the community, and I could make no difference between my clients and co-workers; for the clients also helped me in my public work.

1. *nectar: a sugary fluid secreted within flowers to encourage pollination by insects, collected by bees to make into honey*
2. *bestowed: confer*

One of the gifts was a gold necklace/worth fifty guineas, meant for my wife. But even that gift was given because of my public work, and so it could not be separated from the rest.

The evening I was presented with the bulk of these things I had a sleepless night. I walked up and down my room deeply agitated, but could find no solution. It was difficult for me to forego gifts worth hundreds, it was more difficult to keep them.

And even if I could keep them, what about my children? What about my wife? They were being trained to a life of service and to an understanding that service was its own reward.

I had no costly ornaments in the house. We had been fast simplifying our life How then could we afford to have gold watches? How could we afford to wear gold chains and diamond rings? Even then I was exhorting[1] people to conquer the infatuation for jewellery. What was I now to do with the jewellery that had come upon me?

I decided that I could not keep these things. I drafted a letter, creating a trust of them in favour of the community and appointing Parsi Rustomji and other trustees[2]. In the morning I held a consultation with my wife and children and finally go rid of the heavy incubus.

I knew that I should have some difficulty in persuading my wife, and I was sure that I should have none so far as the children were concerned. So I decided to constitute them my attorneys.

The children readily agreed to my proposal. 'We do not need these costly presents, we must return them to the community, and should we ever need them, we could easily purchase them,' they said.

I was delighted.' Then you will plead with mother won't you? 'I asked them.

'Certainly,' said they. 'That is our business. She does not need to wear the ornaments. She would want to keep them for us, and if we don't want them, why should she not agree to part with them?'

But it was easier said than done.

'You may not need them,' said my wife. 'Your children may not need them. Cajoled[3] they will dance to your tune. I can understand your not permitting me to wear them. But what about my daughters-in-law? They will be sure to need them. And who knows what will happen tomorrow? I would be the last person to part with gifts so lovingly given.'

1. *exhorting: obtain by force, threats, or other unfair means*

2. *trustees: an individual or member of a board given powers of administration of property in trust with a legal obligation to administer it solely for the purposes specified*

3. *cajoled: persuade to do something by sustained coaxing or flattery*

And thus the torrent[1] of argument went on, reinforced, in the end, by tears. But the children were adamant. And I was unmoved.

I mildly put in: 'The children have yet to get married. We do not want to see them married young. When they are grown up, they can take care of themselves. And surely we shall not have, for our sons, brides who are fond of ornaments. And if after all, we need to provide them with ornaments, I am there. You will ask me then.' 'Ask you? I know you by this time. You deprived me of my ornaments, you would not leave me in peace with them. Fancy you offering to get ornaments for the daughters-in-law! You who are trying to make *sadhus* of my boys from today! No, the ornaments will not be returned. And pray what right have you to my necklace?'

'But,' I rejoined,' is the necklace given you for your service or for my service?'

'I agree. But service rendered by you is as good as rendered by me. I have toiled and moiled for you day and night. Is that no service? You forced all and sundry[2] on me, making me weep bitter tears, and I slaved for them!'

These were pointed thrusts[3], and some of them went home. But I was determined to return the ornaments. I somehow succeeded in extorting a consent from her. The gifts received in 1896 and 1901 were all returned. A trust-deed was prepared, and they were deposited with a bank, to be used for the service of the community, according to my wishes or to those of the trustees.

Often, when I was in need of funds for public purposes, and felt that I must draw upon the trust, I have been able to raise the requisite[4] amount, leaving the trust money intact. The fund is still there, being operated upon in times of need, and it has regularly accumulated[5].

I have never since regretted the step, and as the years have gone by, my wife has also seen its wisdom. It has saved us from many temptations.

I am definitely of opinion that a public worker should accept no costly gifts.

1. *torrent: an overwhelmingly copious outpouring*
2. *sundry: various items not important enough be mentioned individually*
3. *thrusts: push suddenly or violently in the specified direction*
4. *requisite: made necessary by particular circumstances or regulations*
5. *accumulated: gather together a number or quantity of; build up*

CHAPTER 67

IN INDIA AGAIN

So I sailed for home. Mauritius was one of the ports of call, and as the boat made a long halt[1] there, I went ashore and acquainted myself fairly well with the local conditions. For one night I was the guest of Sir Charles Bruce, the Governor of the Colony.

After reaching India I spent some time in going about the country. It was the year 1901 when the Congress met at Calcutta under the presidentship of Mr. (later Sir) Dinshaw Wacha. And I of course attended it. It was my first experience of the Congress. From Bombay I traveled in the same train as Sir Pherozeshah Mehta, as I had to speak to him about conditions in South Africa. I knew the kingly[2] style in which he lived. He had engaged a special saloon for himself, and I had orders to take my opportunity of speaking to him by traveling in his saloon for one stage. I, therefore, went to the saloon and reported myself at the appointed station. With him were Mr. Wacha, and Mr. (now Sir) Chimanlal Setalvad. They were discussing politics. As soon as Sir Pherozeshah saw me, he said, 'Gandhi, it seems nothing can be done for you. Of course we will pass the resolution you want. But what rights have we in our own country? I believe that, so long as we have no power in our own land, you cannot fare better in the colonies.' I was taken aback. Mr. Setalvad seemed to concur in the view; Mr. Wacha cast a pathetic look at me. I tried to plead with Sir Pherozeshah, but it was out of the question for one like me to prevail[3] upon the uncrowned king of Bombay. I contented myself with the fact that I should be allowed to move my resolution. You will of course show me the resolution,' said Mr. Wacha, to cheer me up. I thanked him and left them at the next stop. So we reached Calcutta. The President was taken to his camp with great *éclat* by the Reception Committee. I asked a volunteer where I was to go. He took me to the Ripon College, where a number of delegates were being put up. Fortune favoured me. Lokamanya was put up in the

1. *halt: bring or come to an abrupt stop*
2. *kingly: typical of a king*
3. *prevail: prove more powerful; be victorious; be widespread or current*

same block as I. I have a recollection that he came a day later. And as was natural, Lokamanya would never be without his darbar. Were I a painter, I could paint him as I saw him seated on his bed – so vivid is the whole scene in my memory. Of the numberless people that called on him, I can recollect today only one, namely the late Babu Motilal Ghose, editor of the *Amrita Bazar Patrika*. Their loud laughter and their talks about the wrong-doings of the ruling race cannot be forgotten. But I propose to examine in some detail the appointments in this camp. The volunteers were clashing against one another. You asked one of them to do something. He delegated it to another, and he in his turn to a third, and so on; and as for the delegates, they were neither here nor there. I made friends with a few volunteers. I told them some things about South Africa, and they felt somewhat ashamed. I tried to bring home to them the secret of service. They seemed to understand, but service is no mushroom[1] growth. It presupposes the will first, and then experience. There was no lack of will on the part of those good simple-hearted young men, but their experience was nil. The Congress would meet three days every year and then go to sleep. What training could one have out of a three days' show once a year? And the delegates were of a piece with the volunteers. They had no better or longer training. They would do nothing themselves. 'Volunteer, do this,' 'Volunteer, do that,' were their constant orders. Even here I was face to face with untouchability in a fair, measure. The Tamilian kitchen was far away from the rest. To the Tamil delegates even the sight of others, whilst they were dining, meant pollution. So a special kitchen had to be made for them in the college compound, walled in by wicker[2]-work. It was full of smoke which choked you. It was a kitchen, dining room, washroom, all in one – a close safe with no outlet. To me this looked like a travesty of *Varnadharma*[3].' If, I said to myself, there was such untouchability[4] between the delegates of the Congress, one could well imagine the extent to which it existed amongst their constituents. I heaved a sigh at the thought. There was no limit to insanitation. Pools of water were everywhere. There were only a few latrines, and the recollection of their stink still oppresses me. I pointed it out to the volunteers. They said pointblank: 'That is not our work, it is the scavenger's work.' I asked for a broom. The man stared at me in wonder. I procured one and cleaned the latrine. But that was

1. *mushroom: increase or develop rapidly*
2. *wicker: pliable twigs, typically of willow, plaited or woven to make items such as furniture and baskets*
3. *Varnadharma: duties of the four fundamental divisions of hindu society*
4. *untouchability: of or belonging to the lowest caste hindu group or the people outside the caste system; a member of the lowest caste hindu group, with whom contact is traditionally held to defile members of higher caste*

for myself. The rush was so great, and the latrines were so few, that they needed frequent cleaning; but that was more than I could do. So I had to content myself with simply ministering to myself. And the others did not seem to mind the stench and the dirt. But that was not all. Some of the delegates did not scruple to use the verandahs outside their rooms for calls of nature at night. In the morning I pointed out the spots to the volunteers. No one was ready to undertake the cleaning, and I found no one to share the honour with me of doing it. Conditions have since considerably improved, but even today thoughtless delegates are not wanting who disfigure[1] the Congress camp by committing nuisances wherever they choose, and all the volunteers are not always ready to clean up after them. I saw that, if the Congress session were to be prolonged, conditions would be quite favourable for the outbreak of an epidemic.

1. *disfigure: spoil the appearance of*

CHAPTER 68

CLERK AND BEARER

There were yet two days for the Congress session to begin. I had made up my mind to offer my services to the Congress office in order to gain some experience. So as soon as I had finished the daily ablutions on arrival at Calcutta, I proceeded to the Congress office.

Babu Bhupendranath Basu and Sjt. Ghosal were the secretaries. I went to Bhupenbabu and offered my services. He looked at me, and said: 'I have no work, but possibly Ghosalbabu might have something to give you. Please go to him.'

So I went to him. He scanned me and said with a smile: 'I can give you only clerical[1] work. Will you do it?'

'Certainly,' said I. 'I am here to do anything that is not beyond my capacity.'

'That is the right spirit, young man,' he said. Addressing the volunteers who surrounded him, he added, 'Do you hear what this young man says?'

Then turning to me he proceeded: 'Well then, here is a heap of letters for disposal. Take that chair and begin. As you see, hundreds of people come to see me. What am I to do? Am I to meet them, or am I to answer these busybodies inundating[2] me with letters? I have no clerks to whom I can entrust this work. Most of these letters have nothing in them, but you will please look them through. Acknowledge those that are worth it, and refer to me those that need a considered reply.'

I was delighted at the confidence reposed[3] in me.

Sjt. Ghosal did not know me when he gave me the work. Only later did he enquire about my credentials.

I found my work very easy - the disposal of that heap of correspondence. I had done with it in no time, and Sjt. Ghosal was very glad. He was talkative. He would talk away for hours together. When he learnt something from me about my history, he felt rather sorry to have given me clerical work. But I reassured him: 'Please don't worry. What am

1. *clerical: concerned with or relating to the routine work of an office clerk*
2. *inundating: overwhelm with things to be dealt with*
3. *reposed: place something, especially one's confidence or trust in*

I before you? You have grown gray in the service of the Congress, and are as an elder to me. I am but an inexperienced youth. You have put me under a debt of obligation by entrusting me with this work. For I want to do Congress work, and you have given me the rare opportunity of understanding the details.'

'To tell you the truth,' said Sjt. Ghosal, 'that is the proper spirit. But young men of today do not realize it. Of course I have known the Congress since its birth. In fact I may claim a certain share with Mr. Hume in bringing the Congress into being.'

And thus we became good friends. He insisted on my having lunch with him.

Sjt. Ghosal used to get his shirt buttoned by his bearer. I volunteered to do the bearer's duty, and I loved to do it, as my regard for elders was always great. When he came to know this, he did not mind my doing little acts of personal service for him. In fact he was delighted. Asking me to button his shirt, he would say, 'You see, now, the Congress secretary has no time even to button his shirt. He has always some work to do.' Sjt. Ghosal's naiveté amused me, but did not create any dislike in me for service of that nature. The benefit I received from this service in incalculable.

In a few days I came to know the working of the Congress. I met most of the leaders. I observed the movements of stalwarts like Gokhale and Surendranath. I also noticed the huge waste of time there. I observed too, with sorrow even then, the prominent[1] place that the English language occupied in our affairs. There was little regard for economy of energy. More than one did the work of one, and many an important thing was no one's business at all.

Critical as my mind was in observing these things, there was enough charity in me, and so I always thought that it might, after all, be impossible to do better in the circumstances, and that saved me from undervaluing any work.

1. *prominent: important; famous*

CHAPTER 69

IN THE CONGRESS

In the Congress at last. The immense pavilion and the volunteers in stately array, as also the elders seated on the dais, overwhelmed me. I wondered where I should be in that vast assemblage.

The presidential address was a book by itself. To read it from cover to cover was out of the question. Only a few passages were therefore read.

After this came the election of the Subjects Committee. Gokhale took me to the Committee meetings.

Sir Pherozeshah had of course agreed to admit my resolution, but I was wondering who would put it before the Subjects Committee, and when. For there were lengthy speeches to every resolution, all in English to boot, and every resolution had some well-known leader to back it. Mine was but a feeble[1] pipe amongst those veteran drums, and as the night was closing in, my heart beat fast. The resolutions coming at the fag-end were, so far as I can recollect, rushed through at lighting speed. Everyone was hurrying to go. It was eleven o'clock. I had not the courage to speak. I had already met Gokhale, who had looked at my resolution. So I drew near his chair and whispered to him: 'Please do something for me.' He said: 'Your resolution is not out of my mind.

You see the way they are rushing through the resolutions. But I will not allow yours to be passed over.'

'So we have done?' said Sir Pherozeshah Mehta.

'No, no, there is still the resolution on South Africa. Mr. Gandhi has been waiting long,' cried out Gokhale.

'Have you seen the resolution?' asked Sir Pherozeshah.

'Of course.'

'Do you like it?'

'It is quite good.'

'Well then, let us have it, Gandhi.'

1. *feeble: lacking physical strength; lacking strength of character; falling to convince or impress*

I read it trembling.

Gokhale supported it.

'Unanimously[1] passed,' cried out everyone.

'You will have five minutes to speak on it Gandhi,' said Mr. Wacha.

The procedure was far from pleasing to me. No one had troubled to understand the resolution, everyone was in a hurry to go and, because Gokhale had seen the resolution, it was not thought necessary for the rest to see it or understand it!

The morning found me worrying about my speech. What was I to say in five minutes? I had prepared myself fairly well but the words would not come to me. I had decided not to read my speech but to speak *extempore*. But the faculty for speaking that I had acquired in South Africa seemed to have left me for the moment.

As soon as it was time for my resolution, Mr. Wacha called out my name. I stood up. My head was reeling. I read the resolution somehow. Someone had printed and distributed amongst the delegates copies of a poem he had written in praise of foreign emigration. I read the poem[2] and referred to the grievances of the settlers in South Africa. Just at this moment Mr. Wacha rang the bell. I was sure I had not yet spoken for five minutes. I did not know that the bell was rung in order to warn me to finish in two minutes more. I had heard others speak for half an hour or three quarters of an hour, and yet no bell was rung for them. I felt hurt and sat down as soon as the bell was rung. But my childlike intellect thought then that the poem contained an answer to Sir Pherozeshah. There was no question about the passing of the resolution. In those days there was hardly any difference between visitors and delegates. Everyone raised his hand and all resolutions passed unanimously. My resolution also fared in this wise and so lost all its importance for me. And yet the very fact that it was passed by the Congress was enough to delight my heart, The knowledge that the *imprimatur* of the Congress meant that of the whole country was enough to delight anyone.

1. *unanimously: of one mind; without dissent*
2. *poem: a literary composition that is given intensity by particular attention to diction rhythm, and imagery*

CHAPTER 70

LORD CURZON'S DARBAR

The Congress was over, but as I had to meet the Chamber of Commerce and various people in connection with work in South Africa, I stayed in Calcutta for a month. Rather than stay this time in a hotel, I arranged to get the required introduction for a room in the India Club. Among its members were some prominent Indians, and I looked forward to getting into touch with them and interesting them in the work in South Africa. Gokhale frequently went to this Club to play billiards, and when he knew that I was to stay in Calcutta for some time, he invited me to stay with him, I thankfully accepted the invitation, but did not think it proper to go there by myself. He waited for a day or two and then took me personally. He discovered my reserve and said: 'Gandhi, you have to stay in the country, and this sort of reserve will not do. You must get into touch with as many people as possible. I want you to do Congress work.'

I shall record here an incident in the India Club, before I proceed to talk of my stay with Gokhale.

Lord Curzon held his darbar about this time. Some Rajas and Maharajas who had been invited to the darbar were members of the Club. In the Club I always found them wearing fine Bengali *dhotis* and shirts and scarves. On the darbar day they put on trousers befitting *khansamas*[1] and shining boots. I was pained and inquired of one of them the reason for the change.

'We alone know our unfortunate condition. We alone know the insults we have to put up with, in order that we may possess our wealth and titles,' he replied.

'But what about these *khansama* turbans and these shining[2] boots?' I asked.

'Do you see any difference between *khansamas* and us?' he replied, and added, 'they are our *khansamas*, we are Lord Cruzon's *khansamas*. If I were to absent myself from the *levée*, I should have to suffer the consequences.

1. *khansamas: waiters*

2. *shining: give out a bright light; glow with reflected light; direct somewhere; be bright with the expression of emotion*

If I were to attend it in my usual dress, it would be an offence. And do you think I am going to get any opportunity there of talking to Lord Curzon? Not a bit of it!'

I was moved to pity for this plain-spoken friend. This reminds me of another darbar.

At the time when Lord Hardinge laid the foundation stone of the Hindu[1] University, there was a darbar. There were Rajas and Maharajas of course, but Pandit Malaviyaji specially invited me also to attend it, and I did so.

I was distressed to see the Maharajas bedecked like women - silk *pyjamas* and silk *achkans*, pearl[2] necklaces round their necks, bracelets[3] on their wrists, pearl and diamond tassels on their turbans and besides all this swords with golden hilts[4] hanging from their waist-bands.

I discovered that these were insignia not of their royalty, but of their slavery. I had thought that they must be wearing these badges of impotence of their own free will, but I was told that it was obligatory for these Rajas to wear all their costly jewels at such functions. I also gathered that some of them had a positive dislike for wearing these jewels, and that they never wore them except on occasions like the darbar.

I do not know how far my information was correct. But whether they wear them on other occasions or not, it is distressing enough to have to attend viceregal darbars in jewels that only some women wear.

How heavy is the toll of sins and wrongs that wealth, power and prestige exact from man!

1. *Hindu: a major religious and cultural tradition of the indian subcontinent, including belief in reincarnation and the worship of a large pantheon of deities*
2. *bracelets: an ornamental band or chain worn on the wrist or arm*
3. *pearl: a hard, lustrous spherical mass, typically white or bluish-gray, formed within the shell of an oyster or other bivalve mollusk and highly prized as a gem; an artificial imitation of this*
4. *hilts: handle of a sword, dagger, weapon, tool*

CHAPTER 71

A MONTH WITH GOKHALE – I

From the very first day of my stay with him Gokhale made me feel completely at home. He treated me as though I were his younger brother, he acquainted himself with all my requirements and arranged to see that I got all I needed. Fortunately my wants were few, and as I had cultivated the habit of self-help, I needed very little personal attendance. He was deeply impressed with my habit of fending for myself, my personal cleanliness, perseverance and regularity, and would often overwhelm me with praise.

He seemed to keep nothing private[1] from me. He would introduce me to all the important people that called on him. Of these the one who stands foremost in my memory is Dr. (now Sir) P. C. Ray. He lived practically[2] next door and was a very frequent visitor.

This is how he introduced Dr. Ray: 'This is Professor Ray who having a monthly salary of Rs. 800, keeps just Rs. 40 for himself and devotes the balance to public purposes. He is not, and does not want to get, married.

I see little difference between Dr. Ray as he is today and as he used to be then. His dress used to be nearly as simple as it is, with this difference of course that whereas it is Khadi now, it used to be Indian mill[3]-cloth in those days. I felt I could never hear too much of the talks between Gokhale and Dr. Ray, as they all pertained to public good or were of educative value. At times they were painful too, containing as they did, strictures on public men. As a result, some of those whom I had regarded as stalwart fighters began to look quite puny[4].

To see Gokhale at work was as much a joy as an education. He never wasted a minute. His private relations and friendships were all for public good. All his talks had reference only to the good of the country and were absolutely free from any trace of untruth or insincerity. India's poverty and subjection were matters of constant and intense concern to him. Various people sought to interest him in different things. But he gave

1. *private: for or belonging to one particular person or group only; not to be shared or revealed; not choosing to share their thoughts and feelings; secluded; alone and undisturbed by others*
2. *practically: so nearly the case that it can be regarded as so; virtual*
3. *mill: a building fitted with machinery for a manufacturing process; a steel mill; a piece of manufacturing machinery*
4. *puny: small and weak*

every one of them the same reply: 'You do the thing yourself. Let me do my own work. What I want is freedom for my country. After that is won, we can think of other things. Today that one thing is enough to engage all my time and energy.'

His reverence for Ranade could be seen every moment. Ranade's authority was final in every matter, and he would cite[1] it at every step. The anniversary of Ranade's death (or birth, I forget which) occurred during my stay with Gokhale, who observed it regularly. There were with him then, besides myself, his friends Professor Kathavate and a Sub-Judge. He invited us to take part in the celebration, and in his speech he gave us his reminiscences of Ranade. He compared incidentally Ranade, Telang and Mandlik. He eulogized Telang's charming style and Mandlik's greatness as a reformer. Citing an instance of Mandlik's solicitude for his clients, he told us an anecdote as to how once, having missed his usual train, he engaged a special train so as to be able to attend the court in the interest of his client. But Ranade, he said, towered[2] above them all, as a versatile genius. He was not only a great judge, he was an equally great historian[3], economist and reformer[4]. Although he was a judge, he fearlessly attended the Congress, and everyone had such confidence in his sagacity that they unquestioningly accepted his decisions. Gokhale's joy knew no bounds, as he described these qualities of head and heart which were all combined in his master.

Gokhale used to have a horse-carriage in those days. I did not know the circumstances that had made a horse-carriage a necessity for him, and so I remonstrated with him: 'Can't you make use of the tramcar in going about from place to place? Is it derogatory to a leader's dignity?'

Slightly pained he said, 'So you also have failed to understand me! I do not use my Council allowances for my own personal comforts. I envy your liberty to go about in tramcars, but I am sorry I cannot do likewise. When you are the victim of as wide a publicity as I am, it will be difficult, if not impossible, for you to go about in a tramcar. There is no reason to suppose that everything that the leaders do is with a view to personal comfort. I love your simple habits. I live as simply as I can, but some expense is almost inevitable for a man like myself.'

He thus satisfactorily disposed of one of my complaints, but there was another which he could not dispose of to my satisfaction.

1. *cite: quote as evidence for an argument*
2. *towered: very important or influential*
3. *historian: an expert in or student of history*
4. *reformer: a disputant who advocates reform*

'But you do not even go out for walks,' said I. 'Is it surprising that you should be always ailing[1]? Should public work leave no time for physical exercise?'

'When do you ever find me free to go out for a walk?' he replied.

I had such a great regard for Gokhale that I never strove with him. Though this reply was far from satisfying me, I remained silent. I believed then and I believe even now, that, no matter what amount of work one has, one should always find some time for exercise, just as one does for one's meals. It is my humble opinion that, far from taking away from one's capacity for work, it adds to it.

1. *ailing: trouble or afflict in mind or body*

CHAPTER 72

A MONTH WITH GOKHALE - II

Whilst living under Gokhlae's roof I was far from being a stay-at-home.

I had told my Christian friends in South Africa that in India I would meet the Christian Indians and acquaint myself with their condition. I had heard of Babu Kalicharan Banerji and held him in high regard. He took a prominent part in the Congress, and I had none of the misgivings[1] about him that I had about the average Christian Indian, who stood aloof from the Congress and isolated himself from Hindus and Musalmans. I told Gokhale that I was thinking of meeting him. He said: 'What is good of your seeing him? He is a very good man, but I am afraid he will not satisfy you. I know him very well. However, you can certainly meet him if you like?.'

I sought an appointment, which he readily gave me. When I went, I found that his wife was on her death-bed. His house was simple. In the Congress I had seen him in a coat and trousers, but I was glad to find him now wearing a Bengal *dhoti* and shirt. I liked his simple mode of dress, though I myself then wore a Parsi coat and trousers. Without much ado I presented my difficulties to him. He asked: 'Do you believe in the doctrine of original sin?'

'I do,' said I.

'Well then, Hinduism offers no absolution therefrom, Christianity does, and added: The wages of sin is death, and the Bible says that the only way of deliverance is surrender unto Jesus.'

I put forward *Bhakti-marga* (the path of devotion) of the *Bhagavad Gita*, but to no avail. I thanked him for his goodness. He failed to satisfy me, but I benefited by the interview.

During these days I walked up and down the streets of Calcutta. I went to most places on foot. I met Justice Mitter and Sir Gurdas Banerji, whose help I wanted in my work in South Africa. And about this time I met Raja Sir Pyarimohan Mukarji.

1. *misgivings: a feeling of doubt of apprehension about something*

Kalicharan Banerji had spoken to me about the Kali temple, which I was eager to see, especially as I had read about it in books. So I went there one day, Justice Mitter's house was in the same locality, and I therefore went to the temple on the same day that I visited him. On the way I saw a stream of sheep going to be sacrificed to Kali. Rows of beggars lined the lane leading to the temple. There were religious mendicants[1] too, and even in those days I was sternly opposed to giving alms to sturdy[2] beggars. A crowd of them pursued me. One of such men was found seated on a verandah. He stopped me, and accosted[3] me: 'Whither are you going, my boy?' I replied to him.

He asked my companion and me to sit down, which we did.

I asked him: 'Do you regard this sacrifice as religion?'

'Who would regard killing of animals as rcligion?'

'Then, why don't you preach against it?'

'That's not my business. Our business is to worship God.'

'But could you not find any other place in which to worship God?'

'All places are equally good for us. The people are like a flock of sheep, following where leaders lead them. It is no business of us *sadhus*.'

We did not prolong the discussion but passed on to the temple. We were greeted by rivers of blood. I could not bear to stand there. I was exasperated and restless. I have never forgotten that sight.

That very evening I had an invitation to dinner at a party of Bengali friends. There I spoke to a friend about this cruel form of worship. He said: 'The sheep don't feel anything. The noise and the drum-beating there deaden all sensation of pain.'

I could not swallow this. I told him that, if the sheep had speech, they would tell a different tale. I felt that the cruel custom ought to be stopped. I thought of the story of Buddha, but I also saw that the task was beyond my capacity.

I hold today the same opinion as I held then. To my mind the life of a lamb is no less precious than that of a human being. I should be unwilling to take the life of a lamb for the sake of the human body. I hold that, the more helpless a creature, the more entitled is to protection by man from the cruelty of man. But he who has not qualified himself for such service is unable to afford to it any protection. I must go through more

1. *mendicants: a beggar; a member of a mendicant order*
2. *sturdy: strongly and solidly built or made; confident and determined; a sturdy independence*
3. *accosted: approach and address boldly or aggressively*

self-purification and sacrifice. before I can hope to save these lambs from this unholy sacrifice. It is my constant prayer that there may be born on earth some great spirit, man or woman, fired with divine pity, who will deliver us from this heinous sin, save the lives of the innocent creatures, and purify the temple. How is it that Bengal with all its knowledge, intelligence, sacrifice, and emotion tolerates[1] this slaughter[2]?

1. *tolerates: allow the existence or occurrence of without interference*
2. *slaughter: the killing of farm animals for food*

CHAPTER 73

A MONTH WITH GOKHALE - III

The terrible sacrifice offered to Kali in the name of religion enhanced my desire to know Bengali life. I had read and heard a good deal about the Brahmo Samaj. I knew something about the life of Pratap Chandra Mazumdar. I had attended some of the meetings addressed by him. I secured his life of Keshav Chandra Sen, read it with great interest, and understood the distinction between Sadharan Brahmo Samaj, and Adi Brahmo Samaj. I met Pandit Shivanath Shastri and in company with Professor Kathavate went to see Maharshi Devendranath Tagore, but as no interviews with him were allowed then, we could not see him. We were, however, invited to a celebration of the Brahmo Samaj held at his place, and there we had the privilege of listening to fine Bengali music. Ever since I have been a lover of Bengali music.

Having seen enough of the Brahmo Samaj, it was impossible to be satisfied without seeing Swami Vivekanand. So with great enthusiasm I went to Belur Math, mostly, or maybe all the way, on foot. I loved the sequestered site of the Math. I was disappointed and sorry to be told that the Swami was at his Calcutta house, lying ill, and could not be seen.

I then ascertained the place of residence of Sister Nivedita, and met her in a Chowringhee mansion. I was taken aback by the splendour[1] that surrounded her, and even in our conversation there was not much meeting ground. I spoke to Gokhale about this, and he said he did not wonder that there could be no point of contact between me and a volatile person like her.

I met her again at Mr. Pestonji Padshah's place. I happened to come in just as she was talking to his old mother, and so I became an interpreter between the two. In spite of my failure to find any agreement with her, I could not but notice and admire her overflowing love for Hinduism. I came to know of her books later.

I used to divide my day between seeing the leading people in Calcutta regarding the work in South Africa, and visiting and studying the religious

1. *splendour: splendid appearance*

and public institutions of the city. I once addressed a meeting, presided over by Dr. Mullick, on the work of the Indian Ambulance Corps in the Boer War. My acquaintance with *The Englishman* stood me in good stead on this occasion too. Mr. Saunders was ill then, but rendered me as much help as in 1896. Gokhale liked this speech of mine, and he was very glad to hear Dr. Ray praising it.

Thus my stay under the roof of Gokhale made my work in Calcutta very easy, brought me into touch with the foremost Bengali families, and was the beginning of my intimate contact with Bengal.

I must needs skip over many a reminiscence of this memorable month. Let me simply mention my flying visit to Burma, and the *foongis*[1] there. I was pained by their lethargy[2]. I saw the golden pagoda. I did not like the innumerable[3] little candles burning in the temple, and the rats running about the sanctum brought to my mind thoughts of Swami Dayanand's experience at Morvi. The freedom and energy of the Burmese women charmed just as the indolence[4] of the men pained me. I also saw, during my brief sojourn, that just as Bombay was not India, Rangoon was not Burma, and that just as we in India have become commission agents of English merchants, even so in Burma have we combined with the English merchants, in making the Burmese people our commission agents.

On my return from Burma I took leave of Gokhale. The separation was a wrench, but my work in Bengal, or rather Calcutta, was finished, and I had no occasion to stay any longer.

Before settling down I had thought of making a tour through India travelling third class, and acquainting myself with the hardships of third class passengers. I spoke to Gokhale about this. To begin with he ridiculed the idea, but when I explained to him what I hoped to see, he cheerfully approved. I planned to go first to Benares to pay my respects to Mrs. Besant, who was then ill.

It was necessary to equip myself anew for the third class tour. Gokhale himself gave me a metal tiffin-box and got it filled with sweet-balls and *puris*. I purchased a canvas bag worth twelve annas and a long coat made of Chhaya[5] wool. The bag was to contain this coat, a *dhoti*, a towel and a shirt. I had a blanket as well to cover myself with and a water jug. Thus equipped I set forth on my travels, Gokhale and Dr. Ray came to the station to see me off. I had asked them both not to trouble to come,

1. *foongis: monks*
2. *lethargy: a lack of energy and enthusiasm*
3. *innumerable: too many to be counted*
4. *indolence: laziness avoiding activities*
5. *Chhaya: a place in porbandar state noted for its coarse woolen fabrics*

but they insisted. "I should not have come if you had gone first class, but now I had to,' said Gokhale.

No one stopped Gokhale from going on to the platform. He was in his silk[1] turban, jacket and *dhoti*. Dr. Ray was in his Bengali dress. He was stopped by the ticket collector, but on Gokhale telling him that he was his friend, he was admitted.

Thus with their good wishes I started on my journey.

1. *silk: a fine, strong, soft lustrous fiber produced by silkworms in making cocoons*

CHAPTER 74

IN BENARES

The journey was from Calcutta to Rajkot, and I planned to halt at Benares, Agra, Jaipur and Palanpur *en route*. I had not the time to see any more places than these. In each city I stayed one day and put up in *dharmashalas* or with *pandas*[1] like the ordinary pilgrims, excepting at Palanpur. So far as I can remember, I did not spend more than Rs. 31 (including the train fare) on this journey.

In travelling third class I mostly preferred the ordinary to the mail trains, as I knew that the latter were more crowded and the fares in them higher.

The third class compartments are practically as dirty, and the closet arrangements as bad, today as they were then, There may be a little improvement now, but the difference between the facilities provided for the first and the third classes is out of all proportion to the difference between the fares for the two classes. Third class passengers are treated like sheep and their comforts are sheep's comforts. In Europe I travelled third and only once first, just to see what it was like but there I noticed no such difference between the first and the third classes. In South Africa third class passengers are mostly negros, yet the third class comforts are better there than here. In parts of South Africa third class compartments are provided with sleeping accommodation and cushioned seats. The accommodation is also regulated, so as to prevent overcrowding, whereas here I have found the regulation limit usually exceeded.

The indifference of the railway authorities to the comforts of the third class passengers, combined with the dirty and inconsiderate habits of the passengers themselves, makes third class travelling a trial for a passenger of cleanly ways. These unpleasant habits commonly include throwing of rubbish on the floor of the compartment, smoking at all hours and in all places, betel and tobacco chewing, converting of the whole carriage into a spittoon, shouting and yelling, and using foul language, regardless

1. *pandas: priests*

of the convenience or comfort of fellow passengers. I have noticed little difference between my experience of the third class travelling in 1902 and that of my unbroken third class tours from 1915 to 1919.

I can think of only one remedy for this awful state of things that educated men should make a point of travelling third class and reforming the habits of the people, as also of never letting the railway authorities rest in peace, sending in complaints wherever necessary, never resorting to bribes or any unlawful means for obtaining their own comforts, and never putting up with infringements of rules on the part of anyone concerned. This, I am sure, would bring about considerable improvement.

My serious illness in 1918–19 has unfortunately compelled me practically to give up third class travelling, and it has been a matter of constant pain and shame to me, especially because the disability came at a time when the agitation for the removal of the hardships of third class passengers was making fair headway. The hardships of poor railway and steamship passengers, accentuated by their bad habits, the undue facilities allowed by Government to foreign trade, and such other things, make an important group of subjects, worthy to be taken up by one or two enterprising workers who could devote their full time to it.

But I shall leave the third class passengers at that, and come to my experience in Benares. I arrived there in the morning. I had decided to put up with a *panda*. Numerous Brahmans surrounded me, as soon as I got out of the train, and I selected one who struck me to be comparatively cleaner and better than the rest. It proved to be a good choice. There was a cow in the courtyard of his house and an upper storey where I was given a lodging. I did not want to have any food without ablution in the Ganges in the proper orthodox[1] manner. The *panda* made preparations for it. I had told him beforehand that on no account could I give him more than a rupee and four annas as *dakshina*[2], and that he should therefore keep this in mind while making the preparations.

The *panda* readily assented. 'Be the pilgrim rich or poor,' said he, 'the service is the same in every case. But the amount of *dakshina* we receive depends upon the will and the ability of the pilgrim.' I did not find that the *panda* at all abridged the usual formalities in my case. The *puja*[3] was over at twelve o'clock, and I went to the Kashi Vishvanath temple for *darshan*. I was deeply pained by what I saw there. When practising

1. *orthodox: conforming with traditional or generally accepted beliefs*
2. *dakshina: gift*
3. *puja: worship*

as a barrister in Bombay in 1891. I had occasion to attend a lecture on 'Pilgrimage to Kashi' in the Prarthana Samaj hall. I was therefore prepared for some measure of disappointment. But the actual disappointment was greater than I had bargained for.

The approach was through a narrow and slippery[1] lane. Quiet there was none. The swarming flies and the noise made by the shopkeepers and pilgrims were perfectly insufferable[2].

Where one expected an atmosphere of meditation and communion[3] it was conspicuous by its absence. One had to seek that atmosphere in oneself. I did observe devout[4] sisters, who were absorbed in meditation, entirely unconscious of the environment. But for this the authorities of the temple could scarcely claim any credit. The authorities should be responsible for creating and maintaining about the temple a pure sweet and serene atmosphere, physical as well as moral. Instead of this I found a *bazar* where cunning shopkeepers were selling sweets and toys of the latest fashion.

When I reached the temple. I was greeted at the entrance by a stinking mass of rotten flowers. The floor was paved with fine marble, which was however broken by some devotee innocent of aesthetic taste who had set it with rupees serving as an excellent receptacle for dirt.

I went near the *Jnana-vapi* (Well of knowledge). I searched here for God but failed to find Him. I was not therefore in a particularly good mood. The surroundings of the *Jnana-vapi* too I found to be dirty. I had no mind to give any *dakshina*. So I offered a pie. The *panda* in charge got angry and threw away the pie. He swore at me and said, 'This insult will take you straight to hell.'

This did not perturb me. 'Maharaj,' said I, 'whatever fate has in store for me, it does not behove one of your class to indulge in such language. You may take this pie if you like, or you will lose that too.'

'Go away,' he replied, 'I don't care for your pie.' And then followed a further volley of abuse.

I took up the pie and went my way, flattering myself that the Brahman had lost a pie and I had saved one. But the Maharaj was hardly the man to let the pie go. He called me back and said, 'All right, leave the pie here, I would rather not be as you are. If I refuse your pie, it will be bad for you.'

1. *slippery: difficult to hold firmly or stand on through being smooth, wet, or slimy*
2. *insufferable: intolerable; unbearably arrogant or conceited*
3. *communion: the sharing or exchanging of intimate thoughts and feelings*
4. *devout: having or showing deep religious feeling or commitment*

I silently gave him the pie and, with a sigh, went away.

Since then I have twice been to Kashi Vishvanath, but that has been after I had already been afflicted with the title of *Mahatma* and experiences such as I have detailed above had become impossible. People eager to have my *darshan* would not permit me to have a *darshan* of the temple. The woes of *Mahatmas* are known to *Mahatmas* alone. Otherwise the dirt and the noise were the same as before.

If anyone doubts the infinite[1] mercy of God, let him have a look at these sacred places. How much hypocrisy and irreligion[2] does the Prince of Yogis suffer to be perpetrated in His holy name? He proclaimed long ago:

ये यथा मां प्रपद्यन्ते तांस्तथैव भजाम्यहम्।

'Whatever a man sows, that shall he reap.' The law of Karma is inexorable and impossible of evasion. There is thus hardly any need for God to interfere. He laid down the Law and, as it were, retired.

After this visit to the temple, I waited upon Mrs. Besant. I knew that she had just recovered from an illness. I sent in my name. She came at once. As I wished only to pay my respects to her, I said, 'I am aware that you are in delicate health. I only wanted to pay my respects. I am thankful that you have been good enough to receive me in spite of your indifferent health. I will not detain[3] you any longer.'

So saying, I took leave of her.

1. *infinite: limitless in space, extent, or size; very great in amount or degree*
2. *irreligion: hostile to religion*
3. *detain: keep from proceeding by holding them back or making claims on their attention*

CHAPTER 75

SETTLED IN BOMBAY

Gokhale was very anxious that I should settle down in Bombay, practise at the bar and help him in public work. Public work in those days meant Congress work, and the chief work of the institution which he had assisted to found was carrying on the Congress administration.

I liked Gokhale's advice, but I was not overconfident of success as a barrister. The unpleasant memories of past failure were yet with me, and I still hated as poison the use of flattery for getting briefs.

I therefore decided to start work first at Rajkot. Kevalram Mavji Dave, my old well-wisher, who had induced me to go to England, was there, and he started me straightaway with three briefs. Two of them were appeals before the Judicial Assistant to the Political Agent in Kathiawad and one was an original case in Jamnagar. This last was rather important. On my saying that I could not trust myself to do it justice, Kevalram Dave exclaimed: 'Winning or losing is no concern of yours. You will simply try your best, and I am of course there to assist you.'

The counsel[1] on the other side was the late Sjt. Samarth. I was fairly well prepared. Not that I knew much of Indian law, but Kevalram Dave had instructed me very thoroughly. I had heard friends say, before I went out to South Africa, that Sir Pherozeshah Mehta had the law of evidence at his finger-tips and that was the secret of his success. I had borne[2] this in mind, and during the voyage had carefully studied the Indian Evidence Act with commentaries thereon. There was of course also the advantage of my legal experience in South Africa.

I won the case and gained some confidence. I had no fear about the appeals, which were successful. All this inspired a hope in me that after all I might not fail even in Bombay.

But before I set forth the circumstances in which I decided to go to Bombay, I shall narrate my experience of the inconsiderateness and ignorance of English officials. The Judicial Assistant's court was peripatetic.

1. *counsel: a barrister or other legal adviser conducting a case*

2. *borne: carried or transported by the thing specified*

He was constantly touring, and vakils and their clients had to follow him wherever he moved his camp. The vakils would charge more whenever they had to go out of headquarters, and so the clients had naturally to incur[1] double the expenses. The inconvenience was no concern of the judge.

The appeal of which I am talking was to be heard at Veraval where plague was raging. I have a recollection that there were as many as fifty cases daily in the place with a population of 5,500. It was practically deserted, and I put up in a deserted *dharamshala* at some distance from the town. But where were the clients to stay? If they were poor, they had simply to trust themselves to God's mercy.

A friend who also had cases before the court had wired that I should put in an application for the camp to be moved to some other station because of the plague at Veraval. On my submitting the application, the sahib asked me. 'Are you afraid?'

I answered: 'It is not a question of my being afraid. I think I can shift for myself, but what about the clients?'

'The plague has come to stay in India,' replied the sahib. 'Why fear it? The climate of Veraval is lovely. (The sahib lived far away from the town in a palatial[2] tent[3] pitched on the seashore.] Surely people must learn to live thus in the open.'

It was no use arguing against this philosophy. The sahib told his shirastedar: 'Make a note of what Mr. Gandhi says, and let me know if it is very inconvenient for the vakils or the clients.'

The sahib of course had honestly done what he thought was the right thing. But how could the man have an idea of the hardships of poor India? How was he to understand the needs, habits, idiosyncrasies[4] and customs of the people? How was one, accustomed to measure things in gold sovereigns, all at once to make calculations in tiny bits of copper? As the elephant is powerless to think in the terms of the ant, in spite of the best intentions in the world, even so is the Englishman powerless to think in the terms of, or legislate for, the Indian.

But to resume the thread of story. In spite of my successes, I had been thinking of staying on in Rajkot for some time longer, when one day Kevalram Dave came to me and said: 'Gandhi, we will not suffer you to vegetate here. You must settle in Bombay.'

1. *incur: become subject to as a result of one's actions*
2. *palatial: resembling a palace, especially in being spacious or grand*
3. *tent: a portable shelter made of cloth supported by one or more poles and starched tight by cords or loops attached to pegs driven into ground*
4. *idiosyncrasies: a mode of behavioror way of thought peculiar to an individual, a distinctive characteristic of a thing*

'But who will find work for me there?' I asked. 'Will you find the expenses?'

'Yes, yes, I will,' said he. 'We shall bring you down here sometimes as a big barrister from Bombay and drafting work we shall send you there. It lies with us vakils to make or mar a barrister. You have proved your worth in Jamnagar and Veraval, and I have therefore not the least anxiety about you. You are destined to do public work, and we will not allow you to be buried in Kathiawad. So tell me, then, when you will go to Bombay.'

'I am expecting a remittance[1] from Natal. As soon as I get it I will go,' I replied.

The money came in about two weeks, and I went to Bombay. I took chambers in Payne, Gilbert and Sayani's offices, and it looked as though I had settled down.

1. *remittance: a sum of money remitted; the action of remitting money*

CHAPTER 76

FAITH ON ITS TRIAL

Though I had hired chambers in the Fort and a house in Girgaum, God would not let me settle down. Scarcely had I moved into my new house when my second son Manilal, who had already been through an acute attack of smallpox[1] some years back, had a severe attack of typhoid, combined with pneumonia[2] and signs of delirium[3] at night.

The doctor was called in. He said medicine would have little effect, but eggs and chicken broth might be given with profit.

Manilal was only ten years old. To consult his wishes was out of the question. Being his guardian I had to decide. The doctor was a very good Parsi. I told him that we were all vegetarians and that I could not possibly give either of the two things to my son. Would he therefore recommend something else?

'Your son's life is in danger,' said the good doctor. 'We could give him milk diluted with water, but that will not give him enough nourishment. As you know, I am called in by many Hindu families, and they do not object to anything I prescribe. I think you will be well advised not to be so hard on your son.'

'What you say is quite right,' said I. 'As a doctor you could not do otherwise. But my responsibility is very great. If the boy had been grown up, I should certainly have tried to ascertain his wishes and respected them. But here I have to think and decide for him. To my mind it is only on such occasions, that a man's faith is truly tested Rightly or wrongly it is part of my religious conviction that man may not eat meat, eggs, and the like. There should be a limit even to the means of keeping ourselves alive. Even for itself we may not so certain things. Religion, as I understand it, does not permit me to use meat or eggs for me or mine even on occasions like this, and I must therefore take the risk that you say is likely. But I beg of you one thing. As I cannot avail myself of your treatment, I propose to try some hydropathic remedies which I happen

1. *smallpox: an acute contagious viral disease, with fever and pustules usually leaving permanent scars*
2. *pneumonia: a lung infection in which the air sacs is fulled with pus*
3. *delirium: in a state of wild excitement or ecstasy*

to know. But I shall not know how to examine[1] the boy's pulse, chest, lungs, etc. If you will kindly look in from time to time to examine him and keep me informed of his condition, I shall be grateful to you.'

The good doctor appreciated my difficulty and agreed to my request. Though Manilal could not have made his choice, I told him what had passed between the doctor and myself and asked him his opinion.

'Do try your hydropathic treatment,' he said. 'I will not have eggs or chicken broth.'

This made me glad, though I realized that, if I had given him either of these, he would have taken it.

I knew Kuhne's treatment and had tried it too. I knew as well that fasting also could be tried with profit. So I began to give Manilal hip baths according to Kuhne, never keeping him in the tub for more than three minutes, and kept him on orange juice mixed with water for three days.

But the temperature persisted[2], going up to 104. At night he would be delirious. I began to get anxious. What would people say of me? What would my elder brother think of me? Could we not call in another doctor? Why not have an Ayurvedic physician? What right had the parents to inflict their fads on their children?

I was haunted by thoughts like these. Then a contrary current would start. God would surely be pleased to see that I was giving the same treatment to my son as I would give myself. I had faith in hydropathy[3], and little faith in allopathy. The doctors could not guarantee recovery. At best they could experiment. The thread of life was in the hands of God. Why not trust it to Him and in His name go on with what I thought was the right treatment?

My mind was torn between these conflicting thoughts. It was night. I was in Manilal's bed lying by his side. I decided to give him a wet sheet pack. I got up, wetted a sheet, wrung the water out of it and wrapped it about Manilal, keeping only his head out and then covered him with two blankets. To the head I applied a wet towel. The whole body was burning like hot iron, and quite parched. There was absolutely no perspiration.

I was sorely tired. I left Manilal in the charge of his mother, and went out for a walk on Chaupati to refresh myself. It was about ten o'clock. Very few pedestrians were out. Plunged in deep thought, I scarcely

1. *examine: inspect (someone or something) thoroughly in order to determine their nature or condition*
2. *persisted: continue to exist; be prolonged*
3. *hydropathy: the treatment of illness through the use of water, either internally or through external means such as steam baths (not now a part of orthodox medicine)*

looked at them, 'My honour is in Thy keeping oh Lord, in this hour of trial,' I repeated to myself. *Ramanama* was on my lips. After a short time I returned, my heart beating within my breast.

No sooner had I entered the room than Manilal said, 'You have returned, Bapu?'

'Yes, darling.'

'Do please pull me out. I am burning.'

'Are you perspiring, my boy?'

'I am simply soaked. Do please take me out.'

I felt his forehead. It was covered with beads of perspiration. The temperature was going down. I thanked God.

'Manilal, your fever is sure to go now. A little more perspiration and then I will take you out.'

'Pray, no. Do deliver me from this furnace. Wrap me some other time if you like.'

I just managed to keep him under the pack for a few minutes more by diverting[1] him. The perspiration streamed down his forehead. I undid the pack and dried his body. Father and son fell asleep in the same bed.

And each slept like a log. Next morning Manilal had much less fever. He went on thus for forty days on diluted milk and fruit juices. I had no fear now. It was an obstinate type of fever, but it had been got under control.

Today Manilal is the healthiest of my boys. Who can say whether his recovery was due to God's grace, or to hydropathy, or to careful dietary and nursing? Let everyone decide according to his own faith. For my part I was sure that God had saved my honour, and that belief remains unaltered to this day.

1. *diverting: entertaining or amusing*

CHAPTER 77

TO SOUTH AFRICA AGAIN

Manilal was restored to health, but I saw that the Girgaum house was not habitable[1]. It was damp and ill-lighted. So in consultation with Shri Revashankar Jagjivan I decided to hire some well-ventilated bungalow in a suburb of Bombay. I wandered about in Bandra and Santa Cruz. The slaughter house in Bandra prevented our choice falling there. Ghatkopar and places near it were too far from the sea. At last we hit upon a fine bungalow in Santa Cruz. which we hired as being the best from the point of view of sanitation.

I took a first class season ticket from Santa Cruz to Churchgate, and remember having frequently felt a certain pride in being the only first class passenger in my compartment. Often I walked to Bandra in order to take the fast train from there direct to Churchgate.

I prospered in my profession better than I had expected. My South African clients often entrusted me with some work, and it was enough to enable me to pay my way.

I had not yet succeeded in securing any work in the High Court, but I attended the 'moot' that used to be held in those days, though I never ventured to take part in it. I recall Jamiatram Nanabhai taking a prominent part. Like other fresh barristers I made a point of attending the hearing of cases in the High Court, more, I am afraid, for enjoying the soporific breeze coming straight from the sea than for adding to my knowledge. I observed that I was not the only one to enjoy this pleasure. It seemed to be the fashion and therefore nothing to be ashamed of.

However I began to make use of the High Court library and make fresh acquaintances and felt that before long I should secure work in the High Court.

Thus whilst on the one hand I began to feel somewhat at ease about my profession, on the other hand Gokhale, whose eyes were always on me, had been busy making his own plans on my behalf. He peeped[2] in at my chambers twice or thrice every week, often in company with friends

1. *habitable: suitable to live in*

2. *peeped: look quickly and furtively*

whom he wanted me to know, and he kept me acquainted with his mode[1] of work.

But it may be said that God has never allowed any of my own plans to stand. He has disposed them in His own way.

Just when I seemed to be settling down as I had intended I received an unexpected cable from South Africa: 'Chamberlain expected here. Please return immediately.' I remembered my promise and cabled to say that I should be ready to start the moment they put me in funds. They promptly responded, I gave up the chambers and started for South Africa.

I had an idea that the work there would keep me engaged for at least a year, so I kept the bungalow and left my wife and children there.

I believed then that enterprising[1] youths who could not find an opening in the country should emigrate to other lands. I therefore took with me four or five such youths, one of whom was Maganlal Gandhi.

The Gandhis were and are a big family. I wanted to find out all those who wished to leave the trodden path and venture abroad. My father used to accommodate a number of them in some state service. I wanted them to be free from this spell. I neither could nor would secure other service for them; I wanted them to be self-reliant.

But as my ideals advanced, I tried to persuade these youths also to conform their ideals to mine, and I had the greatest success in guiding Maganlal Gandhi. But about this later.

The separation from wife and children, the breaking up of a settled establishment, and the going from the certain to the uncertain - all this was for a moment painful, but I had inured myself to an uncertain life. I think it is wrong to expect certainties in this world, where all else but God that is Truth is an uncertainty. All that appears and happens about and around us is uncertain transient. But there is a Supreme Being hidden therein as a Certainty, and one would be blessed if one could catch a glimpse of that Certainty and hitch one's wagon to it. The quest for that Truth is the *summum bonum* of life.

I reached Durban not a day too soon. There was work waiting for me. The date for the deputation[3] to wait on Mr. Chamberlain had been fixed. I had to draft the memorial to be submitted to him and accompany the deputation.

1. *mode: a way in which something occurs or is done; a way of operating a system; any of the kinds or patterns of vibration of an oscillating system; the character of a modal proposition; another term for mood*
2. *enterprising: showing initiative and resourcefulness*
3. *deputation: a group of people who undertake a mission on behalf of a larger group*

CHAPTER 78

'LOVE'S LABOUR'S LOST'?

Mr. Chamberlain had come to get a gift of 35 million pounds from South Africa, and to win the hearts of Englishmen and Boers. So he gave a cold shoulder to the Indian deputation.

'You know,' he said 'that the Imperial Government has little control over self-governing Colonies. Your grievances seem to be genuine. I shall do what I can, but you must try your best to placate the Europeans, if you wish to live in their midst.'

The reply cast a chill over the members of the deputation. I was also disappointed. It was an eye-opener for us all, and I saw that we should start with our work *de novo*. I explained the situation to my colleagues.

As a matter of fact there was nothing wrong about Mr. Chamberlain's reply. It was well that he did not mince matters. He had brought home to us in a rather gentle way the rule of might being right or the law of the sword.

But sword we had none. We scarcely had the nerve and the muscle even to receive sword-cuts.

Mr. Chamberlain had given only a short time to the sub-continent. If Shrinagar to Cape Comorin is 1,900 miles, Durban to Capetown is not less than 1,100 miles, and Mr. Chamberlain had to cover the long distance at hurricane[1] speed.

From Natal he hastened to the Transvaal. I had to prepare the case for the Indians there as well and submit it to him. But how was I to get to Pretoria? Our people there were not in a position to procure the necessary legal facilities for my getting to them in time. The War had reduced the Transvaal to a howling wilderness. There were neither provisions nor clothing available. Empty or closed shops were there, waiting to be replenished[2] or opened, but that was a matter of time. Even refugees could not be allowed to return until the shops were ready with provisions.

1. *hurricane: a storm with a violent wind, in particular a tropical cyclone in the caribbean*

2. *replenished: fill up again*

Every Transvaaller had therefore to obtain a permit. The European had no difficulty in getting one, but the Indian found it very hard.

During the War many officers and soldiers had come to South Africa from India and Ceylon, and it was considered to be the duty of the British authorities to provide for such of them as decided to settle there. They had in any event to appoint new officers, and these experienced men came in quite handy. The quick ingenuity[1] of some of them created a new department. It showed their resourcefulness. There was a special department for the negroes. Why then should there not be one for the Asiatics? The argument seemed to be quite plausible[2]. When I reached the Transvaal, this new department had already been opened and was gradually spreading its tentacles[3]. The officers who issued permits to the returning refugees might issue them to all, but how could they do so in respect of the Asiatics without the intervention of the new department? And if the permits were to be issued on the recommendation of the new department, some of the responsibility and burden of the permit officers could thus be lessened. This was how they had argued. The fact, however, was that the new department wanted some apology for work, and the men wanted money. If there had been no work, the department would have been unnecessary and would have been discontinued. So they found this work for themselves.

The Indians had to apply to this department. A reply would be vouchsafed many days after. And as there were large numbers wishing to return to the Transvaal, there grew up an army of intermediaries or touts, who with the officers, looted the poor Indians to the tune of thousands. I was told that no permit could be had without influence, and that in some cases one had to pay up to a hundred pounds in spite of the influence which one might bring to bear. Thus there seemed to be no way open to me. I went to my old friend, the Police Superintendent of Durban, and said to him: 'Please introduce me to the Permit Officer and help me to obtain a permit. You know that I have been a resident of the Transvaal.' He immediately put on his hat, came out and secured me a permit. There was hardly an hour left before my train was to start. I had kept my luggage ready. I thanked Superintendent Alexander and started for Pretoria.

1. *ingenuity: the quality of being ingenious*

2. *plausible: apparently reasonable or probable, without necessarily being so*

3. *tentacles: an insidious spread of influence and control*

I now had a fair idea of the difficulties ahead. On reaching Pretoria I drafted the memorial. In Durban I do not recollect the Indians having been asked to submit in advance the names of their representatives, but here there was the new department and it asked to do so. The Pretoria Indians had already come to know that the officers wanted to exclude me.

But another chapter is necessary for this painful[1] though amusing incident.

1. painful: affected with or causing pain

CHAPTER 79

AUTOCRATS FROM ASIA

The officers at the head of the new department were at a loss to know how I had entered the Transvaal. They inquired of the Indians who used to go to them, but these could say nothing definite. The officers only ventured a guess that I might have succeeded in entering without a permit on the strength of my old connections. If that was the case, I was liable to be arrested!

It is a general practice, on the termination of a big war, to invest the government of the day with special powers. This was the case in South Africa. The government had passed a Peace Preservation Ordinance, which provided that anyone entering the Transvaal without a permit should be liable to arrest and imprisonment. The question of arresting me under this provision was mooted, but no one could summon up courage enough to ask me to produce my permit.

The officers had of course sent telegrams to Durban, and when they found that I had entered with a permit, they were disappointed. But they were not the men to be defeated by such disappointment. Though I had succeeded in entering the Transvaal, they could still successfully prevent me from waiting on Mr. Chamberlain.

So the community was asked to submit the names of the representatives who were to form the Deputation. Colour prejudice was of course in evidence everywhere in South Africa, but I was not prepared to find here the dirty and underhand dealing among officials that I was familiar with in India. In South Africa the public departments were maintained for the good of the people and were responsible to public opinion. Hence officials in charge had a certain courtesy of manner and humility about them, and coloured people also got the benefit of it more or less. With the coming of the officers from Asia, came also its autocracy[1], and the habits that the autocrats[2] had imbibed there. In South Africa there was a kind of responsible government or democracy, whereas the commodity[3] imported from Asia was autocracy pure and simple; for the Asiatics had no responsible government, there being a foreign power governing them.

1. *autocracy: a system of government by one person with absolute power*

2. *autocrats: a ruler who has absolute power*

In South Africa the Europeans were settled emigrants. They had become South African citizens and had control over the departmental officers. But the autocrats from Asia now appeared on the scene, and the Indians in consequence found themselves between the devil[1] and the deep sea.

I had a fair taste of this autocracy. I was first summoned to see the chief of the department, an officer from Ceylon. Lest I should appear to exaggerate when I say that I was 'summoned' to see the chief, I shall make myself clear. No written order was sent to me. Indian leaders often had to visit the Asiatic officers. Among these was the late Sheth Tyeb Haji Khanmahomed. The chief of the office asked him who I was and why I had come there.

'He is our adviser,' said Tyeb Sheth, 'and he has come here at our request.'

'Then what are we here for? Have we not been appointed to protect you? What can Gandhi know of the conditions here?' asked the autocrat.

Tyeb Sheth answered the charge as best he could: 'Of course you are there. But Gandhi is our man. He knows our language and understands us. You are after all officials.'

The Sahib ordered Tyeb Sheth to fetch me before him. I went to the Sahib in company with Tyeb Sheth and others. No seats were offered, we were all kept standing.

'What brings you here?' said the Sahib addressing me.

'I have come here at the request of my fellow countrymen to help them with my advice,' I replied.

'But don't you know that you have no right to come here? The permit you hold was given you by mistake. You cannot be regarded as a domiciled Indian. You must go back. You shall not wait on Mr. Chamberlain. It is for the protection of the Indians here that the Asiatic Department has been especially created. Well, you may go.' With this he bade me good-bye, giving me no opportunity for a reply.

But he detained my companions. He gave them a sound scolding[2] and advised them to send me away.

They returned chagrined. We were now confronted with an unexpected situation.

1. *devil: a very wicked or cruel person; a mischievously clever or self-willed person*

2. *scolding: angrily remonstrate with or rebuke*

CHAPTER 80

POCKETED THE INSULT

I smarted[1] under the insult, but as I had pocketed many such in the past I had become inured to them. I therefore decided to forget this latest one and take what course a dispassionate view of the case might suggest.

We had a letter from the Chief of the Asiatic Department to the effect that, as I had seen Mr. Chamberlain in Durban, it had been found necessary to omit my name from the deputation which was to wait on him.

The letter was more than my co-workers could bear. They proposed to drop the idea of the deputation altogether. I pointed out to them the awkward[2] situation of the community.

If you do not represent your case before Mr. Chamberlain,' said I, 'it will be presumed that you have no case at all. After all, the representation has to be made in writing, and we have got it ready. It does not matter in the least whether I read it or someone else reads it. Mr. Chamberlain is not going to argue the matter with us. I am afraid we must swallow the insult.'

I had scarcely finished speaking when Tyeb Sheth cried out, 'Does not an insult to you amount to an insult to the community? How can we forget that you are our representative?'

'Too true.' said I. 'But even the community will have to pocket insults like these. Have we any alternative?'

'Come what may, why should we swallow a fresh insult? Nothing worse can possibly happen to us. Have we many rights to lose?' asked Tyeb Sheth.

It was a spirited[3] reply, but of what avail was it? I was fully conscious of the limitations of the community. I pacified my friends and advised them to have, in my place, Mr. George Godfrey, an Indian barrister.

So Mr. Godfrey led the deputation. Mr. Chamberlain referred in his reply to my exclusion. 'Rather than hear the same representative over and over again, is it not better to have someone new?' he said, and tried to heal the wound.

1. *smarted: feel upset and annoyed*
2. *awkward: hard to do or deal with*
3. *spirited: courage, energy, and determination*

But all this, far from ending the matter, only added to the work of the community and also to mine. We had to start afresh[1].

'It is at your instance that the community helped in the war, and you see the result now,' were the words with which some people taunted[2] me. But the taunt had no effect. 'I do not regret my advice,' said I. 'I maintain that we did well in taking part in the war. In doing so we simply did our duty. We may not look forward to any reward for our labours, but it is my firm conviction that all good action is bound to bear fruit in the end. Let us forget the past and think of the task before us.' With which the rest agreed.

I added: 'To tell you the truth the work for which you had called me is practically finished. But I believe I ought not to leave the Transvaal, so far as it is possible, even if you permit me to return home. Instead of carrying on my work from Natal, as before, I must now do so from here. I must no longer think of returning to India within a year, but must get enrolled in the Transvaal Supreme Court. I have confidence enough to deal with this new department. If we do not do this, the community will be hounded out of the country, besides being thoroughly[3] robbed. Every day it will have fresh insults heaped upon it. The facts that Mr. Chamberlain refused to see me and that the official insulted me, are nothing before the humiliation of the whole community. It will become impossible to put up with the veritable[4] dog's life that we shall be expected to lead.'

So I set the ball rolling, discussed things with Indians in Pretoria and Johannesburg and ultimately decided to set up office in Johannesburg.

It was indeed doubtful whether I would be enrolled in the Transvaal Supreme[5] Court. But the Law Society did not oppose my application, and the Court allowed it. It was difficult for an Indian to secure rooms for office in a suitable locality. But I had come in fairly close contact with Mr. Ritch, who was then one of the merchants there. Through the good offices of a house agent known to him, I succeeded in securing suitable rooms for my office in the legal quarters of the city, and I started on my professional work.

1. *afresh: in a new or different way*
2. *taunted: a jeering or mocking remark made in order to wound or provoke*
3. *thoroughly: complete with regard to every detail; performed with or showing great care and completeness*
4. *veritable: genuine; actual; properly so called used to qualify a metaphor: a veritable price explosion*
5. *supreme: highest in authority or rank*

CHAPTER 81

QUICKENED SPIRIT OF SACRIFICE

Before I narrate the struggle for the Indian settlers rights in the Transvaal and their dealing with the Asiatic Department, I must turn to some other aspects[1] of my life.

Up to now there had been in me a mixed desire. The spirit of self-sacrifice was tempered by the desire to lay by something for the future.

About the time I took up chambers in Bombay, an American insurance agent had come there a man with a pleasing countenance[2] and a sweet tongue. As though we were old friends he discussed my future welfare. 'All men of your status in America have their lives insured. Should you not also insure yourself against the future? Life is uncertain. We in America regard it as a religious obligation to get insured. Can I not tempt you to take out a small policy[3]?'

Up to this time I had given the cold shoulder to all the agents I had met in South Africa and India, for I had though that life assurance implied fear and want of faith in God. But now I succumbed to the temptation of the American agent. As he proceeded with his argument, I had before my mind's eye a picture of my wife and children. 'Man, you have sold almost all the ornaments of your wife,' I said to myself. 'If something were to happen to you, the burden of supporting her and the children would fall on your poor brother, who has so nobly filled the place of father. How would that become you?' With these and similar arguments I persuaded myself to take out a policy for Rs. 10,000.

But when my mode of life changed in South Africa, my outlook[4] changed too. All the steps I took at this time of trial were taken in the name of God and for His service. I did not know how long I should have to stay in South Africa. I had a fear that I might never be able to get back to India: so I decided to keep my wife and children with me and earn enough to support them. This plan made me deplore the life policy and feel ashamed of having been caught in the net of the insurance agent.

1. *aspects: a particular part or feature; a particular appearance or quality*
2. *countenance: a person's face or facial expression*
3. *policy: course or principle of action adopted or proposed by an organization or individual*
4. *outlook: a person's point of view or attitude to life*

If, I said to myself, my brother is really in the position of my father, surely he would not consider it too much of a burden to support my widow, if it came to that, And what reason had I to assume that death would claim me earlier than the others? After all the real protector[1] was neither I nor my brother, but the Almighty[2]. In getting my life insured I had robbed my wife and children of their self-reliance. Why should they not be expected to take care of themselves? What happened to the families of the numberless poor in the world? Why should I not count myself as one of them?

A multitude of such thoughts passed though my mind, but I did not immediately act upon them. I recollect having paid at least one insurance premium in South Africa.

Outward circumstances too supported this train of thought. During my first sojourn[3] in South Africa it was Christian influence that had kept alive in me the religious sense. Now it was theosophical influence that added strength to it. Mr. Ritch was a theosophist and put me in touch with the society at Johannesburg. I never became a member, as I had my differences, but I came in close contact with almost every theosophist. I had religious discussions with them every day. There used to be readings from theosophical books and sometimes I had occasion to address their meetings. The chief thing about theosophy is to cultivate and promote the idea of brotherhood. We had considerable discussion over this, and I criticized the members where their conduct did not appear to me to square with their ideal. The criticism was not without its wholesome effect on me. It led to introspection.

1. *protector: a person or thing that protects*
2. *Almighty: a name or title for god*
3. *sojourn: a temporary stay*

CHAPTER 82

RESULT OF INTROSPECTION

When, in 1893, I came in close contact with Christian friends. I was a mere novice. They tried hard to bring home to me, and make me accept, the message of Jesus, and I was a humble and respectful listener with an open mind. At that time I naturally studied Hinduism to the best of my ability and endeavoured to understand other religions.

In 1903 the position was somewhat changed. Theosophist friends certainly intended to draw me into their society, but that was with a view to getting something from me as a Hindu. Theosophical literature is replete[1] with Hindu influence, and so these friends expected that I should be helpful to them. I explained that my Samskrit study was not much to speak of, that I had not read the Hindu scriptures in the original, and that even my acquaintance with the translations was of the slightest. But being believers in *samskara* (tendencies caused by previous births) and *punarjanma* (rebirth), they assumed that I should be able to render at least some help. And so I felt like a Triton among the minnows. I started reading Swami Vivekananda's *Rajayoga* with some of these friends and M. N. Dvivedi's *Rajayoga* with others. I had to read Patanjali's *Yoga Sutras* with one friend and the *Bhagavadgita* with quite a number. We formed a sort of Seekers' Club where we had regular readings. I already had faith in the Gita, which had a fascination for me. Now I realized the necessity of diving deeper into it. I had one or two translations, by means of which I tried to understand the original Samskrit. I decided also to get by heart one or two verses every day. For this purpose I employed the time of my morning ablutions. The operation took me thirty-five minutes, fifteen minutes for the tooth brush and twenty for the bath. The first I used to do standing in western fashion. So on the wall opposite I stuck slips of paper on which were written the Gita verses and referred to them now and then to help my memory. This time was found sufficient for memorising the daily portion and recalling the verses already learnt. I remember having thus committed to memory thirteen chapters. But the memorising[2] of

1. *replete: filled or well-supplied with something*
2. *memorising: learn by heart*

the Gita had to give way to other work and the creation and nurture of Satyagraha, which absorbed all my thinking time, as the latter may be said to be doing even now.

What effect this reading of the Gita had on my friends only they can say, but to me the Gita became an infallible guide of conduct. It became my dictionary of daily reference. Just as I turned to the English dictionary for the meanings of English words that I did not understand, I turned to this dictionary of conduct for a ready solution of all my troubles and trials. Words like *aparigraha* (non-possession) and *sambhava* (equability) gripped me. How to cultivate and preserve that equability was the question. How was one to treat alike insulting, insolent[1] and corrupt[2] officials, co-workers of yesterday raising meaningless opposition, and men who had always been good to one? How was one to divest oneself of all possessions? Was not the body itself possession enough? Were not wife and children possessions? Was I to destroy all the cupboards of books I had? Was I to give up all I had and follow Him? Straight came the answer: I could not follow Him unless I gave up all I had. My study of English law came to my help. Snell's discussion of the maxims of Equity came to my memory. I understood more clearly in the light of the Gita teaching the implication of the word 'trustee'. My regard for jurisprudence[3] increased, I discovered in it religion. I understood the Gita teaching of non-possession to mean that those who desired salvation should act like the trustee who, though having control over great possessions, regards not an iota of them as his own. It became clear to me as daylight that non-possession and equability presupposed a change of heart, a change of attitude. I then wrote to Revashankarbhai to allow the insurance policy to lapse and get whatever could be recovered, or else to regard the premiums already paid as lost, for I had become convinced that God, who created my wife and children as well as myself, would take care of them. To my brother, who had been as father to me, I wrote explaining that I had given him all that I had saved up to that moment, but that henceforth he should expect nothing from me, for future savings, if any, would be utilized for the benefit of the community.

I could not easily make my brother understand this. In stern language he explained to me my duty towards him. I should not, he said, aspire to be wiser than our father. I must support the family as he did. I pointed out

1. *insolent: rude and disrespectful*
2. *corrupt: willing to act dishonestly in return for money or personal gain; evil or morally depraved*
3. *jurisprudence: the theory or philosophy of law*

to him that I was doing exactly what our father had done. The meaning of 'family' had but to be slightly widened and the wisdom of my step would become clear.

My brother gave me up and practically stopped all communication. I was deeply distressed, but it would have been a greater distress[1] to give up what I considered to be my duty, and I preferred the lesser. But that did not affect my devotion to him, which remained as pure and great as ever. His great love for me was at the root of his misery. He did not so much want my money as that I should be well-behaved towards the family. Near the end of his life, however, he appreciated my viewpoint. When almost on his death-bed, he realized that my step had been right and wrote me a most pathetic[2] letter. He apologized to me, if indeed a father may apologize to his son. He commended his sons to my care, to be brought up as I thought fit, and expressed his impatience to meet me. He cabled that he would like to come to South Africa and I cabled in reply that he could. But that was not to be. Nor could his desire as regards his sons be fulfilled. He died before he could start for South Africa. His sons had been brought up in the old atmosphere and could not change their course of life. I could not draw them to me. It was not their fault. 'Who can say thus far, no further, to the tide of his own nature?' Who can erase the impressions with which he is born? It is idle to expect one's children and wards necessarily to follow the same course of evolution as oneself.

This instance to some extent serves to show what a terrible[3] responsibility it is to be a parent.

1. *distress: extreme anxiety or suffering*
2. *pathetic: arousing pity, especially through vulnerability or sadness*
3. *terrible: extremely bad, serious, or unpleasant*

CHAPTER 83

A SACRIFICE TO VEGETARIANISM

As the ideals of sacrifice and simplicity were becoming more and more realized, and the religious, consciousness was becoming more and more quickened[1] in my daily life, the passion for vegetarianism as a mission went on increasing. I have known only one way of carrying on missionary work, *viz.*, by personal example and discussion with searchers for knowledge.

There was in Johannesburg a vegetarian restaurant conducted by a German who believed in Kuhne's hydropathic treatment. I visited the restaurant myself and helped it by taking English friends there. But I saw that it could not last as it was always in financial difficulties. I assisted it as much as I thought it deserved, and spent some money on it, but it had ultimately to be closed down.

Most theosophists are vegetarians more or less, and an enterprising lady belonging to that society now came upon the scene with a vegetarian restaurant on a grand scale. She was fond of art, extravagant and ignorant of accounts. Her circle of friends was fairly large. She had started in a small way, but later decided to extend the venture by taking large rooms, and asked me for help. I knew nothing of her finances when she thus approached me, but I took it that her estimate must be fairly accurate. And I was in a position to accommodate her. My clients used to keep large sums as deposits with me. Having received the consent of one of these clients, I lent about a thousand pounds from the amount to his credit. This client was most large-hearted and trusting. He had originally come to South Africa as an indentured labourer. He said: 'Give away the money, if you like. I know nothing in these matters. I only know you.' His name was Badri. He afterwards took a prominent part in Satyagraha, and suffered imprisonment[2] as well. So I advanced the loan[3] assuming that this consent was enough.

In two or three months' time I came to know that the amount would not be recovered. I could ill afford to sustain such a loss. There were many

1. *quickened: make or become quicker*
2. *imprisonment: put or keep in prison*
2. *loan: a thing that is borrowed, especially a sum of money that is expected to be paid back with interest; the action of lending; short for loanword*

other purposes to which I could have applied this amount. The loan was never repaid. But how could trusting Badri be allowed to suffer? He had known me only. I made good the loss.

A client friend to whom I spoke about this transaction sweetly chided[1] me for my folly.

'Bhai,' - I had fortunately not yet become 'Mahatma', nor even 'Bapu' (father) friends used to call me by the loving name of 'Bhai' (brother) - said he, 'this was not for you to do. We depend upon you in so many things. You are not going to get back this amount. I know you will never allow Badri to come to grief, for you will pay him out of your pocket, but if you go on helping your reform schemes by operating on your clients' money, the poor fellows will be ruined, and you will soon become a beggar. But you are our trustee and must know that, if you become a beggar, all our public work will come to a stop.'

The friend I am thankful to say, is still alive. I have not yet come across a purer[2] man than he, in South Africa or anywhere else. I have known him to apologize to people and to cleanse himself, when, having happened to suspect them, he had found his suspicion to be unfounded[3].

I saw that he had rightly warned me. For though I made good Badri's loss, I should not have been able to meet any similar loss and should have been driven to incur debt - a thing I have never done in my life and always abhorred. I realized that even a man's reforming zeal ought not to make him exceed his limits. I also saw that in thus lending trust-money I had disobeyed the cardinal teaching of the Gita, *viz*, the duty of a man of equipoise to act without desire for the fruit. The error became for me a beacon-light of warning.

The sacrifice offered on the altar[4] of vegetarianism was neither intentional nor expected. It was a virtue of necessity.

1. *chided: scold or rebuke*
2. *purer: innocent or morally good*
3. *unfounded: having no foundation or basis in fact*
4. *altar: the table in a christian church at which the bread and wine are consecrated in communion services*

CHAPTER 84

EXPERIMENTS IN EARTH AND WATER TREATMENT

With the growing simplicity of my life, my dislike for medicines steadily increased. While practising in Durban, I suffered for some time from debility and rheumatic[1] inflammation. Dr. P. J. Mehta, who had come to see me, gave me treatment, and I got well. After that, up to the time when I returned to India, I do not remember having suffered from any ailment to speak of.

But I used to be troubled with constipation and frequent headaches, while at Johannesburg. I kept myself fit with occasional laxatives and a well-regulated diet. But I could hardly call myself healthy, and always wondered when I should get free from the incubus of these laxative medicines.

About this time I read of the formation of a 'No Breakfast Association' in Manchester. The argument of the promoters was that Englishmen ate too often and too much, that their doctors' bills were heavy because they ate until midnight, and that they should at least give up breakfast, if they wanted to improve this state of affairs. Though all these things could not be said of me, I felt that the argument did partly apply[2] in my case. I used to have three square meals daily in addition to afternoon tea. I was never a spare eater and enjoyed as many delicacies as could be had with a vegetarian and spiceless diet. I scarcely ever got up before six or seven. I therefore argued that, if I also dropped the morning breakfast, I might become free from headaches. So I tried the experiment. For a few days it was rather hard, but the headaches entirely disappeared. This led me to conclude that I was eating more than I needed.

But the change was far from relieving me of constipation. I tried Kuhne's hipbaths, which gave some relief but did not completely cure me. In the meantime the German who had a vegetarian restaurant, or some other friend, I forget who, placed in my hands Just's *Return of Nature*. In this book I read about earth treatment. The author also

1. *rheumatic: of, relating to, caused by, or suffering from rheumatism*
2. *apply: bring into operation of use; be relevant*

advocated fresh fruit and nuts as the natural diet of man. I did not at once take to the exclusive fruit diet, but immediately began experiments in earth treatment, and with wonderful results. The treatment consisted in applying to the abdomen a bandage of clean earth moistened with cold water and spread like a poultice on fine linen. This I applied at bed time, removing it during the night or in the morning, whenever, I happened to wake up. It proved a radical cure. Since then I have tried the treatment on myself and my friends and never had reason to regret it. In India I have not been able to try this treatment with equal confidence. For one thing. I have never had time to settle down in one place to conduct the experiments. But my faith in the earth and water treatment remains practically the same as before. Even today I give myself the earth treatment to a certain extent and recommend it to my co-workers, whenever the occasion arises.

Though I have had two serious illnesses in my life, I believe that man has little need to drug himself. Nine hundred and ninety nine cases out of a thousand can be brought round by means of a well-regulated diet, water and earth treatment and similar household remedies. He who runs to the doctor, *vaidya* or *hakim* for every little aliment, and swallows all kinds of vegetable and mineral drugs[1], not only curtails his life, but, by becoming the slave of his body instead of remaining its master, loses self-control, and ceases to be a man.

Let no one discount these observations because they are being written in a sickbed. I know the reasons for my illnesses. I am fully conscious that I alone am responsible for them, and it is because of that consciousness that I have not lost patience. In fact I have thanked God for them as lessons and successfully resisted the temptation of taking numerous drugs. I know my obstinacy often tries my doctors, but they kindly bear with me and do not give me up.

However, I must not digress. Before proceeding further, I should give the reader a word of warning[2]. Those who purchase Just's book on the strength of this chapter should not take everything in it to be gospel truth. A writer almost always presents one aspect of a case, whereas every case can be seen from no less than seven points of view, all of which are probably correct by themselves, but not correct at the same time and in the same circumstances. And then many books are written with a view

1. *drugs: a medicine or other substance which has a marked physiological effect when taken into the body; a substance with narcotic or stimulant effects*
2. *warning: a statement or event that warns or serves as a cautionary example*

to gaining customers and earning name and fame. Let those, therefore, who read such books as these do so with discernment[1], and take advice of some experienced man before trying any of the experiments set forth, or let them read the books with patience and digest them thoroughly before acting upon them.

3. *discernment: recognize or find out; distinguish with difficulty by sight or with the other senses*

CHAPTER 85

A WARNING

I am afraid I must continue the digression until the next chapter. Along with my experiments in earth treatment, those in dietetics were also being carried on, and it may not be out of place here to make a few observations as regards the latter, though I shall have occasion to refer to them again later.

I may not, now or hereafter, enter into a detailed account of the experiments in dietetics, for I did so in a series of Gujarati articles which appeared years ago in *Indian Opinion*, and which were afterwards published in the form of a book popularly known in English as *A Guide to Health*. Among my little books this has been the most widely read alike in the East and in the West, a thing that I have not yet been able to understand. It was written for the benefit of the readers of *Indian Opinion*. But I know that the booklet[1] has profoundly influenced the lives of many, both in the East and in the West, who have never seen *Indian Opinion*. For they have been corresponding with me on the subject. It has therefore appeared necessary to say something here about the booklet, for though I see no reason to alter the views set forth in it, yet I have made certain radical changes in my actual practice, of which all readers of the book do not know, and of which, I think, they should be informed.

The booklet was written, like all my other writings, with a spiritual end, which has always inspired every one of my actions, and therefore it is a matter for deep distress to me that I am unable today to practise some of the theories propounded[2] in the book.

It is my firm conviction that man need take no milk at all, beyond the mother's milk that he takes as a baby. His diet should consist of nothing but sunbaked fruits and nuts. He can secure enough nourishment both for the tissues and the nerves from fruits like grapes and nuts like almonds. Restraint of the sexual and other passions becomes easy for a man who lives on such food. My co-workers and I have seen by experience that

1. *booklet: a small, thin book with paper covers*

2. *propounded: put forward an idea, theory, etc. for consideration*

there is much truth in the Indian proverb that as a man eats, so shall he become. These views have been set out elaborately in the book.

But unfortunately in India I have found myself obliged to deny some of my theories in practice. Whilst I was engaged on the recruiting campaign in Kheda, an error in diet laid me low, and I was at death's door. I tried in vain to rebuild a shattered constitution without milk. I sought the help of the doctors, *vaidyas* and scientists whom I knew, to recommend a substitute for milk. Some suggested *mung* water, some *mowhra* oil, some almond-milk. I wore out my body in experimenting on these, but nothing could help me to leave the sick-bed. The *vaidyas* read verses to me from Charaka to show that religious scruples about diet have no place in therapeutics[1]. So they could not be expected to help me to live without milk. And how could those who recommended beef-tea and brandy[2] without hesitation help me to persevere with a milkless diet?

I might not take cow's or buffalo's milk, as I was bound by a vow. The vow of course meant the giving up of all milks, but as I had mother cow's and mother buffalo's only in mind when I took the vow, and as I wanted to live, I somehow beguiled myself into emphasizing the letter of the vow and decided to take goat's milk. I was fully conscious, when I started taking mother goat's milk, that the spirit of my vow was destroyed.

But the idea of leading a campaign[3] against the Rowlatt Act had possessed me. And with it grew the desire to live. Consequently one of the greatest experiments in my life came to a stop.

I know it is argued that the soul has nothing to do with what one eats or drinks, as the soul neither eats nor drinks; that it is not what you put inside from without, but what you express outwardly from within, that matters. There is no doubt some force in this. But rather than examine this reasoning. I shall content myself with merely declaring my firm conviction that, for the seeker who would live in fear of God and who would see Him face to face, restraint in diet both as to quantity and quality is as essential as restraint in thought and speech.

In a matter, however, where my theory has failed me, I should not only give the information, but issue a grave warning against adopting it. I would therefore urge those who, on the strength of the theory propounded by me, may have given up milk, not to persist in the experiment, unless they

1. *therapeutics: of or relating to the healing of disease; having a good effect on the body or mind*
2. *brandy: a strong alcoholic spirit distilled from wine or fermented fruit juice*
3. *campaign: an organized course of action to achieve a goal*

find it beneficial[1] in every way, or unless they are advised by experienced physicians. Up to now my experience here has shown me that for those with a weak digestion and for those who are confined to bed there is no light and nourishing diet equal to that of milk.

I should be greatly obliged if anyone with experience in this line, who happens to read this chapter, would tell me, if he has known from experience, and not from reading, of a vegetable substitute for milk, which is equally nourishing and digestible.

1. *beneficial: resulting in good; favourable or advantageous*

CHAPTER 86

A TUSSLE WITH POWER

To turn now to the Asiatic Department.

Johannesburg was the stronghold[1] of the Asiatic officers. I had been observing that, far from protecting the Indians, Chinese and others, these officers were grinding them down. Every day I had complaints like this: 'The rightful ones are not admitted, whilst those who have no right are smuggled[2] in on payment of £100. If you will not remedy this state of things, who will?' I shared the feeling. If I did not succeed in stamping[3] out this evil, I should be living in the Transvaal in vain.

So I began to collect evidence, and as soon as I had gathered a fair Amount, I approached the Police Commissioner. He appeared to be a just man. Far from giving me the cold shoulder, he listened to me patiently and asked me to show him all the evidence in my possession. He examined the witnesses himself and was satisfied, but he knew as well as I that it was difficult in South Africa to get a white jury to convict a white offender against coloured men. 'But,' said he, 'let us try at any rate. It is not proper either, to let such criminals go scot-free for fear of the jury acquitting them, I must get them arrested. I assure you I shall leave no stone unturned.'

I did not need the assurance. I suspected quite a number of officers, but as I had no unchallengeable evidence against them all, warrants of arrest were issued against the two about whose guilt I had not the slightest doubt.

My movements could never be kept secret. Many knew that I was going to the Police Commissioner practically daily. The two officers against whom warrants had been issued had spies more or less efficient. They used to patrol my office and report my movements to the officers. I must admit, however, that these officers were so bad that they could not have had many spies. Had the Indians and the Chinese not helped me, they would never have been arrested.

One of these absconded. The Police Commissioner obtained an extradition warrant against him and got him arrested and brought to the

1. *stronghold: a place of strong support for a cause or political party*
2. *smuggled: convey secretly and illicitly*
3. *stamping: suppress or put an end to something*

Transvaal. They were tried, and although there was strong evidence against them, and in spite of the fact that the jury had evidence of one of them having absconded[1], both were declared to be not guilty and acquitted.

I was sorely disappointed. The Police Commissioner also was very sorry. I was disgusted with the legal profession. The very intellect became an abomination[2] to me inasmuch as it could be prostituted for screening[3] crime.

However, the guilt of both these officers was so patent[4] that in spite of their acquittal the Government could not harbour them. Both were cashiered, and the Asiatic department became comparatively clean, and the Indian community was somewhat reassured.

The event enhanced my prestige and brought me more business. The bulk, though not all, of the hundreds of pounds that thc community was monthly squandering in peculation, was saved. All could not be saved, for the dishonest still plied their trade. But it was now possible for the honest man to preserve his honesty.

I must say that, though these officers were so bad, I had nothing against them personally. They were aware of this themselves, and when in their straits they approached me, I helped them too. They had a chance of getting employed by the Johannesburg Municipality in case I did not oppose the proposal. A friend of theirs saw me in this connection and I agreed not to thwart them, and they succeeded.

This attitude of mine put the officials with whom I came in contact perfectly at ease, and though I had often to fight with their department and use strong language, they remained quite friendly with me. I was not then quite conscious that such behaviour was part of my nature. I learnt later that it was an essential part of Satyagraha, and an attribute of *ahimsa*.

Man and his deed are two distinct things. Whereas a good deed should call forth approbation and a wicked deed disapprobation, the doer of the deed, whether good or wicked always deserves respect or pity as the case may be. 'Hate the sin and not the sinner' is a precept which, though easy enough to understand, is rarely practised, and that is why the poison of hatred spreads in the world.

This *ahimsa* is the basis of the search for truth. I am realizing every day that the search is in vain unless it is founded on *ahimsa* as the basis.

1. *absconded: leave hurriedly and secretly to escape from custody or avoid arrest*
2. *abomination: detest*
3. *screening: conceal, protect, or shelter with a screen; protect from something dangerous or unpleasant*
4. *patent: easily recognizable; obvious*

It is quite proper to resist and attack a system, but to resist and attack its author is tantamount[1] to resisting and attacking oneself. For we are all tarred with the same brush, and are children of one and the same Creator, and as such the divine powers within us are infinite. To slight a single human being is to slight those divine powers, and thus to harm not only that being but with him the whole world.

1. *tantamount: equivalent in seriousness to; virtually the same as*

CHAPTER 87

A SACRED RECOLLECTION AND PENANCE

A variety of incidents in my life have conspired to bring me in close contact with people of many creeds[1] and many communities, and my experience with all of them warrants the statement that I have known no distinction between relatives and strangers, countrymen and foreigners, white and coloured, Hindus and Indians of other faiths, whether Musalmans, Parsis, Christians or Jews. I may say that my heart has been incapable of making any such distinctions. I cannot claim this as a special virtue, as it is in my very nature. rather than a result of any effort on my part, whereas in the case of *ahimsa* (non-violence), *brahmacharya* (celibacy), *aparigraha* (non-possession) and other cardinal virtues, I am fully conscious of a continuous striving for their cultivation.

When I was practising in Durban, my office clerks often stayed with me, and there were among them Hindus and Christians, or to describe them by their provinces, Gujaratis and Tamilians. I do not recollect having ever regarded them as anything but my kith and kin[2]. I treated them as members of my family, and had unpleasantness with my wife if ever she stood in the way of my treating them as such. One of the clerks was a Christian, born of Panchama parents.

The house was built after the Western model and the rooms rightly had no outlets for dirty water. Each room had therefore chamber-pots. Rather than have these cleaned by a servant or a sweeper[3], my wife or I attended to them. The clerks who made themselves completely at home would naturally clean their own pots, but the Christian clerk was a newcomer, and it was our duty to attend to his bedroom. My wife managed the pots of the others, but to clean those used by one who had been a Panchama seemed to her to be the limit, and we fell out. She could not bear the pots being cleaned by me, neither did she like doing it herself. Even today I can recall the picture of her chiding me, her eyes red with anger, and pearl drops streaming down her cheeks, as she descended the

1. *creeds: a system of religious belief; a faith; a formal statement of christian beliefs*
2. *kith and kin: one's family and relations*
3. *sweeper: a person or device that cleans by sweeping*

ladder, pot in hand. But I was a cruelly kind husband. I regarded myself as her teacher, and so harassed her out of my blind love for her.

I was far from being satisfied by her merely carrying the pot. I would have her do it cheerfully. So I said, raising my voice: 'I will not stand this nonsense[1] in my house.'

The words pierced[2] her like an arrow.

She shouted back: 'Keep your house to yourself and let me go.' I forgot myself, and the spring of compassion dried up in me. I caught her by the hand, dragged the helpless woman to the gate, which was just opposite the ladder, and proceeded to open it with the intention of pushing her out. The tears were running down her cheeks in torrents, and she cried: 'Have you no sense of shame? Must you so far forget yourself? Where am I to go? I have no parents or relatives here to harbour me. Being your wife, you think I must put up with your cuffs and kicks? For Heaven's sake behave yourself, and shut the gate. Let us not be found making scenes like this!'

I put on a brave face, but was really ashamed and shut the gate. If my wife could not leave me, neither could I leave her. We have had numerous bickerings[3], but the end has always been peace between us. The wife, with her matchless powers of endurance, has always been the victor.

Today I am in a position to narrate the incident with some detachment, as it belongs to a period out of which I have fortunately emerged. I am no longer a blind, infatuated husband, I am no more my wife's teacher. Kasturba can, if she will, be as unpleasant to me today, as I used to be to her before. We are tried friends, the one no longer regarding the other as the object of lust. She has been a faithful nurse throughout my illnesses, serving without any thought of reward.

The incident in question occurred in 1898, when I had no conception of *brahmacharya*. It was a time when I thought that the wife was the object of the husband's lust, born to do her husband's behest, rather than a helpmate[4], a comrade and a partner in the husband's joys and sorrows.

It was in the year 1900 that these ideas underwent a radical transformation, and in 1906 they took concrete shape. But of this I propose to speak in its proper place. Suffice it to say that with the gradual disappearance in me of the carnal appetite, my domestic life became and is becoming more and more peaceful, sweet and happy.

1. *nonsense: foolish or unacceptable behavior; an absurd or unthinkable scheme, situation, etc.*
2. *pierced: force or cut a way through*
3. *bickerings: argue about petty and trivial matters*
4. *helpmate: a helpful companion or partner*

Let no one conclude from this narrative of a sacred recollection that we are by any means an ideal couple, or that there is a complete identity of ideals between us. Kasturba herself does not perhaps know whether she has any ideals independently of me. It is likely that many of my doings have not her approval even today. We never discuss them, I see no good in discussing them. For she was educated neither by her parents nor by me at the time when I ought to have done it. But she is blessed with one great quality to a very considerable degree, a quality which most Hindu wives possess in some measure. And it is this; willingly or unwillingly, consciously[1] or unconsciously, she has considered herself blessed in following in my footsteps, and has never stood in the way of my endeavour to lead a life of restraint. Though, therefore, there is a wide difference between us intellectually, I have always had the feeling that ours is a life of contentment, happiness and progress.

1. *consciously: aware of and responding to one's surroundings*

CHAPTER 88

INTIMATE EUROPEAN CONTACTS

This chapter has brought me to a stage where it becomes necessary for me to explain to the reader how this story is written from week to week.

When I began writing it, I had no definite plan before me. I have no diary[1] or documents on which to base the story of my experiments. I write just as the Spirit moves me at the time of writing. I do not claim to know definitely that all conscious thought and action on my part is directed by the Spirit. But on an examination of the greatest steps that I have taken in my life, as also of those that may be regarded as the least, I think it will not be improper to say that all of them were directed by the Spirit.

I have not seen Him, neither have I known Him. I have made the world's faith in God my own, and as my faith is ineffaceable[2], I regard that faith as amounting to experience. However, as it may be said that to describe faith as experience is to tamper[3] with truth, it may perhaps be more correct to say that I have no word for characterizing my belief in God.

It is perhaps now somewhat easy to understand why I believe that I am writing this story as the Spirit prompts me. When I began the last chapter I gave it the heading I have given to this, but as I was writing it, I realized that before I narrated my experiences with Europeans, I must write something by way of a preface. This I did and altered the heading.

Now again, as I start on this chapter, I find myself confronted with a fresh problem. What things to mention and what to omit[4] regarding the English friends of whom I am about to write is a serious problem. If things that are relevant are omitted, truth will be dimmed. And it is difficult to decide straightway what is relevant, when I am not even sure about the relevancy of writing this story.

I understand more clearly today what I read long ago about the inadequacy of all autobiography as history. I know that I do not set down

1. *diary: a book in which one keeps a daily record of events and experiences; a book with spaces for each day of the year in which to note appointments*
2. *ineffaceable: unable to be erased or forgotten*
3. *tamper: interfere with something without authority or so as to cause damages*
4. *omit: leave out or exclude; fail to do*

in this story all that I remember. Who can say how much I must give and how much omit in the interests of truth? And what would be the value in a court of law of the inadequate *ex parte* evidence being tendered by me of certain events in my life? If some busybody were to cross-examine me on the chapters already written, he could probably shed much more light on them, and if it were a hostile critic's cross-examination, he might even flatter himself for having shown up 'the hollowness of many of my pretensions.'

I, therefore, wonder for a moment whether it might not be proper to stop writing these chapters. But so long as there is no prohibition from the voice within, I must continue the writing. I must follow the sage maxim that nothing once begun should be abandoned unless it is proved to be morally wrong.

I am not writing the autobiography[1] to please critics[2]. Writing it is itself one of the experiments with truth. One of its objects is certainly to provide some comfort and food for reflection for my co-workers. Indeed I started writing it in compliance with their wishes. It might not have been written, if Jeramdas and Swami Anand had not persisted in their suggestion. If, therefore, I am wrong in writing the autobiography, they must share the blame.

But to take up the subject indicated in the heading. Just as I had Indians living with me as members of my family, so had I English friends living with me in Durban. Not that all who lived with me liked it. But I persisted in having them. Nor was I wise in every case. I had some bitter[3] experiences, but these included both Indians and Europeans. And I do not regret the experiences. In spite of them, and in spite of the inconvenience and worry that I have often caused to friends, I have not altered my conduct and friends have kindly borne with me. Whenever my contacts with strangers have been painful to friends,I have not hesitated to blame[4] them. I hold that believers who have to see the same God in others that they see in themselves, must be able to live amongst all with sufficient detachment. And the ability to live thus can be cultivated, not by fighting shy of unsought opportunities for such contacts, but by hailing them in a spirit of service and withal keeping oneself unaffected by them.

Though, therefore, my house was full when the Boer War broke out, I received two Englishmen who had come from Johannesburg. Both were

1. *autobiography: an account of a person's life written by that person*
2. *critics: a person who judges the merits of literary, artistic, or musical works, especially one who does so professionally*
3. *bitter: causing pain or unhappiness; feeling or showing angry hurt or resentment; harsh and british beer that is strongly flavored with hops and has a bitter taste*
4. *blame: assign responsibility for a fault or wrong to*

theosophists, one of them being Mr. Kitchin, of whom we shall have occasion to know more later. These friends often cost my wife bitter tears. Unfortunately she has had many such trials on my account. This was the first time that I had English friends to live with me as intimately as members of my family. I had stayed in English houses during my days in England, but there I conformed to their ways of living, and it was more or less like living in a boarding house. Here it was quite the contrary. The English friends became members of the family. They adopted the Indian style[1] in many matters. Though the appointments in the house were in the Western fashion, the internal life was mostly Indian. I do remember having had some difficulty in keeping them as members of the family, but I can certainly say that they had no difficulty in making themselves perfectly at home under my roof. In Johannesburg these contacts developed further than in Durban.

1. *style: a manner of doing something; a way of painting, writing, etc. characteristic of a particular period, person, etc.*

CHAPTER 89

EUROPEAN CONTACTS (*Contd.*)

In Johannesburg I had at one time as many as four Indian clerks, who were perhaps more like my sons than clerks. But even these were not enough for my work. It was impossible to do without typewriting, which, among us, if at all, only I knew. I taught it to two of the clerks, but they never came up to the mark because of their poor English. And then one of these I wanted to train as an accountant. I could not get anyone from Natal, for nobody could enter the Transvaal without a permit, and for my own personal convenience I was not prepared to ask a favour of the Permit Officer.

I was at my wits' end. Arrears were fast mounting up, so much so that it seemed impossible for me, however much I might try, to cope[1] with professional and public work. I was quite willing to engage a European clerk, but I was not sure to get a white man or woman to serve a coloured man like myself. However I decided to try. I approached a typewriter's agent whom I knew, and asked him to get me a stenographer[2]. There were girls available, and he promised to try to secure the services of one. He came across a Scots girl called Miss Dick, who had just come fresh from Scotland. She had no objection to earning an honest livelihood, wherever available, and she was in need. So the agent[3] sent her on to me. She immediately prepossessed me.

'Don't you mind serving under an Indian?' I asked her.

'Not at all,' was her firm reply.

'What salary do you expect?'

'Would £17 10s be too much?'

'Not too much if you will give me the work I want from you. When can you join?'

'This moment if you wish.'

I was very pleased and straightaway started dictating letters to her.

Before very long she became more a daughter or a sister to me than a mere stenotypist. I had scarcely any reason to find fault with her work.

1. *cope: deal effectively with something difficult*
2. *stenographer: one who takes notes in short hand and transcribes the same on a typewriter*
3. *agent: a person that provides a particular service, typically one organizing transactions between two other parties; a person who manages financial or contractual matters for an actor, performer, or writer*

She was often entrusted[1] with the management of funds amounting to thousands of pounds, and she was in charge of account books. She won my complete confidence, but what was perhaps more, she confided to me her innermost thoughts and feelings. She sought my advice in the final choice of her husband, and I had the privilege to give her away in marriage. As soon as Miss Dick became Mrs. Macdonald, she had to leave me, but even after her marriage she did not fail to respond, whenever under pressure I made a call upon her.

But a permanent stenotypist was now needed in her place, and I was fortunate in getting another girl. She was Miss Schlesin, introduced to me by Mr. Kallenbach, whom the reader will know in due course. She is at present a teacher in one of the High Schools in the Transvaal. She was about seventeen when she came to me. Some of her idiosyncrasies were at times too much for Mr. Kallenbach and me. She had come less to work as a stenotypist than to gain experience. Colour prejudice was foreign to her temperament. She seemed to mind neither age nor experience. She would not hesitate even to the point of insulting a man and telling him to his face what she thought of him. Her impetuosity[2] often landed me in difficulties, but her open and guileless temperament removed them as soon as they were created. I have often signed without revision letters typed by her, as I considered her English to be better than mine, and had the fullest confidence in her loyalty[3].

Her sacrifice was great. For a considerable period she did not draw more than £6, and refused ever to receive more than £10 a month. When I urged her to take more, she would give me a scolding and say, 'I am not here to draw a salary from you. I am here because I like to work with you and I like your ideals.'

She had once an occasion to take £40 from me, but she insisted on having it as a loan, and repaid the full amount last year. Her courage was equal to her sacrifice. She is one of the few women I have been privileged to come across, with a character as clear as crystal and courage that would shame a warrior. She is a grown up woman now. I do not know her mind quite as well as when she was with me, but my contact with this young lady will ever be for me a sacred[4] recollection. I would therefore be false to truth if I kept back what I know about her.

1. *entrusted: assign a responsibility to; put into someone's care*
2. *impetuosity: acting quickly and carelessly*
3. *loyalty: showing firm and constant support or allegiance to a person or institution*
4. *sacred: connected with a deity and so deserving veneration; holy; embodying the doctrines of a religion; sacrosanct*

She knew neither night nor day in toiling[1] for the cause. She ventured out on errands in the darkness of the night all by herself, and angrily scouted any suggestion of an escort. Thousands of stalwart Indians looked up to her for guidance. When during the Satyagraha days almost every one of the leaders was in jail, she led the movement single-handed. She had the management of thousands, a tremendous amount of correspondence, and *Indian Opinion* in her hands, but she never wearied.

I could go on without end writing thus about Miss Schlesin, but I shall conclude this chapter with citing Gokhale's estimate of her. Gokhale knew every one of my co-workers. He was pleased with many of them, and would often give his opinion of them. He gave the first place to Miss Schlesin amongst all the Indian and European co-workers. 'I have rarely met with the sacrifice, the purity and the fearlessness I have seen in Miss Schlesin,' said he. 'Amongst your co-workers, she takes the first place in my estimation.'

1. *toiling: work extremely hard or incessantly; move somewhere slowly and with difficulty*

CHAPTER 90

'INDIAN OPINION'

Before I proceed with the other intimate European contacts, I must note two or three items of importance. One of the contacts, however, should be mentioned at once. The appointment of Miss Dick was not enough for my purpose. I needed more assistance. I have in the earlier chapters referred to Mr. Ritch. I knew him very well. He was manager in a commercial firm. He approved my suggestion of leaving the firm and getting articled under me, and he considerably lightened my burden.

About this time Sjt. Madanjit approached me with a proposal to start *Indian Opinion* and sought my advice. He had already been conducting a press, and I approved of his proposal. The journal was launched in 1904, and Sjt. Mansukhlal Naazar became the first editor. But I had to bear the brunt of the work, having for most of the time to be practically in charge of the journal. Not that Sjt. Mansukhlal could not carry it on. He had been doing a fair amount of journalism whilst in India, but he would never venture to write on intricate[1] South African problems so long as I was there. He had the greatest confidence in my discernment, and therefore threw on me the responsibility of attending to the editorial columns. The journal has been until this day a weekly, In the beginning it used to be issued in Gujarati, Hindi, Tamil and English. I saw, however, that the Tamil and Hindi sections were a make-believe. They did not serve the purpose for which they were intended, so I discontinued[2] them as I even felt that there would be a certain amount of deception involved in their continuance.

I had no notion that I should have to invest any money in this journal, but I soon discovered that it could not go on without my financial help. The Indians and the Europeans both knew that, though I was not avowedly the editor of *Indian Opinion*, I was virtually responsible for its conduct. It would not have mattered if the journal had never been started, but to stop it after it had once been launched would have been both a loss and

1. *intricate: very complicated or detailed*
2. *discontinued: stop doing, providing, or making*

a disgrace. So I kept on pouring out my money, until ultimately I was practically sinking all my savings in it. I remember a time when I had to remit £75 each month.

But after all these years I feel that the journal has served the community well. It was never intended to be a commercial concern. So long as it was under my control, the changes in the journal were indicative of changes in my life. *Indian Opinion* in those days, like *Young India* and *Navajivan* today, was a mirror of part of my life. Week after week I poured out my soul in its columns, and expounded[1] the principles and practice of Satyagraha as I understood it. During ten years, that is, until 1914, excepting the intervals of my enforced rest in prison, there was hardly an issue of *Indian Opinion* without an article from me. I cannot recall a word in those articles set down without thought or deliberation, or a word of conscious exaggeration, or anything merely to please. Indeed the journal became for me a training in self-restraint, and for friends a medium through which to keep in touch with my thoughts. The critic found very little to which he could object. In fact the tone of *Indian Opinion* compelled the critic to put a curb on his own pen. Satyagraha would probably have been impossible without *Indian Opinion*. The readers looked forward to it for a trustworthy account of the Satyagraha campaign as also of the real condition of Indians in South Africa. For me it became a means for the study of human nature in all its casts and shades, as I always aimed at establishing an intimate and clean bond between the editor and the readers. I was inundated with letters containing the outpourings of my correspondents' hearts. They were friendly, critical or bitter, according to the temper of the writer. It was a fine education for me to study, digest and answer all this correspondence. It was as though the community thought audibly[2] through this correspondence with me. It made me thoroughly understand the responsibility of a journalist, and the hold I secured in this way over the community made the future campaign workable, dignified and irresistible.

In the very first month of *Indian Opinion*, I realized that the sole aim of journalism should be service. The newspaper press is a great power, but just as an unchained torrent of water submerges whole countrysides and devastates crops, even so an uncontrolled pen serves but to destroy. If the control is from without, it proves more poisonous than want of

1. *expounded: present and explain*
2. *audibly: in an audible manner*

control. It can be profitable only when exercised from within. If this line of reasoning is correct, how many of the journals in the world would stand the test? But who would stop those that are useless? And who should be the judge? The useful and the useless must, like good and evil generally, go on together, and man must make his choice.

CHAPTER 91

COOLIE LOCATIONS OR GHETTOS?

Some of the classes which render us the greatest social service, but which we Hindus have chosen to regard as 'untouchables,' are relegated to remote quarters of a town or a village, called in Gujarati *dhedvado*, and the name has acquired[1] a bad odour[2]. Even so in Christian Europe the Jews were once 'untouchables' and the quarters that were assigned to them had the offensive name of 'ghettoes.' In a similar way today we have become the untouchables of South Africa. It remains to be seen how far the sacrifice of Andrews and the magic wand of Sastri succeed in rehabilitating[3] us.

The ancient Jews regarded themselves as the chosen people of God, to the exclusion of all others, with the result that their descendants were visited with a strange and even unjust retribution[4]. Almost in a similar way the Hindus have considered themselves *Aryas* or civilized, and a section of their own kith and kin as *Anaryas* or untouchables, with the result that a strange, if unjust, nemesis is being visited not only upon the Hindus in South Africa, but the Musalmans and Parsis as well, inasmuch as they belong to the same country and have the same colour as their Hindu brethren.

The reader will have now realized to some extent the meaning of the word 'locations' with which I have headed this chapter. In South Africa we have acquired the odious name of 'coolies'. The word 'coolie' in India means only a porter or hired workman, but in South Africa it has a contemptuous connotation. It means what a pariah or an untouchable means to us, and the quarters assigned to the 'coolies' are known as 'coolie locations'. Johannesburg had one such location, but unlike other places with locations where the Indians had tenancy rights, here they acquired their plots on a lease of ninety-nine years. People were densely packed in the location, the area of which never increased with the increase in population. Beyond arranging to clean the latrines in the location in a haphazard way, the Municipality did nothing to provide any sanitary

1. *acquired: come to possess*
2. *odour: a distinctive smell; a lingering quality or impression*
3. *rehabilitating: restore the standing or reputation of*
4. *retribution: punishment inflicted in the spirit of moral outrage or personal vengeance*

facilities, much less good roads or lights. It was hardly likely that it would safeguard its sanitation, when it was indifferent to the welfare of the residents. These were too ignorant of the rules of municipal sanitation and hygiene[1] to do without the help or supervision of the Municipality. If those who went there had all been Robinson Crusoes, theirs would have been a different story. But we do not know of a single emigrant colony of Robinson Crusoes in the world. Usually people migrate abroad in search of wealth and trade, but the bulk[2] of the Indians who went to South Africa were ignorant, pauper agriculturists, who needed all the care and protection that could be given them. The traders and educated Indians who followed them were very few.

The criminal[3] negligence of the Municipality and the ignorance of the Indian settlers thus conspired to render the location thoroughly insanitary. The Municipality, far from doing anything to improve the condition of the location, used the insanitation, caused by their own neglect, as a pretext[4] for destroying the location, and for that purpose obtained from the local legislature authority to dispossess the settlers. This was the condition of things when I settled in Johannesburg.

The settlers, having proprietary rights in their land, were naturally entitled to compensation. A special tribunal was appointed to try the land acquisition cases. If the tenant was not prepared to accept the offer of the Municipality, he had a right to appeal to the tribunal, and if the latter's award exceeded the Municipality's offer, the Municipality had to bear the costs.

Most of the tenants engaged me as their legal adviser. I had no desire to make money out of these cases, so I told the tenants that I should be satisfied with whatever costs the tribunal awarded, in case they won, and a fee of £10 on every lease, irrespective of the result of the case. I also told them that I proposed to set apart half of the money paid by them for the building of a hospital or similar institution for the poor. This naturally pleased them all.

Out of about seventy cases only one was lost. So the fees amounted to a fairly big figure. But *Indian Opinion* was there with its persistent claim and devoured, so far as I can recollect, a sum of £1,600. I had worked hard for these cases. The clients always surrounded me. Most of them were originally indentured labourers from South India. For the redress

1. *hygiene: conditions or practices conducive to maintaining health and preventing disease, especially cleanliness*
2. *bulk: the greater part*
3. *criminal: deplorable and shocking*
4. *pretext: an ostensible or false reason used to justify an action*

of their peculiar grievances they had formed an association of their own, separate from that of the free Indian merchants and traders. Some of them were open-hearted, liberal men and had high character. Their leaders were Sjt. Jairamsing, the president, and Sjt. Badri, who was as good as the president. Both of them are now no more. They were exceedingly helpful to me. Sjt. Badri came in very close contact with me and took a prominent[1] part in Satyagraha. Through these and other friends I came in intimate contact with numerous Indian settlers from North and South India. I became more their brother than a mere[2] legal adviser, and shared in all their private and public sorrows and hardships.

It may be of some interest to know how the Indians used to name me. Abdulla Sheth refused to address me as Gandhi. None, fortunately, ever insulted me by calling or regarding me as 'saheb'. Abdulla Sheth hit upon a fine appellation-'bhai', i.e., brother. Others followed him and continued to address me as 'bhai' until the moment I left South Africa. There was a sweet flavour about the name when it was used by the ex-indentured Indians.

1. *prominent: important; famous*

2. *mere: that is solely or no more or better than what is specified*

CHAPTER 92

THE BLACK PLAGUE – I

The Indians were not removed from the location as soon as the Municipality secured its ownership. It was necessary to find the residents suitable new quarters before dislodging them, but as the Municipality could not easily do this, the Indians were suffered to stay in the same 'dirty' location, with this difference that their condition became worse than before. Having ceased to be proprietors they became tenants of the Municipality, with the result that their surroundings became more insanitary than ever. When they were proprietors, they had to maintain some sort of cleanliness, if only for fear of the law. The Municipality had no such fear! The number of tenants increased, and with them the squalor[1] and the disorder.

While the Indians were fretting over this state of things, there was a sudden outbreak of the black plague, also called the pneumonic plague, more terrible and fatal than the bubonic.

Fortunately it was not the location but one of the gold mines in the vicinity of Johannesburg that was responsible for the outbreak. The workers in this mine were for the most part negroes, for whose cleanliness their white employers were solely responsible. There were a few Indians also working in connection with the mine, twenty-three of whom suddenly caught the infection, and returned one evening to their quarters in the location with an acute attack of the plague. Sjt. Madanjit, who was then canvassing subscribers for *Indian Opinion* and realizing subscriptions, happened to be in the location at this moment. He was a remarkably fearless[2] man. His heart wept to see these victims of the scourge, and he sent a pencil-note to me to the following effect: 'There has been a sudden outbreak of the black plague. You must come immediately and take prompt measures, otherwise we must be prepared for dire[3] consequences. Please come immediately.'

Sjt. Madanjit bravely broke open the lock of a vacant house, and put all the patients there. I cycled to the location, and wrote to the Town Clerk

1. *squalor: the state of being squalid*
2. *fearless: brave or not scared*
3. *dire: extremely serious or urgent*

to inform him of the circumstances in which we had taken possession of the house.

Dr. William Godfrey, who was practising in Johannesburg, ran to the rescue as soon as he got the news, and became both nurse and doctor to the patients. But twenty-three patients were more than three of us could cope with.

It is my faith, based on experience, that if one's heart is pure, calamity brings in its train men and measures to fight it. I had at that time four Indians in my office Sjts. Kalyandas, Maneklal, Gunvantrai Desai and another whose name I cannot recollect. Kalyandas had been entrusted to me by his father. In South Africa I have rarely come across anyone more obliging and willing to render implicit obedience than Kalyandas. Fortunately he was unmarried[1] then, and I did not hesitate to impose on him duties involving risks, however great Maneklal I had secured in Johannesburg. He too, so far as I can remember, was unmarried. So I decided to sacrifice all four - call them clerks, co-workers or sons. There was no need at all to consult Kalyandas. The others expressed their readiness as soon as they were asked. 'Where you are, we will also be', was their short and sweet reply.

Mr. Ritch had a large family. He was ready to take the plunge[2], but I prevented him. I had not the heart to expose him to the risk. So he attended to the work outside the danger zone.

It was a terrible night - that night of vigil and nursing. I had nursed a number of patients before, but never any attacked by the black plague. Dr. Godfrey's pluck proved infectious. There was not much nursing required. To give them their doses of medicine, to attend to their wants, to keep them and their beds clean and tidy, and to cheer them up was all that we had to do.

The indefatigable zeal and fearlessness with which the youths worked rejoiced me beyond measure. One could understand the bravery of Dr. Godfrey and of an experienced man like Sjt. Madanjit. But the spirit of these callow[3] youths!

So far as I can recollect, we pulled all the patients through that night.

But the whole incident, apart from its pathos[4], is of such absorbing interest and, for me, of such religious value, that I must devote to it at least two more chapters.

1. *unmarried: not married; single*
2. *plunge: fall or move suddenly and uncontrollably; jump or dive quickly and energetically*
3. *callow: inexperienced and immature*
4. *pathos: a quality that evokes pity or sadness*

CHAPTER 93

THE BLACK PLAGUE – II

The Town Clerk expressed his gratitude to me for having taken charge of the vacant house and the patients. He frankly confessed that the Town Council had no immediate means to cope with such an emergency, but promised that they would render all the help in their power. Once awakened to a sense of their duty, the Municipality made no delay[1] in taking prompt measures.

The next day they placed a vacant godown[2] at my disposal, and suggested that the patients be removed there, but the Municipality did not undertake to clean the premises. The building was unkempt[3] and unclean. We cleaned it up ourselves, raised a few beds and other necessaries through the offices of charitable Indians, and improvised a temporary hospital. The Municipality lent the services of a nurse, who came with brandy and other hospital equipment. Dr. Godfrey still remained in charge.

The nurse was a kindly lady and would fain have attended to the patients, but we rarely allowed her to touch them, lest she should catch the contagion.

We had instructions to give the patients frequent doses of brandy. The nurse even asked us to take it for precaution, just as she was doing herself. But none of us would touch it. I had no faith in its beneficial effect even for the patients. With the permission of Dr. Godfrey, I put three patients, who were prepared to do without brandy, under the earth treatment, applying wet earth bandages to their heads and chests. Two of these were saved. The other twenty died in the godown.

Meanwhile the Municipality was busy taking other measures. There was a lazaretto for contagious diseases about seven miles from Johannesburg. The two surviving patients were removed to tents near the lazaretto, and arrangements were made for sending any fresh cases there. We were thus relieved of our work.

In the course of a few days we learnt that the good nurse had had an attack and immediately succumbed[4]. It is impossible to say how the two

1. *delay: become or cause to become late or slow*
2. *godown: a warehouse*
3. *unkempt: untidy or disheveled*
4. *succumbed: die from the effect of a disease or injury*

patients were saved and how we remained immune, but the experience enhanced my faith in earth treatment, as also my scepticism of the efficacy of brandy, even as a medicine. I know that neither this faith nor this scepticism[1] is based upon any solid grounds, but I still retain the impression which I then received, and have therefore thought it necessary to mention it here.

On the outbreak of the plague, I had addressed a strong letter to the press, holding the Municipality guilty of negligence after the location came into its possession and responsible for the outbreak of the plague itself. This letter secured me Mr. Henry Polak, and was partly responsible for the friendship of the late Rev. Joseph Doke.

I have said in an earlier chapter that I used to have my meals at a vegetarian restaurant. Here I met Mr. Albert West. We used to meet in this restaurant every evening and go out walking after dinner. Mr. West was a partner in a small printing concern. He read my letter in the press about the outbreak of the plague and, not finding me in the restaurant, felt uneasy.

My co-workers and I had reduced our diet since the outbreak, as I had long made it a rule to go on a light diet during epidemics[2]. In these days I had therefore given up my evening dinner. Lunch also I would finish before the other guests arrived. I knew the proprietor of the restaurant very well, and I had informed him that, as I was engaged in nursing the plague patients, I wanted to avoid the contact of friends as much as possible.

Not finding me in the restaurant for a day or two, Mr. West knocked at my door early one morning just as I was getting ready to go out for a walk. As I opened the door Mr. West said: 'I did not find you in the restaurant and was really afraid lest[3] something should have happened to you. So I decided to come and see you in the morning in order to make sure of finding you at home. Well, here I am at your disposal. I am ready to help in nursing the patients. You know that I have no one depending on me.'

I expressed my gratitude, and without taking even a second to think, replied: 'I will not have you as a nurse. If there are no more cases, we shall be free in a day or two. There is one thing however.'

'Yes, what is it?'

1. *scepticism: a person inclined to question or doubt accepted opinions; a person who doubts the [philosophy] a philosopher who denies the possibility of knowledge, or even rational belief, in certain spheres*
2. *epidemics: a widespread occurrence of an infectious disease in a community at a particular time; a sudden, widespread occurrence of an undesirable phenomenon*
3. *lest: with the intention of preventing; to avoid the risk of*

'Could you take charge of the *Indian Opinion* press at Durban? Mr. Madanjit is likely to be engaged here, and someone is needed at Durban. If you could go, I should feel quite relieved on that score.'

'You know that I have a press. Most probably I shall be able to go, but may I give my final reply in the evening? We shall talk it over during our evening walk.

I was delighted. We had the talk. He agreed to go. Salary was no consideration to him, as money was not his motive, But a salary £10 per month and a part of the profits, if any, was fixed up. The very next day Mr. West left for Durban by the evening mail, entrusting me with the recovery of his dues. From that day until the time I left the shores of South Africa, he remained a partner of my joys and sorrows.

Mr. West belonged to a peasant[1] family in Louth (Lincolnshire). He had had an ordinary school education, but had learnt a good deal in the school of experience and by dint[2] of self-help. I have always known him to be a pure, sober[3], god-fearing, humane Englishman.

We shall know more of him and his family in the chapters to follow.

1. *peasant: a poor small-holder or agricultural laborer of low social status*
2. *dint: a blow or stroke*
3. *sober: serious; thoughtful*

CHAPTER 94

LOCATION IN FLAMES

Though my co-workers and I were relieved of the charge of the patients, there remained many things arising out of the black plague still to be dealt with.

I have referred to the negligence of the Municipality regarding the location. But it was wide awake so far as the health of its white citizens was concerned. It had spent large amounts for the preservation of their health and now it poured forth money like water in order to stamp out the plague. In spite of the many sins of omission[1] and commission against the Indians that I had laid at the door of the Municipality, I could not help commending its solicitude for the white citizens, and I rendered it as much help as I could in its laudable[2] efforts. I have an impression that, if I had withheld my co-operation, the task would have been more difficult for the Municipality, and that it would not have hesitated to use armed force and do its worst.

But all that was averted[3]. The Municipal authorities were pleased at the Indians' behaviour, and much of the future work regarding plague measures was simplified. I used all the influence I could with the Indians to make them submit to the Municipality's requirements and I do not remember anyone having resisted my advice.

The location was put under a strong guard, passage in and out being made impossible without permission. My co-workers and I had free permits of entry and exit. The decision was to make the whole location population vacate, and live under canvas[4] for three weeks in an open plain about thirteen miles from Johannesburg, and then to set fire to the location. To settle down under canvas with provisions and other necessaries was bound to take some time, and a guard became necessary during the interval.

The people were in a terrible fright, but my constant presence was a consolation to them. Many of the poor people used to hoard their scanty

1. *omission: someone or something that has been left out*
2. *laudable: deserving praise and commendation*
3. *averted: prevent or ward off*
4. *canvas: a strong, coarse unbleached cloth used to make sails, tents, etc., and a surface for oil painting; a piece of canvas prepared for use as the surface for an oil painting; the floor of a boxing or wrestling ring, having a canvas covering*

savings underground. This had to be unearthed[1]. They had no bank, they knew none. I became their banker. Streams of money poured into my office. I could not possibly charge any fees for my labours in such a crisis. I coped with the work somehow. I knew my bank manager very well. I told him that I should have to deposit these moneys with him. The banks were by no means anxious[2] to accept large amounts of copper and silver. There was also the fear of bank clerks refusing to touch money coming from a plague-affected area. But the manager accommodated me in every way. It was decided to disinfect[3] all the money before sending it to the bank. So far as I can remember, nearly sixty thousand pounds were thus deposited. I advised such of the people as had enough money to place it as fixed deposit, and they accepted the advice. The result was some of them became accustomed[4] to invest their money in banks.

The location residents were removed by special train to Klipspruit Farm near Johannesburg, where they were supplied with provisions by the Municipality at public expense. This city under canvas looked like a military camp. The people who were unaccustomed to this camp life were distressed and astonished over the arrangements; but they did not have to put up with any particular inconvenience. I used to cycle out to them daily. Within twenty-four hours of their stay they forgot all their misery and began to live merrily. Whenever I went there I found them enjoying themselves with song and mirth. Three weeks' stay in the open air evidently improved their health.

So far as I recollect, the location was put to the flames on the very next day after its evacuation. The Municipality showed not the slightest inclination to save anything from the conflagration. About this very time, and for the same reason, the Municipality burnt down all its timber in the market, and sustained a loss of some £10000. The reason for this drastic step was the discovery of some dead rats in the market.

The Municipality had to incur heavy expenditure, but it successfully arrested the further progress of the plague, and the city once more breathed freely.

1. *unearthed: discover by investigation or searching*
2. *anxious: experiencing worry or unease*
3. *disinfect: make clean and free from infection, especially by the use of a chemical disinfectant*
4. *accustomed: be used to*

CHAPTER 95

THE MAGIC SPELL OF A BOOK

The black plague enhanced[1] my influence with the poor Indians, and increased my business and my responsibility. Some of the new contacts with Europeans became so close that they added considerably to my moral obligations.

I made the acquaintance of Mr. Polak in the vegetarian restaurant, just as I had made that of Mr. West. One evening a young man dining at a table a little way off sent me his card expressing a desire to see me. I invited him to come to my table, which he did.

'I am sub-editor of the *The Critic*,' he said 'When I read your letter to the press about the plague. I felt a strong desire to see you. I am glad to have this opportunity.'

Mr. Polak's candour[2] drew me to him. The same evening we got to know each other. We seemed to hold closely similar views on the essential things of life. He liked simple life. He had a wonderful faculty of translating into practice anything that appealed to his intellect. Some of the changes that he had made in his life were as prompt as they were radical.

Indian Opinion was getting more and more expensive every day. The very first report from Mr. West was alarming. He wrote: 'I do not expect the concern to yield the profit that you had thought probable[3]. I am afraid there may be even a loss. The books are not in order. There are heavy arrears to be recovered, but one cannot make head or tail of them. Considerable overhauling[4] will have to be done. But all this need not alarm you. I shall try to put things right as best I can. I remain on, whether there is profit or not.'

Mr. West might have left when he discovered that there was no profit, and I could not have blamed him. In fact, he had a right to arraign me for having described the concern as profitable without proper proof. But he never so much as uttered one word of complaint. I have, however, an

1. *enhanced: improve the quality, value, or extent of*
2. *candour: the quality of being open and honest*
3. *probable: likely to happen or be the case*
4. *overhauling: examine and repair it if necessary*

impression that this discovery led Mr. West to regard me as credulous. I had simply accepted Sjt. Madanjit's estimate[1] without caring to examine it, and told Mr. West to expect a profit.

I now realize that a public worker should not make statements of which he has not made sure. Above all, a votary of truth must exercise the greatest caution. To allow a man to believe a thing which one has not fully verified is to compromise truth. I am pained to have to confess that, in spite of this knowledge, I have not quite conquered my credulous habit, for which my ambition to do more work than I can manage is responsible. This ambition has often been a source of worry more to my co-workers than to myself.

On receipt of Mr. West's letter I left for Natal. I had taken Mr. Polak into my fullest confidence. He came to see me off at the station, and left with me a book to read during the journey, which he said I was sure to like. It was Ruskin's *Unto*[2] *This Last*.

The book was impossible to lay aside, once I had begun it. It gripped me. Johannesburg to Durban was a twenty-four hours' journey. The train reached there in the evening. I could not get any sleep that night. I determined to change my life in accordance with the ideals of the book.

This was the first book of Ruskin I had ever read. During the days of my education I had read practically nothing outside text-books, and after I launched into active life I had very little time for reading. I cannot therefore claim much book knowledge. However, I believe I have not lost much because of this enforced restraint. On the contrary, the limited reading may be said to have enabled me thoroughly to digest what I did read. Of these books, the one that brought about an instantaneous and practical transformation in my life was *Unto This Last*. I translated it later into Gujarati, entitling it *Sarvodaya* (the welfare of all).

I believe that I discovered some of my deepest convictions reflected in this great book of Ruskin, and that is why it so captured me and made me transform my life. A poet is one who can call forth the good latent in the human breast. Poets do not influence all alike, for everyone is not evolved in an equal measure.

The teaching of *Unto This Last* I understood to be:

1. That the good of the individual is contained in the good of all.
2. That a lawyer's work has the same value as the barber's inasmuch as all have the same right of earning their livehood from their work.

1. *estimate: an approximate calculation or judgment; a written statement indicated the likely price that will be charged for specified work*
2. *unto: archaic term for 'to'*

3. That a life of labour, i.e., the life of the tiller[1] of the soil and the handicraftsman is the life worth living.

The first of these I knew. The second I had dimly realized. The third had never occured to me. *Unto This Last* made it as clear as daylight for me that the second and the third were contained in the first. I arose with the dawn, ready to reduce these principles to practice.

1. tiller: an implement or machine for breaking up soil; a plough or cultivator

CHAPTER 96

THE PHOENIX SETTLEMENT

I talked over the whole thing with Mr. West, described to him the effect *Unto This Last* had produced on my mind, and proposed that *Indian Opinion* should be removed to a farm, on which everyone should labour, drawing the same living wage[1], and attending to the press work in spare[2] time. Mr. West approved of the proposal, and £3 was laid down as the monthly allowance per head, irrespective of colour or nationality.

But it was a question whether all the ten or more workers in the press would agree to go and settle on an out-of-the-way farm, and be satisfied with bare maintenance. We therefore proposed that those who could not fit in with the scheme should continue to draw their salaries and gradually try to reach the ideal of becoming members of the settlement.

I talked to the workers in the terms of this proposal. It did not appeal to Sjt. Madanjit, who considered my proposal to be foolish and held that it would ruin a venture on which he had staked his all; that the workers would bolt, *Indian Opinion* would come to a stop, and the press would have to be closed down.

Among the men working in the press was Chhaganlal Gandhi, one of my cousins. I had put the proposal to him at the same time as to West. He had a wife and children, but he had from childhood chosen to be trained and to work under me. He had full faith in me. So without any argument he agreed to the scheme and has been with me ever since. The machinist Govindaswami also fell in with the proposal. The rest did not join the scheme, but agreed to go wherever I removed the press.

I do not think I took more than two days to fix up these matters with the men. Thereafter I at once advertised for a piece of land situated near a railway station in the vicinity of Durban. An offer came in respect of Phoenix. Mr. West and I went to inspect the estate. Within a week we purchased twenty acres of land. It had a nice little spring and a few orange and mango trees. Adjoining it was a piece of 80 acres which had many

1. *wage: a fixed regular payment for work, typically paid on a daily or weekly basis*

2. *spare: additional to what is required for ordinary use; not currently in use or occupied*

more fruit trees and a dilapidated cottage. We purchased this too, the total cost being a thousand pounds.

The late Mr. Rustomji always supported me in such enterprises. He liked the project. He placed at my disposal second-hand corrugated iron sheets of a big godown and other building material, with which we started work. Some Indian carpenters and masons, who had worked with me in the Boer War, helped me in erecting a shed for the press. This structure, which was seventy-five feet long and fifty feet broad, was ready in less than a month. Mr. West and others, at great personal risk, stayed with the carpenters and masons. The place, uninhabited and thickly overgrown[1] with grass, was infested with snakes and obviously dangerous to live in. At first all lived under canvas. We carted most of our things to Phoenix in about a week. It was 14 miles from Durban, and two and a half miles from Phoenix station.

Only one issue of *Indian Opinion* had to be printed outside, in the Mercury press.

I now endeavoured to draw to Phoenix those relations and friends who had come with me from India to try their fortune, and who were engaged in business of various kinds. They had come in search of wealth, and it was therefore difficult to persuade them; but some agreed. Of these I can single out here only Manganlal Gandhi's name. The others went back to business. Manganlal Gandhi left his business for good to cast in his lot with me, and by ability, sacrifice and devotion stands foremost among my original co-workers in my ethical experiments. As a self-taught handicraftsman his place among them is unique.

Thus the Phoenix Settlement was started in 1904, and there in spite of numerous odds *Indian Opinion* continues to be published.

But the initial difficulties, the changes made, the hopes and the disappointments demand a separate chapter.

1. *overgrown: grown over with vegetation*

CHAPTER 97

THE FIRST NIGHT

It was no easy thing to issue the first number of *Indian Opinion* from Phoenix. Had I not taken two precautions, the first issue would have had to be dropped or delayed. The idea of having an engine to work the press had not appealed to me. I had thought that hand-power would be more in keeping with an atmosphere where agricultural[1] work was also to be done by hand. But as the idea had not appeared feasible, we had installed[2] an oil-engine. I had, however, suggested to West to have something handy[3] to fall back upon in case the engine failed. He had therefore arranged a wheel which could be worked by hand. The size of the paper, that of a daily, was considered unsuitable for an out-of-the-way place like Phoenix. It was reduced to foolscap size, so that, in case of emergency, copies might be struck off with the help of a treadle[4].

In the initial stages, we all had to keep late hours before the day of publication. Everyone, young and old, had to help in folding the sheets. We usually finished our work between ten o'clock and midnight. But the first night was unforgettable. We had got out an engineer from Durban to put up the engine and set it going. He and West tried their hardest, but in vain. Everyone was anxious. West, in despair, at last came to me, with tears in his eyes, and said, 'The engine will not work, I am afraid we cannot issue the paper in time.'

'If that is the case, we cannot help it. No use shedding tears. Let us do whatever else is humanly possible. What about the hand-wheel?' I said, comforting him.

'Where have we the men to work?' he replied. 'We are not enough to cope with the job. It requires relays of four men each, and our own men are all tired.'

Building work had not yet been finished so the carpenters were still with us. They were sleeping on the press floor. I said pointing to them, 'But can't we make use of these carpenters? And we may have a whole night of work. I think this device is still open to us.'

1. *agricultural: the science or practice of farming, including the rearing of crops and animals*
2. *installed: established in a new place*
3. *handy: convenient to handle or use; useful*
4. *treadle: a lever worked by the foot and imparting motion to a machine*

'I dare not wake up the carpenters[1]. And our men are really too tired,' said West.

'Well, that's for me to negotiate,' said I.

'Then it is possible that we may get through the work,' West replied.

I woke up the carpenters and requested their co-operation. They needed no pressure. They said, 'If we cannot be called upon in an emergency, what use are we? You rest yourselves and we will work the wheel. For us it is easy work.' Our own men were of course ready.

West was greatly delighted and started singing a hymn[2] as we set to work. I partnered the carpenters, all the rest joined turn by turn, and thus we went on until 7 a.m. There was still a good deal to do. I therefore suggested to West that the engineer[3] might now be asked to get up and try again to start the engine, so that if we succeeded we might finish in time.

West woke him up, and he immediately went into the engine room. And lo and behold[4]! the engine worked almost as soon as he touched it. The whole press rang with peals of joy. 'How can this be? How is it that all our labours last night were of no avail, and this morning it has been set going as though there were nothing wrong with it?' I enquired.

'It is difficult to say,' said West or the engineer, I forget which. 'Machines also sometimes seem to behave as though they required rest like us.'

For me the failure of the engine had come as a test for us all, and its working in the nick of time as the fruit of our honest and earnest labours.

The copies were despatched in time, and everyone was happy.

This initial insistence ensured the regularity of the paper, and created an atmosphere of self-reliance in Phoenix. There came a time we deliberately gave up the use of the engine and worked with hand-power only. Those were, to my mind, the days of the highest moral uplift for Phoenix.

1. *carpenters: a person who makes wooden objects and structures*
2. *hymn: a religious song of praise, typically a christian song in praise of god*
3. *engineer: a person qualified in engineering*
4. *behold: see or observe*

CHAPTER 98

POLAK TAKES THE PLUNGE

It has always been my regret that, although I started the Settlement at Phoenix, I could stay there only for brief periods. My original idea had been gradually to retire from practice, go and live at the Settlement, earn my livelihood by manual work there, and find the joy of service in the fulfillment of Phoenix. But it was not to be. I have found by experience that man makes his plans to be often upset by God, but, at the same time where the ultimate[1] goal is the search of truth, no matter how a man's plans are frustrated[2], the issue is never injurious[3] and often better than anticipated. The unexpected turn that Phoenix took and the unexpected happenings were certainly not injurious, though it is difficult to say that they were better than our original expectations.

In order to enable every one of us to make a living by manual labour, we parceled out the land round the press in pieces of three acres each. One of these fell to my lot. On all these plots we, much against our wish, built houses with corrugated iron. Our desire had been to have mud huts thatched with straw or small brick houses such as would become ordinary peasants, but it could not be. They would have been more expensive and would have meant more time, and everyone was eager to settle down as soon as possible.

The editor was still Mansukhlal Nazar. He had not accepted the new scheme and was directing the paper from Durban where there was a branch office for *Indian Opinion*. Though we had paid compositors, the idea was for every member of the Settlement to learn type-setting, the easiest, if the most tedious, of the processes in a printing press. Those, therefore, who did not already know the work learnt it. I remained a dunce[4] to the last. Maganlal Gandhi surpassed us all. Though he had never before worked in a press, he became an expert compositor and not only achieved great speed but, to my agreeable surprise, quickly mastered all the other branches of press work. I have always thought that he was not conscious of his own capacity.

1. *ultimate: being or happening at the end of a process*
2. *frustrated: causing or likely to cause injury*
3. *injurious: prevent from progressing, succeeding, or being fulfilled; prevent from doing or achieving something*
4. *dunce: a person who is slow at learning*

We had hardly settled down, the buildings were hardly ready, when I had to leave the newly constructed[1] nest[2] and go to Johannesburg. I was not in a position to allow the work there to remain without attention for any length of time.

On return to Johannesburg, I informed Polak of the important changes I had made. His joy knew no bounds when he learnt that the loan of his book had been so fruitful. 'Is it not possible,' he asked, 'for me to take part in the new venture?'. 'Certainly,' said I. 'You may if you like join the Settlement.' 'I am quite ready,' he replied, 'If you will admit me.'

His determination captured[3] me. He gave a month's notice to his chief to be relieved from *The Critic*, and reached Phoenix in due course. By his sociability he won the hearts of all and soon became a member of the family. Simplicity was so much a part of his nature that, far from feeling the life at Phoenix in any way strange or hard, he took to it like a duck takes to water. But I could not keep him there long. Mr. Ritch had decided to finish his legal studies in England, and it was impossible for me to bear the burden of the office single-handed, so I suggested to Polak that he should join the office and qualify as an attorney. I had thought that ultimately both of us would retire and settle at Phoenix, but that never came to pass. Polak's was such a trustful nature that, when he reposed his confidence in a friend, he would try to agree with him instead of arguing with him. He wrote to me from Phoenix that though he loved the life there, was perfectly happy, and had hopes of developing the Settlement, still he was ready to leave and join the office to qualify as an attorney, if I thought that thereby we should more quickly realize our ideals. I heartily welcomed the letter. Polak left Phoenix, came to Johannesburg and signed his articles with me.

About the same time a Scots theosophist, whom I had been coaching for a local legal examination, also joined as an articled clerk, on my inviting him to follow Polak's example. His name was Mr. MacIntyre.

Thus, with the laudable object of quickly realizing the ideals at Phoenix, I seemed to be going deeper and deeper into a contrary current, and had God not willed otherwise, I should have found myself entrapped in this net spread in the name of simple life.

It will be after a few more chapters that I shall describe how I and my ideals were saved in a way no one had imagined or expected.

1. *nest: a snug or secluded retreat*
2. *constructed: build or erect*
3. *captured: absorb*

CHAPTER 99

WHOM GOD PROTECTS

I had now given up all hope of returning to India in the near future. I had promised my wife that I would return home within a year. The year was gone without any prospect of my return, so I decided to send for her and the children.

On the boat bringing them to South Africa, Ramdas, my third son, broke his arm while playing with the ship's captain. The captain looked after him well and had him attended to by the ship's doctor. Ramdas landed with his hand in a sling. The doctor had advised that, as soon as we reached home, the wound[1] should be dressed by a qualified[2] doctor. But this was the time when I was full of faith in my experiments in earth treatment[3]. I had even succeeded in persuading some of my clients who had faith in my quackery to try the earth and water treatment.

What then was I to do for Ramdas? He was just eight years old. I asked him if he would mind my dressing[4] his wound. With a smile he said he did not mind at all. It was not possible for him at that age to decide what was the best thing for him, but he knew very well the distinction between quackery and proper medical treatment. And he knew my habit of home treatment and had faith enough to trust himself to me. In fear and trembling I undid the bandage, washed the wound, applied a clean earth poultice and tied the arm up again. This sort of dressing went on daily for about a month until the wound was completely healed. There was no hitch, and the wound took no more time to heal than the ship's doctor had said it would under the usual treatment.

This and other experiments enhanced my faith in such household remedies, and I now proceeded with them with more self-confidence. I widened the sphere of their application, trying the earth and water and fasting treatment in cases of wounds, fevers, dyspepsia, jaundice and other complaints, with success on most occasions. But nowadays I have not the confidence I had in South Africa and experience has even shown that these experiments involve obvious risks.

1. *wound: an injury to living tissue caused by a cut, blow, or other impact*
2. *qualified: certified as being trained to perform a job*
3. *treatment: medical care for an illness or injury*
4. *dressing: clean, treat, or apply a dressing to a wound*

The reference here, therefore, to these experiments is not meant to demonstrate their success. I cannot claim complete success for any experiment. Even medical men can make no such claim for their experiments. My object is only to show that he who would go in for novel experiments must begin with himself. That leads to a quicker discovery of truth, and God always protects the honest experimenter.

The risks involved in experiments in cultivating intimate contacts with Europeans were as grave as those in the nature cure experiments. Only those risks were of a different kind. But in cultivating those contacts I never so much as thought of the risks.

I invited Polak to come and stay with me, and we began to live like blood brothers. The lady who was soon to be Mrs. Polak and he had been engaged for some years, but the marriage had been postponed for a propitious time. I have an impression that Polak wanted to put some money by before he settled down to a married life. He knew Ruskin much better than I, but his Western surroundings were a bar against his translating Ruskin's teaching immediately into practice. But I pleaded with him: 'When there is a heart union, as in your case, it is hardly right to postpone marriage merely for financial considerations. If poverty is a bar, poor men can never marry. And then you are now staying with me. There is no question of household expenses. I think you should get married as soon as possible. As I have said in a previous chapter, I had never to argue a thing twice with Polak. He appreciated the force of my argument, and immediately opened correspondence on the subject with Mrs. Polak, who was then in England. She gladly accepted the proposal and in a few months reached Johannesburg. Any expense over the wedding was out of the question, not even a special dress was thought necessary. They needed no religious rites[1] to seal the bond. Mrs. Polak was a Christian by birth and Polak a Jew. Their common religion was the religion of ethics.

I may mention in passing an amusing incident in connection with this wedding. The Registrar of European marriages in the Transvaal could not register between black or coloured people. In the wedding in question, I acted as the best man. Not that we could not have got a European friend for the purpose, but Polak would not brook the suggestion. So we three went to the Registrar of marriages. How could he be sure that the parties to a marriage in which I acted as the best man would be whites? He proposed to postpone

1. *rites: a religious or other solemn ceremony or event, e.g. marriage, marking an important stage in someone's life*

registration pending inquiries. The next day was a Sunday. The day following was New Year's Day, a public holiday. To postpone the date of a solemnly arranged wedding on such a flimsy[1] pretext[2] was more than one could put up with. I knew the Chief Magistrate, who was head of the Registration Department. So I appeared before him with the couple. He laughed and gave me a note to the Registrar and the marriage was duly[3] registered.

Up to now the Europeans living with us had been more or less known to me before. But now an English lady who was an utter stranger to us entered the family. I do not remember our ever having had a difference with the newly married couple, but even if Mrs. Polak and my wife had some unpleasant experiences, they would have been no more than what happens in the best-regulated homogeneous families. And let it be remembered that mine would be considered an essentially heterogeneous family, where people of all kinds and temperaments were freely admitted. When we come to think of it, the distinction between heterogeneous and homogeneous is discovered to be merely imaginary. We are all one family.

I had better celebrate West's wedding also in this chapter. At this stage of my life, my ideas about *brahmacharya* had not fully matured, and so I was interesting myself in getting all my bachelor friends married. When, in due course, West made a pilgrimage to Louth to see his parents, I advised him to return married if possible. Phoenix was the common home, and as we were all supposed to have become farmers, we were not afraid of marriage and its usual consequences. West returned with Mrs. West, a beautiful young lady from Leicester. She came of a family of shoemakers working in a Leicester factory. I have called her beautiful, because it was her moral beauty that at once attracted me. True beauty after all consists in purity of heart. With Mr. West had come his mother-in-law too. The old lady is still alive. She put us all to shame by her industry and her buoyant, cheerful nature.

In the same way as I persuaded these European friends to marry, I encouraged the Indian friends to send for their families from home. Phoenix thus developed into a little village, half a dozen families having come and settled and begun to increase there.

1. *flimsy: weak and insubstantial, light and thin, weak; unconvincing*
2. *pretext: an ostensible or false reason used to justify an action*
3. *duly: in accordance with what is required or appropriate; as might be expected*

CHAPTER 100

A PEEP INTO THE HOUSEHOLD

It has already been seen that, though household expenses were heavy, the tendency towards simplicity began in Durban. But the Johannesburg house came in for much severer overhauling in the light of Ruskin's teaching.

I introduced as much simplicity as was possible in a barrister's house. It was impossible to do without a certain amount of furniture. The change was more internal than external[1]. The liking for doing personally all the physical labour increased. I therefore began to bring my children also under that discipline.

Instead of buying baker's bread, we began to prepare unleavened wholemeal bread at home according to Kuhne's recipe. Common mill flour was no good for this, and the use of hand-ground flour, it was thought, would ensure more simplicity, health and economy. So I purchased a hand-mill for £7. The iron wheel was too heavy to be tacked by one man, but easy for two. Polak and I and the children usually worked it. My wife also occasionally lent a hand, though the grinding hour was her usual time for commencing[2] kitchen work. Mrs. Polak now joined us on her arrival. The grinding proved a very beneficial exercise for the children. Neither this nor any other work was ever imposed on them, but it was a pastime to them to come and lend a hand, and they were at liberty to break off whenever tired. But the children, including those whom I shall have occasion to introduce later, as a rule never failed me. Not that I had no laggards at all, but most did their work cheerfully enough. I can recall few youngsters in those days fighting shy of work or pleading fatigue[3].

We had engaged a servant to look after the house. He lived with us as a member of the family, and the children used to help him in his work. The municipal sweeper removed the night-soil, but we personally attended to the cleaning of the closet instead of asking or expecting the

1. *external: belonging to, situated on, or forming the outside*
2. *commencing: begin*
3. *fatigue: extreme tiredness resulting from mental or physical exertion or illness, a reduction in the efficiency of a muscle or organ after prolonged activity, a lessening in one's response to or enthusiasm for something, caused by overexposure*

servant to do it. This proved a good training for the children. The result was that none of my sons developed any aversion for scavenger's work, and they naturally got a good grounding[1] in general sanitation. There was hardly any illness in the home at Johannesburg, but whenever there was any, the nursing was willingly done by the children. I will not say that I was indifferent to their literary education, but I certainly did not hesitate to sacrifice it. My sons have therefore some reason for a grievance against me. Indeed they have occasionally given expression to it, and I must plead guilty to a certain extent. The desire to give them a literary education was there. I even endeavoured to give it to them myself, but every now and then there was some hitch or other. As I had made no other arrangement for their private tuition[2], I used to get them to walk with me daily to the office and back home a distance of about five miles in all. This gave them and me a fair amount of exercise. I tried to instruct them by conversation during these walks, if there was no one else claiming my attention. All my children, excepting the eldest, Harilal, who had stayed away in India, were brought up in Johannesburg in this manner. Had I been able to devote at least an hour to their literary education with strict regularity, I should have given them, in my opinion, an ideal education. But it was been their, as also my, regret that I failed to ensure them enough literary training. The eldest son has often given vent to his distress privately before me and publicly in the press; the other sons have generously forgiven the failure as unavoidable[3]. I am not heart broken over it and the regret, if any, is that I did not prove an ideal father. But I hold that I sacrificed their literary training to what I genuinely, though may be wrongly, believed to be service to the community. I am quite clear that I have not been negligent in doing whatever was needful for building up their character. I believe it is the bounden duty of every parent to provide for this properly. Whenever, in spite of my endeavour, my sons have been found wanting, it is my certain conviction that they have reflected, not want of care on my part, but the defects of both their parents.

Children inherit the qualities of the parents, no less than their physical features. Environment does play an important part, but the original capital on which a child starts in life is inherited from its ancestors. I have also seen children successfully surmounting the effects of an evil inheritance. That is due to purity being an inherent attribute[4] of the soul.

1. *grounding: basic training or instruction in a subject*
2. *tuition: teaching or instruction, especially of individuals or small groups; a fee charged for this*
3. *unavoidable: not able to be avoided or prevented; inevitable*
4. *attribute: a quality or feature regarded as characteristic or inherent*

Polak and I had often very heated discussions about the desirability or otherwise of giving the children an English education. It has always been my conviction that Indian parents who train their children to think and talk in English from their infancy betray their children and their country. They deprive them of the spiritual and social heritage of the nation, and render them to that extent unfit for the service of the country. Having these convictions, I made a point of always talking to my children in Gujarati. Polak never liked this. He thought I was spoiling their future. He contended, with all the vigour and love at his command, that, if children were to learn a universal language like English from their infancy, they would easily gain considerable advantage over others in the race of life. He failed to convince me. I do not now remember whether I convinced him of the correctness of my attitude, or whether he gave me up as too obstinate. This happened about twenty years ago, and my convictions have only deepened with experience. Though my sons have suffered for want of full literary education, the knowledge of the mother-tongue that they naturally acquired has been all to their and the country's good, inasmuch as they do not appear the foreigners they would otherwise have appeared. They naturally become bilingual[1], speaking and writing English with fair ease, because of daily contact with a large circle of English friends, and because of their stay in a country where English was the chief language spoken.

1. *bilingual: speaking two languages fluently; expressed in or using two languages*

CHAPTER 101

THE ZULU 'REBELLION'

Even after I thought I had settled down in Johannesburg, there was to be no settled life for me. Just when I felt that I should be breathing in peace, an unexpected event happened. The papers brought the news of the out break of the Zulu 'rebellion' in Natal. I bore no grudge[1] against the Zulus, they had harmed no Indian. I had doubts about the 'rebellion' itself. But I then believed that the British Empire[2] existed for the welfare of the world. A genuine sense of loyalty prevented me from even wishing ill to the Empire. The rightness or otherwise of the 'rebellion' was therefore not likely to affect my decision. Natal had a Volunteer Defence Force, and it was open to it to recruit more men. I read that this force had already been mobilized to quell the 'rebellion'.

I considered myself a citizen of Natal, being intimately connected with it. So I wrote to the Governor, expressing my readiness, if necessary, to form an Indian Ambulance Corps. He replied immediately accepting the offer.

I had not expected such prompt acceptance. Fortunately I had made all the necessary arrangements even before writing the letter. If my offer was accepted, I had decided to break up the Johannesburg home. Polak was to have a smaller house, and my wife was to go and settle at Phoenix. I had her full consent to this decision. I do not remember her having ever stood in my way in matters like this. As soon, therefore, as I got the reply from the Governor, I gave the landlord the usual month's notice of vacating the house, sent some of the things to Phoenix and left some with Polak.

I went to Durban and appealed for men. A big contingent was not necessary. We were a party of twenty-four, of whom, besides me, four were Gujaratis. The rest were ex-indentured men from South India, excepting one who was a free Pathan.

In order to give me a status and to facilitate work, as also in accordance with the existing convention[3], the Chief Medical Officer appointed me

1. *grudge: a persistent feeling of ill will or resentment resulting from a past insult or injury*
2. *empire: an extensive group of states ruled over by a singly monarch, an oligarchy, or a sovereign state*
3. *convention: a way in which something is usually done; socially acceptable behavior*

to the temporary rank of Sergeant Major and three men selected by me to the rank of sergeants[1] and one to that of corporal[2]. We also received our uniforms[3] from the Government. Our Corps was on active service for nearly six weeks. On reaching the scene of the 'rebellion', I saw that there was nothing there to justify the name of 'rebellion'. There was no resistance that one could see. The reason why the disturbance had been magnified into a rebellion was that a Zulu chief had advised non-payment of a new tax imposed on his people, and had assagaied a sergeant who had gone to collect the tax. At any rate my heart was with the Zulus, and I was delighted, on reaching headquarters, to hear that our main work was to be the nursing of the wounded Zulus. The Medical Officer in charge welcomed us. He said the white people were not willing nurses for the wounded Zulus, that their wounds were festering[4], and that he was at his wits' end. He hailed our arrival as a godsend for those innocent people, and he equipped us with bandages, disinfectants, etc., and took us to the improvised hospital. The Zulus were delighted to see us. The white soldiers used to peep through the railings that separated us from them and tried to dissuade us from attending to the wounds. And as we would not heed them, they became enraged and poured unspeakable abuse on the Zulus.

Gradually I came into closer touch with these soldiers, and they ceased to interfere. Among the commanding officers were Colonel Sparks and Colonel Wylie, who had bitterly opposed me in 1896. They were surprised at my attitude and specially called and thanked me. They introduced me to General Mackenzie. Let not the reader think that these were professional soldiers. Colonel Wylie was a well-known Durban lawyer. Colonel Sparks was well known as the owner of a butcher's shop in Durban. General Mackenzie was a noted Natal farmer. All these gentlemen were volunteers, and as such had received military training and experience.

The wounded in our charge were not wounded in battle. A section of them had been taken prisoners as suspects. The General had sentenced them to be flogged. The flogging had caused severe sores. These, being unattended to, were festering. The others were Zulu friendlies. Although these had badges given them to distinguish them from the 'enemy', they had been shot at by the soldiers by mistake.

1. *sergeants: a rank of non-commissioned officer in the army or air force, above corporal and below staff sergeant*
2. *corporal: a rank of non-commissioned officer in the army, above lance corporal or private first class and below sergeant*
3. *uniforms: the distinctive clothing worn by members of the same organization or body or by children attending certain school*
4. *festering: of a wound or sore become septic; become rotten*

Besides this work I had to compound and dispense prescriptions for the white soldiers. This was easy enough for me as I had received a year's training in Dr. Booth's little hospital. This work brought me in close contact with many Europeans[1].

We were attached to a swift-moving column. It had orders to march wherever danger was reported. It was for the most part mounted infantry. As soon as our camp was moved, we had to follow on foot with our stretchers on our shoulders. Twice or thrice we had to march forty miles a day. But wherever we went, I am thankful that we had God's good work to do, having to carry to the camp on our stretchers those Zulu friendlies who had been inadvertently wounded, and to attend upon them as nurses.

1. *Europeans: inhabitants of Europe*

CHAPTER 102

HEART SEARCHINGS

The Zulu 'rebellion' was full of new experiences and gave me much food for thought. The Boer War had not brought home to me the horrors[1] of war with anything like the vividness that the 'rebellion' did. This was no war but a man-hunt, not only in my opinion, but also in that of many Englishmen with whom I had occasion to talk. To hear every morning reports of the soldiers' rifles exploding like crackers in innocent hamlets, and to live in the midst of them was a trial. But I swallowed the bitter draught, especially as the work of my Corps consisted only in nursing the wounded Zulus. I could see that but for us the Zulus would have been uncared for. This work, therefore, eased my conscience.

But there was much else to set one thinking. It was a sparsely[2] populated part of the country. Few and far between in hills and dales were the scattered[3] Kraals of the simple and so-called 'uncivilized' Zulus. Marching, with or without the wounded, through these solemn[4] solitudes, I often fell into deep thought.

I pondered over *brahmacharya* and its implications, and my convictions took deep root. I discussed it with my co-workers. I had not realized then how indispensable it was for self-realization, but I clearly saw that one aspiring to serve humanity with his whole soul could not do without it. It was borne in upon me that I should have more and more occasions for service of the kind I was rendering, and that I should find myself unequal to my task if I were engaged in the pleasures of family life and in the propagation and rearing of children.

In a word, I could not live both after the flesh and the spirit. On the present occasion, for instance, I should not have been able to throw myself into the fray, had my wife been expecting a baby. Without the observance of *brahmacharya* service of the family would be inconsistent with service of the community. With *brahmacharya* they would be perfectly consistent.

1. *horrors: an intense feeling of fear, shock, or disgust; a thing causing such a feeling; intense dismay*
2. *sparsely: thinly dispersed*
3. *scattered: throw in various random directions; separate or cause to separate and move off in different directions; occur or be found at various places rather than all together*
4. *solemn: formal and dignified; a solemn procession*

So thinking, I became somewhat impatient to take a final vow. The prospect of the vow brought a certain kind of exultation. Imagination also found free play and opened out limitless vistas[1] of service.

Whilst I was thus in the midst of strenuous physical and mental work, a report came to the effect that the work of suppressing the 'rebellion' was nearly over, and that we should soon be discharged. A day or two after this our discharge came and in a few days we got back to our homes.

After a short while I got a letter from the Governor specially thanking the Ambulance Corps for its services.

On my arrival at Phoenix I eagerly broached the subject of *brahmacharya* with Chhaganlal, Maganlal, West and others. They liked the idea and accepted the necessity of taking the vow, but they also represented the difficulties of the task. Some of them set themselves bravely to observe it, and some, I know, succeeded also.

I too took the plunge the vow to observe *brahmacharya* for life. I must confess that I had not then fully realized the magnitude and immensity of the task I undertook. The difficulties are even today staring[2] me in the face. The importance of the vow is being more and more borne in upon me. Life without *brahmacharya* appears to me to be insipid and animal-like. The brute by nature knows no self-restraint. Man is man because he is capable of, and only in so far as he exercises, self-restraint. What formerly appeared to me to be extravagant praise of *brahmacharya* in our religious books seems now, with increasing clearness every day, to be absolutely proper and founded on experience.

I saw that *brahmacharya*, which is so full of wonderful potency, is by no means an easy affair, and certainly not a mere matter of the body. It begins with bodily restraint, but does not end there. The perfection of it precludes even an impure thought. A true *brahmachari* will not even dream of satisfying the fleshly[3] appetite, and until he is in that condition, he has a great deal of ground to cover.

For me the observance of even bodily *brahmacharya* has been full of difficulties. Today I may say that I feel myself fairly safe, but I had yet to achieve complete mastery over thought, which is so essential. Not that the will or effort is lacking, but it is yet a problem to me wherefrom undesirable thoughts spring their insidious invasions[4]. I have no doubt

1. *vistas: a pleasing view, especially on seen through a long, narrow opening*
2. *staring: look fixedly at someone or something with the eyes wide open; look fixedly at someone until they feel forced to look away*
3. *fleshly: the soft substance in the body consisting of muscle tissue and fat*
4. *invasions: an instance of invading; the action or process of being invaded*

that there is a key to lock out undesirable[1] thoughts, but every one has to find it out for himself. Saints and seers have left their experiences for us, but they have given us no infallible and universal prescription. For perfection or freedom from error comes only from grace, and so seekers after God have left us *mantras*, such as *Ramanama*, hallowed by their own austerities[2] and charged with their purity. Without an unreserved surrender to His grace, complete mastery over thought is impossible. This is the teaching of every great book of religion, and I am realizing the truth of it every moment of my striving after that perfect *brahmacharya.*

But part of the history of that striving and struggle will be told in chapters to follow. I shall conclude this chapter with an indication of how I set about the task. In the first flush of enthusiasm, I found the observance quite easy. The very first change I made in my mode of life was to stop sharing the same bed with my wife or seeking privacy with her.

Thus *brahmacharya* which I had been observing willy-nilly since 1900, was sealed with a vow in the middle of 1906.

1. *undesirable: not wanted or desirable because harmful, objectionable, or unpleasant*
2. *austerities: the trait of great self-denial*

CHAPTER 103

THE BIRTH OF SATYAGRAHA

Events were so shaping themselves in Johannesburg as to make this self-purfication on my part a preliminary[1] as it were to Satyagraha. I can now see that all the principal events of my life, culminating[2] in the vow of *brahmacharya*, were secretly preparing me for it. The principle called Satyagraha came into being before that name was invented[3]. Indeed when it was born, I myself could not say what it was. In Gujarati also we used the English phrase 'passive[4] resistance' to describe it. When in a meeting of Europeans I found that the term 'passive resistance' was too narrowly construed, that it was supposed to be a weapon of the weak, that it could be characterized by hatred, and that it could finally manifest itself as violence, I had to demur to all these statements and explain the real nature of the Indian movement. It was clear that a new word must be coined by the Indians to designate their struggle.

But I could not for the life of me find out a new name, and therefore offered a nominal prize through *Indian Opinion* to the reader who made the best suggestion on the subject. As a result Maganlal Gandhi coined the word 'Sadagraha' (Sat=truth, Agraha=firmness) and won the prize. But in order to make it clearer I changed the word to 'Satyagraha' which has since become current in Gujarati as a designation for the struggle.

The history of this struggle is for all practical purposes a history of the remainder of my life in South Africa and especially of my expriments with truth in that sub-continent. I wrote the major portion of this history in Yeravda jail and finished it after I was released. It was published in *Navajivan* and subsequently issued in book form. Sjt. Valji Govindji Desai has been translating it into English for *Current Thought*, but I am now arranging to have the English translation published in book form at an early date, so that those who will may be able to familiarize themselves with my most important experiments in South Africa. I would recommend a perusal of my history of Satyagraha in South Africa to such readers as

1. *preliminary: preceding or done in preparation for something fuller or more important*
2. *culminating: reach or be a climax or point of highest development*
3. *invented: create or design a new device, process, etc. make up especially as to deceive*
4. *passive: accepting or allowing what happens or what others do, without active response or resistance*

have not seen it already. I will not repeat what I have put down there, but in the next few chapters will deal only with a few personal incidents of my life in South Africa which have not been covered by that history. And when I have done with these, I will at once proceed to give the reader[1] some idea of my experiments in India. Therefore, anyone who wishes to consider these experiments in their strict chronological order will now do well to keep the history of Satyagraha in South Africa before him.

1. reader: a person who reads

CHAPTER 104

MORE EXPERIMENTS IN DIETETICS

I was anxious to observe *brahmacharya* in thought, word and deed, and equally anxious to devote the maximum of time to the Satyagraha struggle and fit myself for it by cultivating purity. I was therefore led to make further changes and to impose[1] greater restraints upon myself in the matter of food. The motive for the previous changes had been largely hygienic, but the new experiments were made from a religious standpoint.

Fasting and restriction in diet now played a more important part in my life. Passion in man is generally co-existent with a hankering[2] after the pleasures of the palate. And so it was with me. I have encountered many difficulties in trying to control passion as well as taste, and I cannot claim even now to have brought them under complete subjection[3]. I have considered myself to be a heavy eater. What friends have thought to be my restraint has never appeared to me in that light. If I had failed to develop restraint to the extent that I have, I should have descended lower than the beasts and met my doom long ago. However, as I had adequately realized my shortcomings, I made great efforts to get rid of them, and thanks to this endeavour I have all these years pulled on with my body and put in with it my share of work.

Being conscious of my weakness and unexpectedly coming in contact with congenial[4] company, I began to take an exclusive fruit diet or to fast on the *Ekadashi* day, and also to observe *Janmashtami* and similar holidays.

I began with a fruit diet, but from the standpoint of restraint I did not find much to choose between a fruit diet and a diet of food grains. I observed that the same indulgence of taste was possible with the former as with the latter, and even more, when one got accustomed to it. I therefore came to attach greater importance to fasting or having only one meal a day on holidays. And if there was some occasion for penance or the like, I gladly utilized it too for the purpose of fasting.

1. *impose: force to be accepted, undertaken, or complied with*
2. *hankering: feel a strong desire for or to do something*
3. *subjection: cause or force to undergo*
4. *congenial: pleasant because of qualities or interests similar to one's own; suited to one's taste or inclination*

But I also saw that, the body now being drained more effectively, the food yielded greater relish and the appetite grew keener. It dawned upon me that fasting could be made as powerful a weapon of indulgence as of restraint. Many similar later experiences of mine as well as of others can be adduced[1] as evidence of this startling fact. I wanted to improve and train my body, but as my chief object now was to achieve restraint and a conquest[2] of the palate, I selected first one food and then another, and at the same time restricted the amount. But the relish was after me, as it were. As I gave up one thing and took up another, this latter afforded me a fresher and greater relish than its predecessor[3].

In making these experiments I had several companions, the chief of whom was Hermann Kallenbach. I have already written about this friend in the history of Satyagraha in South Africa, and will not go over the same ground here. Mr. Kallenbach was always with me whether in fasting or in dietetic changes. I lived with him at his own place when the Satyagraha struggle was at its height. We discussed our changes in food and derived more pleasure from the new diet than from the old. Talk of this nature sounded quite pleasant in those days, and did not strike me as at all improper. Experience has taught me, however, that it was wrong to have dwelt upon the relish of food. One should eat not in order to please the palate, but just to keep the body going. When each organ of sense subserves the body and through the body the soul, its special relish disappears, and then alone does it begin to function in the way nature intended it to do.

Any number of experiments is too small and no sacrifice is too great for attaining this symphony with nature. But unfortunately the current is nowadays flowing strongly in the opposite direction.

We are not ashamed to sacrifice a multitude of other lives in decorating the perishable body and trying to prolong it existence for a few fleeting moments, with the result that we kill ourselves, both body and soul[4]. In trying to cure one old disease, we give rise to a hundred new ones: in trying to enjoy the pleasures of sense, we lose in the end even our capacity for enjoyment. All this is passing before our very eyes, but there are none so blind as those who will not see.

Having thus set forth their object and the train of ideas which led up to them, I now propose to describe the dietetic experiments at some length.

1. *adduced: cite as evidence*
2. *conquest: the action of conquering; a territory gained in such a way*
3. *predecessor: a thing that has been followed or replaced by another*
4. *soul: the spiritual or immaterial part of a human, regarded as immortal; one's moral or emotional nature or sense of identity; emotional or intellectual energy or intensity*

CHAPTER 105

KASTURBAI'S COURAGE

Thrice in her life my wife narrowly escaped death through serious illness. The cures were due to household remedies. At the time of her first attack Satyagraha was going on or was about to commence. She had frequent haemorrhage[1]. A medical friend advised a surgical operation, to which she agreed after some hesitation. She was extremely emaciated[2], and the doctor had to perform the operation without chloroform[3]. It was successful, but she had to suffer much pain. She, however, went through it with wonderful bravery. The doctor and his wife who nursed her were all attention. This was in Durban. The doctor gave me leave to go to Johannesburg, and told me not to have any anxiety about the patient.

In a few days, however, I received a letter to the effect that Kasturbai was worse, too weak to sit up in bed, and had once become unconscious. The doctor knew that he might not, without my consent, give her wines or meat. So he telephoned to me at Johannesburg for permission to give her beef tea. I replied saying I could not grant the permission, but that, if she was in a condition to express her wish in the matter she might be consulted and she was free to do as she liked. 'But,' said the doctor, 'I refuse to consult the patient's wishes in the matter. You must come yourself. If you do not leave me free to prescribe[4] whatever diet I like, I will not hold myself responsible for your wife's life.'

I took the train for Durban the same day, and met the doctor who quietly broke this news to me: 'I had already given Mrs. Gandhi beef tea when I telephoned to you.'

'Now, doctor, I call this a fraud,' said I.

'No question of fraud in prescribing medicine or diet for a patient. In fact we doctors consider it a virtue to deceive patients or their relatives, if thereby we can save our patients, said the doctor with determination.

1. *haemorrhage: an escape of blood from a ruptured blood vessel*
2. *emaciated: abnormally thin and weak*
3. *chloroform: a volatile sweet-smelling liquid used as a solvent and formerly as a general anesthetic; [chcl$_3$] make unconscious with this substance*
4. *prescribe: advise and authorize the use of especially in writing*

I was deeply pained, but kept cool. The doctor was a good man and a personal friend. He and his wife had laid me under a debt[1] of gratitude[2], but I was not prepared to put up with his medical morals.

'Doctor, tell me what you propose to do now. I would never allow my wife to be given meat or beef, even if the denial meant her death, unless of course she desired to take it.'

'You are welcome to your philosophy. I tell you that, so long as you keep your wife under my treatment, I must have the option to give her anything I wish. If you don't like this, I must regretfully ask you to remove her. I can't see her die under my roof.'

'Do you mean to say that I must remove her at once?'

'Whenever did I ask you to remove her? I only want to be left entirely free. If you do so, my wife and I will do all that is possible for her, and you may go back without the least anxiety on her score. But if you will not understand this simple thing, you will compel me to ask you to remove your wife from my place.'

I think one of my sons was with me. He entirely agreed with me, and said his mother should not be given beef tea. I next spoke to Kasturbai herself. She was really too weak to be consulted in this matter. But I thought it my painful duty to do so. I told her what had passed between the doctor and myself. She gave a resolute[3] reply: 'I will not take beef tea. It is a rare thing in this world to be born as a human being, and I would far rather die in your arms than pollute my body with such abominations.'

I pleaded with her. I told her that she was not bound to follow me. I cited to her the instances of Hindu friends and acquaintances who had no scruples about taking meat or wine as medicine. But she was adamant[4]. 'No,' said she, 'pray remove me at once.'

I was delighted. Not without some agitation I decided to take her away. I informed the doctor of her resolve. He exclaimed in a rage: 'What a callous man you are! You should have been ashamed to broach the matter to her in her present condition. I tell you your wife is not in a fit state to be removed. She cannot stand the least little hustling. I shouldn't surprised if she were to die on the way. But if you must persist, you are free to do so. If you will not give her beef tea, I will not take the risk of keeping her under my roof even for a single day.'

1. *gratitude: thankfulness; appreciation of kindness*
2. *debt: money or services owed or due*
3. *resolute: determined; unwavering*
4. *adamant: refusing to be persuaded or to change one's mind*

So we decided to leave the place at once. It was drizzling and the station was some distance. We had to take the train from Durban for Phoenix, whence our Settlement was reached by a road of two miles and a half, I was undoubtedly taking a very great risk, but I trusted in God, and proceeded with my task. I sent a messenger to Phoenix in advance, with a message to West to receive us at the station with a hammock, a bottle of hot milk and one of hot water, and six men to carry Kasturbai in the hammock[1]. I got a rickshaw to enable me to take her by the next available train, put her into it in that dangerous condition, and marched away.

Kasturbai needed no cheering up. On the contrary, she comforted me, saying: 'Nothing will happen to me. Don't worry.'

She was mere skin and bone, having had no nourishment for days. The station platform was very large, and as the rickshaw could not be taken inside, one had to walk some distance before one could reach the train. So I carried her in my arms and put her into the compartment. From Phoenix we carried her in the hammock, and there she slowly picked up strength under hydropathic treatment.

In two or three days of our arrival at Phoenix a Swami came to our place. He had heard of the resolute way in which we had rejected the doctor's advice, and he had, out of sympathy, come to plead with us. My second and third sons Manilal and Ramdas were, so far as I can recollect, present when the Swami came. He held forth on the religious harmlessness[2] of taking meat, citing authorities from Manu. I did not like his carrying on this disputation in the presence of my wife, but I suffered him to do so out of courtesy. I knew the verses from the *Manusmriti*, I did not need them for my conviction. I knew also that there was a school which regarded these verses as interpolations: but even if they were not, I held my views on vegetarianism independently of religious texts, and Kasturbai's faith was unshakable. To her the scriptural texts were a sealed book, but the traditional religion of her forefathers was enough for her. The children swore by their father's creed and so they made light of the Swami's discourse. But Kasturbai put an end to the dialogue at once. 'Swamiji,' she said, 'whatever you may say, I do not want to recover by means of beef tea. Pray don't worry me any more. You may discuss the thing with my husband and children if you like. But my mind is made up.'

1. *hammock: a wide strip of canvas or rope mesh suspended by two ends, used as a bed*
2. *harmlessness: not able or likely to cause harm*

CHAPTER 106

DOMESTIC SATYAGRAHA

My first experience of jail life was in 1908. I saw that some of the regulations that the prisoners had to observe were such as should voluntarily be observed by a *brahmachari*, that is, one desiring to practise self-restraint. Such, for instance, was the regulation requiring the last meal to be finished before sunset. Neither the Indian nor the African prisoners were allowed tea or coffee. They could add salt to the cooked food if they wished, but they might not have anything for the mere satisfaction of the palate. When I asked the jail medical officer to give us curry powder, and to let us add salt to the food whilst it was cooking, he said: 'You are not here for satisfying your palate. From the point of view of health, curry powder is not necessary, and it makes no difference whether you add salt during or after cooking.'

Ultimeately these restrictions were modified, though not without much difficulty, but both were wholesome rules of self-restraint. Inhabitations imposed from without rarely succeed, but when they are self-imposed, they have a decidedly salutary[1] effect. So, immediately after release from jail, I imposed on myself the two rules. As far as was then possible, I stopped taking tea, and finished my last meal before sunset. Both these now require no effort in the observance.

There came, however, an occasion which compelled me to give up salt altogether, and this restriction I continued for an unbroken[2] period of ten years. I had read in some books on vegetarianism that salt was not a necessary article of diet for man, that on the contrary saltless diet was better for the health. I had deduced that a *brahmachar*i benefited by a saltless diet, I had read and realized that the weak-bodied should avoid pulses. I was very fond of them.

Now it happened that Kasturbai, who had a brief respite after her operation, had again begun getting haemorrhage, and the malady seemed to be obstinate. Hydropathic treatment by itself did not answer. She had not much faith in my remedies, though she did not resist them.

1. salutary: health-giving *2. unbroken: not broken; intact*

She certainly did not ask for outside help. So when all my remedies had failed. I entreated her to give up salt and pulses. She would not agree, however much I pleaded with her, supporting myself with authorities. At last she challenged me, saying that even I could not give up these articles if I was advised to do so, I was pained and equally delighted, delighted in that I got an opportunity to shower[1] my love on her. I said to her: 'You are mistaken. If I was ailing and the doctor advised me to give up these or any other articles, I should unhesitatingly do so. But there! Without any medical advice, I give up salt and pulses for one year, whether you do so or not.'

She was rudely shocked and exclaimed in deep sorrow: 'Pray forgive me. Knowing you, I should not have provoked you. I promise to abstain from these things, but for heaven's sake take back your vow. This is too hard on me.'

'It is very good for you to forego these articles. I have not the slightest doubt that you will be all the better without them. As for me, I cannot retract[2] a vow seriously taken. And it is sure to benefit me, for all restraint, whatever prompts it, is wholesome for men. You will therefore leave me alone. It will be a test for me, and a moral support to you in carrying out your resolve.'

So she gave me up. 'You are too obstinate. You will listen to none,' she said, and sought relief in tears.

I would like to count this incident as an instance of Satyagraha, and it is one of the sweetest recollections of my life.

After this Kasturbai began to pick up quickly whether as a result of the saltless and pulseless diet or of the other consequent changes in her food, whether as a result of my strict vigilance in exacting observance of the other rules of life, or as an effect of the mental exhilaration produced by the incident, and if so to what extent, I cannot say. But she rallied quickly, haemorrhage completely stopped, and I added somewhat to my reputation as a quack[3].

As for me, I was all the better for the new denials. I never craved for the things I had left, the year sped away, and I found the senses to be more subdued[4] than ever. The experiment stimulated the inclination for self-restraint, and I continues the abstention from the articles until long after I returned to India. Only once I happened to take both the articles

1. *shower: give a great number of things to someone*
2. *retract: draw or be drawn back or back in*
3. *quack: a person who claims to have special skills but does not*
4. *subdued: overcome, quieten, or brig under control; bring under control by force*

whilst I was in London in 1914. But of that occasion, and as to how I resumed both, I shall speak in a later chapter.

I have tried the experiment of a saltles and pulseless diet on many of my co-workers, and with good results in South Africa. Medically there may be two opinions as to the value of this diet, but morally[1] I have no doubt that all self-denial is good for the soul. The diet of a man of self-restraint must be different from that of a man of pleasure, just as their ways of life must be different. Aspirants after *brahmacharya* often defeat their own end by adopting courses suited to a life of pleasure.

1. *morally: principles of right or wrong behaviour*

CHAPTER 107

TOWARDS SELF-RESTRAINT

I have described in the last chapter how Kasturbai's illness was instrumental in bringing about some changes in my diet. At a later stage more changes were introduced for the sake of supporting *brahmacharya*.

The first of these was the giving up of milk. It was from Raychandbhai that I first learnt that milk stimulated animal passion[1]. Books on vegetarianism strengthened the idea, but so long as I had not taken the *brahmacharya* vow I could not make up my mind to forego milk. I had long realized that milk was not necessary for supporting the body, but it was not easy to give it up. While the necessity for avoiding milk in the interests of self-restraint was growing upon me, I happened to come across some literature from Calcutta, describing the tortures to which cows and buffaloes were subjected by their keepers. This had a wonderful effect on me. I discussed it with Mr. Kallenbach.

Though I have introduced Mr. Kallenbach to the readers of the history of Satyagraha in South Africa, and referred to him in a previous chapter, I think it necessary to say something more about him here. We met quite by accident. He was a friend of Mr. Khan's, and as the latter had discovered deep down in him a vein of other-worldliness he introduced him to me.

When I came to know him I was startled at his love of luxury and extravagance. But at our very first meeting, he asked searching questions concerning matters of religion. We incidentally talked of Gautama Buddha's renunciation. Our acquaintance soon ripened[2] into very close friendship, so much so that we thought alike, and he was convinced that he must carry out in his life the changes I was making in mine.

At that time he was single, and was expending[3] Rs. 1,200 monthly on himself, over and above house rent. Now he reduced himself to such simplicity that his expenses[4] came to Rs. 120 per month. After the breaking up of my household and my first release from jail, we began to live together. It was a fairly hard life that we led.

1. *passion: strong and barely controllable emotion; an outburst of such emotion*
2. *ripened: become or make ripe*
3. *expending: spend or use up a resource*
4. *expenses: cost incurred or required; costs incurred in the performance of a job or task*

It was during this time that we had the discussion about milk. Mr. Kallenbach said, 'We constantly talk about the harmful effects of milk. Why then do not we give it up? It is certainly not necessary.' I was agreeably surprised at the suggestion, which I warmly welcomed, and both of us pledged ourselves to abjure milk there and then. This was at Tolstoy Farm in the year 1912.

But this denial was not enough to satisfy me. Soon after this I decided to live on a pure fruit diet, and that too composed of the cheapest fruit possible, Our ambition was to live the life of the poorest people.

The fruit diet turned out to be very convenient also. Cooking was practically done away with. Raw groundnuts[1], bananas, dates, lemons, and olive[2] oil composed our usual diet.

I must here utter a warning for the aspirants of *brahmacharya*. Though I have made out an intimate connection between diet and *brahmacharya*, it is certain that mind is the principal thing. A mind consciously unclean cannot be cleansed by fasting. Modifications in diet have no effect on it. The concupiscence of the mind cannot be rooted out except by intense self-examination, surrender to God and lastly, grace. But there is an intimate connection between the mind and the body, and carnal mind always lusts for delicacies and luxuries. To obviate this tendency dietetic restrictions and fasting would appear to be necessary. The carnal mind, instead of controlling the senses, becomes their slave, and therefore the body always needs clean non-stimulating foods and periodical[3] fasting.

Those who make light of dietetic restriction and fasting are as much in error as those who stake their all on them. My experience teaches me that, for those whose minds are working towards self-restraint, dietetic restrictions and fasting are very helpful. In fact without their help concupiscence cannot be completely rooted out the mind.

1. *groundnuts: another term for peanut*
2. *olive: a small oval fruit with a hard stone and bitter flesh, green when unripe and blusih black when ripe, used as food and as a source of oil*
3. *periodical: occurring or appearing at intervals, published at regular intervals*

CHAPTER 108

FASTING

Just about the time when I gave up milk and cereals, and started on the experiment of a fruit diet, I began fasting as a means of self-restraint. In this Mr. Kallenbach also joined me. I had been used to fasting now and again, but for purely health reasons. That fasting was necessary for self-restraint I learnt from a friend.

Having been born in a Vaishnava family and of a mother who was given to keeping all sorts of hard vows, I had observed, while in India, the *Ekadashi* and other fasts, but in doing so I had merely copied my mother and sought to please my parents.

At that time I did not understand, nor did I believe in, the efficacy[1] of fasting. But seeing that the friend I have mentioned was observing it with benefit, and with the hope of supporting the *brahmacharya* vow, I followed his example and began keeping the *Ekadashi* fast. As a rule Hindus allow themselves milk and fruit on a fasting day, but such fast I had been keeping daily. So now I began complete fasting, allowing myself only water.

When I started on this experiment, the Hindu month of Shravan and the Islamic month of Ramzan happened to coincide. The Gandhis used to observe not only the Vaishnava but also the Shaivite vows, and visited the Shaivite as also the Vaishnava temples. Some of the members of the family used to observe *pradosha*[2] in the whole of the month of Shravan. I decided to do likewise.

These important experiments were undertaken while we were at Tolstoy Farm, where Mr. Kallenbach and I were staying with a few Satyagrahi families, including young people and children. For these last we had a school. Among them were four or five Musalmans. I always helped and encouraged them in keeping all their religious observances. I took care to see that they offered their daily *namaz*. There were Christians and Parsi youngsters too, whom I considered it my duty to encourage to follow their respective religious observances[3].

1. *efficacy: ability to produce results*
2. *pradosha: fasting until evening*
3. *observances: the practice of observing the requirements of law, morality, or ritual*

During this month, therefore, I persuaded the Musalman youngsters to observe the *ramzan* fast. I had of course decided to observe *pradosha* myself, but I now asked the Hindu, Parsi and Christian youngsters to join me. I explained to them that it was always a good thing to join with others in any matter of self-denial. Many of the Farm inmates welcomed my proposal. The Hindu and the Parsi youngsters did not copy the Musalman ones in every detail; it was not necessary. The Musalman youngsters had to wait for their breakfast until sunset, whereas the others did not do so, and were thus able to prepare delicacies for the Musalman friends and serve them. Nor had the Hindu and other youngsters to keep the Musalmans company when they had their last meal before sunrise next morning, and of course all except the Musalmans allowed themselves water.

The result of these experiments was that all were convinced of the value of fasting, and a splendid *esprit de corps* grew up among them.

We were all vegetarians on Tolstoy Farm, thanks, I must gratefully confess, to the readiness of all to respect my feelings. The Musalman youngsters must have missed their meat during *ramzan*, but none of them ever let me know that they did so. They delighted in and relished the vegetarian diet, and the Hindu youngsters often prepared vegetarian delicacies for them, in keeping with the simplicity of the Farm.

I have purposely digressed in the midst of this chapter on fasting, as I could not have given these pleasant reminiscences[1] anywhere else, and I have indirectly described a characteristic of mine, namely that I have always loved to have my co-workers with me in anything that has appealed to me as being good. They were quite new to fasting, but thanks to the *pradosha* and *ramzan* fasts, it was easy for me to interest them in fasting as a means of self-restraint.

Thus an atmosphere of self-restraint naturally sprang up on the Farm. All the Farm inmates now began to join us in keeping partial and complete fasts, which, I am sure, was entirely to the good. I cannot definitely say how far this self-denial touched their hearts and helped them in their striving to conquer[2] the flesh. For my part, however, I am convinced that I greatly benefited by it both physically and morally. But I know that it does not necessarily follow that fasting and similar disciplines would have the same effect for all.

1. *reminiscences: tending to remind one of something*
2. *conquer: overcome and take control of by military force*

Fasting can help to curb animal passion, only if it is undertaken with a view to self-restraint. Some of my friends have actually found their animal passion and palate stimulated as an after-effect of fasts. That is to say, fasting is futile unless it is accompanied by an incessant longing for self-restraint. The famous verse from the second chapter of the *Bhagavad Gita* is worth noting in this connection:

'For a man who is fasting his senses Outwardly, the sense-objects disappear, Leaving the yearning behind; but when He has seen the Highest, Even the yearning[1] disappears.'

Fasting and similar discipline is, therefore, one of the means to the end of self-restraint, but it is not all, and if physical fasting is not accompanied by mental fasting, it is bound to end in hypocrisy and disaster.

1. *yearning: have an intense feeling of loss and longing for something*

CHAPTER 109

AS SCHOOLMASTER

The reader will, I hope, bear in mind the fact that I am, in these chapters, describing things not mentioned, or only cursorily mentioned, in the history of Satyagraha in South Africa. If he does so, he will easily see the connection between the recent chapters.

As the Farm grew, it was found necessary to make some provision for the education of its boys and girls. There were, among these, Hindu, Musalman, Parsi and Christian[1] boys and some Hindu girls. It was not possible, and I did not think it necessary, to engage special teachers for them. It was not possible, for qualified Indian teachers were scarce, and even when available, none would be ready to go to a place twenty one miles distant from Johannesburg on a small salary. Also we were certainly not overflowing with money. And I did not think it necessary to import[2] teachers from outside the Farm[3]. I did not believe in the existing system of education, and I had a mind to find out by experience and experiment the true system. Only this much I knew-that, under ideal conditions, true education could be imparted only by the parents, and that then there should be the minimum of outside help, that Tolstoy Farm was a family, in which I occupied the place of the father, and that I should so far as possible shoulder the responsibility for the training of the young.

The conception no doubt was not without its flaws. All the young people had not been with me since their childhood, they had been brought up in different conditions and environments, and they did not belong to the same religion[4]. How could I do full justice to the young people, thus circumstanced, even if I assumed the place of paterfamilias?

But I had always given the first place to the culture of the heart or the building of character, and as I felt confident that moral training could be given to all alike, no matter how different their ages and their upbringing, I decided to live amongst them all the twenty-four hours of the day as their father. I regarded character building as the proper foundation for

1. *Christian: of, relating to, or professing Christianity or its teachings*
2. *farm: an area of land and its buildings used for growing crops and rearing animals, an establishment for breeding or growing something, or devoted to a particular thing; a fish farm, a wind farm*
3. *import: bring into a country from abroad*
4. *religion: the belief in and worship of a superhuman controlling power, especially a personal god or gods; a particular system of faith and worship*

their education and, if the foundation was firmly laid, I was sure that the children could learn all the other things themselves or with the assistance of friends.

But as I fully appreciated the necessity of a literary training in addition, I started some classes with the help of Mr. Kallenbach and Sjt. Pragji Desai. Nor did I underrate[1] the building up of the body. This they got in the course of their daily routine. For there were no servants on the Farm, and all the work, from cooking down to scavenging, was done by the inmates. There were many fruit trees to be looked after, and enough gardening to be done as well. Mr. Kallenbach was fond of gardening and had gained some experience of this work in one of the Governmental model gardens. It was obligatory on all, young and old, who were not engaged in the kitchen, to give some time to gardening. The children had the lion's share of this work, which included digging pits, felling timber[2] and lifting loads. This gave them ample exercise. They took delight in the work, and so they did not generally need any other exercise or games. Of course some of them, and sometimes all them, malingered and shirked[3]. Sometimes I connived at their pranks, but often I was strict with them, I dare say they did not like the strictness, but I do not recollect their having resisted it. Whenever I was strict, I would, by argument, convince them that it was not right to play with one's work. The conviction would, however, be short-lived, the next moment they would again leave their work and go to play. All the same we got along, and at any rate they built up fine physiques. There was scarcely any illness on the Farm, though it must be said that good air and water and regular hours of food were not a little responsible for this.

A word about vocational training. It was my intention to teach every one of the youngsters some useful manual vocation. For this purpose Mr. Kallenbach went to a Trappist monastery and returned having learnt shoe-making. I learnt it from him and taught the art to such as were ready to take it up. Mr. Kallenbach had some experience of carpentry, and there was another inmate who knew it; so we had a small class in carpentry. Cooking almost all the youngsters knew.

All this was new to them. They had never even dreamt that they would have to learn these things some day. For generally the only training that Indian children received in South Africa was in the three R's.

1. *underrate: underestimate the extent, value, or importance of*
2. *timber: wood prepared for use in building and carpentry; trees grown for such wood; a wooden beam or board used in building and shipbuilding*
3. *shirked: avoid or neglect a duty or responsibility*

On Tolstoy Farm we made it a rule that the youngsters should not be asked to do what the teachers did not do, and therefore, when they were asked to do any work, there was always a teacher co-operating and actually working with them. Hence whatever the youngsters learnt, they learnt cheerfully.

Literary training and character[1] building must be dealt with in the following chapters.

1. *character: typical of a particular person, place, or thing*

CHAPTER 110

LITERARY TRAINING

It was seen in the last chapter how we provided for the physical training on Tolstoy Farm, and incidentally for the vocational. Though this was hardly done in a way to satisfy me, it may be claimed to have been more or less successful.

Literary training, however, was a more difficult matter. I had neither the resources nor the literary equipment necessary; and I had not the time I would have wished to devote to the subject. The physical work that I was doing used to leave me thoroughly exhausted at the end of the day, and I used to have the classes just when I was most in need of some rest. Instead, therefore, of my being fresh for the class, I could with the greatest difficulty keep myself awake. The mornings had to be devoted to work on the farm and domestic duties, so the school hours had to be kept after the midday meal. There was no other time suitable for the school.

We gave three periods at the most to literary training. Hindi, Tamil, Gujarati and Urdu were all taught, and tuition was given through the vernaculars[1] of the boys. English was taught as well. It was also necessary to acquaint the Gujarati Hindu children with a little Samskrit, and to teach all the children elementary history, geography and arithmetic[2].

I had undertaken[3] to teach Tamil and Urdu. The little Tamil I knew was acquired during voyages and in jail. I had not got beyond Pope's excellent Tamil handbook. My knowledge of the Urdu script was all that I had acquired on a single voyage, and my knowledge of the language was confined to the familiar Persian and Arabic words that I had learnt from contact with Musalman friends. Of Samskrit I knew no more than I had learnt at the high school, even my Gujarati was no better than that which one acquires at the school.

Such was the capital with which I had to carry on. In poverty[4] of literary equipment my colleagues went one better than I. But my love for the languages of my country, my confidence in my capacity as a teacher,

1. *vernaculars: the language or dialect spoken by the ordinary people of a country or region*
2. *arithmetic: the branch of mathematics concerned with the properties and manipulation of numbers; the use of numbers in counting and calculation*
3. *undertaken: commit oneself to and begin an enterprise or responsibility; take on*
4. *poverty: the state of being extremely poor; the renunciation of the right to individual ownership of property as part of a religious vow*

as also the ignorance of my pupils, and more than that, their generosity, stood me in good stead.

The Tamil boys were all born in South Africa, and therefore knew very little Tamil, and did not know the script at all. So I had to teach them the script[1] and the rudiments[2] of grammar. That was easy enough. My pupils knew that they could any day beat me in Tamil conversation, and when Tamilians, not knowing English, came to see me, they became my interpreters. I got along merrily, because I never attempted to disguise my ignorance from my pupils. In all respects I showed myself to them exactly as I really was. Therefore in spite of my colossal[3] ignorance of the language I never lost their love and respect. It was comparatively easier to teach the Musalman boys Urdu. They knew the script. I had simply to stimulate in them an interest in reading and to improve their handwriting.

These youngsters were for the most part unlettered and unschooled. But I found in the course of my work that I had very little to teach them, beyond weaning them from their laziness, and supervising their studies. As I was content with this, I could pull on with boys of different ages and learning different subjects in one and the same class room.

Of text-books, about which we hear so much, I never felt the want. I do not even remember having made much use of the books that were available. I did not find it at all necessary to load the boys with quantities of books. I have always felt that the true text-book for the pupil is his teacher. I remember very little that my teachers taught me from books, but I have even now a clear recollection of the things they taught me independently of books.

Children take in much more and with less labour through their ears than through their eyes. I do not remember having read any book from cover to cover with my boys. But I gave them, in my own language, all that I had digested from my reading of various books, and I dare say they are still carrying a recollection of it in their minds. It was laborious for them to remember what they learnt from books, but what I imparted to them by word of mouth, they could repeat with the greatest ease. Reading was a task for them, but listening to me was a pleasure, when I did not bore them by failure to make my subject interesting. And from the questions that my talks prompted them to put, I had a measure of their power of understanding.

1. *rudiments: the first principles of a subject; an elementary or primitive form of something*
2. *script: handwriting as distinct from print: written characters; writing using a particular alphabet: russian script*
3. *colossal: extremely large; sculpture at least twice life size*

CHAPTER 111

TRAINING OF THE SPIRIT

The spiritual training of the boys was a much more difficult matter than their physical and mental training. I relied little on religious books for the training of the spirit. Of course, I believed that every student should be acquainted with the elements of his own religion and have a general knowledge of his own scriptures, and therefore I provided for such knowledge as best I could. But that, to my mind, was part of the intellectual[1] training. Long before I undertook the education of the youngsters of the Tolstoy Farm I had realized that the training of the spirit was a thing by itself. To develop the spirit is to build character and to enable one to work towards a knowledge of God and self-realization. And I held that this was an essential part of the training of the young, and that all training without culture of the spirit was of no use, and might be even harmful.

I am familiar with the superstition that self-realization is possible only in the fourth stage of life, i.e., sannyasa (renunciation). But it is a matter of common knowledge that those who defer preparation for this invaluable experience until the last stage of life attain not self-realization but old age amounting to a second and pitiable[2] childhood, living as a burden on this earth. I have a full recollection that I held these views even whilst I was teaching i. e., in 1911-12, though I might not then have expressed them in identical[3] language.

How then was this spiritual training to be given? I made the children memorize and recite hymns, and read to them from books on moral training. But that was far from satisfying me. As I came into closer contact with them I saw that it was not through books that one could impart[4] training of the spirit. Just as physical training was to be imparted through physical exercise, and intellectual through intellectual exercise, even so the training of the spirit was possible only through the exercise of the spirit. And the exercise of the spirit entirely depended on the life and character of the teacher. The teacher had always to be mindful[5] of his p's and q's, whether he was in the midst of his boys or not.

1. *intellectual: of, relating to, or appealing to the intellect; having a highly developed intellect*
2. *pitiable: deserving or arousing pity*
3. *identical: exactly alike*
4. *impart: communicate; bestow a quality*
5. *mindful: conscious or aware or responses planned for their psychological effect on another*

It is possible for a teacher situated miles away to affect the spirit of the pupils by his way of living. It would be idle for me, if I were a liar, to teach boys to tell the truth. A cowardly teacher would never succeed in making his boys valiant, and a stranger to self-restraint could never teach his pupils the value of self-restraint. I saw therefore that I must be an eternal object-lesson to the boys and girls living with me. They thus became my teachers, and I learnt I must be good and live straight, if only for their sakes. I may say that the increasing discipline and restraint I imposed on myself at Tolstoy Farm was mostly due to those wards[1] of mine.

One of them was wild, unruly[2], given to lying, and quarrelsome. On one occasion he broke out most violently. I was exasperated. I never punished my boys, but this time I was very angry. I tried to reason with him. But he was adamant and even tried to over-reach me. At last I picked up a ruler lying at hand and delivered a blow on his arm. I trembled as I struck him. I dare say he noticed it. This was an entirely novel experience for them all. The boy cried out and begged to be forgiven. He cried not because the beating was painful to him; he could, if he had been so minded, have paid me back in the same coin, being a stoutly built youth of seventeen; but he realized my pain in being driven to this violent resource. Never again after this incident did he disobey me. But I still repent that violence. I am afraid I exhibited before him that day not the spirit, but the brute[3], in me.

I have always been opposed to corporal punishment. I remember only one occasion on which I physically punished one of my sons. I have therefore never until this day been able to decide whether I was right or wrong in using the ruler. Probably it was improper, for it was prompted by anger and a desire to punish. Had it been an expression only of my distress, I should have considered it justified. But the motive in this case was mixed.

This incident set me thinking and taught me a better method of correcting students. I do not know whether that method would have availed on the occasion in question. The youngster soon forgot the incident, and I do not think he ever showed great improvement. But the incident made me understand better the duty of a teacher towards his pupils.

1. *wards: a child or young person under the care and control of a guardian appointed by their parents or a court, guardianship*
2. *unruly: disorderly and disruptive; difficult to control*
3. *brute: a violent or savage person or animal; (informal) a cruel or insensitive person*

Cases of misconduct on the part of the boys often occurred after this, but I never resorted to corporal[1] punishment. Thus in my endeavour to impart spiritual training to the boys and girls under me, I came to understand better and better the power of the spirit.

1. *corporal: relating to the human body*

CHAPTER 112

TARES AMONG THE WHEAT

It was at Tolstoy Farm that Mr. Kallenbach drew my attention to a problem that had never before struck me. As I have already said, some of the boys at the Farm were bad and unruly. There were loafers, too, amongst them. With these my three boys came in daily contact, as also did other children of the same type as my own sons. This troubled Mr. Kallenbach, but his attention was centred on the impropriety of keeping my boys with these unruly[1] youngsters.

One day he spoke out: 'Your way of mixing your own boys with the bad ones does not appeal to me. It can have only one result. They will become demoralized[2] through this bad company.'

I do not remember whether the question puzzled me at the moment, but I recollect what I said to him:

'How can I distinguish between my boys and the loafers? I am equally responsible for both. The youngsters have come because I invited them. If I were to dismiss them with some money, they would immediately run off to Johannesburg and fall back into their old ways. To tell you the truth, it is quite likely that they and their guardians believe that, by having come here, they have laid me under an obligation. That they have to put up with a good deal of inconvenience here, you and I know very well. But my duty is clear. I must have them here, and therefore my boys also must needs live with them. And surely you do not want me to teach my boys to feel from today that they are superior[3] to other boys. To put that sense of superiority into their heads would be to lead them astray. This association with other boys will be a good discipline for them. They will, of their own accord[4], learn to discriminate between good and evil. Why should we not believe that, if there is really anything good in them, it is bound to react on their companions? However that may be, I cannot help keeping them here, and if that means some risk, we must run it.'

1. *unruly: disorderly and disruptive; difficult to control*
2. *demoralized: cause to lose confidence or hope*
3. *superior: higher in rank, status, or quality; of high standard or quality; greater in size or power*
4. *accord: an official agreement or treaty*

Mr. Kallenbach shook his head.

The result, I think, cannot be said to have been bad. I do not consider my sons were any the worse for the experiment. On the contrary I can see that they gained something. If there was the slightest trace of superiority[1] in them, it was destroyed and they learnt to mix with all kinds of children. They were tested and disciplined.

This and similar experiments have shown me that, if good children are taught together with bad ones and thrown into their company, they will lose nothing, provided the experiment is conducted under the watchful care of their parents and guardians.

Children wrapped up in cotton wool are not always proof against all temptation or contamination. It is true, however, that when boys and girls of all kinds of upbringing[2] are kept and taught together, the parents and the teachers are put to the severest test. They have constantly to be on the alert.

1. *superiority: state of being superior*

2. *upbringing: the treatment and instruction received from one's parents throughout childhood*

CHAPTER 113

FASTING AS PENANCE

Day by day it became increasingly clear to me how very difficult it was to bring up and educate boys and girls in the right way. If I was to be their real teacher and guardian, I must touch their hearts. I must share their joys and sorrows, I must help them to solve the problems that faced them, and I must take along the right channel the surging[1] aspirations of their youth.

On the release of some of the Satyagrahis from jail, Tolstoy Farm was almost denuded[2] of its inmates. The few that remained mostly belonged to Phoenix. So I removed them there. Here I had to pass through a fiery[3] ordeal[4].

In those days I had to move between Johannesburg and Phoenix. Once when I was in Johannesburg I received tidings of the moral fall of two of the inmates of the Ashram. News of an apparent failure or reverse in the Satyagraha struggle would not have shocked me, but this news came upon me like a thunderbolt. The same day I took the train for Phoenix. Mr. Kallenbach insisted on accompanying me. He had noticed the state I was in. He would not brook the thought of my going alone, for he happened to be the bearer of the tidings which had so upset me.

During the journey my duty seemed clear to me. I felt that the guardian or teacher was responsible, to some extent at least, for the lapse of his ward or pupil. So my responsibility regarding the incident in question became clear to me as daylight. My wife had already warned me in the matter, but being of a trusting nature, I had ignored her caution. I felt that the only way the guilty parties could be made to realize my distress and the depth of their own fall would be for me to do some penance. So I imposed upon myself a fast for seven days and a vow to have only one meal a day for a period of four months and a half. Mr. Kallenbach tried to dissuade me, but in vain. He finally conceded the propriety of the penance, and insisted on joining me. I could not resist his transparent affection.

I felt greatly relieved, for the decision meant a heavy load off my mind. The anger against the guilty parties subsided and gave place to the purest

1. *surging: a sudden large temporary increase*
2. *denuded: strip of covering or possessions; make bare*
3. *fiery: resembling or consisting of fire; too quick-tempered or passionate*
4. *ordeal: a prolonged painful or horrific experience*

pity for them. Thus considerably eased, I reached Phoenix. I made further investigation and acquainted myself with some more details I needed to know.

My penance[1] pained everybody, but it cleared the atmosphere. Everyone came to realize what a terrible thing it was to be sinful, and the bond that bound me to the boys and girls became stronger and truer.

A circumstance arising out of this incident compelled me, a little while after, to go into a fast for fourteen days, the results of which exceeded even my expectations.

It is not my purpose to make out from these incidents that it is the duty of a teacher to resort to fasting whenever there is a delinquency on the part of his pupils. I hold, however, that some occasions do call for this drastic remedy. But it presupposes[2] clearness of vision and spiritual fitness. Where there is no true love between the teacher and the pupil, where the pupil's delinquency has not touched the very being of the teacher and where the pupil has no respect for the teacher, fasting is out of place and may even be harmful. Though there is thus room for doubting the propriety of fasts in such cases, there is no question about the teacher's responsibility for the error of his pupil.

The first penance did not prove difficult for any of us. I had to suspend or stop none of my normal activities. It may be recalled that during the whole of this period of penance I was a strict fruitarian. The latter part of the second fast went fairly hard with me. I had not then completely understood the wonderful efficacy[3] of Ramanama, and my capacity for suffering was to that extent less. Besides, I did not know the technique of fasting, especially the necessity of drinking plenty of water, however nauseating or distasteful it might be. Then the fact that the first fast had been an easy affair had made me rather careless as to the second. Thus during the first I took Kuhne baths every day, but during the second I gave them up after two or three days, and drank very little water, as it was distasteful and produced nausea[4]. The throat became parched and weak and during the last days I could speak only in a very low voice. In spite of this, however, my work was carried on through dictation where writing was necessary. I regularly listened to readings from the Ramayana and other sacred books. I had also sufficient strength to discuss and advise in all urgent matters.

1. *penance: voluntary self-punishment as an open expression of repentance for wrongdoing*
2. *presupposes: require as a precondition of possibility or coherence; tacitly assume to be the case*
3. *efficacy: ability to produce results*
4. *nausea: a feeling of sickness with an inclination to vomit*

CHAPTER 114

TO MEET GOKHALE

I must skip many of the recollections of South Africa. At the conclusion of the Satyagraha struggle in 1914, I received Gokhale's instruction to return home via London. So in July Kasturbai, Kallenbach and I sailed for England.

During Satyagraha I had begun traveling third class. I therefore took third class passages for this voyage. But there was a good deal of difference between third class accommodation on the boat on this route and that provided on Indian coastal boats or railway trains. There is hardly sufficient sitting, much less sleeping, accommodation in the Indian service, and little cleanliness. During the voyage to London, on the other hand, there was enough room and cleanliness, and the steamship company had provided special facilities for us. The company had provided reserved closet accommodation for us, and as we were fruitarians, the steward had orders to supply us with fruits and nuts. As a rule third class passengers get little fruit or nuts. These facilities made our eighteen days on the boat quite comfortable.

Some of the incidents during the voyage are well worth recording. Mr. Kallenbach was very fond of binoculars, and had one or two costly pairs. We had daily discussions over one of these. I tried to impress on him that this possession was not in keeping with the ideal of simplicity[1] that we aspired to reach. Our discussions came to a head one day, as we were standing near the porthole[2] of our cabin.

'Rather than allow these to be a bone of contention[3] between us, why not throw them into the sea and be done with them?' said I.

'Certainly throw the wretched things away.' said Mr. Kallenbach.

'I mean it,' said I.

'So do I,' quickly came the reply.

And forthwith I flung them into the sea. They were worth some £7, but their value lay less in their price than in Mr. Kallenbach's infatuation for them. However, having got rid of them, he never regretted it.

1. *simplicity: the quality or condition of being simple*
2. *porthole: a small window on the outside of a ship or an aircraft*
3. *contention: heated disagreement*

This is but one out of the many incidents that happened between Mr. Kallenbach and me.

Every day we had to learn something new in this way, for both of us were trying to tread[1] the path of Truth. In the march towards Truth, anger, selfishness, hatred, etc., naturally give way, for otherwise Truth would be impossible to attain. A man who is swayed by passions may have good enough intentions, may be truthful in word, but he will never find the Truth. A successful search for Truth means complete deliverance from the dual throng such as of love and hate, happiness and misery.

Not much time had elapsed since my fast when we started on our voyage. I had not regained my normal strength. I used to stroll on deck to get a little exercise, so as to revive my appetite and digest what I ate. But even this exercise was beyond me, causing me pain in the calves, so much so that on reaching London I found that I was worse rather than better. There I came to know Dr. Jivraj Mehta. I gave him the history of my fast and subsequent pain, and he said, 'If you do not take complete rest for a few days, there is a fear of your legs going out of use.'

It was then that I learned that a man emerging from a long fast should not be in a hurry to regain lost strength, and should also put a curb on his appetite[2]. More caution[3] and perhaps more restraint are necessary in breaking a fast than in keeping it.

In Madeira we heard that the great War might break out at any moment. As we entered the English Channel, we received the news of its actual outbreak. We were stopped for some time. It was a difficult business to tow the boat through the submarine[4] mines which had been laid throughout the Channel, and it took about two days to reach Southampton.

War was declared on the 4th of August. We reached London on the 6th.

1. *tread: walk in a specified way; walk on or along*
2. *appetite: a natural desire to satisfy a bodily need, especially for food*
3. *caution: care taken to avoid danger or mistakes*
4. *submarine: a streamlined warship designed to operate completely submerged in the sea for long periods*

CHAPTER 115

MY PART IN THE WAR

On arrival in England I learned that Gokhale had been stranded in Paris where he had gone for reasons of health, and as communication between Paris and London had been cut off, there was no knowing when he would return. I did not want to go home without having seen him, but no one could say definitely when he would arrive.

What then was I to do in the meanwhile? What was my duty as regards the war? Sorabji Adajania, my comrade in jail and a Satyagrahi, was then reading for the bar[1] in London. As one of the best Satyagrahis he had been sent to England to qualify himself as a barrister, so that he might take my place on return to South Africa. Dr. Pranjivandas Mehta was paying his expenses. With him, and through him, I had conferences with Dr. Jivraj Mehta and others who were per suing their studies in England. In consultation with them, a meeting of the Indian residents in Great Britain and Ireland was called. I placed my views before them.

I felt that Indians residing[2] in England ought to do their bit in the war. English students had volunteered to serve in the army, and Indians might do no less. A number of objections were taken to this line of argument. There was, it was contended, a world of difference between the Indians and the English. We were slaves and they were masters. How could a slave co-operate with the master in the hour of the latter's need? Was it not the duty of the slave, seeking to be free, to make the master's need his opportunity? This argument failed to appeal to me then. I knew the difference of status between an Indian and an Englishman, but I did not believe that we had been quite reduced to slavery. I felt then that it was more the fault of individual British officials than of the British system, and that we could convert[3] them by love. If we would improve our status through the help and co-operation of the British, it was our duty to win their help by standing by them in their hour of need. Though the system was faulty, it did not seem to me to be intolerable[4], as it does today. But

1. *bar: the profession of barrister; [british] barristers collectively; [north american] lawyers collectively*
2. *residing: have one's permanent home in a particular place*
3. *convert: change or cause to change in form, character, or function; change into others of a different kind; adapt to make it suitable for a new purpose*
4. *intolerable: unable to be endured*

if, having lost my faith in the system, I refuse to co-operate with the British Government today, how could those friends do so, having lost their faith[1] not only in the system but in the officials as well?

The opposing friends felt that that was the hour for making a bold[2] declaration of Indian demands and for improving the status of Indians.

I thought that England's need should not be turned into our opportunity, and that it was more becoming and far-sighted not to press our demands while the war lasted. I therefore adhered to my advice and invited those who would to enlist as volunteers. There was a good response, practically all the provinces and all the religions being represented among the volunteers.

I wrote a letter to Lord Crewe, acquainting him with these facts, and expressing our readiness to be trained for ambulance work, if that should be considered a condition precedent to the acceptance of our offer.

Lord Crewe accepted the offer after some hesitation, and thanked us for having tendered our services to the Empire at that critical hour.

The volunteers began their preliminary training in first aid to the wounded[3] under the well-known Dr. Cantlie. It was a short course of six weeks, but it covered the whole course of first aid.

We were a class of about eighty. In six weeks we were examined, and all except one passed. For these the Government now provided military drill and other training. Colonel Baker was placed in charge of this work.

London in these days was a sight worth seeing. There was no panic, but all were busy helping to the best of their ability. Able-bodied adults began training as combatants, but what were the old, the infirm[4] and the women to do? There was enough work for them, if they wanted. So they employed themselves in cutting and making clothes and dressings for the wounded.

The Lyceum, a ladies' club, undertook to make as many clothes for the soldiers as they could. Shrimati Sarojini Naidu was a member of this club, and threw herself whole-heartedly into the work. This was my first acquaintance with her. She placed before me a heap of clothes which had been cut to pattern, and asked me to get them all sewn up and return them to her. I welcomed her demand and with the assistance of friends got as many clothes made as I could manage during my training for first aid.

1. *faith: complete trust or confidence*
2. *bold: confident and daring or courageous; audacious; impudent*
3. *wounded: an injury to living tissue caused by a cut, blow, or other impact*
4. *infirm: not physically strong, especially through age*

CHAPTER 116

A SPIRITUAL DILEMMA

As soon as the news reached South Africa that I along with other Indians had offered my services in the war, I received two cables. One of these was from Mr. Polak who questioned the consistency of my action with my profession of ahimsa.

I had to a certain extent anticipated this objection, for I had discussed the question in my Hind Swaraj (Indian Home Rule), and used to discuss it day in and day out with friends in South Africa. All of us recognized the immorality[1] of war. If I was not prepared to prosecute my assailant[2], much less would I be willing to participate in a war, especially when I knew nothing of the justice or otherwise of the cause of the combatants. Friends of course knew that I had previously served in the Boer War, but they assumed that my views had since undergone a change.

As a matter of fact the very same line of argument that persuaded me to take part in the Boer War had weighed with me on this occasion. It was quite clear to me that participation in war could never be consistent with ahimsa. But it is not always given to one to be equally clear about one's duty. A votary of truth is often obliged to grope in the dark.

Ahimsa is a comprehensive principle. We are helpless mortals caught in the conflagration of himsa. The saying that life lives on life has a deep meaning in it. Man cannot for a moment live without consciously or unconsciously committing outward himsa. The very fact of his living eating, drinking and moving about necessarily involves some himsa, destruction of life, be it ever so minute. A votary of ahimsa therefore remains true to his faith if the spring of all his actions is compassion, if he shuns[3] to the best of his ability the destruction of the tiniest creature, tries to save it, and thus incessantly strives to be free from the deadly coil[4] of himsa. He will be constantly growing in self-restraint and compassion, but he can never become entirely free from outward himsa.

1. *immorality: not conforming to accepted standards of morality*
2. *assailant: make a concerned or violent attack on*
3. *shuns: persistently avoid, ignore, or reject*
4. *coil: a length of something round in a joined sequence of concentric rings*

Then again, because underlying[1] ahimsa is the unity of all life, the error of one cannot but affect all, and hence man cannot be wholly free from himsa. So long as he continues to be a social being, he cannot but participate in the himsa that the very existence of society involves. When two nations are fighting, the duty of a votary of ahimsa is to stop the war. He who is not equal to that duty, he who has no power of resisting war, he who is not qualified to resist war, may take part in war, and yet whole-heartedly try to free himself, his nation and the world from war.

I had hoped to improve my status and that of my people through the British Empire. Whilst in England I was enjoying the protection of the British Fleet, and taking shelter as I did under its armed might, I was directly participating in its potential violence. Therefore if I desired to retain my connection with the Empire and to live under its banner, one of three courses was open to me: I could declare open resistance to the war and, in accordance with the law of Satyagraha, boycott the Empire until it changed its military policy; or I could seek imprisonment by civil disobedience of such of its laws as were fit to be disobeyed; or I could participate in the war on the side of the Empire and thereby acquire the capacity and fitness for resisting the violence of war. I lacked this capacity and fitness, as I thought there was nothing for it but to serve in the war.

I make no distinction, from the point of view of ahimsa, between combatants and non-combatants. He who volunteers to serve a band of dacoits, by working as their carrier, or their watchman while they are about their business, or their nurse when they are wounded, is as much guilty of dacoity as the dacoits[2] themselves. In the same way those who confine themselves to attending to the wounded in battle cannot be absolved from the guilt of war.

I had argued the whole thing out to myself in this manner, before I received Polak's cable, and soon after its receipt, I discussed these views with several friends and concluded that it was my duty to offer to serve in the war. Even today I see no flaw in that line of argument, nor am I sorry for my action, holding, as I then did, views favourable to the British connection.

I know that even then I could not carry conviction with all my friends about the correctness of my position. The question is subtle[3]. It admits of differences of opinion, and therefore I have submitted my argument as

1. *underlying: be the cause or basis of*
2. *dacoits: a member of a band of armed robbers in India or Burma*
3. *subtle: so delicate or precise as to be difficult to analyze or describe; a subtle distinction; capable of making fine distinctions; delicately complex and understated; subtle lighting*

clearly as possible to those who believe in ahimsa and who are making serious efforts to practise it in every walk of life. A devotee[1] of Truth may not do anything in deference to convention. He must always hold himself open to correction, and whenever he discovers himself to be wrong he must confess it at all costs and atone for it.

1. *devotee: enthusiast*

CHAPTER 117
MINIATURE SATYAGRAHA

Though I thus took part in the war as a matter of duty, it chanced that I was not only unable directly to participate in it, but actually compelled to offer what may be called miniature Satyagraha even at that critical[1] juncture.

I have already said that an officer was appointed in charge of our training, as soon as our names were approved and enlisted. We were all under the impression that this Commanding Officer was to be our chief only so far as technical matters were concerned, and that in all other matters I was the head of our Corps, which was directly responsible to me in matters of internal discipline; that is to say, the Commanding Officer had to deal with the Corps through me. But from the first the Officer left us under no such delusion[2].

Mr. Sorabji Adajania was a shrewd[3] man. He warned me. 'Beware of this man,' he said. 'He seems inclined[4] to lord it over us. We will have none of his orders. We are prepared to look upon him as our instructor. But the youngsters he has appointed to instruct us also feel as though they had come as our masters.'

These youngsters were Oxford students who had come to instruct us and whom the Commanding Officer had appointed to be our section leaders.

I also had not failed to notice the high-handedness of the Commanding Officer, but I asked Sorabji not to be anxious and tried to pacify him. But he was not the man to be easily convinced.

'You are too trusting. Those people will deceive you with wretched words, and when at last you see through them, you will ask us to resort to Satyagraha, and so come to grief, and bring us all to grief along with you,' said he with a smile.

'What else but grief can you hope to come to after having cast in your lot with me?' said I. 'A Satyagrahi is born to be deceived. Let the

1. *critical: decisive*
2. *delusion: an idiosyncratic belief or impression that is not in accordance with a generally accepted reality*
3. *shrewd: having or showing sharp powers of judgment; astute*
4. *inclined: favorable disposed towards something*

Commanding Officer deceive us. Have I not told you times without number that ultimately a deceiver only deceives himself?'

Sorabji gave a loud laugh. 'Well, then,' said he, 'continue to be deceived. You will some day meet your death in Satyagraha and drag poor mortals like me behind you.'

These words put me in mind of what the late Miss Emily Hobhouse wrote to me with regard to non-co-operation: 'I should not be surprised if one of these days you have to go to the gallows for the sake of truth. May God show you the right path and protect you.'

The talk with Sorabji took place just after the appointment of the Commanding Officer. In a very few days our relations with him reached the breaking point. I had hardly regained my strength after the fourteen days' fast, when I began to take part in the drill, often walking to the appointed place about two miles from home. This gave me pleurisy and laid me low. In this condition I had to go week-end camping. Whilst the others stayed there, I returned home. It was here that an occasion arose for Satyagraha.

The Commanding Officer began to exercise his authority somewhat[1] freely. He gave us clearly to understand that he was our head in all matters, military and non-military, giving us at the same time a taste of his authority. Sorabji hurried to me. He was not at all prepared to put up with this high-handedness. He said: 'We must have all orders through you. We are still in the training camp and all sorts of absurd orders are being issued. Invidious distinctions are made between ourselves and those youths who have been appointed to instruct us. We must have it out with the Commanding Officer, otherwise we shall not be able to go on any longer. The Indian students and others who have joined our Corps are not going to abide by any absurd[2] orders. In a cause which has been taken up for the sake of self-respect, it is unthinkable[3] to put up with loss of it.'

I approached the Commanding Officer and drew his attention to the complaints I had received. He wrote asking me to set out the complaints in writing, at the same time asking me 'to impress upon those who complain that the proper direction in which to make complaints is to me through their section[4] commanders, now appointed, who will inform me through the instructors.'

1. *somewhat: to some extent*
2. *absurd: wildly unreasonable, illogical or inappropriate*
3. *unthinkable: too unlikely or undesirable to be considered a possibility*
4. *section: a distinct group within a larger body of people or things; a subdivision of an army platoon*

To this I replied saying that I claimed no authority, that in the military sense I was no more than any other private, but that I had believed that as Chairman of the Volunteer Corps, I should be allowed unofficially to act as their representative. I also set out the grievances and requests that had been brought to my notice, namely, that grievous dissatisfaction had been caused by the appointment of section leaders without reference to the feeling of the members of the Corps; that they be recalled, and the Corps be invited to elect section leaders, subject to the Commander's approval.

This did not appeal to the Commanding Officer, who said it was repugnant[1] to all military discipline that the section leaders should be elected by the Corps, and that the recall of appointments already made would be subversive[2] of all discipline.

So we held a meeting and decided upon withdrawal. I brought home to the members the serious consequences of Satyagraha. But a very large majority voted for the resolution, which was to the effect that, unless the appointments of Corporals already made were recalled and the members of the Corps given an opportunity of electing their own Corporals, the members would be obliged to abstain from further drilling and week-end camping.

I then addressed a letter to the Commanding Officer telling him what a severe disappointment his letter rejecting my suggestion had been. I assured him that I was not fond of any exercise of authority and that I was most anxious to serve. I also drew his attention to a precedent. I pointed out that, although I occupied no official rank in the South African Indian Ambulance Corps at the time of the Boer War, there was never a hitch between Colonel Gallwey and the Corps, and the Colonel never took a step without reference to me with a view to ascertain[3] the wishes of the Corps. I also enclosed a copy of the resolution we had passed the previous evening.

This had no good effect on the Officer, who felt that the meeting and the resolution were a grave breach[4] of discipline.

Hereupon I addressed a letter to the Secretary of State for India, acquainting him with all the facts and enclosing a copy of the resolution. He replied explaining that conditions in South Africa were different, and drawing my attentions to the fact that under the rules the section

1. *repugnant: extremely distasteful; unacceptable*
2. *subversive: seeking or intended to subvert an established system or institution*
3. *ascertain: find out for certain*
4. *breach: an act of breaking a law, agreement, or code of conduct; a break in relations*

commanders were appointed by the Commanding Officer, but assuring me that in future, when appointing section commanders, the Commanding Officer would consider my recommendations.

A good deal of correspondence passed between us after this, but I do not want to prolong the bitter tale. Suffice it to say that my experience was of a piece with the experiences we daily have in India. What with threats and what with adroitness the Commanding Officer succeeded in creating a division in our Corps. Some of those who had voted for the resolution yielded to the Commander's threats or persuasions[1] and went back on their promise.

About this time an unexpectedly large contingent of wounded soldiers arrived at the Netley Hospital, and the services of our Corps were requisitioned[2]. Those whom the Commanding Officer could persuade went to Netley. The others refused to go. I was on my back, but was in communication with the members of the Corps. Mr. Roberts, the Under-Secretary of State, honoured me with many calls during those days. He insisted on my persuading the others to serve. He suggested that they should form a separate Corps and that at the Netley Hospital they could be responsible only to the Commanding Officer there, so that there would be no question of loss of self-respect, Government would be placated[3], and at same time helpful service would be rendered to the large number of wounded received at the hospital. This suggestion appealed both to my companions and to me, with the result that those who had stayed away also went to Netley.

Only I remained away, lying on my back and making the best of a bad job.

1. *persuasions: the action of persuading someone to do or believe in something*
2. *requisitioned: an official order laying claim to the use of property or materials*
3. *placated: calm, pacify or appease*

CHAPTER 118

GOKHALE'S CHARITY

I have already referred to the attack of pleurisy I had in England. Gokhale returned to London soon after. Kallenbach and I used regularly to go to him. Our talks were mostly about the war, and as Kallenbach had the geography of Germany at his finger tips, and had travelled much in Europe, he used to show him on the map the various places in connection with the war.

When I got pleurisy this also became a topic of daily discussion. My dietetic experiments were going on even then. My diet consisted, among other things, of groundnuts, ripe and unripe[1] bananas, lemon, olive oil, tomatoes and grapes. I completely eschewed milk, cereals[2], pulses[3] and other things.

Dr. Jivraj Mehta treated me. He pressed me hard to resume milk and cereals, but I was obdurate[4]. The matter reached Gokhale's ears. He had not much regard for my reasoning in favour of a fruitarian diet, and he wanted me to take whatever the doctor prescribed for my health.

It was no easy thing for me not a yield to Gokhale's pressure. When he would not take a refusal, I begged him to give me twenty-four hours for thinking over the question. As Kallenbach and I returned home that evening, we discussed where my duty lay. He had been with me in my experiment. He liked it, but I saw that he was agreeable to my giving it up if my health demanded it. So I had to decide for myself according to the dictates of the inner voice.

I spent the whole night thinking over the matter. To give up the experiment would mean renouncing all my ideas in that direction, and yet I found no flaw in them. The question was how far I should yield to Gokhale's loving pressure, and how far I might modify my experiment in the so-called interests of health. I finally decided to adhere to the experiment in so far as the motive behind was chiefly religious, and to yield to the doctor's advice where the motive was mixed. Religious

1. *unripe: not ripe*

2. *cereals: a grain used for food, for example wheat, maize, or rye; a grass producing such grain, grown as an agricultural crop*

2. *pulses: the edible seeds of various leguminous plants, e.g. lentils; the plant or plants producing such seeds*

4. *obdurate: stubbornly refusing to change one's opinion or course of action*

considerations had been predominant in the giving up of milk. I had before me a picture of the wicked[1] processes the govals in Calcutta adopted to extract the last drop of milk from their cows and buffaloes. I also had the feeling that, just as meat was not man's food, even so animal's milk could not be man's food. So I got up in the morning with the determination to adhere to my resolve to abstain from milk. This greatly relieved me. I dreaded to approach Gokhale, but I trusted him to respect my decision.

In the evening Kallenbach and I called on Gokhale at the National Liberal Club. The first question he asked me was: 'Well, have you decided to accept the doctor's advice?'

I gently but firmly replied: 'I am willing to yield on all points except one about which I beg you not to press[2] me. I will not take milk, milk-products or meat. If not to take these things should mean my death, I feel I had better face it.'

'Is this your final decision?' asked Gokhlae.

'I am afraid I cannot decide otherwise,' said I. 'I know that my decision will pain you, but I beg your forgiveness.'

With a certain amount of pain but with deep affection, Gokhale said: 'I do not approve of your decision. I do not see any religion in it. But I won't press you any more.' With these words he turned to Dr. Jivraj Mehta and said: 'Please don't worry him any more. Prescribe anything you like within the limit he has set for himself.'

The doctor expressed dissent[3], but was helpless. He advised me to take mung soup., with a dash of asafoetida[4] in it. To this I agreed. I took it for a day or two, but it increased my pain. As I did not find it suitable, I went back to fruits and nuts. The doctor of course went on with his external treatment. The latter somewhat relieved my pain, but my restrictions were to him a sore handicap.

Meanwhile Gokhale left for home, as he could not stand the October fogs of London.

1. *wicked: evil or morally wrong*
2. *press: force*
3. *dissent: express disagreement witha prevailing view or official decision; disagree with the doctrine of an established or orthodox church*
4. *asafoetida: a fetid resinous gum obtained from the roots of a herbaceous plant, used in herbal medicine and Indian cooking; a plant of the parsley family, from which this gum is obtained*

CHAPTER 119

TREATMENT OF PLEURISY

The persistence of the pleurisy caused some anxiety, but I knew that the cure lay not in taking medicine internally but in dietetic changes assisted by external remedies.

I called in Dr. Allinson of vegetarian fame, who treated diseases by dietetic modifications and whom I had met in 1890. He thoroughly overhauled me. I explained to him how I had pledged myself not to take milk. He cheered me up and said: 'You need not take milk. In fact I want you to do without any fat for some days.' He then advised me to live on plain brown bread, raw vegetables such as beet[1], radish, onion and other tubers[2] and greens, and also fresh fruit, mainly oranges. The vegetables were not to be cooked but merely grated fine, if I could not masticate them.

I adopted this for about three days, but raw vegetables did not quite suit me. My body was not in a condition to enable me to do full justice to the experiment. I was nervous about taking raw vegetables.

Dr. Allinson also advised me to keep all the windows of my room open for the whole twenty-four hours, bathe in tepid water, have an oil massage on the affected parts and a walk in the open for fifteen to thirty minutes. I liked all these suggestions.

My room had French windows which, if kept wide open, would let in the rain. The fanlight could not be opened. I therefore got the glass broken, so as to let in fresh air, and I partially opened the windows in a manner not to let in rain.

All these measures somewhat improved my health, but did not completely cure me.

Lady Cecilia Roberts occasionally called on me. We became friends. She wanted very much to persuade me to take milk. But as I was unyielding, she hunted about for a substitute for milk. Some friend suggested to her malted milk, assuring her quite unknowingly that it was absolutely free from milk, and that it was a chemical preparation with all the properties

1. *beet: a herbaceous plant cultivated as a source of food for humans and livestock, and for processing into sugar*
2. *tubers: a much thickened underground part of a stem or rhizome, e.g. in the potato, serving as a food reserve and bearing buds from which new plants arise; a thickened fleshy root, e.g. of the dahlia*

of milk. Lady Cecilia, I knew, had a great regard for my religious scruples, and so I implicitly trusted her. I dissolved the powder in water and took it only to find that it tasted just like milk. I read the label on the bottle, to find, only too late, that it was a preparation of milk. So I gave it up.

I informed Lady Cecilia about the discovery, asking her not to worry over it. She came post haste to me to say how sorry she was. Her friend had not read the label at all. I begged her not to be anxious and expressed my regret that I could not avail myself of the thing she had procured[1] with so much trouble. I also assured her that I did not at all feel upset or guilty over having taken milk under a misapprehension.

I must skip over many other sweet reminiscences of my contact with Lady Cecilia. I could think of many friends who have been a source of great comfort to me in the midst of trials and disappointments. One who has faith reads in them the merciful providence of God, who thus sweetens sorrow itself.

Dr. Allinson, when he next called, relaxed his restrictions and permitted me to have groundnut butter or olive oil for the sake of fat, and to take the vegetables cooked, if I chose, with rice. These changes were quite welcome, but they were far from giving me a complete cure. Very careful nursing was still necessary, and I was obliged to keep mostly in bed.

Dr. Mehta occasionally looked in to examine me and held out a standing offer to cure me if only I would listen to his advice.

Whilst things were going on in this way, Mr, Roberts one day came to see me and urged me very strongly to go home. 'You cannot possibly go to Netley in this condition. There is still severer[2] cold ahead of us. I would strongly advise you to get back to India, for it is only there that you can be completely cured. If, after your recovery, you should find the war still going on, you will have many opportunities there of rendering help. As it is, I do not regard what you have already done as by any means a mean contribution.'

I accepted his advice and began to make preparations for returning to India.

1. *procured: obtain; as a prostitute for someone else*
2. *severer: strict or harsh*

CHAPTER 120

HOMEWARD

Mr. Kallenbach had accompanied me to England with a view to going to India. We were staying together and of course wanted to sail by the same boat. Germans, however, were under such strict surveillance[1] that we had our doubts about Mr. Kallenbach getting a passport. I did my best to get it, and Mr. Roberts, who was in favour of his getting his passport, sent a cable to the Viceroy in this behalf. But straight came Lord Hardinge's reply: 'Regret Government of India not prepared to take any such risk.' All of us understood the force of the reply.

It was a great wrench for me to part from Mr. Kallenbach, but I could see that his pang was greater. Could he have come to India, he would have been leading today the simple happy life of a farmer and weaver. Now he is in South Africa, leading his old life and doing brisk business as an architect[2].

We wanted a third class passage, but as there was none available on P. & O. boats, we had to go second.

We took with us the dried fruit we had carried from South Africa, as most of it would not be procurable on the boat, where fresh fruit was easily available.

Dr. Jivraj Mehta had bandaged my ribs with 'Mede's Plaster' and had asked me not to remove it till we reached the Red Sea. For two days I put up with the discomfort, but finally it became too much for me. It was with considerable difficulty that I managed to undo the plaster and regain the liberty of having a proper wash and bath.

My diet consisted mostly of nuts and fruits. I found that I was improving every day and felt very much better by the time we entered the Suez Canal. I was weak, but felt entirely out of danger, and I gradually went on increasing my exercise. The improvement I attributed largely to the pure air of the temperate[3] zone.

1. *surveillance: close observation, especially of a suspected spy or criminal*
2. *architect: a person who designs buildings and supervises their construction*
3. *temperate: relating to or denoting a region or climate characterized by mild temperatures*

Whether it was due to past experience or to any other reason, I do not know, but the kind of distance I noticed between the English and Indian passengers on the boat was something I had not observed even on my voyage from South Africa. I did talk to a few Englishmen, but the talk was mostly formal. There were hardly any cordial[1] conversations such as had certainly taken place on the South African boats. The reason for this was, I think, to be found in the conscious or unconscious feeling at the back of the Englishman's mind that he belonged to the ruling race, and the feeling at the back of the Indian's mind that he belonged to the subject[2] race.

I was eager to reach home and get free from this atmosphere.

On arriving at Aden we already began to feel somewhat at home. We knew the Adenwallas very well, having met Mr. Kekobad Kavasji Dinshaw in Durban and come in close contact with him and his wife.

A few days more and we reached Bombay. It was such a joy to get back to the homeland after an exile of ten years.

Gokhale had inspired a reception for me in Bombay, where he had come in spite of his delicate health. I had approached India in the ardent hope of merging myself in him, and thereby feeling free. But fate had willed it otherwise.

1. *cordial: warm and friendly*

2. *subject: a member of a state owing allegiance to its monarch or supreme ruler*

CHAPTER 121

SOME REMINISCENCES OF THE BAR

Before coming to a narrative of the course my life took in India, it seems necessary to recall a few of the South African experiences which I have deliberately left out.

Some lawyer friends have asked me to give my reminiscences[1] of the bar. The number of these is so large that, if I were to describe them all, they would occupy a volume by themselves and take me out of my scope. But it may not perhaps be improper to recall some of those which bear upon the practice of truth.

So far as I can recollect, I have already said that I never resorted to untruth in my profession, and that a large part of my legal practice was in the interest of public work, for which I charged nothing beyond out-of-pocket expenses, and these too I sometimes met myself. I had thought that in saying this I had said all that was necessary as regards my legal practice. But friends want me to do more. They seem to think that, if I described however slightly, some of the occasions when I refused to swerve from the truth, the legal profession might profit by it.

As a student I had heard that the lawyer's profession was a liar's profession. But this did not influence me, as I had no intention of earning either position or money by lying.

My principle was put to the test many a time in South Africa. Often I knew that my opponents had tutored[2] their witnesses, and if I only encouraged my client or his witness to lie, we could win the case. But I always resisted the temptation. I remember only one occasion when, after having won a case, I suspected that my client had deceived me. In my heart of hearts I always wished that I should win only if my client's case was right. In fixing my fees I do not recall ever having made them conditional on my winning the case. Whether my client won or lost, I expected nothing more nor less than my fees.

I warned every new client at the outset[3] that he should not expect me to take up a false case or to coach the witnesses, with the result that

1. *reminiscences: tending to remind one of something*
2. *tutored: coached; taught*
3. *outset: the start or beginning*

I built up such a reputation that no false cases used to come to me. Indeed some of my clients would keep their clean cases for me, and take the doubtful ones elsewhere.

There was one case which proved a severe trial. It was brought to me by one of my best clients. It was a case of highly complicated accounts and had been a prolonged one. It had been heard in parts before several courts. Ultimately the book-keeping portion of it was entrusted by the court to the arbitration of some qualified accountants. The award[1] was entirely in favour[2] of my client, but the arbitrators had inadvertently committed an error in calculation which, however small, was serious, inasmuch as an entry which ought to have been on the debit side was made on the credit side. The opponents had opposed the award on other grounds. I was junior counsel for my client. When the senior counsel became aware of the error, he was of opinion that our client was not bound to admit it. He was clearly of opinion that no counsel was bound to admit anything that went against his client's interest. I said we ought to admit the error.

But the senior counsel contended: 'In that case there is every likelihood of the court canceling the whole award, and no sane counsel would imperil[3] his client's case to that extent. At any rate I would be the last man to take any such risk. If the case were to be sent up for a fresh hearing, one could never tell what expenses our client might have to incur, and what the ultimate result might be!'

The client was present when this conversation took place.

I said: 'I feel that both our client and we ought to run the risk. Where is the certainty of the court upholding[4] a wrong award simply because we do not admit the error? And supposing the admission were to bring the client to grief, what harm is there?'

'But why should we make the admission at all?' said the senior counsel.

'Where is the surety of the court not detecting the error or our opponent not discovering it?' said I.

'Well then, will you argue the case? I am not prepared to argue it on your terms,' replied the senior counsel with decision.

I humbly answered: 'If you will not argue, then I am prepared to do so, if our client so desires. I shall have nothing to do with the case if the error is not admitted.'

1. *award: give or grant officially as a prize or reward*
2. *favour: approval or liking; overgenerous preferential treatment*
3. *imperil: put into danger*
4. *upholding: confirm or support*

With this I looked at my client. He was a little embarrassed. I had been in the case from the very first. The client fully trusted me, and knew me through and through. He said: 'Well, then, you will argue the case and admit the error. Let us lose, if that is to be our lot. God defend the right.'

I was delighted. I had expected nothing less from him. The senior counsel again warned me, pitied me for my obduracy[1], but congratulated me all the same. What happened in the court we shall see in the next chapter.

1. *obduracy: stubborn unyielding*

CHAPTER 122

SHARP PRACTICE?

I had no doubt about the soundness of my advice, but I doubted very much my fitness for doing full justice to the case. I felt it would be a most hazardous[1] undertaking to argue such a difficult case before the Supreme Court, and I appeared before the Bench in fear and trembling.

As soon as I referred to the error in the accounts, one of the judges said:

'Is not this sharp practice, Mr. Gandhi?'

I boiled within to hear this charge. It was intolerable to be accused of sharp practice when there was not the slightest warrant for it.

'With a judge prejudiced from the start like this, there is little chance of success in this difficult case,' I said to myself. But I composed my thoughts and answered:

'I am surprised that your Lordship should suspect sharp practice without hearing me out.'

'No question of a charge,' said the judge. 'It is a mere suggestion.'

'The suggestion here seems to me to amount to a charge. I would ask your Lordship to hear me out and then arraign[2] me if there is any occasion for it.'

'I am sorry to have interrupted you,' replied the judge. 'Pray do go on with your explanation of the discrepancy.'

I had enough material in support of my explanation. Thanks to the judge having raised this question, I was able to rivet the Court's attention on my argument from the very start. I felt much encouraged and took the opportunity of entering into a detailed explanation. The Court gave me a patient hearing, and I was able to convince the judges that the discrepancy[3] was due entirely to inadvertence. They therefore did not feel disposed to cancel the whole award, which had involved considerable labour.

1. *hazardous: risky; dangerous*
2. *arraign: call before a court to answer a criminal charge*
3. *discrepancy: an illogical or surprising lack of compatibility or similarity between two or more facts*

The opposing counsel seemed to feel secure in the belief that not much argument would be needed after the error had been admitted. But the judges continued to interrupt him, as they were convinced that the error was a slip which could easily be rectified. The counsel laboured hard to attack the award, but the judge who had originally started with the suspicion had now come round definitely to my side.

'Supposing Mr. Gandhi had not admitted the error, what would you have done?' he asked.

'It was impossible for us to secure the services of a more competent and honest expert accountant than the one appointed by us.'

'The Court must presume that you know your case best. If you cannot point out anything beyond the slip which any expert accountant is liable to commit, the Court will be loath to compel the parties to go in for fresh litigation and fresh expenses because of a patent[1] mistake. We may not order a fresh hearing when such an error can be easily corrected continued the judge.

And so the counsel's objection was overruled. The Court either confirmed the award, with the error rectified[2], or ordered the arbitrator to rectify the error, I forget which.

I was delighted. So were my client and senior counsel; and I was confirmed in my conviction that it was not impossible to practise law without compromising truth.

Let the reader, however, remember that even truthfulness in the practice of the profession cannot cure it of the fundamental defect that vitiates it.

1. *patent: a government license to an individual or body conferring a right or title for a set period, especially the sole right to make, use, or sell an invention*
2. *rectified: put right; correct; convert to direct current*

CHAPTER 123

CLIENTS TURNED CO-WORKERS

The distinction between the legal practice in Natal and that in the Transvaal was that in Natal there was a joint bar; a barrister, whilst he was admitted to the rank of advocate, could also practise as an attorney; whereas in the Transvaal, as in Bombay, the spheres of attorneys and advocates were distinct. A barrister had the right of election whether he would practise as an advocate or as an attorney. So whilst in Natal I was admitted as an advocate, in the Transvaal I sought admission as an attorney. For as an advocate I could not have come in direct contact with the Indians and the white attorneys in South Africa would not have briefed me.

But even in the Transvaal it was open to attorneys to appear before magistrates. On one occasion, whilst I was conducting a case before a magistrate in Johannesburg, I discovered that my client had deceived me. I saw him completely break down in the witness[1] box. So without any argument I asked the magistrate to dismiss the case. The opposing[2] counsel was astonished, and the magistrate was pleased. I rebuked my client for bringing a false case to me. He knew that I never accepted false cases, and when I brought the thing home to him, he admitted his mistake, and I have an impression that he was not angry with me for having asked the magistrate to decide against him. At any rate my conduct in this case did not affect my practice for the worse, indeed it made my work easier. I also saw that my devotion to truth enhanced my reputation amongst the members of the profession, and in spite of the handicap of colour I was able in some cases to win even their affection.

During my professional work it was also my habit never to conceal[3] my ignorance from my clients or my colleagues. Wherever I felt myself at sea, I would advise my client to consult some other counsel, or if he preferred to stick to me, I would ask him to let me seek the assistance of senior counsel. This frankness earned me the unbounded affection and trust of my clients. They were always willing to pay the fee whenever

1. *witness: a person who sees an event take place*
2. *opposing: different from or in conflict with each other*
3. *conceal: not allow to be seen; hide; keep secret; prevent from being known*

consultation with senior counsel was necessary. This affection and trust served me in good stead in my public work.

I have indicated in the foregoing chapters that my object in practising in South Africa was service of the community. Even for this purpose, winning the confidence of the people was an indispensable condition. The large hearted Indians magnified[1] into service professional work done for money, and when I advised them to suffer the hardships of imprisonment for the sake of their rights, many of them cheerfully accepted the advice, not so much because they had reasoned out the correctness of the course, as because of their confidence in, and affection for, me.

As I write this, many a sweet reminiscence comes to my mind. Hundreds of clients became friends and real co-workers in public service, and their association sweetened a life that was otherwise full of difficulties and dangers.

1. *magnified: make something appear bigger than it actually is*

CHAPTER 124

HOW A CLIENT WAS SAVED

The reader, by now, will be quite familiar with Parsi Rustomji's name. He was one who became at once my client and co-worker, or perhaps it would be truer to say that he first became co-worker and then client. I won his confidence to such an extent that he sought and followed my advice also in private domestic matters. Even when he was ill, he would seek my aid, and though there was much difference between our ways of living, he did not hesitate to accept my quack treatment.

This friend once got into a very bad scrape[1]. Though he kept me informed of most of his affairs, he had studiously kept back one thing. He was a large importer of goods from Bombay and Calcutta, and not infrequently he resorted to smuggling. But as he was on the best terms with customs officials, no one was inclined to suspect him. In charging duty, they used to take his invoices on trust. Some might even have connived[2] at the smuggling.

But to use the telling simile of the Gujarati poet Akho, theft like quicksilver won't be suppressed, and Parsi Rustomji's proved no exception. The good friend ran post haste to me, the tears rolling down his cheeks as he said: 'Bhai, I have deceived you. My guilt has been discovered today. I have smuggled and I am doomed. I must go to jail and be ruined. You alone may be able to save me from this predicament. I have kept back nothing else from you, but I thought I ought not to bother you with such tricks of the trade, and so I never told you about this smuggling. But now, how much I repent it!'

I calmed him and said: 'To save or not to save you is in His hands. As to me you know my way. I can but try to save you by means of confession.'

The good Parsi felt deeply mortified.

'But is not my confession before you enough?' he asked.

'You have wronged[3] not me but Government. How will the confession made before me avail[4] you?' I replied gently.

1. *scrape: an embarrassing or difficult predicament*
2. *connived: secretly allow a wrongdoing; conspire*
3. *wronged: act unjustly or dishonestly towards*
4. *avail: use or take advantage of*

'Of course I will do just as you advise, but will you not consult with my old counsel Mr.---? He is a friend too,' said Parsi Rustomji.

Inquiry revealed that the smuggling had been going on for a long time, but the actual offence detected involved a trifling sum. We went to his counsel. He perused the papers, and said: 'The case will be tried by a jury, and a Natal jury will be the last to acquit[1] an Indian. But I will not give up hope.'

I did not know this counsel intimately. Parsi Rustomji intercepted: 'I thank you, but I should like to be guided by Mr. Gandhi's advice in this case. He knows me intimately. Of course you will advise him whenever necessary.'

Having thus shelved the counsel's question, we went to Parsi Rustomji's shop.

And now explaining my view I said to him: 'I don't think this case should be taken to court at all. It rests with the Customs Officer to prosecute you or to let you go, and he in turn will have to be guided by the Attorney General. I am prepared to meet both. I propose that you should offer to pay the penalty they fix, and the odds are that they will be agreeable. But if they are not, you must be prepared to go to jail. I am of opinion that the shame lies not so much in going to jail as in committing the offence. The deed of shame has already been done. Imprisonment you should regard as a penance. The real penance lies in resolving[2] never to smuggle again.'

I cannot say that Parsi Rustomji took all this quite well. He was a brave man, but his courage failed him for the moment. His name and fame were at stake, and where would he be if the edifice[3] he had reared with such care and labour should go to pieces?

'Well, I have told you,' he said, 'that I am entirely in your hands. You may do just as you like.'

I brought to bear on this case all my powers of persuasion. I met the Customs Officer and fearlessly apprised[4] him of the whole affair. I also promised to place all the books at his disposal and told him how penitent Parsi Rustomji was feeling The Customs Officer said: 'I like the old Parsi. I am sorry he has made a fool of himself. You know where my duty lies. I must be guided by the Attorney General and so I would advise you to use all your persuasion with him.'

1. *acquit: formally declare not guilty of a criminal charge*
2. *resolving: decide firmly on a course of action take a decision by a formal vote*
3. *edifice: a building, especially a large, imposing one*
4. *apprised: assess the value, quality, or performance of; set a price on*

'I shall be thankful,' said I, 'if you do not insist on dragging him into court.'

Having got him to promise this, I entered into correspondence[1] with the Attorney General and also met him. I am glad to say that he appreciated my complete frankness and was convinced that I had kept back nothing.

I now forget whether it was in connection with this or with some other case that my persistence and frankness extorted from him the remark: 'I see you will never take a no for an answer.'

The case against Parsi Rustomji was compromised. He was to pay a penalty equal to twice the amount he had confessed to having smuggled. Rustomji reduced to writing the facts of the whole case, got the paper framed and hung it up in his office to serve as a perpetual[2] reminder to his heirs and fellow merchants.

These friends of Rustomji warned me not to be taken in by this transitory contrition. When I told Rustomji about this warning he said: 'What would be my fate if I deceived you?'

1. *correspondence: communicate by exchanging letters*

2. *perpetual: never ending or changing; denoting or having a position or trophy held for life rather than a limited period; having no fixed maturity date*

CHAPTER 125

THE FIRST EXPERIENCE

Before I reached home, the party which had started from Phoenix had already arrived. According to our original plan I was to have preceded them, but my preoccupation in England with the war had upset all our calculations, and when I saw that I had to be detained in England indefinitely, I was faced with the question of a place for accommodating the Phoenix party. I wanted them all to stay together in India, if possible, and to live the life they had led at Phoenix. I did not know of any Ashram to which I could recommend them to go, and therefore cabled to them to meet Mr. Andrews and do as he advised.

So they were first put in the Gurukul, Kangri, where the late Swami Shraddhanandji treated them as his own children. After this they were put in the Shantiniketan Ashram, where the Poet and his people showered similar love upon them. The experiences they gathered at both these places too stood them and me in good stead[1].

The Poet, Shraddhanandji and Principal Sushil Rudra, as I used to say to Andrews, composed this trinity[2]. When in South Africa he was never tired of speaking of them, and of my many sweet memories of South Africa, Mr. Andrews' talks, day in and day out, of this great trinity, are amongst the sweetest and most vivid. Mr. Andrews naturally put the Phoenix party in touch with Sushil Rudra. Principal Rudra had no Ashram, but he had a home which he placed completely at the disposal of the Phoenix family. Within a day of their arrival, his people made them feel so thoroughly at home that they did not seem to miss Phoenix at all.

It was only when I landed in Bombay that I learnt that the Phoenix party was at Shantiniketan. I was therefore impatient[3] to meet them as soon as I could after my meeting with Gokhale.

The receptions in Bombay gave me an occasion for offering what might be called a little Satyagraha.

1. *stead: the place or role that someone or something should have or fill; appointed in his stead*
2. *trinity: a group of three people or things*
3. *impatient: tendency of restlessness*

At the party given in my honour at Mr. Jehangir Petit's place, I did not dare to speak in Gujarati. In those palatial surroundings of dazzling[1] splendour[2] I, who had lived my best life among indentured labourers, felt myself a complete rustic. With my Kathiawadi cloak, turban and dhoti, I looked somewhat more civilized than I do today, but the pomp[3] and splendour of Mr. Petit's mansion made me feel absolutely out of my element. However, I acquitted myself tolerably[4] well, having taken shelter under Sir Pherozeshah's protecting wing.

Then there was the Gujarati function. The Gujaratis would not let me go without a reception, which was organized by the late Uttamlal Trivedi. I had acquainted myself with the programme beforehand. Mr. Jinnah was present, being a Gujarati, I forget whether as president or as the principal speaker. He made a short and sweet little speech in English. As far as I remember most of the other speeches were also in English. When my turn came, I expressed my thanks in Gujarati explaining my partiality for Gujarati and Hindustani, and entering my humble protest against the use of English in a Gujarati gathering. This I did, not without some hesitation, for I was afraid lest it should be considered discourteous for an inexperienced man, returned home after a long exile, to enter his protest against established practices. But no one seemed to misunderstand my insistence on replying in Gujarati. In fact I was glad to note that everyone seemed reconciled to my protest.

The meeting thus emboldened me to think that I should not find it difficult to place my new-fangled notions before my countrymen.

After a brief stay in Bombay, full of these preliminary experiences, I went to Poona whither Gokhale had summoned me.

1. *dazzling: overwhelm with an impressive quality*
2. *splendour: splendid appearance*
3. *pomp: ceremony and splendid display*
4. *tolerably: able to endure specified conditions or treatment*

CHAPTER 126

WITH GOKHALE IN POONA

The moment I reached Bombay Gokhale sent me word that the Governor was desirous of seeing me, and that it might be proper for me to respond[1] before I left for Poona. Accordingly I called on His Excellency. After the usual inquiries, he said:

'I ask one thing of you. I would like you to come and see me whenever you propose to take any steps concerning Government.'

I replied:

'I can very easily give the promise, inasmuch as it is my rule, as a Satyagrahi, to understand the viewpoint of the party I propose to deal with, and to try to agree with him as far as may be possible. I strictly observed the rule in South Africa and I mean to do the same here.'

Lord Willingdon thanked me and said:

'You may come to me whenever you like, and you will see that my Government do not willfully do anything wrong.'

To which I replied: 'It is that faith which sustains me.'

After this I went to Poona. It is impossible for me to set down all the reminiscences of this precious time. Gokhale and the members of the Servants of India Society overwhelmed me with affection. So far as I recollect, Gokhale had summoned all of them to meet me. I had a frank talk with them all on every sort of subject.

Gokhale was very keen that I should join the Society and so was I. But the members felt that, as there was a great difference between my ideals and methods of work and theirs, it might not be proper for me to join the Society. Gokhale believed that, in spite of my insistence[2] on my own principles, I was equally ready and able to tolerate[3] theirs.

'But,' he said, 'the members of the Society have not yet understood your readiness for compromise. They are tenacious[4] of their principles, and quite independent. I am hoping that they will accept you, but if they

1. *respond: say or do something in reply or as a reaction*
2. *insistence: repeated and demanding attention: a telephone started ringing, loud and insistent*
3. *tolerate: endure with forbearance*
4. *tenacious: not readily relinquishing something; keeping a firm hold*

don't you will not for a moment think that they are lacking in respect or love for you. They are hesitating to take any risk lest[1] their high regard for you should be jeopardized. But whether you are formally admitted as a member or not, I am going to look upon you as one.'

I informed Gokhale of my intentions. Whether I was admitted as a member or not, I wanted to have an Ashram where I could settle down with my Phoenix family, preferably somewhere in Gujarat, as, being a Gujarati, I thought I was best fitted to serve the country through serving Gujarat. Gokhale liked the idea. He said: 'You should certainly do so. Whatever may be the result of your talks with the members, you must look to me for the expenses of the Ashram, which I will regard as my own.'

My heart overflowed with joy. It was a pleasure to feel free from the responsibility of raising funds, and to realize that I should not be obliged to set about the work all on my own, but that I should be able to count on a sure guide whenever I was in difficulty. This took a great load[2] off my mind.

So the late Dr. Dev was summoned and told to open an account for me in the Society's books and to give me whatever I might require for the Ashram and for public expenses.

I now prepared to go to Shantiniketan. On the eve of my departure Gokhale arranged a party of selected friends, taking good care to order refreshments[3] of my liking, i.e., fruits and nuts. The party was held just a few paces from his room, and yet he was hardly in a condition to walk across and attend it. But his affection for me got the better of him and he insisted on coming. He came, but fainted and had to be carried away. Such fainting was not a new thing with him and so when he came to, he sent word that we must go on with the party.

This party was of course no more than a conversazione in the open space opposite the Society's guesthouse, during which friends had heart-to-heart chats over light refreshments of groundnuts, dates and fresh fruits of the season.

But the fainting fit was to be no common event in my life.

1. *lest: with the intention of preventing; to avoid the risk of*
2. *load: a heavy or bulky thing that is being carried or is about to be carried; the total number or amount that can be carried in a vehicle or container: a carload of people*
3. *refreshments: a light snack or drink*

CHAPTER 127

WAS IT A THREAT?

From Poona I went to Rajkot and Porbandar, where I had to meet my brother's widow and other relatives.

During the Satyagraha in South Africa I had altered my style of dress so as to make it more in keeping with that of the indentured labourers, and in England also I had adhered to the same style for indoor use. For landing in Bombay I had a Kathiawadi suit of clothes consisting of a shirt, a dhoti, a cloak and a white scarf, all made of Indian mill cloth. But as I was to travel third from Bombay, I regarded the scarf and the cloak as too much of an encumbrance[1], so I shed them, and invested in an eight-to-ten-annas Kashmiri cap. One dressed in that fashion was sure to pass muster as a poor man.

On account of the plague prevailing at that time third class passengers were being medically inspected at Viramgam or Wadhwan I forget which. I had slight[2] fever. The inspector on finding that I had a temperature asked me to report myself to the Medical Officer at Rajkot and noted down my name.

Someone had perhaps sent the information that I was passing through Wadhwan, for the tailor Motilal, a noted public worker of the place, met me at the station. He told me about the Viramgam customs, and the hardships[3] railway passengers had to suffer on account of it. I had little inclination to talk because of my fever, and tried to finish with a brief reply which took the form of a question:

'Are you prepared to go to jail?'

I had taken Motilal to be one of those impetuous youths who do not think before speaking. But not so Motilal. He replied with firm deliberation:

'We will certainly go to jail, provided you lead us. As kathiawadis, we have the first right on you. Of course we do not mean to detain you now, but you must promise to halt here on your return. You will be delighted

1. *encumbrance: a burden or impediment*

2. *slight: small in degree; inconsiderable; not profound or substantial*

3. *hardships: severe suffering or privation*

to see the work and the spirit of our youths, and you may trust us to respond as soon as you summon us.'

Motilal captivated me. His comrade eulogizing him, said:

'Our friend is but a tailor[1]. But he is such a master of his profession that he easily earns Rs. 15 a month which is just what he needs working an hour a day, and gives the rest of his time to public work. He leads us all, putting our education to shame.

Later I came in close contact with Motilal, and I saw that there was no exaggeration in the eulogy. He made a point of spending some days in the then newly started Ashram every month to teach the children tailoring and to do some of the tailoring of the Ashram himself. He would talk to me every day of Viramgam, and the hardships of the passengers, which had become absolutely unbearable[2] for him. He was cut off in the prime[3] of youth by a sudden illness, and public life at Wadhwan suffered without him.

On reaching Rajkot, I reported myself to the Medical officer the next morning. I was not unknown there. The Doctor felt ashamed and was angry with the inspector. This was unnecessary, for the inspector had only done his duty. He did not know me, and even if he had known me, he should not have done otherwise. The Medical Officer would not let me go to him again insisted on sending an inspector to me instead.

Inspection of third class passangers for sanitary reasons is essential on such occasions. If big men choose to travel third, whatever their position in life, they must voluntarily submit themselves to all the regulations that the poor are subject to, and the officials ought to be impartial. My experience is that the officials, instead of looking upon third class passengers as fellowmen, regard them as so many sheep[4]. They talk to them contemptuously, and brook no reply or argument. The third class passenger has to obey the official as though he were his servant, and the letter may with impunity belabour and blackmail him, and book him his ticket only after putting him to the greatest possible inconvenience, including often missing the train. All this I have seen with my own eyes. No reform is possible unless some of the educated and the rich voluntarily accept the status of the poor, travel third, refuse to enjoy the amenities denied to the poor and, instead of taking avoidable hardships, discourtesies and injustice as a matter of course, fight for their removal.

1. *tailor: a person whose occupation is making clothes, especially men's outer garments for individual customers*
2. *unbearable: not able to be endured or tolerated*
3. *prime: of the best possible quality; excellent; having all the expected characteristics; most suitable or likely*
4. *sheep: a perso who is too easily influenced or led*

Wherever I went in Kathiawad I heard complaints about the Viramgam customs hardships. I therefore decided immediately to make use of Lord Willingdon's offer. I collected and read all the literature available on the subject, convinced myself that the complaints were well founded, and opened correspondence with the Bombay Government. I called on the Private Secretary to Lord Willingdon and waited on His Excellency also. The latter expressed his sympathy but shifted the blame[1] on Delhi. 'If it had been in our hands, we should have removed the cordon long ago. You should approach the Government of India,' said the Secretary.

I communicated with the Government of India, but got no reply beyond an acknowledgment. It was only when I had an occasion to meet Lord Chelmsford later that redress could be had. When I placed the facts before him, he expressed his astonishment. He had known nothing of the matter. He gave me a patient hearing, telephoned[2] that very moment for papers about Viramgam, and promised to remove the cordon if the authorities had no explanation or defence to offer. Within a few days of this interview I read in the papers that the Viramgam customs cordon had been removed.

I regarded this event as the advent of Satyagraha in India. For during my interview with the Bombay Government the Secretary had expressed his disapproval of a reference to Satyagraha in a speech[3] which I had delivered in Bagasra (in Kathiawad).

'Is not this a threat?' he had asked. 'And do you think a powerful Government will yield to threats?'

'This was no threat,' I had replied. 'It was educating the people. It is my duty to place before the people all the legitimate remedies for grievances. A nation that wants to come into its own ought to know all the ways and means to freedom. Usually they include violence as the last remedy. Satyagraha, on the other hand, is an absolutely non-violent weapon. I regard it as my duty to explain its practice and its limitations. I have no doubt that the British Government is a powerful Government, but I have no doubt also that Satyagraha is a sovereign remedy.'

The clever Secretary nodded his head and said: 'We shall see.'

1. *blame: responsibility for a fault or wrong*
2. *telephoned: ring or speak to someone using the telephone; make a telephone call*
3. *speech: a formal address delivered to an audience; a sequence of lines written for one character in a play*

CHAPTER 128

SHANTINIKETAN

From Rajkot I proceeded to Shantiniketan. The teachers and students overwhelmed me with affection. The reception was a beautiful combination of simplicity, art and love. It was here I met Kakasaheb Kalelkar for the first time.

I did not know then why Kalelkar was called 'Kakasaheb'. But I learnt later on that Sjt. Keshavrao Deshpande, who was a contemporary and a close friend of mine in England, and who had conducted a school in the Baroda State called 'Ganganath Vidyalaya', had given the teachers family names with a view to investing the Vidyalaya with a family atmosphere. Sjt. Kalelkar who was a teacher there came to be called, 'Kaka' (literally paternal uncle), Phadke was called 'Mama' (literally maternal uncle), and Harihar Sharma received the name 'Anna' (literally brother). Others also got similar names. Anandanand (Swami) as Kaka's friend and Patwardhan (Appa) as Mama's friend later joined the family, and all in course of time became my co-workers one after another. Sjt. Deshpande himself used to be called 'Saheb'. When the Vidyalaya had to be dissolved, the family also broke up, but they never gave up their spiritual[1] relationship or their assumed names.

Kakasaheb went out to gain experience of different institutions, and at the time I went to Shantiniketan, he happened to be there. Chintaman Shastri, belonging to the same fraternity[2], was there also. Both helped in teaching Samskrit.

The Phoenix family had been assigned separate quarters at Shantiniketan. Maganlal Gandhi was at their head, and he had made it his business to see that all the rules of the Phoenix Ashram should be scrupulously[3] observed. I saw that, by dint of his love, knowledge and perseverance, he had made his fragrance[4] felt in the whole of Shantiniketan.

1. *spiritual: of, relating to, or affecting the human spirit as opposed to material or physical things*
2. *fraternity: a brotherhood, especially with a religious or charitable purpose*
3. *scrupulously: a pleasant, sweet, smell; a perfume or aftershave*
4. *fragrance: diligent, thorough, and attentive to details*

Andrews was there, and also Pearson. Amongst the Bengali teachers with whom we came in fairly close contact were Jagadanandbabu, Nepalbabu, Santoshbabu, Kshitimohanbabu, Nagenbabu, Sharadbabu and Kalibabu.

As is my wont, I quickly mixed with the teachers and students, and engaged them in a discussion on self-help. I put it to the teachers that, if they and the boys dispensed with the services of paid cooks and cooked their food themselves, it would enable the teachers to control the kitchen from the point of view of the boy's physical and moral health, and it would afford to the students an object-lesson in self-help. One or two of them were inclined to shake their heads. Some of them strongly approved of the proposal. The boys welcomed it, if only because of their instinctive taste for novelty. So we launched the experiment. When I invited the Poet to express his opinion, he said that he did not mind it provided the teachers were favourable. To the boys he said, 'The experiment contains the key to Swaraj.'

Pearson began to wear away his body in making the experiment a success. He threw himself into it with zest. A batch was formed to cut vegetables, another to clean the grain, and so on. Nagenbabu and others undertook to see to the sanitary cleaning of the kitchen and its surroundings. It was a delight to me to see them working spade[1] in hand.

But it was too much to expect the hundred and twenty-five boys with their teachers to take to this work of physical labour like ducks to water. There used to be daily discussion. Some began early to show fatigue. But Pearson was not the man to be tired. One would always find him with his smiling face doing something or other in or about the kitchen. He had taken upon himself the cleaning of the bigger utensils. A party of students played on their *sitar* before this cleaning party in order to beguile the tedium of the operation. All alike took the thing up with zest and Shantiniketan became a busy hive.

Changes like these when once begun always develop. Not only was the Phoenix party's kitchen self-conducted, but the food cooked in it was of the simplest. Condiments were eschewed[2]. Rice, *dal*, vegetables and even wheat flour were all cooked at one and the same time in a steam cooker. And Shantiniketan boys started a similar kitchen with a view to introducing reform in the Bengali kitchen. One or two teachers and some students ran this kitchen.

1. *spade: a tool with a sharp edged, rectangular metal blade and a long handle, used for digging*
2. *eschewed: abstain from*

The experiment was, however, dropped after some time. I am of the opinion that the famous institution lost nothing by having conducted the experiment for a brief interval, and some of the experiences gained could not but be of help to the teachers.

I had intended to stay at Shantiniketan for some time but fate willed otherwise. I had hardly been there a week when I received from Poona a telegram announcing Gokhale's death. Shantiniketan was immersed in grief. All the members came over to me to express their condolences[1]. A special meeting was called in the Ashram temple to mourn the national loss. It was a solemn function. The same day I left for Poona with my wife and Maganlal. All the rest stayed at Shantiniketan.

Andrews accompanied me up to Burdwan. 'Do you think,' he asked me, 'that a time will come for Satyagraha in India? And if so, have you any idea when it will come?'

'It is difficult to say,' said I. 'For one year I am to do nothing. For Gokhale took from me a promise that I should travel in India for gaining experience, and express no opinion on public questions until I have finished the period of probation. Even after the year is over, I will be in no hurry to speak and pronounce opinions. And so I do not suppose there will be any occasion for Satyagraha for five years or so.'

I may note in this connection that Gokhale used to laugh at some of my ideas in *Hind Swaraj (Indian Home Rule)* and say: 'After you have stayed a year in India, your views will correct themselves.'

1. *condolences: express sympathy for*

CHAPTER 129

WOES OF THIRD CLASS PASSENGERS

At Burdwan we came face to face with the hardships[1] that a third class passenger has to go through even in securing[2] his ticket. 'Third class tickets are not booked so early,' we were told. I went to the Station Master, though that too was a difficult business. Someone kindly directed me to where he was, and I represented to him our difficulty. He also made the same reply. As soon as the booking window opened, I went to purchase the tickets. But it was no easy thing to get them. Might was right, and passengers, who were forward and indifferent to others, coming one after another, continued to push me out. I was therefore about the last of the first crowd to get a ticket.

The train arrived, and getting into it was another trial. There was a free exchange of abuse and pushes between passengers already in the train and those trying to get in. We ran up and down the platform[3], but were everywhere met with the same reply: 'No room here.' I went to the guard. He said, 'You must try to get in where you can or take the next train.'

'But I have urgent business,' I respectfully replied. He had no time to listen to me. I was disconcerted[4]. I told Maganlal to get in wherever possible, and I got into an inter-class compartment with my wife. The guard saw us getting in. At Asansol station he came to charge us excess fares. I said to him:

'It was your duty to find us room. We could not get any, and so we are sitting here. If you can accommodate us in a third class compartment, we shall be only too glad to go there.'

'You may not argue with me,' said the guard. 'I cannot accommodate you. You must pay the excess fare, or get out.'

I wanted to reach Poona somehow. I was not therefore prepared to fight the guard. So I paid the excess fare he demanded, i.e., up to Poona. But I resented the injustice.

In the morning we reached Mogalsarai. Maganlal had managed to get a seat in the third class, to which I now shifted. I acquainted the

1. *hardships: severe suffering or privation*
2. *securing: succeed in obtaining; seek to guarantee repayment of by having a right to take possession of an asset in the event of non-payment*
3. *platform: a raised structure along the side of a railway track where passengers get on and off trains*
4. *disconcerted: disturb the composure of*

ticket examiner with all the facts, and asked him to give me a certificate to the effect that I had shifted to a third class compartment at Mogalsarai. This he declined to do. I applied to the railway authorities for redress, and got a reply to this effect: 'It is not our practice to refund excess fares without the production of a certificate, but we make an exception in your case. It is not possible, however, to refund the excess fare from Burdwan to Mogalsarai.'

Since this I have had experiences of third class travelling which, if I wrote them all down, would easily fill a volume[1]. But I can only touch on them causally in these chapters. It has been and always will be my profound regret that physical incapacity should have compelled me to give up third class travelling.

The woes of third class passengers are undoubtedly due to the high-handedness of railway authorities. But the rudeness, dirty habits, selfishness and ignorance[2] of the passengers[3] themselves are no less to blame. The pity is that they often do not realize that they are behaving ill, dirtily or selfishly. They believe that everything they do is in the natural way. All this may be traced to the indifference towards them of us 'educated' people.

We reached Kalyan dead tried. Maganlal and I got some water from the station water-pipe and had our bath. As I was proceeding to arrange for my wife's bath, Sjt Kaul of the Servants of India Society recognizing us came up. He too was going to Poona. He offered to take my wife to the second class bath room. I hesitated to accept the courteous offer. I knew that my wife had no right to avail herself of the second class bathroom, But I ultimately connived at the impropriety. This, I know, does not become a votary of truth. Not that my wife was eager to use the bath room, but a husband's partiality for his wife got the better of his partiality for Truth. The face of truth is hidden behind the golden veil of *maya*, says the Upanishad.

1. *volume: a single book or a bound collection of printed sheets*
2. *ignorance: lack of knowledge or information*
3. *passengers: a traveler on a public or private conveyance other than the driver, pilot, or crew*

CHAPTER 130
WOOING

On arrival in Poona, we found ourselves, after the performance of the *shradha* ceremonies, discussing the future of the Society, and the question as to whether I should join it or not. This question of membership proved a very delicate matter for me to handle. Whilst Gokhale was there I did not have to seek admission as a member. I had simply to obey[1] his wish, a position I loved to be in. Launching on the stormy sea of Indian public life, I was in need of a sure pilot[2]. I had one in Gokhale and had felt secure in his keeping. Now that he was gone, I was thrown on my own resources, and I felt that it was my duty to seek admission. That, I thought, would please Gokhale's spirit. So, without hesitation and with firmness, I began the wooing.

Most of the members of the Society were in Poona at this juncture. I set about pleading with them and tried to dispel[3] their fears about me. But I saw that they were divided. One section favoured my admission, the other was strongly against it. I knew that neither yielded to the other in its affection for me, but possibly their loyalty to the Society was greater, at any rate not less than their love for me. All our discussions were therefore free from bitterness, and strictly confined to matters of principle. The section that was opposed to me held that they and I were as the poles asunder in various vital matters, and they felt my membership was likely to imperil[4] the very objects for which the Society was founded. This naturally was more than they could bear.

We dispersed after prolonged discussions, the final decision being postponed to a later date.

I was considerably agitated as I returned home. Was it right for me to be admitted by a majority vote? Would it be consonant with my loyalty to Gokhale? I saw clearly that, when there was such a sharp division amongst the members of the Society over admitting me, by far the best course for me was to withdraw my application for admission and save

1. *obey: submit to the authority of; carry out a command or instruction; behave in accordance with a general principle, natural law, etc.*
2. *pilot: a person who operates the flying controls of an aircraft*
3. *dispel: make doubt, feeling, or belief disappear*
4. *imperil: put into danger*

those opposed to me from a delicate situation. Therein I thought lay my loyalty to the Society and Gokhale. The decision came to me in a flash[1], and immediately I wrote to Mr. Shastri asking him not to have the adjourned meeting at all. Those who had opposed my application fully appreciated the decision. It saved them from an awkward position and bound us in closer bonds of friendship. The withdrawal of my application made me truly a member of the Society.

Experience now tells me that it was well that I did not formally become a member, and that the opposition of those who had been against me was justified. Experience has shown too that our views on matters of principle were widely divergent. But the recognition of the differences has meant no estrangement[2] or bitterness between us. We have remained as brothers, and the Society's Poona home has

It is true that I did not officially become a member of the Society, but I have ever been a member in spirit. Spiritual relationship is far more precious than Physical relationship divorced[3] from spiritual is body without soul.

1. *flash: burst forth into or as if into flame, give off light or be lighted in sudden or intermittent bursts, appear or occur suddenly*
2. *estrangement: cause to feel less close or friendly; alienate*
3. *divorced: detach or dissociate*

CHAPTER 131

KUMBHA MELA

I next went to Rangoon to meet Dr. Mehta, and on my way I halted at Calcutta. I was the guest[1] of the late Babu Bhupendranath Basu. Bengali hospitality reached its climax[2] here. In those days I was a strict fruitarian, so all the fruits and nuts available in Calcutta were ordered for me. The ladies of the house kept awake all night skinning various nuts. Every possible care was taken in dressing fresh fruit in the Indian style. Numerous delicacies were prepared for my companions, amongst whom was my son Ramdas. Much as I could appreciate this affectionate hospitality, I could not bear the thought of a whole household being occupied in entertaining two or three guests. But as yet I saw no escape from such embarrassing attentions.

On the boat going to Rangoon I was a deck passenger. If excess of attention embarrassed us in Sjt. Basu's house, grossest inattention, even to the elementary comforts of deck passengers, was our lot on the boat. What was an apology for a bath room was unbearably dirty, the latrines were stinking sinks. To use the latrine one had to wade[3] through urine and excreta[4] or jump over them.

This was more than flesh and blood could bear. I approached the Chief Officer without avail. If anything was lacking to complete the picture of stink and filth, the passengers furnished it by their thoughtless habits. They spat where they sat, dirtied the surroundings with the leavings of their food, tobacco and betel leaves. There was no end to the noise, and everyone tried to monopolize as much room as possible. Their luggage took up more room than they. We had thus two days of the severest trial.

On reaching Rangoon I wrote to the Agent of the Steamship Company, acquainting him with all the facts. Thanks to this letter and to Dr. Mehta's efforts in the matter, the return journey though on deck was less unbearable.

In Rangoon my fruitarian diet was again a source of additional trouble to the host. But since Dr. Mehta's home was as good as my own, I could

1. *guest: a person who is invited to visit someone's home or take part in a function; a visiting performer invited to take part in an entertainment*
2. *climax: the most intense, exciting, or important point of something*
3. *wade: walk through a liquid or viscous substance*
4. *excreta: waste discharged from the body, especially feces and urine*

control somewhat the lavishness of the menu. However, as I had not set any limit to the number of articles I might eat, the palate[1] and the eyes refused to put an effective check on the supply of varieties ordered. There were no regular hours for meals. Personally I preferred having the last meal before night fall. Nevertheless as a rule it could not be had before eight or nine.

This year 1915 was the year of the Kumbha fair, which is held at Hardvar once every 12 years. I was by no means eager to attend the fair, but I was anxious to meet Mahatma Munshiramji who was in his Gurukul. Gokhale's Society had sent a big volunteer corps for service at the Kumbha. Pandit Hridayanath Kunzru was at the head, and the late Dr. Dev was the medical officer. I was invited to send the Phoenix party to assist them, and so Maganlal Gandhi had already preceded me. On my return from Rangoon, I joined the band.

The journey from Calcutta to Hardvar was particularly trying. Sometimes the compartments had no lights. From Saharanpur we were huddled[2] into carriages for goods or cattle. These had no roofs, and what with the blazing midday sun overhead and the scorching iron floor beneath, we were all but roasted. The pangs of thirst, caused by even such a journey as this, could not persuade orthodox Hindus to take water, if it was 'Musalmani.' They waited until they could get the 'Hindu' water. These very Hindus, let it be noted, do not so much as hesitate or inquire[3] when during illness the doctor administers them wine or prescribes beef tea or a Musalman or Christian compounder gives them water.

Our stay in Shantiniketan had taught us that the scavenger's work would be our special function in India. Now for the volunteers in Hardvar tents had been pitched in a *dharamshala*, and Dr. Dev had dug some pits to be used as latrines. He had to depend on paid scavengers for looking after these. Here was work for the Phoenix party. We offered to cover up the excreta with earth and to see to their disposal, and Dr. Dev gladly accepted our offer. The offer was naturally made by me, but it was Maganlal Gandhi who had to execute it. My business was mostly to keep sitting in the tent giving *darshan* and holding religious and other discussions with numerous pilgrims who called on me. This left me not a minute which I could call my own. I was followed even to the bathing *ghat* by these *darshan-seekers*, nor did they leave me alone

1. *palate: a person's ability to distinguish between and appreciate different flavors*
2. *huddled: crowd together*
3. *inquire: another term for enquire*

whilst I was having my meals. Thus it was in Hardvar that I realized what a deep impression my humble services in South Africa had made throughout the whole of India.

But this was no enviable position to be in. I felt as though I was between the devil and the deep sea. Where no one recognized me, I had to put up with the hardships that fall to the lot of the millions[1] in this land, e.g., in railway travelling. Where I was surrounded by people who had heard of me I was the victim of their craze for *darshan*. Which of the two conditions was more pitiable, I have often been at a loss to determine. That at least I know that the *darshanvalas*' blind love has often made me angry, and more often sore[2] at heart. Whereas travelling, though often trying, has been uplifting and has hardly ever roused[3] me to anger.

I was in those days strong enough to roam about a lot, and was fortunately not so known as not to be able to go in the streets without creating much fuss[4]. During these roamings I came to observe more of the pilgrims' absent mindedness, hypocrisy and slovenliness[5], than of their piety. The swarm of sadhus, who had descended there, seemed to have been born to enjoy the good things of life.

Here I saw a cow with five feet! I was astonished, but knowing men soon disillusioned me. The poor five-footed cow was a sacrifice to the greed of the wicked. I learnt that the fifth foot was nothing else but a foot cut off from a live calf and grafted upon the shoulder of the cow! The result of this double cruelty was exploited to fleece the ignorant of their money. There was no Hindu but would be attracted by a five-footed cow, and no Hindu but would lavish his charity on such a miraculous cow.

The day of the fair was now upon us. It proved a red letter day for me. I had not gone to Hardvar with the sentiments of a pilgrim. I have never thought of frequenting places of pilgrimage in search of piety. But the seventeen lakhs of men that were reported to be there could not all be hypocrites or mere sight-seers. I had no doubt that countless people amongst them had gone there to earn merit and for self-purification. It is difficult, if not impossible, to say to what extent this kind of faith uplifts the soul.

I therefore passed the whole night immersed in deep thought. There were those pious souls in the midst of the hypocrisy that surrounded them. They would be free of guilt before their Maker. If the visit to

1. *millions: the number equivalent to the product of a thousand and a thousand; 1,000,000 or 10^6*
2. *sore: painful or aching; suffering pain*
3. *roused: stir*
4. *fuss: a display of unnecessary or excessive excitement, activity, or interest*
5. *slovenliness: untidy and dirty*

Hardvar was in itself a sin, I must publicly protest against it, and leave Hardvar on the day Kumbha. If the pilgrimage to Hardvar and to the Kumbha fair was not sinful, I must impose some act of self-denial on myself in atonement for the iniquity[1] prevailing there and purify myself. This was quite natural for me. My life is based on disciplinary[2] resolutions. I thought of the unnecessary trouble I had caused to my hosts at Calcutta and Rangoon, who had so lavishly entertained me. I therefore decided to limit the articles of my daily diet and to have my final meal before sunset. I was convinced that, if I did not impose these restrictions on myself, I should put my future hosts to considerable inconvenience and should engage them in serving me rather than engage myself in service. So I pledged myself never whilst in India to take more than five articles in twenty-four hours, and never to eat after dark. I gave the fullest thought to the difficulties I might have to face. But I wanted to leave no loophole. I rehearsed[3] to myself what would happen during an illness, if I counted medicine among the five articles, and made no exception in favour of special articles of diet. I finally decided that there should be no exception on any account whatsoever.

I have been under these vows for now thirteen years. They have subjected me to a severe test, but I am able to testify that they have also served as my shield. I am of opinion that they have added a few years to my life and saved me from many an illness.

1. *iniquity: injustice or immoral behavior*
2. *disciplinary: having to do with discipline*
3. *rehearsed: practice for later public performance*

CHAPTER 132

LAKSHMAN JHULA

It was a positive relief to reach the Gurukul and meet Mahatma Munshiramji with his giant frame. I at once felt the wonderful contrast between the peace of the Gurukul and the din and noise of Hardvar.

The Mahatma overwhelmed me with affection. The *Brahmacharis* were all attention. It was here that I was first introduced to Acharya Ramadevji, and I could immediately see what a force and a power[1] he must be. We had different viewpoints in several matters, nevertheless our acquaintance soon ripened into friendship.

I had long discussions with Acharya Ramadevji and other professors[2] about the necessity of introducing industrial training into the Gurukul. When the time came for going away it was a wrench to leave the place.

I had heard much in praise of the Lakshman Jhula (a hanging bridge over the Ganges) some distance from Hrishikesh, and many friends pressed me not to leave Hardvar without having gone as far as the bridge[3]. I wanted to do this pilgrimage[4] on foot and so I did it in two stages.

Many *sannyasis* called on me at Hrishikesh. One of them was particularly attracted towards me. The Phoenix party was there and their presence drew from the Swami many questions.

We had discussions about religion and he realized that I felt deeply about matters of religion. He saw me bareheaded and shirtless as I had returned from my bath in the Ganges. He was pained to miss the *shikha* (tuft of hair) on my head and the sacred thread about my neck and said:

'It pains me to see you, a believing Hindu, going without a sacred thread and the *shikha*. These are the two external symbols of Hinduism and every Hindu ought to wear them.'

Now there is a history as to how I came to dispense with both. When I was an urchin of ten, I envied the Brahman lads sporting bunches of keys tied to their sacred threads, and I wished I could do likewise. The practice of wearing the sacred thread was not then common among the

1. *power: the ability to do something or act in a particular way*
2. *professors: a university academic of the highest rank; the holder of a university chair*
3. *bridge: a structure that allows people or vehicles to cross on obstacle such as a river or and or railway etc.*
4. *pilgrimage: a pilgrim's journey*

vaishya families in Kathiawad. But a movement had just been started for making it obilgatory for the first three *varnas*. As a result several members of the Gandhi clan adopted the sacred thread. The Brahman who was teaching two or three of us boys *Ramraksha* invested us with the thread, and although I had no occasion to possess a bunch of keys, I got one and began to sport[1] it. Later, when the thread gave way, I do not remember whether I missed it very much. But I know that I did not go in for a fresh one.

As I grew up several well-meaning attempts were made both in India and South Africa to re-invest me with the sacred thread, but with little success. If the *shudras* may not wear it, I argued, what right have the other *varnas* to do so? And I saw no adequate[2] reason for adopting what was to me an unnecessary custom. I had no objection to the thread as such, but the reasons for wearing it were lacking.

As a *vaishnava* I had naturally worn round my neck the *kanthi*, and the *shikha* was considered obligatory[3] by elders. On the eve of my going to England, however, I got rid of the *shikha*, lest when I was bare-headed it should expose me to ridicule and make me look, as I then thought, a barbarian in the eyes of the Englishmen. In fact this cowardly feeling carried me so far that in South Africa I got my cousin Chhaganlal Gandhi, who was religiously wearing the *shikha*, to do away with it. I feared that it might come in the way of his public work and so, even at the risk of paining him, I made him get rid of it.

I therefore made a clean breast of the whole matter to the Swami and said:

'I will not wear the sacred thread, for I see no necessity for it, when countless Hindus can go without it and yet remain Hindus, Moreover, the sacred thread should be a symbol of spiritual regeneration, presupposing a deliberate attempt on the part of the wearer at a higher and purer life. I doubt whether in the present state of Hinduism and of India, Hindus can the right to wear a symbol charged with such a meaning. That the right can come only after Hinduism has purged itself of untouchability, has removed all distinctions of superiority and inferiority, and shed a host of other evils and shams that have become rampant in it. My mind therefore rebels against the idea of wearing the sacred thread. But I am sure your suggestion about the *shikha* is worth considering. I once used to have it,

1. *sport: wear or display*
2. *adequate: satisfactory or acceptable*
3. *obligatory: compulsory; having binding force*

and I discarded it from a false sense of shame. And so I feel that I should start growing it again. I shall discuss the matter with my comrades[1].'

The Swami did not appreciate my position with regard to the sacred thread. The very reasons that seemed to me to point to not wearing it appeared to him to favour its wearing. Even today my position remains about the same as it was at Hrishikesh. So long as there are different religions, every one of them may need some outward distinctive symbol. But when the symbol is made into a fetish and an instrument of proving the superiority of one's religion over others', it is fit only to be discarded. The sacred thread does not appear to me today to be a means of uplifting[2] Hinduism. I am therefore indifferent to it.

As for the *shikha*, cowardice having been the reason for discarding[3] it, after consultation with friends I decided to re-grow it.

But to return to Lakshman Jhula. I was charmed with the natural scenery about Hrishikesh and the Lakshman Jhula, and bowed my head in reverence[4] to our ancestors for their sense of the beautiful in Nature, and for their foresight in investing beautiful manifestations of nature with a religious significance.

But the way in which men were using these beauty spots was far from giving me peace. As at Hardvar, so at Hrishikesh, people dirtied the roads and the fair banks of the Ganges. They did not even hesitate to desecrate the sacred water of the Ganges. It filled me with agony to see people performing natural functions on the thoroughfares and river banks, when they could easily have gone a little farther away from public haunts.

Lakshman Jhula was, I saw, nothing but an iron suspension bridge over the Ganges. I was told that originally there had been a fine rope-bridge. But a philanthropic Marwadi got it into his head to destroy the rope-bridge and erect an iron one at a heavy cost and then entrusted the keys to the Government! I am at a loss to say anything about the rope-bridge as I have never seen it, but the iron bridge is entirely out of place in such surroundings and mars their beauty. The making over of the keys of this pilgrims' bridge to the Government was too much even for my loyalty of those days.

The *Svargashram* which one reaches after crossing the bridge was a wretched place, being nothing but a number of shabby-looking sheds

1. *comrades: a companion who shares one's activities or is a fellow member of an organization*
2. *uplifting: the rise of something*
3. *discarding: get rid of as no longer useful or desirable*
4. *reverence: deep respect*

of galvanized iron sheets. These, I was told, were made for *sadhakas* (aspirants[1]). There were hardly any living there at the moment. Those who were in the main building gave one an unfavourable[2] impression.

But the Hardvar experiences proved for me to be of inestimable[3] value. They helped me in no small way to decide where I was to live and what I was to do.

1. *aspirants: aspiring towards a particular achievement or status*
2. *unfavourable: adverse; inauspicious*
3. *inestimable: not able to be measured; very great*

CHAPTER 133

FOUNDING OF THE ASHRAM

The pilgrimage to the Kumbha fair was my second visit to Hardvar.

The Satyagraha Ashram was founded on the 25th of May, 1915. Shraddhanandji wanted me to settle in Hardvar. Some of my Calcutta friends recommended Vaidyanathadham. Others strongly urged me to choose Rajkot. But when I happened to pass through Ahmedabad, many friends pressed me to settle down there, and they volunteered to find the expenses of the Ashram, as well as a house for us to live in.

I had a predilection for Ahmedabad. Being a Gujarati I thought I should be able to render the greatest service to the country through the Gujarati language. And then, as Ahmedabad was an ancient centre of handloom weaving, it was likely to be the most favourable field for the revival of the cottage industry of hand-spinning. There was also the hope that, the city being the capital of Gujarat, monetary help from its wealthy citizens would be more available here than elsewhere.

The question of untouchability was naturally among the subjects discussed with the Ahmedabad friends. I made it clear to them that I should take the first opportunity of admitting an untouchable candidate to the Ashram if he was otherwise worthy.

'Where is the untouchable who will satisfy your condition?' said a *vaishnava* friend self-complacently[1]. I finally decided to found the Ashram at Ahmedabad.

So far as accommodation was concerned, Sjt. Jivanlal Desai, a barrister in Ahmedabad, was the principal man to help me. He offered to let, and we decided to hire, his Kochrab bungalow.

The first thing we had to settle was the name of the Ashram. I consulted friends. Amongst the names suggested were 'Sevashram' (the abode of service), 'Tapovan' (the abode[2] of austerities[3]), etc. I liked the name 'Sevashram' but for the absence of emphasis on the method of service. 'Tapovan' seemed to be a pretentious[4] title, because though *tapas*

1. *complacently: smug and uncritically satisfied with oneself or one's achievements*
2. *abode: a house or home*
3. *austerities: the trait of great self-denial*
4. *pretentious: attempting to impress by affecting greater importance or merit than is actually possessed*

was dear to us we would not presume to be *tapasvins* (men of austerity). Our creed was devotion to truth, and our business was the search for and insistence on truth. I wanted to acquaint India with the method I had tried in South Africa, and I desired to test in India the extent to which its application might be possible.

So my companions and I selected the name 'Satyagraha Ashram,' as conveying both our goal and our method of service.

For the conduct of the Ashram a code of rules and observances was necessary. A draft was therefore prepared, and friends were invited to express their opinions on it. Amongst the many opinions that were received, that of Sir Gurudas Banerji is still in my memory. He liked the rules, but suggested that humility should be added as one of the observances, as he believed that the younger generation sadly lacked humility. Though I noticed this fault, I feared humility would cease to be humility the moment it became a matter of vow. The true connotation of humility is self-effacement[1]. Self-effacement is *moksha* (salvation), and whilst it cannot, by itself, be an observance, there may be other observances[2] necessary for its attainment[3]. If the acts of an aspirant after *moksha* or a servant have no humility[4] or selflessness about them, there is no longing for *moksha* or service. Service without humility is selfishness and egotism.

There were at this time about thirteen Tamilians in our party. Five Tamil youngsters had accompanied me from South Africa, and the rest came from different parts of the country. We were in all about twenty-five men and women.

This is how the Ashram started. All had their meals in a common kitchen and strove to live as one family.

1. *effacement: make oneself appear insignificant or inconspicuous*
2. *observances: the practice of observing the requirements of law, morality or ritual*
3. *attainment: succeed in accomplishing*
4. *humility: a humble view of one's own importance*

CHAPTER 134

ON THE ANVIL

The Ashram had been in existence only a few months when we were put to a test such as I had scarcely expected. I received a letter from Amritlal Thakkar to this effect: 'A humble and honest untouchable family is desirous of joining your Ashram. Will you accept them?'

I was perturbed[1]. I had never expected that an untouchable family with an introduction from no less a man than Thakkar Bapa would so soon be seeking admission to the Ashram. I shared the letter with my companions. They welcomed it.

I wrote to Amritlal Thakkar expressing our willingness to accept the family, provided all the members were ready to abide[2] by the rules of the Ashram.

The family consisted of Dudabhai, his wife Danibehn and their daughter Lakshmi, then a mere toddling babe. Dudabhai had been a teacher in Bombay. They all agreed to abide by the rules and were accepted.

But their admission created a flutter[3] amongst the friends who had been helping the Ashram. The very first difficulty was found with regard to the use of the well, which was partly controlled by the owner of the bungalow. The man in charge of the water-lift objected that drops of water from our bucket would pollute him. So he took to swearing at us and molesting Dudabhai. I told everyone to put up with the abuse and continue drawing water at any cost. When he saw that we did not return his abuse[4], the man became ashamed and ceased to bother us.

All monetary help, however was stopped. The friend who had asked that question about an untouchable being able to follow the rules of the Ashram had never expected that any such would be forthcoming.

With the stopping of monetary help came rumours of proposed social boycott. We were prepared for all this. I had told my companions that, if we were boycotted and denied the usual facilities, we would not leave Ahmedabad. We would rather go and stay in the untouchables' quarters and live on whatever we could get by manual labour.

1. *perturbed: anxious or unsettled*
2. *abide: accept act in accordance with (a rule or decision)*
3. *flutter: an act of fluttering, a state or sensation of tremulous excitement*
4. *abuse: address in an insulting and offensive way*

Matters came to such a pass that Maganlal Gandhi one day gave me this notice: 'We are out of funds[1] and there is nothing for the next month.'

I quietly replied: 'Then we shall go to the untouchables' quarter.'

This was not the first time I had been faced with such a trial. On all such occasions God has sent help at the last moment,. One morning, shortly after Maganlal had given me warning of our monetary[2] plight[3], one of the children came and said that a Sheth who was waiting in a car outside wanted to see me. I went out to him. 'I want to give the Ashram some help.' Will you accept it?' 'Most certainly,' said I. 'And I confess I am at the present moment at the end of my resources.'

'I shall come tomorrow at this time,' he said. 'Will you be here?'

'Yes,' said I, and he left.

Next day, exactly at the appointed hour, the car drew up near our quarters, and the horn was blown. The children came with the news. The Sheth did not come in. I went out to see him. He placed in my hands currency notes of the value of Rs. 13,000, and drove away.

I had never expected this help, and what a novel way of rendering it! The gentleman had never before visited the Ashram. So far as I can remember, I had met him only once. No visit, no enquiries, simply rendering help and going away! This was a unique experience for me. The help deferred the exodus to the untouchables' quarter. We now felt quite safe for a year.

Just as there was a storm outside so there was a storm in the Ashram itself. Though in South Africa untouchable friends used to come to my place and live and feed with me, my wife and other women did not seem quite to relish the admission into the Ashram of the untouchable friends. My eyes and ears easily detected their indifference, if not their dislike, towards Danibehn. The monetary difficulty had caused me no anxiety, but this internal storm[4] was more than I could bear. Danibehn was an ordinary woman. Dudabhai was a man with slight education but of good understanding. I liked his patience. Sometimes he did flare up, but on the whole I was well impressed with his forbearance. I pleaded with him to swallow minor insults. He not only agreed, but prevailed upon his wife to do likewise.

The admission of this family proved a valuable lesson to the Ashram. In the very beginning we proclaimed to the world that the Ashram

1. *funds: financial resources*
2. *plight: a dangerous, difficult, or otherwise unfortunate situation*
3. *monetary: of or relating to money or currency*
4. *storm: a violent disturbance of the atmosphere with strong winds and usually rain, thunder, lighting, or snow*

would not countenance untouchability. Those who wanted to help the Ashram were thus put on their guard, and the work of the Ashram in this direction was considerably simplified. The fact that it is mostly the real orthodox Hindus who have met the daily growing expenses of the Ashram is perhaps a clear indication that untouchability is shaken[1] to its foundation. There are indeed many other proofs of this, but the fact that good Hindus do not scruple to help an Ashram where we go the length of dining with the untouchables is no small proof.

I am sorry that I should have to skip over quite a number of things pertaining[2] to this subject, how we tackled delicate questions arising out of the main question, how we had to overcome some unexpected difficulties, and various other matters which are quite relevant to a description of experiments with Truth. The chapters that follow will also suffer from the same drawback. I shall have to omit important details, because most of the characters in the drama are still alive, and it is not proper without permission to use their names in connection with events with which they are concerned. It is hardly practicable[3] to obtain their consent or to get them every now and then to revise the chapters concerning themselves. Besides such procedure is outside the limit of this autobiography. I therefore fear that the rest of the story, valuable as it in my opinion to seekers after Truth, will be told with inevitable omissions. Nevertheless, it is my desire and hope, God willing, to bring this narrative down to the days of Non-co-opeartion.

1. *shaken: shock or astonish; cause a change of mood by shocking or disturbing; weaken or impair*
2. *pertaining: be appropriate, related, or applicable*
3. *practicable: able to be done or put into practice successfully*

CHAPTER 135

ABOLITION OF INDENTURED EMIGRATION

We shall, for a moment, take leave of the Ashram, which in the very beginning had to weather internal and external storms, and briefly advert to a matter that engaged my attention.

Indentured labourers were those who had emigrated from India to labour under an indenture for five years or less. Under the Smuts-Gandhi settlement of 1914, the £3 tax in respect of the indentured emigrants to Natal had been abolished, but the general emigration from India still needed treatment.

In March 1916 Pandit Madan Mohan Malaviyaji moved a resolution in the Imperial Legislative Council for the abolition of the indenture system. In accepting the motion Lord Hardinge announced that he had 'obtained from His Majesty's Government the promise of the abolition[1] in due course' of the system. I felt however, that India could not be satisfied with so very vague an assurance, but ought to agitate for immediate abolition. India had tolerated the system through sheer negligence, and I believed the time had come when people could successfully agitate for this redress[2]. I met some of the leaders, wrote in the press, and saw that public opinion was solidly in favour of immediate abolition. Might this be a fit subject for Satyagraha? I had no doubt that it was, but I did not know the *modus operandi*.

In the meantime the Viceroy had made no secret of the meaning of 'the eventual abolition', which, as he said, was abolition 'within such reasonable time as will allow of alternative arrangements introduced,' So in February 1917, Pandit Malaviyaji asked for leave to introduce a bill for the immediate abolition of the system. Lord Chelmsford refused[3] permission[4]. It was time for me to tour the country for an all-India agitation.

Before I started the agitation I thought it proper to wait upon the Viceroy. So I applied for an interview. He immediately granted it. Mr. Maffey, now Sir John Maffey, was his private secretary. I came in close

1. *abolition: the act of abolishing a system practice or invitation*
2. *redress: remedy or set right*
3. *permission: authorization*
4. *refused: indicate unwillingness; indicate unwillingness to accept or grant something offered or requested; decline to jump a fence or other obstacle*

contact with him. I had a satisfactory talk with Lord Chelmsford who, without being definite, promised to be a helpful.

I began my tour from Bombay. Mr. Jehangir Petit undertook to convene the meeting under the auspices of the Imperial Citizenship Association. The Executive Committee of the Association met first for framing the resolutions to be moved at the meeting. Dr. Stanley Reed, Sjt. (now Sir) Lallubhai Samaldas, Sjt. Natarajan and Mr. Petit were present at the Committee meeting. The discussion centred round the fixing of the period within which the Government was to be asked to abolish the system. There were three proposals, viz, for abolition 'as soon as possible,' abolition 'by the 31st July,' and 'immediate[1] abolition.' I was for a definite date, as we could then decide what to do if the Government failed to accede to our request within the time limit. Sjt. Lallubhai was for 'immediate' abolition. He said 'immediate' indicated a shorter period than the 31st July. I explained that the people would not understand the word 'immediate'. If we wanted to get them to do something, they must have a more definite word. Everyone would interpret 'immediate' in his own way, Government one way, the people another way. There was no question of misunderstanding 'the 31st of July,' and if nothing was done by that date, we could proceed further. Dr. Reed saw the force of the argument, and ultimately Sjt. Lallubhai also agreed. We adopted the 31st July as the latest date by which the abolition should be announced, a resolution to that effect was passed at the public meeting, and meetings throughout India resolved[2] accordingly[3].

Mrs. Jaiji Petit put all her energies into the organization of a ladies' deputation to the Viceroy. Amongst the ladies from Bombay who formed the deputation, I remember the names of Lady Tata and the late Dilshad Begam. The deputation had a great effect. The Viceroy gave an encouraging reply.

I visited Karachi, Calcutta and various other places. There were fine meetings everywhere, and there was unbounded[4] enthusiasm. I had not expected anything like it when the agitation was launched.

In those days I used to travel alone, and had therefore wonderful experiences. The C.I.D. men were always after me. But as I had nothing to conceal, they did not molest me, nor did I cause them any trouble. Fortunately I had not then received the stamp of Mahatmaship, though the shout of that name was quite common where people knew me.

1. *immediate: at once*
2. *accordingly: as stated by or in; in a manner corresponding or in proportion to*
3. *resolved: settle or find a solution to; medicine cause to heal or disappear*
4. *unbounded: having no limits*

On one occasion the detectives disturbed me at several stations, asked for my ticket[1] and took down the number. I, of course, readily replied to all questions they asked. My fellow passengers had taken me to be a 'sadhu' or a 'fakir'. When they saw that I was being molested at every station, they were exasperated and swore at the detectives. 'Why are you worrying the poor sadhu for nothing?' they protested. 'Don't you show these scoundrels[2] your ticket,' they said, addressing me.

I said to them gently: 'It is no trouble to show them my ticket. They are doing their duty.' The passengers were not satisfied, they evinced[3] more and more sympathy, and strongly objected to this sort of ill-treatment of innocent men.

But the detectives were nothing. The real hardship was the third class travelling. My bitterest experience was from Lahore to Delhi. I was going to Calcutta from Karachi *via* Lahore where I had to change trains. It was impossible to find a place in the train. It was full, and those who could get in did so by sheer force, often sneaking[4] through windows if the doors were locked. I had to reach Calcutta on the date fixed for the meeting, and if I missed this train I could not arrive in time. I had almost given up hope of getting in. No one was willing to accept me, when a porter discovering my plight came to me and said, 'Give me twelve annas and I'll get you a seat.' 'Yes,' said I, 'you shall have twelve annas if you do procure me a seat.' The young man went from carriage to carriage entreating passengers but no one heeded him. As the train was about to start, some passengers said, 'There is no room here, but you can shove him in if you like. He will have to stand.' 'Well?' asked the young porter. I readily agreed, and he shoved me in bodily through the window. Thus I got in and the porter earned his twelve annas.

The night was a trial. The other passengers were sitting somehow. I stood two hours, holding the chain of the upper bunk. Meanwhile some of the passengers kept worrying me incessantly. 'Why will you not sit down?' they asked. I tried to reason with them saying there was no room, but they could not tolerate my standing, though they were lying full length on the upper bunks. They did not tire of worrying me neither did I tire of gently replying to them. This at last mollified them.

Some of them asked me my name, and made room for me. Patience was thus rewarded. I was dead tired, and my head was reeling. God sent help just when it was most needed.

1. *ticket: a piece of paper or card giving the holder a right to admission to a place or event or to travel on public transport*
2. *scoundrels: a dishonest or unscrupulous person; a rogue*
3. *evinced: formal reveal the presence of; indicate a quality or feeling*
4. *sneaking: move, go, or convey in a furtive or stealthy manner; stealthily acquire or obtain: she sneaked a glance at her watch*

In that way I somehow reached Delhi and thence Calcutta. The Maharaja of Cassimbazar, the president of the Calcutta meeting, was my host. Just as in Karachi, here also there was unbounded enthusiasm. The meeting was attended by several Englishmen.

Before the 31st July the Government announced that indentured emigration[1] from India was stopped.

It was in 1894 that I drafted the first petition protesting against the system, and I had then hoped that this 'semi-slavery,' as Sir W. W. Hunter used to call the system, would some day be brought to an end.

There were many who aided in the agitation which was started in 1894, but I cannot help saying that potential Satyagraha hastened[2] the end.

For further details of that agitation[3] and of those who took part in it, I refer the reader to my *Satyagraha in South Africa*.

1. *emigration: the act of relocating to another country*
2. *hastened: be quick to do something move quickly, cause to happen sooner than anticipated*
3. *agitation: a state of turbulent change or development*

CHAPTER 136

THE STAIN OF INDIGO

Champaran is the land of King Janaka. Just as it abounds in mango groves[1], so used it to be full of indigo plantations until the year 1917. The Champaran tenant was bound by law to plant three out of every twenty parts of his land with indigo for his landlord. This system was known as the *tinkathis* system, as three *kathas* out of twenty (which make one acre) had to be planted with indigo.

I must confess that I did not then know even the name, much less the geographical position, of Champaran, and I had hardly any notion of indigo plantations[2]. I had seen packets of indigo, but little dreamed that it was grown and manufactured in Champaran at great hardship to thousands of agriculturists.

Rajkumar Shukla was one of the agriculturists who had been under this harrow, and he was filled with a passion to wash away the stain[3] of indigo for the thousands who were suffering as he had suffered.

This man caught hold of me at Lucknow, where I had gone for the Congress of 1916. 'Vakil Babu will tell you everything about our distress,' he said, and urged me to go to Champaran. 'Vakil Babu' was none other than Babu Brajkishore Prasad, who became my esteemed co-worker in Champaran, and who is the soul of public work in Bihar. Rajkumar Shukla brought him to my tent. He was dressed in a black alpaca[4] *achkan* and trousers. Brijkishore Babu failed then to make an impression on me. I took it that he must be some vakil exploiting the simple agriculturists. Having heard from him something of Champaran, I replied as was my wont: 'I can give no opinion without seeing the condition with my own eyes. You will please move the resolution in the Congress, but leave me free for the present.' Rajkumar Shukla of course wanted some help from the Congress. Babu Brajkishore Prasad moved the resolution, expressing sympathy for the people of Champaran, and it was unanimously passed.

1. *groves: a small wood, orchard, or group of trees*
2. *plantations: a large estate on which crops such as coffee, sugar, and tobacco are grown*
3. *stain: damage*
4. *alpaca: a long-haired domesticated south american mammal related to the llama; the wool of the alpaca, or fabric made from it*

Rajkumar Shukla was glad, but far from satisfied. He wanted me personally to visit Champaran and witness the miseries of the ryots there. I told him that I would include Champaran in the tour which I had contemplated[1] and give it a day or two. 'One day will be enough,' said he, 'and you will see things with your own eyes.'

From Lucknow I went to Cawnpore Rajkumar Shukla followed me there. 'Champaran is very near here. Please give a day,' he insisted.' Pray excuse me this time. But I promise that I will come,' said I, further committing myself.

I returned to the Ashram. The ubiquitous Rajkumar was there too. 'Pray fix the day now,' he said. 'Well,' said I, 'I have to be in Calcutta on such and such a date, come and meet me then, and take me from there.' I did not know where I was to go, what to do, what things to see.

Before I reached Bhupen Babu's place in Calcutta, Rajkumar Shukla had gone and established himself there. Thus this ignorant, unsophisticated but resolute agriculturist captured me.

So early in 1917, we left Calcutta for Champaran, looking just like fellow rustics[2]. I did not even know the train. He took me to it, and we travelled together, reaching Patna in the morning.

This was my first visit to Patna. I had no friend or acquaintance with whom I could think of putting up. I had an idea that Rajkumar Shukla, simple agriculturist as he was, must have some influence in Patna. I had come to know him a little more on the journey, and on reaching Patna I had no illusions left concerning him. He was perfectly innocent of every thing. The vakils that he had taken to be his friends were really nothing of the sort. Poor Rajkumar was more or less as a menial to them. Between such agriculturist clients and their vakils there is a gulf[3] as wide as the Ganges in flood.

Rajkumar Shukla took me to Rajendra Babu's place in Patna. Rajendra Babu had gone to Puri or some other place, I now forget which. There were one or two servants at the bungalow who paid us no attention. I had with me something to eat. I wanted dates which my companion procured for me from the bazaar.

There was strict untouchability in Bihar. I might not draw water at the well whilst the servants were using it, lest drops of water from my bucket might pollute them, the servants not knowing to what caste I belonged.

1. *contemplated: look at thoughtfully; think about; think profoundly and at length; have as a probable intention*
2. *rustics: of or characteristic of life in the country; having a simplicity and charm that is considered typical of the countryside*
3. *gulf: a deep ravine, chasm, or abyss*

Rajkumar directed me to the indoor latrine, the servant promptly directed me to the outdoor[1] one. All this was far from surprising or irritating to me, for I was inured to such things. The servants were doing the duty, which they thought Rajendra Babu would wish them to do.

These entertaining experiences enhanced my regard for Rajkumar Shukla, if they also enabled me to know him better. I saw now that Rajkumar Shukla could not guide me, and that I must take the reins[2] in my own hands.

1. *outdoor: done, situated, or used outdoors; liking the outdoors*
2. *reins: a long, narrow strap attached at one end to a horse's bit, typically used in paris to guide or check a horse in riding or driving; a similar device used to restrain a young child*

CHAPTER 137

THE GENTLE BIHARI

I knew Maulana Mazharul Haq in London when he was studying for the bar, and when I met him at the Bombay Congress in 1915 the year in which he was President of the Muslim League he had renewed the acquaintance, and extended me an invitation to stay with him whenever I happened to go to Patna. I bethought myself of this invitation and sent him a note indicating the purpose of my visit. He immediately came in his car, and pressed me to accept his hospitality. I thanked him and requested him to guide me to my destination by the first available train, the railway guide being useless to an utter stranger like me. He had a talk with Rajkumar Shukla and suggested that I should first go to Muzaffarpur. There was a train for that place the same evening and he sent me off by it.

Principal Kripalani was then in Muzaffarpur. I had known of him ever since my visit to Hyderabad. Dr. Choithram had told me of his great sacrifice, of his simple life, and of the Ashram that Dr. Choithram was running out of funds provided by Professor Kripalani. He used to be a professor in the Government College, Muzaffarpur, and had just resigned the post when I went there. I had sent a telegram informing him of my arrival, and he met me at the station with a crowd of students, though the train reached there at midnight. He had no rooms of his own, and was staying with Professor Malkani who therefore virtually became my host[1]. It was an extraordinary[2] thing in those days for a Government professor to harbour a man like me.

Professor Kripalani spoke to me about the desperate condition of Bihar, particularly of the Tirhut division and gave me an idea of the difficulty of my task. He had established very close contact[3] with the Biharis, and had already spoken to them about the mission that took me to Bihar.

In the morning a small group of vakils called on me. I still remember Ramnavmi Prasad among them, as his earnestness specially appealed to me.

1. *host: a person who receives or entertains other people as guests*
2. *extraordinary: very unusual or remarkable*
3. *contact: get in touch or communication with*

'It is not possible,' he said, 'for you to do the kind of work you have come for, if you stay here (meaning Professor Malkani's quarters). You must come and stay with one of us. Gaya Babu is a well-known vakil here. I have come on his behalf in invite you to stay with him. I confess we are all afraid of Government, but we shall render what help we can. Most of the things Rajkumar Shukla has told you are true. It is a pity our leaders are not here today. I have, however, wired to them both, Bapu Brajkishore Prasad and Babu Rajendra Prasad. I expect them to arrive shortly, and they are sure to be able to give you all the information you want and to help you considerably. Pray come over to Gaya Babu's place.'

This was a request that I could not resist, though I hesitated for fear of embarrassing Gaya Babu. But he put me at ease, and so I went over to stay with him. He and his people showered all their affection on me.

Brajkishore Babu now arrived from Darbhanga and Rajendra Babu from Puri. Brajkishore Babu was not the Babu Brajkishore Prasad I had met in Lucknow. He impressed me this time with his humility, simplicity, goodness and extraordinary faith, so characteristic of the Biharis, and my heart was joyous over it. The Bihar vakils' regard for him was an agreeable surprise to me.

Soon I felt myself becoming bound to this circle of friends in life-long friendship. Brajkishore Babu acquainted me with the facts of the case. He used to be in the habit of taking up the cases of the poor tenants. There were two such cases pending when I went there. When he won any such case, he consoled himself that he was doing something good for these poor people. Not that he did not charge fees from these simple peasants. Lawyers labour under the belief that, if they do not charge fees, they will have no wherewithal[1] to run their households, and will not be able to render effective help to the poor people. The figures of the fees they charged and the standard of a barrister's fees in Bengal and Bihar staggered[2] me.

'We gave Rs. 10,000 to so and so for his opinion,' I was told. Nothing less than four figures in any case.

The friends listened to my kindly reproach[3] and did not misunderstand me.

'Having studied these cases,' said I, 'I have come to the conclusion that we should stop going to law courts. Taking such cases to the courts

1. *wherewithal: the money or other resources needed for a particular purpose*
2. *staggered: hesitate*
3. *reproach: express to someone one's disapproval of or disappointment in their actions*

does little good. Where the ryots are so crushed and fear-stricken[1], law courts are useless[2]. The real relief for them is to be free from fear. We cannot sit still until we have driven *tinkathia* out of Bihar. I had thought that I should be able to leave here in two days, but I now realize that the work might take even two years. I am prepared to give that time, if necessary. I am now feeling my ground, but I want your help.'

I found Brajkishore Babu exceptionally coolheaded. 'We shall render all the help we can,' he said quietly, 'but pray tell us what kind of help you will need.'

And thus we sat talking until midnight.

'I shall have little use for your legal knowledge,' I said to them. 'I want clerical assistance and help in interpretation. It may be necessary to face imprisonment, but, much as I would love you to run that risk, you would go only so far as you feel yourselves capable of going. Even turning yourselves into clerks and giving up your profession for an indefinite period is no small thing. I find it difficult to understand the local dialect[3] of Hindi, and I shall not be able to read papers written in Kaithi or Urdu. I shall want you to translate them for me. We cannot afford to pay for this work. It should all be done for love and out of a spirit of service.'

Brajkishore Babu understood this immediately, and he now cross-examined me and his companions by turns. He tried to ascertain the implications of all that I had said how long their service would be required, how many of them would be needed, whether they might serve by turns and so on. Then he asked the vakils the capacity of their sacrifice.

Ultimately they gave me this assurance. 'Such and such a number of us will do whatever you may ask. Some of us will be with you for so much time as you may require. The idea of accommodating oneself to imprisonment is a novel[4] thing for us. We will try to assimilate it.'

1. *stricken: seriously affected by an undesirable condition or unpleasant feeling; showing great distress*
2. *useless: serving no purpose*
3. *dialect: a form of a language which is peculiar to a specific region or social group*
4. *novel: the quality of being novel; a new or unfamiliar thing or experience; denoting something intended to be amusing as a result of its originality or unusualness*

CHAPTER 138

FACE TO FACE WITH AHIMSA

My object was to inquire into the condition of the Champaran agriculturists and understand their grievances against the indigo planters. For this purpose it was necessary that I should meet thousands of the ryots. But I deemed it essential, before starting on my inquiry, to know the planters' side of the case and see the Commissioner of the Division. I sought and was granted appointments with both.

The Secretary of the Planters' Association told me plainly that I was an outsider and that I had no business to come between the planters and their tenants, but if I had any representation to make, I might submit it in writing. I politely told him that I did not regard myself as an outsider, and that I had every right to inquire into the condition of the tenants if they desired me to do so. The Commissioner, on whom I called, proceeded to bully me, and advised me forthwith to leave Tirhut.

I acquainted my co-workers with all this, and told them that there was a likelihood[1] of Government stopping me from proceeding further, and that I might have to go to jail earlier than I had expected, and that, if I was to be arrested, it would be best that the arrest[2] should take place in Motihari or if possible in Bettiah. It was advisable, therefore, that I should go to those place as early as possible.

Champaran is a district of the Tirhut division and Motihari is its headquarters. Rajkumar Shukla's place was in the vicinity of Bettiah, and the tenants[3] belonging to the *kothis* in its neighbourhood were the poorest in the district. Rajkumar Shukla wanted me to see them and I was equally anxious to do so.

So I started with my co-workers for Motihari the same day. Babu Gorakh Prasad harboured us in his home, which became a caravanserai. It could hardly contain us all. The very same day we heard that about five miles[4] from Motihari a tenant had been ill-treated. It was decided that, in company with Babu Dharanidhar Prasad, I should go and

1. *likelihood: the state or fact of being likely*
2. *arrest: seize by legal authority and take them into custody*
3. *tenants: a person occupying rented land or property; a person holding real property by private ownership*
4. *miles: a unit of measure equal to 1,760 yards*

see him the next morning, and we accordingly set off for the place on elephant's back. An elephant, by the way, is about as common in Champaran as a bullock-cart in Gujarat. We had scarcely gone half when a messenger from the Police Superintendent overtook us and said that the latter had sent his compliments. I saw what he meant. Having left Dharanidharbabu to proceed to the original destination, I got into the hired carriage which the messenger had brought. He then served on me a notice to leave Champaran, and drove me to my place. On his asking me to acknowledge the service of the notice, I wrote to the effect that I did not propose to comply with it and leave Champaran till my inquiry was finished. Thereupon I received a summons to take my trial the next day for disobeying the order to leave Champaran.

I kept awake that whole night writing letters and giving necessary instructions to Babu Brajkishore Prasad.

The news of the notice and the summons spread like wildfire, and I was told that Motihari that day witnessed unprecedented[1] scenes. Gorakhbabu's house and the court house overflowed with men. Fortunately I had finished all my work during the night and so was able to cope with the crowds. My companions proved the greatest help. They occupied themselves with regulating the crowds, for the latter followed me wherever I went.

A sort of friendliness sprang up between the officials Collector, Magistrate, Police Superintendent and myself. I might have legally resisted the notices served on me. Instead I accepted them all, and my conduct towards the officials was correct. They thus saw that I did not want to offend them personally, but that I wanted to offer civil resistance to their orders. In this way they were put at ease, and instead of harassing me they gladly availed themselves of my and my co-workers' co-operation in regulating[2] the crowds. But it was an ocular demonstration to them of the fact that their authority was shaken. The people had for the moment lost all fear of punishment and yielded obedience to the power of love which their new friend exercised.

It should be remembered that no one knew me in Champaran. The peasants were all ignorant. Champaran, being far up north of the Ganges, and right at the foot of the Himalayas in close proximity[3] to Nepal, was cut off from the rest of India. The Congress was practically unknown in those parts. Even those who had heard the name of the Congress shrank[4]

1. *unprecedented: never done or known before*
2. *regulating: control or maintain the rate or speed of a machine or process*
3. *proximity: nearness in space, time, or relationship*
4. *shrank: move back or away in fear or disgust; be averse to or unwilling to do something*

from joining it or even mentioning it. And now the Congress and its members had entered this land, though not in the name of the Congress, yet in a far more real sense.

In consultation with my co-workers I had decided that nothing should be done in the name of the Congress. What we wanted was work and not name, substance and not shadow[1]. For the name of the Congress was the *bete noire* of the Government and their controllers the planters. To them the Congress was a byword for lawyers' wrangles, evasion of law through legal loopholes[2], a byword for bomb and anarchical crime and for diplomacy and hypocrisy. We had to disillusion them both. Therefore we had decided not to mention the name of the Congress and not to acquaint the peasants with the organization called the Congress. It was enough, we thought, if they understood and followed the spirit of the Congress instead of its letter.

No emissaries had therefore been sent there, openly or secretly, on behalf of the Congress to prepare the ground for our arrival. Rajkumar Shukla was incapable of reaching the thousands of peasants. No political work had yet been done amongst them. The world outside Champaran was not known to them. And yet they received me as though we had been age-long friends. It is no exaggeration, but the literal truth, to say that in this meeting with the peasants I was face to face with God, Ahimsa and Truth.

When I come to examine my title to this realization, I find nothing but my love for the people. And this in turn is nothing but an expression of my unshakable faith in Ahimsa.

That day in Champaran was an unforgettable event in my life and a red-letter day for the peasants and for me.

According to the law, I was to be on my trial, but truly speaking Government was to be on its trial. The Commissioner only succeeded in trapping Government in the net which he had spread[3] for me.

1. *shadow: the dark area or shape produced by a body coming between light rays and a surface; partial or complete darkness; a dark patch or area*
2. *loopholes: an ambiguity or inadequacy in the [law] or a set of rules*
3. *spread: open out so as to increase in surface area, width, or length; stretch out so that they are far apart*

CHAPTER 139

CASE WITHDRAWN

The trial began, The Government pleader, the Magistrate and other officials were at a loss to know what to do. The Government pleader was pressing the Magistrate to postpone the case. But I interfered and requested the Magistrate not to postpone the case, as I wanted to plead guilty to having disobeyed the order to leave Champaran and read a brief[1] statement as follows:

'With the permission of the Court I would like to make a brief statement showing why I have taken the very serious step of seemingly disobeying the order passed under section 144 of Cr. P.C. In my humble opinion it is a question of difference of opinion between the Local Administration and myself. I have entered the country with motives of rendering humanitarian and national service. I have done so in response to a pressing invitation to come and help the ryots, who urge they are not being fairly treated by the indigo planters. I could not render any help without studying the problem. I have, therefore, come to study it with the assistance, if possible, of the Administration and the planters. I have no other motive, and cannot believe that my coming can in any way disturb public peace and cause loss of life. I claim to have considerable experience in such matters. The Administration, however, have thought differently. I fully appreciate their difficulty, and I admit too that they can only proceed upon information they received. As a law-abiding citizen my first instinct would be, as it were, to obey the order served upon me. But I could not do so without doing violence to my sense of duty to those for whom I have come. I feel that I could just now serve them only by remaining in their midst. I could not, therefore, voluntarily retire[2]. Amid this conflict of duties I could only throw the responsibility of removing me from them on the Administration. I am fully conscious of the fact that a person, holding, in the public life of India, a position such as I do, has to be most careful in setting an example. It is my firm belief that in the complex[3] constitution[4] under which we are living, the only safe and

1. *brief: give essential information to someone*
2. *retire: leave one's job and cease to work, especially because one has reached a particular age; of a sports player cease to play competitively*
3. *complex: consisting of many different and connected parts*
4. *constitution: a body of fundamental principle or established precedents according to which a state or organization is governed; [historical] a decree, ordinance, or law*

honourable course for a self-respecting man is, in the circumstances such as face me, to do what I have decided to do, that is, to submit without protest to the penalty of disobedience.

'I venture to make this statement not in any way in extenuation[1] of the penalty to be awarded against me, but to show that I have disregarded the order served upon me not for want of respect for lawful authority, but in obedience to the higher law of our being, the voice[2] of conscience.'

There was now no occasion to postpone the hearing, but as both the Magistrate and the Government pleader had been taken by surprise, the Migistrate postponed judgment. Meanwhile I had wired full details to the Viceroy, to Patna friends, as also to Pandit Madan Mohan Malaviya and others.

Before I could appear before the Court to receive the sentence, the Magistrate sent a written message that the Lieutenant Governor had ordered the case against me to be withdrawn, and the Collector wrote to me saying that I was at liberty to conduct the proposed inquiry, and that I might count on whatever help I needed from the officials. None of us was prepared for this prompt and happy issue.

I called on the Collector Mr. Heycock. He seemed to be a good man, anxious to do justice. He told me that I might ask for whatever papers I desired to see, and that I was at liberty to see him whenever I liked.

The country thus had its first direct object-lesson in Civil Disobedience. The affair was freely discussed both locally and in the press, and my inquiry got unexpected publicity.

It was necessary for my inquiry that the Government should remain neutral. But the inquiry did not need support from press reporters or leading articles in the press. Indeed the situation in Champaran was so delicate and difficult that over-energetic criticism or highly coloured reports might easily damage the cause which I was seeking to espouse. So I wrote to the editors of the principal papers requesting them not to trouble to send any reporters, as I should send them whatever might be necessary for publication and keep them informed.

I knew that the Government attitude countenancing[3] my presence had displeased[4] the Champaran planters, and I know that even the officials, though they could say nothing openly, could hardly have liked it. Incorrect or misleading reports, therefore, were likely to incense them all the more,

1. *extenuation: lessen the seriousness of guilt or an offence by reference to mitigating factor*
2. *voice: an opinion or attitude, or a means or agency by which it is expressed*
3. *countenancing: support or approval; admit as acceptable or possible*
4. *displeased: annoy or upset*

and their ire, instead of descending on me, would be sure to descend on the poor fear-stricken ryots and seriously hinder my search for the truth about the case.

In spite of these precautions the planters engineered against me a poisonous agitation. All sorts of falsehoods appeared in the press about my co-workers and myself. But my extreme cautiousness and my insistence on truth, even to the minutest detail, turned the edge of their sword.

The planters left no stone unturned in maligning Brajkishore Babu, but the more they maligned[1] him, the more he rose in the estimation of the people.

In such a delicate situation as this I did not think it proper to invite any leaders from other provinces. Pandit Malaviyaji had sent me an assurance that, whenever I wanted him, I had only to send him word, but I did not trouble him. I thus prevented the struggle from assuming a political aspect. But I sent to the leaders and the principal papers occasional reports, not for publication, but merely for their information. I had seen that, even where the end might be political, but where the cause was non-political, one damaged it by giving it a political aspect and helped it by keeping it within its non-political limit. The Champaran struggle was a proof of the fact that disinterested service of the people in any sphere ultimately helps the country politically.

1. *maligned: speak ill of*

CHAPTER 140

METHODS OF WORK

To give a full account[1] of the Champaran inquiry would be to narrate the histroy, for the period, of the Champaran ryot, which is out of the question in these chapters. The Champaran inquiry was a bold experiment with Truth and Ahimsa, and I am giving week by week only what occurs to me as worth giving from that point of view. For more details the reader must turn to Sjt. Rajendra Prasad's history of the Champaran Satyagraha in Hindi, of which, I am told, an English edition is now in the press.

But to return to the subject matter of this chapter. The inquiry could not be conducted in Gorakhbabu's house, without practically asking poor Gorakhbabu to vacate it. And the people of Motihari had not yet shed their fear to the extent of renting[2] a house to us. However, Brajkishore Babu tactfully[3] secured one with considerable open space about it, and we now removed there.

It was not quite possible to carry on the work without money. It had not been the practice hitherto to appeal to the public for money for work of this kind. Brajkishore Babu and his friends were mainly vakils who either contributed funds themselves, or found it from friends whenever there was an occasion. How could they ask the people to pay when they and their kind could well afford to do so? That seemed to be the argument. I had made up my mind not to accept anything from the Champaran ryots. It would be bound to be misinterpreted. I was equally determined not to appeal to the country at large for funds to conduct this inquiry. For that was likely to give it an all-India and political aspect[4]. Friends from Bombay offered Rs. 15,000, but I declined the offer with thanks. I decided to get as much as was possible, with Brajkishore Babu's help, from well-to-do Biharis living outside Champaran and, if more was needed, to approach my friend Dr. P.J. Mehta of Rangoon. Dr. Mehta readily agreed to send me whatever might be needed. We were thus free from all anxiety on this score. We were not likely to require large funds,

1. *account: a description of an event or experience*
2. *renting: be let or hired out at a specified rate*
3. *tactfully: adroitness and sensitivity in dealing with others or with difficult issues*
4. *aspect: a particular part or feature; a particular appearance or quality*

as we were bent on exercising the greatest economy in consonance[1] with the poverty of Champaran. Indeed it was found in the end that we did not need any large amount. I have an impression that we expended in all not more than three thousand rupees, and, as far as I remember, we saved a few hundred rupees from what we had collected.

The curious ways of living of my companions in the early days were a constant theme of raillery at their expense. Each of the vakils had a servant and a cook, and therefore a separate kitchen, and they often had their dinner as late as midnight. Though they paid their own expenses, their irregularity worried me, but as we had become close friends there was no possibility of a misunderstanding between us, and they received my ridicule in good part. Ultimately it was agreed that the servants should be dispensed with, that all the kitchens should be amalgamated, and that regular hours should be observed. As all were not vegetarians, and as two kitchens would have been expensive, a common vegetarian kitchen was decided upon. It was also felt necessary to insist on simple meals.

These arrangements considerably reduced the expenses and saved us a lot of time and energy, and both these were badly needed. Crowds of peasants came to make their statements, and they were followed by an army[2] of companions who filled the compound and garden to overflowing. The efforts of my companions to save me from *darshan* seekers were often of no avail, and I had to be exhibited for *darshan* at particular hours. At least five to seven volunteers were required to take down statements, and even then some people had to go away in the evening without being able to make their statements. All these statements were not essential, many of them being repetitions[3], but the people could not be satisfied otherwise, and I appreciated their feeling in the matter.

Those who took down the statements had to observe certain rules. Each peasant had to be closely cross-examined, and whoever failed to satisfy the test was rejected. This entailed a lot of extra time but most of the statements were thus rendered incontrovertible[4].

An officer from the C.I.D. would always be present when these statements were recorded. We might have prevented him, but we had decided from the very beginning not only not to mind the presence of C.I.D. officers, but to treat them with courtesy and to give them all the information that it was possible to give them. This was far from doing

1. *consonance: agreement or compatibility*
2. *army: a large number of similar people or things*
3. *repetitions: the act or an instance of repeating or being repeated; a thing that repeats another*
4. *incontrovertible: not able to be changed in form, function*

us any harm. On the contrary the very fact that the statements were taken down in the presence of the C.I.D. officers made the peasants more fearless. Whilst on the one hand excessive fear of the C.I.D. was driven out of the peasants' minds, on the other, their presence exercised a natural restraint on exaggeration. It was the business of C.I.D. friends to entrap people and so the peasants had necessarily to be cautious.

As I did not want to irritate the planters, but to win them over by gentleness, I made a point of writing to and meeting such of them against whom allegations[1] of a serious nature were made. I met the Planters' Association as well, placed the ryots' grievances before them and acquainted myself with their point of view. Some of the planters hated me, some were indifferent and a few treated me with courtesy.

1. *allegations: a formal accusation against somebody*

CHAPTER 141

COMPANIONS

Brajkishorebabu and Rajendrababu were a matchless pair. Their devotion made it impossible for me to take a single step without their help. Their disciples, or their companions Shambhaubabu, Anugrahababu, Dharanibabu, Ramnavmibabu and other vakils were always with us. Vindhyababu and Janakdharibabu also came and helped us now and then. All these were Biharis. Their principal work was to take down the ryots' statements.

Professor Kripalani could not but cast in his lot with us. Though a Sindhi he was more Bihari than a born Bihari. I have seen only a few workers capable of merging themselves in the province of their adoption. Kripalani is one of those few. He made it impossible for anyone to feel that he belonged to a different province. He was my gatekeeper in chief. For the time being he made it the end and aim of his life to save me from *darshan* seekers. He warded off people, calling to his aid now his unfailing humour, now his non-violent threats. At nightfall he would take up his occupation of a teacher and regale[1] his companions with his historical studies and observations, and quicken[2] any timid visitor into bravery.

Maulana Mazharul Haq had registered his name on the standing list of helpers whom I might count upon whenever necessary, and he made a point of looking in once or twice a month. The pomp and splendour in which he then lived was in sharp contrast to his simple life of today. The way in which he associated with us made us feel that he was one of us, though his fashionable habit gave a stranger a different impression.

As I gained more experience of Bihar, I became convinced that work of a permanent nature was impossible without proper village education. The ryots' ignorance was pathetic. They either allowed their children to roam[3] about, or made them toil on indigo plantations from morning to night for a couple of coppers a day. In those days a male labourer's wage did not exceed ten pice, a female's did not exceed[4] six, and a child's

1. *regale: entertain with conversation*
2. *quicken: stimulate or be stimulated; give or restore life to; make burn brighter*
3. *roam: travel aimlessly over a wide area; wander over, through, or about; pass lightly over*
4. *exceed: be greater in number or size than; go beyond what is allowed or stipulated by a set limit, especially of one's authority; surpass*

three. He who succeeded in earning four annas a day was considered most fortunate.

In consultation with my companions I decided to open primary schools in six villages. One of our conditions with the villagers was that they should provide the teachers with board and lodging while we would see to the other expenses. The village folk had hardly any cash in their hands, but they could well afford to provide foodstuffs. Indeed they had already expressed their readiness to contribute grain and other raw materials.

From where to get the teachers was a great problem. It was difficult to find local teachers who would work for a bare allowance or without remuneration. My idea was never to entrust children to commonplace teachers. Their literary qualification was not so essential as their moral fibre.

So I issued a public appeal for voluntary teachers. It received a ready response. Sjt. Gangadharrao Deshpande sent Babasaheb Soman and Pundalik Shrimati Avantikabai Gokhale came from Bombay and Mrs. Anandibai Vaishampayan from Poona. I sent to the Ashram for Chhotalal, Surendranath and my son Devdas. About this time Mahadev Desai and Narahari Parikh with their wives cast in their lot with me. Kasturbai was also summoned for the work. This was a fairly strong contingent. Shrimati Avantikabai and Shrimati Anandibai were educated enough, but Shrimati Durga Desai and Shrimati Manibehn Parikh had nothing more than a bare knowledge of Gujarati, and Kasturbai not even that. How were these ladies to instruct the children in Hindi?

I explained to them they were expected to teach the children not grammar and the three R's so much as cleanliness and good manners. I further explained that even as regards letters there was not so great a difference between Gujarati, Hindi and Marathi as they imagined, and in the primary classes, at any rate, the teaching of the rudiments[1] of the alphabet and numerals was not a difficult matter. The result was that the classes taken by these ladies were found to be most successful. The experience inspired them with confidence and interest in their work. Avantikabai's became a model school. She threw herself heart and soul into her work. She brought her exceptional gifts[2] to bear on it. Through these ladies we could, to some extent, reach the village women.

But I did not want to stop at providing for primary education. The villages were insanitary, the lanes full of filth, the wells surrounded by

1. *rudiments: the first principles of a subject; an elementary or primitive form of something*
2. *gifts: a natural ability or talent*

mud and stink and the courtyards unbearably untidy[1]. The elder people badly needed education in cleanliness. They were all suffering from various skin[2] diseases. So it was decided to do as much sanitary work as possible and to penetrate every department of their lives.

Doctors were needed for this work. I requested the Servants of India Society to lend us the services of the late Dr. Dev. We had been great friends, and he readily offered his services for six months. The teachers men and women had all to work under him.

All of them had express instructions not to concern themselves with grievances against planters or with politics. People who had any complaints to make were to be referred to me. No one was to venture out of his beat. The friends carried out these instructions with wonderful fidelity. I do not remember a single occasion of indiscipline[3].

1. *untidy: not arranged tidily; of a person not inclined to be neat*

2. *indiscipline: lack of discipline*

CHAPTER 142

PENETRATING THE VILLAGES

As far as was possible we placed each school in charge of one man and one woman. These volunteers had to look after medical relief and sanitation. The womenfolk had to be approached through women.

Medical relief was a very simple affair. Castor oil[1], quinine and sulphur ointment were the only drugs provided to the volunteers. If the patient showed a furred tongue or complained of constipation, castor oil was administered, in case of fever quinine was given after an opening dose of castor oil, and the sulphur ointment was applied in case of boils and itch after thoroughly washing the affected parts. No patient was permitted to take home any medicine. Wherever there was some complication Dr. Dev was consulted. Dr. Dev used to visit each centre on certain fixed days in the week.

Quite a number of people availed themselves of this simple relief. This plan of work will not seem strange when it is remembered that the prevailing ailments were few and amenable to simple treatment, by no means requiring expert help. As for the people the arrangement answered excellently.

Sanitation was a difficult affair. The people were not prepared to do anything themselves. Even the field labourers were not ready to do their own scavenging. But Dr. Dev was not a man easily to lose heart. He and the volunteers concentrated their energies on making a village ideally[2] clean. They swept the roads and the courtyards[3], cleaned out the wells, filled up the pools near by, and lovingly persuaded the villagers to raise volunteers from amongst themselves. In some villages they shamed people into taking up the work, and in others the people were so enthusiastic that they even prepared roads to enable my car to go from place to place. These sweet experiences were not unmixed with bitter ones of people's apathy. I remember some villagers frankly expressing their dislike for this work.

1. *castor oil: a pale yellow purgative oil obtained from the seeds of an african shrub*
2. *ideally: preferably*
3. *courtyards: an open area enclosed by walls or buildings, especially in a castle or large house*

It may not be out of place here to narrate[1] an experience that I have described before now at many meetings. Bhitiharva was a small village in which was one of our schools. I happened to visit a smaller village in its vicinity and found some of the women dressed very dirtily. So I told my wife to ask them why they did not wash their clothes. She spoke to them. One of the women took her into her hut and said: 'Look now, there is no box or cupboard here containing other clothes. The *sari* I am wearing is the only one I have. How am I to wash it? Tell Mahatmaji to get me another *sari*, and I shall then promise to bathe and put on clean clothes every day.'

This cottage[2] was not an exception, but a type to be found in many Indian villages. In countless cottages in India people live without any furniture, and without a change of clothes, merely with a rag to cover their shame.

One more experience I will note. In Champaran there is no lack of bamboo and grass. The school hut they had put up at Bhitiharva was made of these materials. Someone possibly some of the neighbouring planters' men set fire to it one night. It was not thought advisable to build another hut of bamboo[3] and grass. The school was in charge of Sjt. Soman and Kasturbai. Sjt. Soman decided to build a *pukka* house, and thanks to his infectious labour, many co-operated with him, and a brick house was soon made ready. There was no fear now of this building being burnt down.

Thus the volunteers with their schools, sanitation work and medical relief gained the confidence and respect of the village folk, and were able to bring good influence to bear upon them.

But I must confess with regret that my hope of putting this constructive work on a permanent footing[4] was not fulfilled. The volunteers had come for temporary periods, I could not secure any more from outside, and permanent honorary workers from Bihar were not available. As soon as my work in Champaran was finished, work outside, which had been preparing in the meantime, drew me away. The few months' work in Champaran, however, took such deep root that its influence in one form or another is to be observed there even today.

1. *narrate: give a spoken or written account of; provide a commentary to accompany*
2. *cottage: a small simple house, typically one in the country*
3. *bamboo: a giant woody grass with hollow jointed stems, grown chiefly in the*
4. *footing: secure placement of the feet, or something to allow stability*

CHAPTER 143

WHEN A GOVERNOR IS GOOD

Whilst on the one hand social service work of the kind I have described in the foregoing chapters was being carried out, on the other the work of recording statements of the ryots' grievances was progressing apace[1]. Thousands of such statements were taken, and they could not but have their effect. The ever growing number of ryots coming to make their statements increased the planters' wrath[2], and they moved heaven and earth to counteract[3] my inquiry.

One day I received a letter from the Bihar Government to the following effect: 'Your inquiry has been sufficiently prolonged; should you not now bring it to an end and leave Bihar?' The letter was couched in polite language, but its meaning was obvious.

I wrote in reply that the inquiry was bound to be prolonged, and unless and until it resulted in bringing relief to the people, I had no intention of leaving Bihar, I pointed out that it was open to Government to terminate[4] my inquiry by accepting the ryots' grievances as genuine and redressing them, or by recognizing that the ryots had made out a *prima facie* case for an official inquiry which should be immediately instituted.

Sir Edward Gait, the Lieutenant Governor, asked me to see him, expressed his willingness to appoint an inquiry and invited me to be a member of the Committee. I ascertained the names of the other members, and after consultation with my co-workers agreed to serve on the Committee, on condition that I should be free to confer with my co-workers during the progress of the inquiry, that Government should recognize that, by being a member of the Committee, I did not cease to be the ryots' advocate, and that in case the result of the inquiry failed to give me satisfaction, I should be free to guide and advise the ryots as to what line of action they should take.

Sir Edward Gait accepted the condition as just and proper and announced the inquiry. The late Sir Frank Sly was appointed Chairman of the Commitee.

1. *apace: swiftly; quickly*
2. *wrath: extreme anger*
3. *counteract: act against in order to reduce its force or neutralize it*
4. *terminate: bring to an end*

The Committee found in favour of the ryots, and recommended that the planters should refund a portion of the exactions made by them which the Committee had found to be unlawful[1], and that the *tinkathia* system should be abolished by law.

Sir Edward Gait had a large share in getting the Committee to make a unanimous report and in getting the agrarian bill passed in accordance with the Committee's recommendations. Had he not adopted a firm attitude, and had he not brought all his tact to bear on the subject, the report would not have been unanimous[2], and the Agrarian Act would not have been passed. The planters wielded extraordinary power. They offered strenuous[3] opposition to the bill in spite of the report, but Sir Edwin Gait remained firm up to the last and fully carried out the recommendations of the Committee.

The *tinkathia* system which had been in existence for about a century was thus abolished and with it the planters' *raj* came to an end. The ryots, who had all along remained crushed, now somewhat came to their own, and the superstition that the stain of indigo could never be washed out was exploded.

It was my desire to continue the constructive work for some years, to establish more schools and to penetrate the villages more effectively. The ground had been prepared, but it did not please God, as often before, to allow my plans to be fulfilled. Fate decided otherwise and drove me to take up work elsewhere.

1. *unlawful: not conforming to or permitted by the law or rules*
2. *unanimous: fully in agreement*
3. *strenuous: requiring or using great exertion*

CHAPTER 144

IN TOUCH WITH LABOUR

Whilst I was yet winding up my work on the Committee, I received a letter from Sjts. Mohanlal Pandya and Shankarlal Parikh telling me of the failure of crops in the Kheda district, and asking me to guide the peasants, who were unable to pay the assessment. I had not the inclination, the ability or the courage to advise without an inquiry on the spot.

At the same time there came a letter from Shrimati Anasuyabai about the condition of labour in Ahmedabad, Wages were low, the labourers had long been agitating for an increment, and I had a desire to guide them if I could. But I had not the confidence to direct even this comparatively small affair from that long distance. So I seized the first opportunity to go to Ahmedabad. I had hoped that I should be able to finish both these matters quickly and get back to Champaran to supervise the constructive work that had been inaugurated there.

But things did not move as swiftly as I had wished, and I was unable to return to Champaran, with the result that the schools closed down one by one. My co-workers and I had built many castles in the air, but they all vanished[1] for the time being.

One of these was cow protection[2] work in Champaran, besides rural[3] sanitation and education. I had seen, in the course of my travels, that cow protection and Hindi propaganda had become the exclusive[4] concern of the Marwadis. A Marwadi friend had sheltered me in his *dharamshala* whilst at Bettiah. Other Marwadis of the place had interested me in their *goshala* (dairy). My ideas about cow protection had been definitely formed then, and my conception of the work was the same as it is today. Cow protection, in my opinion, included cattle-breeding, improvement of the stock, humane treatment of bullocks, formation of model dairies, etc. The Marwadi friends had promised full co-operation in this work, but as I could not fix myself up in Champaran, the scheme could not be carried out.

1. *vanished: disappear suddenly and completely*
2. *protection: the action or state of protecting or being protected; a person or thing that protects; a document guaranteeing safety to the person specified in it*
3. *rural: in, relating to, or characteristic of the country; side rather than the town*
4. *exclusive: restricted to the person, group, or area concerned; not published or broadcast elsewhere*

The *goshala* in Bettiah is still there, but it has not become a model dairy, the Champaran bullock is still made to work beyond his capacity, and the so-called Hindu still cruelly belabours the poor animal and disgraces his religion.

That this work should have remained unrealized has been, to me, a continual regret, and whenever I go to Champaran and hear the gentle reproaches of the Marwadi and Bihari friends, I recall with a heavy sigh all those plans which I had to drop so abruptly.

The educational work in one way or another is going on in many places. But the cow protection work had not taken firm root, and has not, therefore, progressed in the direction intended.

Whilst the Kheda peasants' question was still being discussed, I had already taken up the question of the mill-hands in Ahmedabad.

I was in a most delicate situation. The mill-hands' case was strong. Shrimati Anasuyabai had to battle against her own brother, Sjt. Ambalal Sarabhai, who led the fray on behalf[1] of the mill-owners. My relations with them were friendly, and that made fighting with them the more difficult. I held consultations with them, and requested them to refer the dispute to arbitration, but they refused to recognize the principle of arbitration.

I had therefore to advise the labourers to go on strike. Before I did so, I came in very close contact with them and their leaders, and explained to them the conditions of a successful strike:

1. never to resort to violence, 2. never to molest[2] blacklegs, 3. never to depend upon alms[3], and 4. to remain firm, no matter how long the strike continued, and to earn bread, during the strike, by any other honest labour.

The leaders of the strike understood and accepted the conditions, and the labourers pledged themselves at a general meeting not to resume work until either their terms were accepted or the mill-owners agreed to refer the dispute to arbitration.

It was during this strike that I came to know intimately Sjts. Vallabhbhai Patel and Shankarlal Banker. Shrimati Anasuyabai I knew well before this.

We had daily meetings of the strikers under the shade of a tree on the bank of the Sabarmati. They attended the meeting in their thousands, and I reminded them in my speeches of their pledge and of the duty to maintain peace and self-respect. They daily paraded[4] the streets of the city

1. *behalf: in the interests of a persons, group, or principle*
2. *molest: pester or harass in a hostile way; assault or abuse sexually*
3. *alms: charitable donations of money of food to the poor*
4. *paraded: a public procession, especially one celebrating a special day or event*

in peaceful procession[1], carrying their banner[2] bearing the inscription '*Ek-Tek*' (keep the pledge).

The strike went on for twenty-one days. During the continuance of the strike I consulted the mill-owners from time to time and entreated them to do justice to the labourers. 'We have our pledge too,' they used to say. 'Our relations with the labourers are those of parents and children.... How can we brook the interference of a third party? Where is the room for arbitration?'

1. *procession: a number of people or vehicles moving forward in an orderly fashion, especially as part of a ceremony; the action of moving in such a way; a relentless succession of people or things*
2. *banner: a long strip of cloth bearing a slogan or design*

CHAPTER 145

A PEEP INTO THE ASHRAM

Before I proceed to describe the progress of the labour dispute it is essential[1] to have a peep into the Ashram. All the while I was in Champaran the Ashram was never out of my mind, and occasionally I paid it flying visits.

At that time the Ashram was in Kochrab, a small village near Ahmedabad. Plague broke out in this village, and I saw evident danger to the safety of the Ashram children. It was impossible to keep ourselves immune from the effects of the surrounding insanitation, however scrupulously[2] we might observe the rules of cleanliness within the Ashram walls. We were not then equal either to getting the Kochrab people to observe these rules nor to serving the village otherwise.

Our ideal was to have the Ashram at a safe distance both from town and village, and yet at a manageable distance from either. And we were determined, some day, to settle on ground of our own.

The plague, I felt, was sufficient notice to quit Kochrab. Sjt. Punjabhai Hirachand, a merchant in Ahmedabad, had come in close contact with the Ashram, and used to serve us in a number of matters in a pure and selfless spirit. He had a wide experience of things in Ahmedabad, and he volunteered to procure[3] us suitable land. I went about with him north and south of Kochrab in search of land, and then suggested to him to find out a piece of land three or four miles to the north. He hit upon the present site. Its vicinity to the Sabarmati Central Jail was for me a special attraction. As jail-going was understood to be the normal lot of Satyagrahis, I liked this position. And I knew that the sites selected for jails have generally clean surroundings.

In about eight days the sale was executed. There was no building on the land and no tree. But its situation on the bank of the river and its solitude were great advantages.

We decided to start by living under canvas, and having a tin shed for a kitchen, till permanent houses were built.

1. *essential: absolutely necessary; extremely important*
2. *scrupulously: diligent, thorough, and attentive to details*
3. *procure: obtain*

The Ashram had been slowly growing. We were now over forty souls, men, women and children, having our meals at a common kitchen. The whole conception about the removal was mine, the execution was as usual left to Maganlal.

Our difficulties, before we had permanent living accommodation, were great. The rains were impending, and provisions had to be got from the city four miles away. The ground, which had been a waste, was infested with snakes, and it was no small risk to live with little children under such conditions. The general rule was not to kill the snakes, though I confess none of us had shed the fear of these reptiles[1], nor have we even now.

The rule of not killing venomous reptiles had been practised for the most part at Phoenix, Tolstoy Farm and Sabarmati. At each of these places we had to settle on waste lands. We have had, however, no loss of life occasioned by snakebite. I see, with the eye of faith, in this circumstance the hand of the God of Mercy. Let no one cavil[2] at this, saying that God can never be partial, and that He has no time to meddle with the humdrum affairs of men. I have no other language to express the fact of the matter, to describe this uniform experience of mine. Human language can but imperfectly describe God's ways. I am sensible of the fact that they are indescribable and inscrutable. But if mortal man will dare to describe them, he has no better medium than his own inarticulate speech. Even if it be a superstition to believe that complete immunity from harm for twenty-five years in spite of a fairly regular practice of non-killing is not a fortuitous accident but a grace of God, I should still hug that superstition.

During the strike of the mill-hands in Ahmedabad the foundation of the Ashram weaving shed was being laid. For the principal activity of the Ashram was then weaving. Spinning had not so far been possible for us.

1. *reptiles: a cold-blooded vertebrate animal of a class that includes snakes, lizards, crocodiles, turtles, and tortoises, typically having a dry scaly skin and laying soft-shelled eggs on land*

2. *cavil: make petty or unnecessary objections*

CHAPTER 146

THE FAST

For the first two weeks the mill-hands exhibited great courage and self-restraint and daily held monster meetings. On these occasions I used to remind them of their pledge, and they would shout back to me the assurance that they would rather die than break their word.

But at last they began to show signs of flagging. Just as physical weakness in men manifests itself in irascibility, their attitude towards the blacklegs became more and more menacing as the strike seemed to weaken, and I began to fear an outbreak of rowdyism on their part. The attendance at their daily meetings began to dwindle by degrees, and despondency and despair were writ large on the faces of those who did attend. Finally the information was brought to me that the strikers had begun to totter[1]. I felt deeply troubled and set to thinking furiously as to what my duty was in the circumstances. I had had experience of a gigantic strike in South Africa, but the situation that confronted me here was different. The mill-hands had taken the pledge at my suggestion. They had repeated it before me day after day, and the very idea that they might now go back upon it was to me inconceivable[2]. Was it pride or was it my love for the labourers and my passionate regard for truth that was at the back of this feeling who can say?

One morning it was at a mill-hands' meeting while I was still groping and unable to see my way clearly, the light came to me. Unbidden and all by themselves the words came to my lips: 'Unless the strikers rally,' I declared to the meeting, 'and continue the strike till a settlement is reached, or till they leave the mills altogether, I will not touch any food.'

The labourers were thunderstruck. Tears began to course down Anasuyabehn's cheeks. The labourers broke out, 'Not you but we shall fast. It would be monstrous[3] if you were to fast. Please forgive us for our lapse[4], we will now remain faithful to our pledge to the end.'

'There is no need for you to fast,' I replied. 'It would be enough if you could remain true to your pledge. As you know we are without funds,

1. *totter: move in an unsteady way*
2. *inconceivable: not capable of being grasped mentally*
3. *monstrous: a brief failure of concentration, memory, or judgement; a decline from previously high standards*
4. *lapse: inhumanly or outrageously evil or wrong*

and we do not want to continue our strike by living on public charity. You should therefore try to eke out a bare existence by some kind of labour, so that you may be able to remain unconcerned, no matter how long the strike may continue. As for my fast, it will be broken only after the strike is settled.'

In the meantime Vallabhbhai was trying to find some employment for the strikers under the Municipality, but there was not much hope of success there. Maganlal Gandhi suggested that, as we needed sand for filling the foundation of our weaving school in the Ashram, a number of them might be employed for that purpose. The labourers welcomed the proposal. Anasuyabehn led the way with a basket on her head and soon an endless stream of labourers carrying baskets of sand on their heads could be seen issuing out of the hollow of the river-bed. It was a sight worth seeing. The labourers felt themselves infused with a new strength, and it became difficult to cope with the task of paying out wages to them.

My fast was not free from a grave defect. For as I have already mentioned in a previous chapter. I enjoyed very close and cordial relations with the mill-owners, and my fast could not but affect their decision. As a Satyagrahi I knew that I might not fast against them, but ought to leave them free to be influenced by the mill-hands' strike alone. My fast was undertaken not on account of lapse of the mill-owners, but on account of that of the labourers in which, as their representative, I felt I had a share. With the mill-owners, I could only plead; to fast against them would amount to coercion. Yet in spite of my knowledge that my fast was bound to put pressure upon them, as in fact it did, I felt I could not help it. The duty to undertake it seemed to me to be clear.

I tried to set the mill-owners at ease. 'There is not the slightest necessity for you to withdraw from your position,' I said to them. But they received my words coldly and even flung keen, delicate bits of sarcasm[1] at me, as indeed they had a perfect[2] right to do.

The principal man at the back of the mill-owners' unbending attitude towards the strike was Sheth Ambalal. His resolute[3] will and transparent[4] sincerity were wonderful and captured my heart. It was a pleasure to be pitched against him. The strain produced by my fast upon the opposition, of which he was the head, cut me, therefore, to the quick. And then,

1. *sarcasm: the use of irony to mock or convey contempt*
2. *perfect: having all the required elements, qualities, or characteristics*
3. *resolute: determined; unwavering*
4. *transparent: obvious or evident*

Sarladevi, his wife, was attached to me with the affection of a blood-sister, and I could not bear to see her anguish[1] on account of my action.

Anasuyabhen and a number of other friends and labourers shared the fast with me on the first day. But after some difficulty I was able to dissuade them from continuing it further.

The net result of it was that an atmosphere of goodwill was created all round. The hearts of the mill-owners were touched, and they set about discovering some means for a settlement. Anasuyabehn's house became the venue of their discussions. Sjt. Anandshankar Dhruva intervened and was in the end appointed arbitrator, and the strike was called off after I had fasted only for three days. The mill-owners commemorated[2] the event by distributing sweets among the labourers, and thus a settlement was reached after twenty-one days' strike.

At the meeting held to celebrate the settlement, both the mill-owners and the Commissioner were present. The advice which the latter gave to the mill-hands on this occasion was: 'You should always act as Mr. Gandhi advises you.' Almost immediately after these events I had to engage in a tussle[3] with this very gentleman. But circumstances were changed, and he had changed with the circumstances. He then set about warning the Patidars of Kheda against following my advice!

I must not close this chapter without noting here an incident, as amusing as it was pathetic[4]. It happened in connection with the distribution of sweets. The mill-owners had ordered a very large quantity, and it was a problem how to distribute it among the thousands of labourers. It was decided that it would be the fittest thing to distribute it in the open, beneath the very tree under which the pledge had been taken, especially as it would have been extremely inconvenient to assemble them all together in any other place.

I had taken it for granted that the men who had observed strict discipline for full twenty-one days would without any difficulty be able to remain standing in an orderly[4] manner while the sweets were being distributed, and not make an impatient scramble for them. But when it came to the test, all the methods that were tried for making the distribution failed. Again and again their ranks would break into confusion after distribution had proceeded for a couple of minutes. The leaders of the mill-hands tried their best to restore order, but in vain. The confusion,

1. *anguish: extreme distress of body or mind*
2. *commemorated: honor the memory of as a mark of respect, especially with a ceremony or memorial*
3. *tussle: a vigorous struggle or scuffle*
4. *pathetic: arousing pity, especially through vulnerability or sadness*
5. *orderly: neatly and methodically arranged*

the crush and the scramble at last became so great that quite a number of the sweets were spoiled by being trampled under foot, and the attempt to distribute them in the open had finally to be given up. With difficulty we succeeded in taking the remaining sweets to Sheth Ambalal's bungalow in Mirzapur. Sweets were distributed comfortably the next day within the compound of that bungalow.

The comic side of this incident is obvious, but the pathetic side bears mention. Subsequent inquiry revealed the fact that the beggar population of Ahmedabad, having got scent of the fact that sweets were to be distributed under the *Ek-Tek* tree, had gone there in large numbers, and it was their hungry scramble for the sweets that had created all the confusion and disorder.

The grinding poverty and starvation with which our country is afflicted is such that it drives more and more men every year into the ranks of the beggars, whose desperate struggle for bread renders[1] them insensible[2] to all feelings of decency and self-respect. And our philanthropists, instead of providing work for them and insisting on their working for bread, give them alms.

1. *renders: cause to be or become*

2. *insensible: unaware of; indifferent to*

CHAPTER 147

THE KHEDA SATYAGRAHA

No breathing time was, however, in store for me. Hardly was the Ahmedabad mill-hands' strike over, when I had to plunge into the Kheda Satyagraha struggle.

A condition approaching famine had arisen in the Kheda district owing to a widespread failure of crops, and the Patidars of Kheda were considering the question of getting the revenue assessment for the year suspended.

Sjt. Amritlal Thakkar had already inquired into and reported on the situation and personally discussed the question with the Commissioner, before I gave definite advice to the cultivators. Sjts. Mohanlal Pandya and Shankarlal Parikh had also thrown themselves into the fight, and had set up an agitation in the Bombay Legislative Council through Sjt. Vithalbhai Patel and the late Sir Gokuldas Kahandas Parekh. More than one deputation[1] had waited upon the Governor in that connection.

I was at this President of the Gujarat Sabha. The Sabha sent petitions and telegrams to the Government and even patiently swallowed the insults and threats[2] of the Commissioner. The conduct of the officials on this occasion was so ridiculous[3] and undignified as to be almost incredible[4] now.

The cultivators' demand was as clear as daylight, and so moderate as to make out a strong case for its acceptance. Under the Land Revenue Rules, if the crop was four annas or under, the cultivators could claim full suspension of the revenue assessment for the year. According to the official figures the crop was said to be over four annas. The contention of the cultivators, on the other hand, was that it was less than four annas. But the Government was in on mood to listen, and regarded the popular demand for arbitration as *lése majesté*. At last all petitioning and prayer having failed, after taking counsel with co-workers, I advised the Patidars ro resort to Satyagraha.

1. *deputation: a group of people who undertake a mission on behalf of a larger group*
2. *threats: a statement of an intention to inflict injury, damage, or other hostile action as retribution; a menace of bodily harm, such as may restrain a person's freedom of action*
3. *ridiculous: inviting ridicule; absurd*
4. *incredible: greater degree, extremely*

Besides the volunteers of Kheda, my principal comrades in this struggle were Sjts. Vallabhbhai Patel, Shankarlal Banker, Shrimati Anasuyabehn, Sjts. Indulal Yajnik, Mahadev Desai and others. Sjt. Vallabhbhai, in joining the struggle, had to suspend a splendid and growing practice at the bar, which for all practical purposes he was never able to resume.

We fixed up our headquarters at the Nadiad Anathashram, no other place being available which would have been large enough to accommodate all of us.

The following pledge was signed by the Satyagrahis:

'Knowing that the crops of our villages are less than four annas, we requested the Government to suspend the collection of revenue assessment till the ensuing[1] year, but the Government has not acceded to our prayer. Therefore, we, the undersigned, hereby solemnly[2] declare that we shall not, of our own accord, pay to the Government the full or the remaining revenue for the year. We shall let the Government take whatever legal steps it may think fit and gladly suffer[3] the consequences of our non-payment. We shall rather let our lands be forfeited than that by voluntary payment we should allow our case to be considered false or should compromise our self-respect. Should the Government, however, agree to suspend collection of the second installment of the assessment[4] throughout the district, such amongst us as are in a position to pay will pay up the whole or the balance of the revenue that may be due. The reason why those who are able to pay still withhold payment is that, if they pay up, the poorer ryots may in a panic sell their chattels or incur debts to pay their dues, and thereby bring suffering upon themselves. In these circumstances we feel that, for the sake of the poor, it is the duty even of those who can afford to pay to withhold payment of their assessment.'

I cannot devote many chapters to this struggle. So a number of sweet recollections in this connection will have to be crowded out. Those who want to make a fuller and deeper study of this important fight would do well to read the full and authentic[5] history of the Kheda Satyagraha by Sjt. Shankarlal Parikh of Kathlal, Kheda.

1. *ensuing: happen or occur afterwards or as a result*
2. *solemnly: formal and dignified; a solemn procession*
3. *suffer: experience or be subjected to something bad or unpleasant; be affected by or subject to an illness or ailment; become or appear worse in quality*
4. *assessment: evaluate or estimate the nature, value, or quality of; set the value of a tax, fine, etc. for (a person or property) at a specified level*
5. *authentic: of undisputed origin or veracity;*

CHAPTER 148

'THE ONION THIEF'

Champaran being in a far away corner of India, and the press having been kept out of the campaign, it did not attract visitors from outside. Not so with the Kheda campaign, of which the happenings were reported in the press from day to day.

The Gujaratis were deeply interested in the fight, which was to them a novel experiment. They were ready to pour forth their riches for the success of the cause. It was not easy for them to see that Satyagraha could not be conducted simply by means of money. Money is the thing that it least needs. In spite of my remonstrance, the Bombay merchants sent us more money than necessary, so that we had some balance left at the end of the campaign.

At the same time the Satyagrahi volunteers had to learn the new lesson of simplicity. I cannot say that they imbibed[1] it fully, but they considerably changed their ways of life.

For the Patidar farmers, too, the fight was quite a new thing. We had, therefore, to go about from village to village explaining the principles of Satyagraha.

The main thing was to rid the agriculturists of their fear by making them realize that the officials were not the masters but the servants of the people, inasmuch as they received their salaries from the taxpayer. And then it seemed well nigh impossible to make them realize the duty of combining civility with fearlessness[2]. Once they had shed the fear of the officials, how could they be stopped from returning their insults? And yet if they resorted to incivility it would spoil their Satyagraha, like a drop of arsenic in milk. I realized later that they had less fully learnt the lesson of civility than I had expected. Experience has taught me that civility is the most difficult part of Satyagraha. Civility does not here mean the mere outward[3] gentleness of speech cultivated for the occasion, but an inborn gentleness and desire to do the opponent[4] good. These should show themselves in every act of a Satyagrahi.

1. *imbibed: drink, absorb*
2. *fearlessness: brave or not scared*
3. *outward: of, on, or from the outside; relating to the external appearance of something rather than its true nature*
4. *opponent: a person who opposes*

In the initial stages, though the people exhibited much courage, the Government did not seem inclined to take strong action. But as the people's firmness showed no signs of wavering, the Government began coercion. The attachment officers sold people's cattle and seized[1] whatever movables[2] they could lay hands on. Penalty notices were served, and in some cases standing crops were attached. This unnerved the peasants, some of whom paid up their dues, while others desired to place safe movables in the way of the officials so that they might attach them to realize the dues. On the other hand some were prepared to fight to the bitter end.

While these things were going on, one of Sjt. Shankarlal Parikh's tenants paid up the assessment in respect of his land. This created a sensation. Sjt. Shankarlal Parikh immediately made amends for his tenant's mistake by giving away for charitable purposes the land for which the assessment had been paid. He thus saved his honour and set a good example to others.

With a view to steeling the hearts of those who were frightened[3], I advised the people, under the leadership of Sjt. Mohanlal Pandya, to remove the crop of onion, from a field which had been, in my opinion wrongly attached. I did not regard this as civil disobedience, but even if it was, I suggested that this attachment of standing crops, though it might be in accordance with law, was morally wrong, and was nothing short of looting, and that therefore it was the people's duty to remove the onion in spite of the order of attachment. This was a good opportunity for the people to learn a lesson in courting fines or imprisonment, which was the necessary consequence of such disobedience. For Sjt. Mohanlal Pandya it was a thing after his heart. He did not like the campaign to end without someone undergoing suffering in the shape of imprisonment for something done consistently with the principles of Satyagraha. So he volunteered to remove the onion crop from the field, and in this seven or eight friends joined him.

It was impossible for the Government to leave them free. The arrest of Sjt. Mohanlal and his companions added to the people's enthusiasm. When the fear of jail disappears, repression puts heart into the people. Crowds of them besieged the court-house on the day of the hearing. Pandya and his companions were convicted and sentenced to a brief

1. *seized: take hold of suddenly and forcibly; take forcible possession of by warrant or legal right*
2. *movables: [law] of the nature of a chattel, as distinct from land or buildings*
3. *frightened: cause to be afraid; drive someone away by fear*

term of imprisonment. I was of opinion that the conviction was wrong, because the act of removing the onion crop could not come under the definition of 'theft' in the Penal Code. But no appeal was filed as the policy was to avoid the law courts.

A procession escorted[1] the 'convicts' to jail, and on that day Sjt. Mohanlal Pandya earned from the people the honoured title of *dungli chor* (onion thief) which he enjoys to this day.

The conclusion of the Kheda Satyagraha I will leave to the next chapter.

1. *escorted: accompany (someone or something) somewhere as an escort*

CHAPTER 149

END OF KHEDA SATYAGRAHA

The campaign came to an unexpected end. It was clear that the people were exhausted, and I hesitated to let the unbending be driven to utter ruin. I was casting about for some graceful way of terminating the struggle which would be acceptable to a Satyagrahi. Such a one appeared quite unexpectedly. The Mamlatdar of the Nadiad Taluka sent me word that, if well-to-do Patidars paid up, the poorer ones would be granted suspension. I asked for a written undertaking to that effect, which was given. But as a Mamlatdar could be responsible only for his Taluka, I inquired of the Collector, who alone could give an undertaking in respect of the whole district, whether the Mamlatdar's undertaking[1] was true for the whole district. He replied that orders declaring suspension in terms of the Mamlatdar's letter had been already issued. I was not aware of it, but if it was a fact, the people's pledge had been fulfilled. The pledge, it will be remembered, had the same things for its object, and so we expressed ourselves satisfied with the orders.

However, the end was far from making me feel happy, inasmuch as it lacked the grace with which the termination of every Satyagraha campaign ought to be accompanied. The Collector carried on as though he had done nothing by way of a settlement. The poor were to be granted suspension, but hardly any got the benefit of it. It was the people's right to determine who was poor, but they could not exercise it. I was sad that they had not the strength to exercise the right. Although, therefore, the termination was celebrated as a triumph of Satyagraha, I could not enthuse over it, as it lacked the essentials of a complete triumph[2].

The end of a Satyagraha campaign can be described as worthy, only when, it leaves the Satyagrahis stronger and more spirited than they are in the beginning.

The campaign was not, however, without its indirect[3] results which we can see today and the benefit of which we are reaping[4]. The Kheda

1. *undertaking: a formal pledge or promise to do something; a task that is taken on; an enterprise*
2. *triumph: a great victory or achievement; the state of being victorious or successful; joy or satisfaction resulting from a success or victory; a highly successful example: the arrest was a triumph of international co-operation*
3. *indirect: not direct*
4. *reaping: receive as a consequence of one's own or others actions*

Satyagraha marks the beginning of an awakening among the peasants of Gujarat, the beginning of their true political education.

Dr. Besant's brilliant Home Rule agitation had certainly touched the peasants, but it was the Kheda campaign that compelled the educated public workers to establish contact with the actual life of the peasants. They learnt to identify themselves with the latter. They found their proper sphere of work, their capacity for sacrifice increased. That Vallabhbhai found himself during this campaign was by itself no small achievement. We could realize its measure during the flood relief operations last year and the Bardoli Satyagraha this year. Public life in Gujarat became instinct with a new energy and a new vigour[1]. The Patidar peasant came to an unforgettable consciousness of his strength. The lesson was indelibly imprinted on the public mind that the salvation[2] of the people depends upon themselves, upon their capacity for suffering and sacrifice. Through the Kheda campaign Satyagraha took firm root in the soil of Gujarat.

Although, therefore, I found nothing to enthuse over in the termination of the Satyagraha, the Kheda peasants were jubilant[3], because they knew that what they had achieved was commensurate with their effort, and they had found the true and infallible method for a redress of their grievances. This knowledge was enough justification for their jubilation.

Nevertheless the Kheda peasants had not fully understood the inner meaning of Satyagraha, and they saw it to their cost, as we shall see in the chapters to follow.

1. *vigour: physical strength and good health*
2. *salvation: deliverance from sin and its consequences, believed by Christians to be brought about by faith in Christ*
3. *jubilant: show great happiness*

CHAPTER 150

PASSION FOR UNITY

The Kheda campaign was launched while the deadly war in Europe was still going on. Now a crisis had arrived, and the Viceroy had invited various leaders to a war conference in Delhi. I had also been urged to attend the conference. I have already referred to the cordial relations between Lord Chelmsford, the Viceroy, and myself.

In response to the invitation I went to Delhi. I had, however, objections to taking part in the conference, the principal one being the exclusion from it of leaders like the Ali Brothers. They were then in jail. I had met them only once or twice, though I had heard much about them. Everyone had spoken highly of their services and their courage. I had not then come in close touch with Hakim Saheb, but Principal Rudra and Dinabandhu Andrews had told me a good deal in his praise. I had met Mr. Shuaib Qureshi and Mr. Khwaja at the Muslim League in Calcutta. I had also come in contact with Drs. Ansari and Abdur Rahman. I was seeking the friendship of good Musalmans. and was eager to understand the Musalman mind through contact with their purest and most patriotic representatives. I therefore never needed any pressure to go with them, wherever they took me, in order to get into intimate touch with them.

I had realized early enough in South Africa that there was no genuine[1] friendship between the Hindus and the Musalmans. I never missed a single opportunity to remove obstacles in the way of unity. It was not in my nature to placate anyone by adulation, or at the cost of self-respect. But my South African experiences had convinced me that it would be on the question of Hindu-Muslim unity that my Ahimsa would be put to its severest test, and that the question presented the widest field for my experiments in Ahimsa. The conviction[2] is still there. Every moment of my life I realize that God is putting me on my trial.

Having such strong convictions on the question when I returned from South Africa, I prized[3] the contact with the Brothers. But before closer touch[4] could be established they were isolated. Maulana Mahomed Ali

1. *genuine: truly what it is said to be; authentic*
2. *conviction: a firmly held belief or opinion; the quality of showing that one is firmly convinced of something*
3. *prized: value highly*
4. *touch: come into or be in contact with; come or bring into mutual contact*

used to write long letters to me from Betul and Chhindwada whenever his jailers allowed him to do so. I applied for permission to visit the Brothers but to no purpose.

It was after the imprisonment of the Ali Brothers that I was invited by Muslim friends to attend the session of the Muslim League at Calcutta. Being requested to speak, I addressed them on the duty of the Muslims to secure[1] the Brother's release. A little while after this I was taken by these friends to the Muslim College at Aligarh. There I invited the young men to be fakirs for the service of the motherland.

Next I opened correspondence with the Government for the release of the Brothers. In that connection I studied the Brothers' views and activities about the Khilafat. I had discussions with Musalman friends. I felt that, if I would become a true friend of the Muslims, I must render[2] all possible help in securing the release of the Brothers, and a just settlement of the Khilafat question. It was not for me to enter into the absolute[3] merits of the question, provided there was nothing immoral in their demands. In matters of religion beliefs differ, and each one's is supreme for himself. If all had the same belief about all matters of religion, there would be only one religion in the world, As time progressed I found that the Muslim demand about the Khilafat was not only not against any ethical principle, but that the British Prime Minister had admitted the justice of the Muslim demand. I felt, therefore, bound to render what help I could in securing a due fulfillment of the prime Minister's pledge. The pledge had been given in such clear terms that the examination of the Muslim demand on the merits was needed only to satisfy my own conscience.

Friends and critics have criticized my attitude regarding the Khilafat question. In spite of the criticism I feel that I have no reason to revise it or to regret my co-operation with the Muslims. I should adopt the same attitude, should a similar occasion arise[4].

When, therefore, I went to Delhi, I had fully intended to submit the Muslim case to the Viceroy. The Khilafat question had not then assumed the shape it did subsequently.

But on my reaching Delhi another difficulty in the way of my attending the conference arose. Dinabandhu Andrews raised a question about the morality of my participation in the war conference. He told me

1. *secure: succeed in obtaining; seek to guarantee repayment of by having a right to take possession of an asset in the event of non-payment*
2. *render: provide or give aservice, help, etc. submit for inspection, consideration, or payment; poetic hand over; surrender*
3. *absolute: not qualified or diminished in any way; total; not subject to any limitation of power*
4. *arise: originate or become apparent; occur as a result of*

of the controversy in the British press regarding secret treaties between England and Italy. How could I participate in the conference, if England had entered into secret treaties with another European power? asked Mr. Andrews. I knew nothing of the treaties. Dinabandhu Andrews' word was enough for me. I therefore addressed a letter to Lord Chelmsford explaining my hesitation to take part in the conference. He invited me to discuss the question with him. I had a prolonged discussion with him and his Private Secretary Mr. Maffey. As a result I agreed to take part in the conference. This was in effect the Viceroy's argument: 'Surely you do not believe that the Viceroy knows everything done by the British Cabinet[1]. I do not claim, no one claims, that the British Government is infallible[2]. But if you agree that the Empire has been, on the whole, a power for good, if you believe that India has, on the whole, benefited by the British connection, would you not admit that it is the duty of every Indian citizen to help the Empire in the hour of its need? I too have read what the British papers say about the secret treaties[3]. I can assure you that I know nothing beyond what the papers say, and you know the canards that these papers frequently start, Can you, acting on a mere newspaper report, refuse help to the Empire at such a critical juncture? You may raise whatever moral issues you like and challenge us as much as you please after the conclusion of the war, not today.'

The argument was not new. It appealed to me as new because of the manner in which, and the hour at which, it was presented, and I agreed to attend the conference. As regards the Muslim demands I was to address a letter to the Viceroy.

1. *Cabinet: the committee of senior ministers responsible for controlling government policy; a body of advisers to the president, composed of the heads of the executive departments of the government*
2. *infallible: never failing; always effective; infallible cures*
3. *treaties: a formally concluded and ratified agreement between states*

CHAPTER 151

RECRUITING CAMPAIGN

So I attended the conference. The Viceroy was very keen on my supporting the resolution about recruiting. I asked for permission to speak in Hindi-Hindustani. The Viceroy acceded to my request, but suggested that I should speak also in English. I had no speech to make. I spoke but one sentence to this effect: 'With a full sense of my responsibility I beg to support the resolution.'

Many congratulated me on my having spoken in Hindustani. That was, they said, the first instance within living memory of anyone having spoken in Hindustani at such a meeting. The congratulations and the discovery that I was the first to speak in Hindustani at a Viceregal meeting hurt my national pride. I felt like shrinking[1] into myself. What a tragedy[2] that the language of the country should be taboo[3] in meetings held in the country, for work relating to the country, and that a speech there in Hindustani by a stray individual like myself should be a matter for congratulation? Incidents like these are reminders of the low state to which we have been reduced.

The one sentence that I uttered at the conference had for me considerable significance. It was impossible for me to forget either the conference or the resolution I supported. There was one undertaking that I had to fulfill while yet in Delhi. I had to write a letter to the Viceroy. This was no easy thing for me. I felt it my duty both in the interests of the Government and of the people to explain therein how and why I attended the conference, and to state clearly what the people expected from Government.

In the letter I expressed my regret for the exclusion from the conference of leaders like Lokamanya Tilak and the Ali Brothers, and stated the people's minimum political demand as also the demands of the Muslims on account of the situation created by the war. I asked for permission to publish the letter, and the Viceroy gladly gave it.

1. *tragedy: an event causing great suffering; destruction, and distress*
2. *shrinking: become or make smaller in size or amount; contract; become smaller as a result of being immersed in water*
3. *taboo: a social or religious custom placing prohibition or restriction on a particular thing or person*

The letter had to be sent to Simla, where the Viceroy had gone immediately after the conference. The letter had for me considerable importance, and sending it by post would have meant delay[1]. I wanted to save time, and yet I was not inclined to send it by any messenger I came across. I wanted some pure man to carry it and hand it personally at the Viceregal Lodge. Dinabandhu Andrews and Principal Rudra suggested the name of the good Reverend. Ireland of the Cambridge Mission. He agreed to carry the letter if he might read it and if it appealed to him as good. I had no objection as the letter was by no means private. He read it, liked it and expressed his willingness to carry out the mission. I offered him the second class fare, but he declined it saying he was accustomed to travelling intermediate. This he did though it was a night journey. His simplicity and his straight and plainspoken manner captivated[2] me. The letter thus delivered at the hands of a pure-minded man had, as I thought, the desired result. It eased my mind and cleared my way.

The other part of my obligation consisted in raising recruits. Where could I make a beginning except in Kheda? And whom could I invite to be the first recruits except my own co-workers? So as soon as I reached Nadiad, I had a conference with Vallabhbhai and other friends. Some of them could not easily take to the proposal. Those who liked the proposal had misgivings[3] about its success. There was no love lost between the Government and the classes to which I wanted to make my appeal. The bitter experience they had had of the Government officials was still fresh in their memory.

And yet they were in favour of starting work. As soon as I set about my task, my eyes were opened. My optimism received a rude shock. Whereas during the revenue campaign the people readily offered their carts free of charge, and two volunteers came forth when one was needed, it was difficult now to get a cart even on hire, to say nothing of volunteers. But we would not be dismayed. We decided to dispense with the use of carts and to do our journeys on foot. At this rate we had to trudge about twenty miles a day. If carts were not forthcoming, it was idle to expect people to feed us. It was hardly proper to ask for food. So it was decided that every volunteer must carry his food in his satchel[4]. No bedding or sheet was necessary as it was summer.

We had meetings wherever we went. People did attend, but hardly one or two would offer themselves as recruits. 'You are a votary of Ahimsa,

1. *delay: become or cause to become late or slow*
2. *captivated: attract and hold the interest and attention of; charm*
3. *misgivings: a feeling of doubt of apprehension about something*
4. *satchel: a shoulder bag with a long strap, used especially for school books*

how can you ask us to take up arms?' 'What good has Government done for India to deserve our co-operation?' These and similar questions used to be put to us.

However, our steady work began to tell. Quite a number of names were registered, and we hoped that we should be able to have a regular supply as soon as the first batch was sent. I had already begun to confer with the Commissioner as to where the recruits were to be accommodated.

The Commissioners in every division were holding conferences on the Delhi model. One such was held in Gujarat. My co-workers and I were invited to it. We attended, but I felt there was even less place for me here than at Delhi. In this atmosphere of servile submission I felt ill at ease. I spoke somewhat at length. I could say nothing to please the officials, and had certainly one or two hard things to say.

I used to issue leaflets asking people to enlist as recruits. One of the arguments I had used was distasteful to the Commissioner: 'Among the many misdeeds of the British rule in India, history will look upon the Act depriving a whole nation of arms as the blackest. If we want the Arms Act to be repealed, if we want to learn the use of arms, here is a golden[1] opportunity. If the middle classes render voluntary help to Government in the hour of its trial, distrust will disappear, and the ban on possessing arms will be withdrawn.' The Commissioner referred to this and said that he appreciated my presence in the conference in spite of the differences between us. And I had to justify my standpoint[2] as courteously[3] as I could.

Here is the letter to the Viceroy referred to above:

'As you are aware, after careful consideration, I felt constrained to convey to Your Excellency that I could not attend the Conference for reasons stated in the letter of the 26th instant (April), but after the interview you were good enough to grant me, I persuaded myself to join it, if for no other cause, then certainly out of my great regard for yourself. One of my reasons for abstention and perhaps the strongest was that Lokamanya Tilak, Mrs. Besant and the Ali Brothers, whom I regard as among the most powerful leaders of public opinion, were not invited to the Conference. I still feel that it was a grave blunder[4] not to have asked them, and I respectfully suggest that blunder might be possibly repaired

1. *golden: made of, colored like, or shining like gold*
2. *courteously: courteous behavior; a polite speech or action, especially one required by convention*
3. *standpoint: an attitude towards a particular issue*
4. *blunder: a stupid or careless mistake*

if these leaders were invited to assist the Government by giving it the benefit of their advice at the Provincial Conferences, which I understand are to follow. I venture to submit that no Government can afford to disregard the leaders, who represent the large masses of the people as these do, even though they may hold views fundamentally different. At the same time it gives me pleasure to be able to say that the views of all parties were permitted to be freely expressed at the Committees of the Conference. For my part, I purposely refrained from stating my views at the Committee at which I had the honour of serving, or at the Conference itself. I felt that I could best serve the objects of the Conference by simply tendering[1] my support to the resolutions submitted to it, and this I have done without any reservation. I hope to translate the spoken word into action as early as the Government can see its way to accept my offer, which I am submitting simultaneously herewith in a separate letter.

'I recognize that in the hour of its danger we must give, as we have decided to give, ungrudging and unequivocal support to the Empire of which we aspire in the near future to be partners in the same sense as the Dominions[2] overseas[3]. But it is the simple truth that our response is due to the expectation that our goal will be reached all the more speedily. On that account, even as performance of duty automatically confers a corresponding right, people are entitled to believe that the imminent reforms[4] alluded to in your speech will embody the main general principles of the Congress-League Scheme, and I am sure that it is this faith which has enabled many members of the Conference to tender to the Government their full-hearted co-operation.

'If I could make my countrymen retrace their steps. I would make them withdraw all the Congress resolutions, and not whisper "Home Rule" or "Responsible Government" during the pendency of the war. I would make India offer all her able-bodied sons as a sacrifice to the Empire at its critical moment, and I know that India, by this very act, would become the most favoured partner in the Empire, and racial distinctions would become a thing of the past. But practically the whole of educated India has decided to take a less effective course, and it is no longer possible to say that educated India does not exercise any influence on the masses. I have been coming into most intimate touch with the

1. *tendering: offer or present formally; make a formal written offer to carry out work, supply goods, etc. for a stated fixed price*
2. *overseas: in or to a foreign country*
3. *Dominions: a self-governing territory of the [British] commonwealth*
4. *reforms: make changes in to relinquish an immoral or criminal lifestyle*

ryots ever since my return from South Africa to India, and I wish to assure you that the desire for Home Rule has widely penetrated them. I was present at the sessions of the last Congress, and I was a party to the resolution session that full Responsible Government should be granted to British India within a period to be fixed definitely by a Parliamentary Statute. I admit that it is a bold step to take, but I feel sure that nothing less than a definite vision of Home Rule to be realized in the shortest possible time will satisfy the Indian people. I know that there are many in India who consider no sacrifice as too great in order to achieve the end, and they are wakeful enough to realize that they must be equally prepared to sacrifice themselves for the Empire in which they hope and desire to reach their final status. It follows then that we can but accelerate our journey to the goal by silently and simply devoting ourselves heart and soul to the work of delivering the Empire from the threatening danger. It will be national suicide not to recognize this elementary truth. We must perceive that, if we serve to save the Empire, we have in that very act secured Home Rule.

'Whilst, therefore, it is clear to me that we should give to the Empire every available man for its defence, I fear that I cannot say the same thing about financial assistance. My intimate intercourse with the ryots convinces me that India has already donated to the Imperial[1] Exchequer beyond her capacity. I know that in making this statement I am voicing the opinion of the majority of my countrymen.

'The conference means for me, and I believe for many of us, a definite step in the consecration of our lives to the common cause, but ours is a peculiar position. We are today outside the partnership. Ours is a consecration[2] based on hope of better future. I should be untrue[3] to you and to my country if I did not clearly and unequivocally[4] tell you what that hope is. I do not bargain for its fulfillment, but you should know that disappointment of hope means disillusion.

'There is one thing I may not omit. You have appealed to us to sink domestic differences. If the appeal involves the toleration of tyranny and wrongdoing on the part of officials, I am powerless to respond. I shall resist organized tyranny to the uttermost. The appeal must be to the officials that they do not ill-treat a single soul, and that they consult and respect popular opinion as never before. In Champaran by resisting

1. *Imperial: rule by an emperor*
2. *untrue: not faithful or loyal*
3. *consecration: make or declare sacred; make into the body and blood of christ*
4. *unequivocally: leaving no doubt; unambiguous*

an age-long tyranny[1] I have shown the ultimate sovereignty of British justice. In Kheda a population that was cursing the Government now feels that it, and not the Government, is the power when it is prepared to suffer for the truth it represents. It is, therefore, losing its bitterness and is saying to itself that the Government must be a Government for people, for it tolerates orderly and respectful disobedience where injustice is felt. Thus Champaran and Kheda affairs are my direct, definite and special contribution to the war. Ask me to suspend my activities in that direction and you ask me to suspend my life. If I could popularize the use of soul-force, which is but another name for love-force, in place of brute force, I know that I could present you with an India that could defy the whole world to do its worst. In season and out of season, therefore, I shall discipline myself to express in my life this eternal law of suffering, and present it for acceptance to those who care, and if I take part in any other activity, the motive is to show the matchless superiority of that law.

'Lastly, I would like you to ask His Majesty's Ministers to give definite assurance about Mohammedan States. I am sure you know that every Mohammedan is deeply interested in them. As a Hindu. I cannot be indifferent to their cause. Their sorrows must be our sorrows. In the most scrupulous regard for the rights of those States and of the Muslim sentiment as to their places of worship, and your just and timely treatment of India's claim to Home Rule lies the safety of the Empire. I write this, because I love the English nation, and I wish to evoke in every Indian the loyalty of Englishmen.'

1. *tyranny: a state under cruel and oppressive government*

CHAPTER 152

NEAR DEATH'S DOOR

I very nearly ruined my constitution during the recruiting campaign. In those days my food principally consisted of groundnut butter and lemons. I knew that it was possible to eat too much butter and injure one's health, and yet I allowed myself to do so. This gave me a slight attack of dysentery. I did not take serious notice of this, and went that evening to the Ashram, as was my wont every now and then. I scarcely took any medicine in those days. I thought I should get well if I skipped a meal, and indeed I felt fairly free from trouble as I omitted[1] the morning meal next day. I knew, however, that to be entirely free I must prolong my fast and, if I ate anything at all, I should have nothing but fruit juices.

There was some festival that day, and although I had told Kasturbai that I should have nothing for my midday[2] meal, she tempted me and I succumbed. As I was under a vow of taking no milk or milk products, she had specially prepared for me a sweet wheaten porridge with oil added to it instead of *ghi*. She had reserved too a bowlful of *mung* for me. I was fond of these things, and I readily took them, hoping that without coming to grief I should eat just enough to please Kasturbai and to satisfy my palate. But the devil had been only waiting for an opportunity. Instead of eating very little I had my fill of the meal. This was sufficient invitation to the angel of death. Within an hour the dysentery appeared in acute form.

The same evening I had to go back to Nadiad. I walked with very great difficulty to the Sabarmati station, a distance of only ten furlongs. Sjt. Vallabhbhai, who joined me at Ahmedabad, saw that I was unwell, but I did not allow him to guess how unbearable[3] the pain was.

We reached Nadiad at about ten o'clock. The Hindu Anathashram where we had our headquarters was only half a mile from the station; but it was as good as ten for me. I somehow managed to reach the quarters, but the griping pain was steadily increasing. Instead of using the usual

1. *omitted: leave out or exclude; fail to do*
2. *midday: noon*
3. *unbearable: not able to be endured or tolerated*

latrine which was a long way off, I asked for a commode to be placed in the adjoining room. I was ashamed to have to ask for this, but there was no escape. Sjt. Fulchand immediately procured a commode. All the friends surrounded me deeply concerned. They were all love and attention, but they could not relieve my pain. And my obstinacy added to their helplessness. I refused all medical aid. I would take no medicine, but preferred to suffer the penalty for my folly. So they looked on in helpless dismay. I must have had thrity or forty motions in twenty-four hours. I fasted, not taking even fruit juices in the beginning. The appetite had all gone. I had thought all along that I had an iron frame, but I found that my body had now become a lump of clay[1]. It had lost all power of resistance. Dr. Kanuga came and pleaded with me to take medicine. I declined. He offered to give me an injection. I declined that too. My ignorance about injections was in those days quite ridiculous. I believed that an injection must be some kind of serum. Later I discovered that the injection that the doctor suggested was a vegetable substance, but the discovery was too late to be of use. The motions still continued, leaving me completely exhausted. The exhaustion brought on a delirious fever. The friends got more nervous, and called in more doctors. But what could they do with a patient who would not listen to them?

Sheth Ambalal with his good wife came down to Nadiad, conferred with my co-workers and removed me with the greatest care to his Mirzapur bungalow in Ahmedabad. It was impossible for anyone to receive more loving and selfless service than I had the privilege of having during this illness. But a sort of low fever persisted, wearing away my body from day to day, I felt that the illness was bound to be prolonged and possibly fatal[2]. Surrounded as I was with all the love and attention that could be showered on me under Sheth Ambalal's roof, I began to get restless and urged him to remove me to the Ashram. He had to yield to my importunity[3].

Whilst I was thus tossing on the bed of pain in the Ashram, Sjt. Vallabhbhai brought the news that Germany had been completely defeated, and that the Commissioner had sent word that recruiting was no longer necessary. The news that I had no longer to worry myself about recruiting came as a very great relief.

I had now been trying hydropathy which gave some relief, but it was a hard job to build up the body. The many medical advisers overwhelmed

1. *clay: a stiff, sticky fine-grained impermeable earth that can be molded when wet and baked to make bricks and pottery*
2. *fatal: causing death; leading to failure or disaster*
3. *importunity: bothering to the point of annoying*

me with advice, but I could not persuade myself to take anything. Two or three suggested meat broth as a way out of the milk vow, and cited authorities from Ayurveda in support of their advice. One of them strongly recommended eggs. But for all of them I had but one answer-no.

For me the question of diet was not one to be determined on the authority of the Shastras. It was one interwoven with my course of life which is guided by principles no longer depending upon outside authority. I had no desire to live at the cost of them. How could I relinquish a principle in respect of myself, when I had enforced it relentlessly in respect of my wife, children and friends?

This protracted[1] and first long illness in my life thus afforded[2] me a unique opportunity to examine my principles and to test them. One night I gave myself up to despair. I felt that I was at death's door. I sent word to Anasuyabehn. She ran down to the Ashram. Vallabhbhai came up with Dr. Kanuga, who felt my pulse and said 'Your pulse is quite good. I see absolutely no danger. This is a nervous breakdown due to extreme weakness.' But I was far from being reassured. I passed the night without sleep.

The morning broke without death coming. But I could not get rid of the feeling that the end was near, and so I began to devote all my waking hours to listening to the Gita being read to me by the inmates of the Ashram. I was incapable of reading. I was hardly inclined to talk. The slightest talk meant a strain on the brain. All interest in living had ceased, as I have never liked to live for the sake of living. It was such an agony[3] to live on in that helpless state, doing nothing, receiving the service of friends and co-workers, and watching the body slowly wearing away.

Whilst I lay thus ever expectant of death, Dr. Talvalkar came one day with a strange creature. He hailed from Maharashtra. He was not known to fame, but the moment I saw him I found that he was a crank like myself. He had come to try his treatment on me. He had almost finished his course of studies in the Grant Medical College without taking the degree. Later I came to know that he was a member of the Brahmo Samaj. Sjt. Kelkar, for that is his name, is a man of an independent and obstinate temperament. He swears by the ice treatment, which he wanted to try on me. We gave him the name of 'Ice Doctor'. He is quite confident that he has discovered certain things which have escaped qualified[4] doctors.

1. *protracted: have sufficient money, time, or means for; be able to do something without risk of adverse consequences*
2. *afforded: lasting for a period longer than expected*
3. *agony: extreme suffering*
4. *qualified: certified as being trained to perform a job*

It is a pity both for him and me that he has not been able to infect me with his faith in his system. I believe in his system up to a certain point, but I am afraid he has been hasty in arriving at certain conclusions.

But whatever may be the merits of his discoveries, I allowed him to experiment on my body. I did not mind external treatment. The treatment consisted in the application of ice all over the body. Whilst I am unable to endorse his claim about the effect his treatment had on me, it certainly infused in me a new hope and a new energy, and the mind naturally reacted on the body. I began to have an appetite[1], and to have a gentle walk for five to ten minutes. He now suggested a reform in my diet. Said he: 'I assure you that you will have more energy and regain your strength quicker if you take raw eggs. Eggs are as harmless as milk. They certainly cannot come under the category of meat. And do you know that all eggs are not fertilized[2]? There are sterilized eggs on the markket.' I was not, however, prepared to take even the sterilized eggs. But the improvement was enough to give me interest in public activities.

1. *appetite: a natural desire to satisfy a bodily need, especially for food*
2. *fertilized: cause to develop a new individual by introducing male reproductive material*

CHAPTER 153

THE ROWLATT BILLS AND MY DILEMMA

Friends and doctors assured me that I should recuperate quicker by a change to Matheran, so I went there. But the water at Matheran being very hard, it made my stay there extremely difficult. As a result of the attack of the dysentery[1] that I had, my anal[2] tract had become extremely tender, and owing to fissures, I felt an excruciating pain at the time of evacuation, so that the very idea of eating filled me with dread. Before the week was over, I had to flee from Matheran. Shankarlal Banker now constituted himself the guardian of my health, and pressed me to consult Dr. Dalal. Dr. Dalal was called accordingly. His capacity for taking instantaneous decisions captured me.

He said: 'I cannot rebuild your body unless you take milk. If in addition you would take iron and arsenic[3] injections, I would guarantee fully to renovate your constitution.'

'You can give me the injections,' I replied, 'but milk is a different question; I have a vow against it.'

'What exactly is the nature of your vow?' the doctor inquired.

I told him the whole history and the reasons behind my vow, how, since I had come to know that the cow and the buffalo were subjected to the process of *phooka*, I had conceived a strong disgust for milk. Moreover, I had always held that milk is not the natural diet of man. I had therefore abjured its use altogether. Kasturbai was standing near my bed listening all the time to this conversation.

'But surely you cannot have any objection to goat's milk then,' she interposed.

The doctor too took up the strain. 'If you will take goat's milk, it will be enough for me,' he said.

I succumbed. My intense eagerness to take up the Satyagraha fight had created in me a strong desire to live, and so I contented myself with adhering[4] to the letter of my vow only, and sacrificed its spirit. For

1. *dysentery: intestinal disease*
2. *anal: of, relating to, or situated near the anus*
3. *arsenic: the chemical element of atomic number 33, a brittle steel-gray semi-metal with many highly poisonous compounds*
4. *adhering: stick fast to*

although I had only the milk of the cow and the she buffalo in mind when I took the vow, by natural implication it covered the milk of all animals. Nor could it be right for me to use milk at all, so long as I held that milk is not the natural diet of man. Yet knowing all this I agreed to take goat's milk. The will to live proved stronger than the devotion to truth, and for once the votary of truth compromised his sacred ideal by his eagerness to take up the Satyagraha fight. The memory of this action even now rankles in my breast and fills me with remorse, and I am constantly thinking how to give up goat's milk. But I cannot yet free myself from that subtlest of temptations, the desire to serve, which still holds me.

My experience in dietetics are dear to me as a part of my researches in Ahimsa. They give me recreation and joy. But my use of goat's milk today troubles me not from the viewpoint of dietetic Ahimsa so much as from that of truth, being no less than a breach of pledge. It seems to me that I understand the ideal of truth better than that of a Ahimsa, and my experience tells me that, if I let go my hold of truth, I shall never be able to solve the riddle of Ahimsa. The ideal of truth requires that vows taken should be fulfilled in the spirit as well as in the letter. In the present case I killed the spirit the soul of my vow by adhering to its outer form only, and that is what galls me. But in spite of this clear knowledge I cannot see my way straight before me. In other words, perhaps, I have not the courage to follow the straight course. Both at bottom mean one and the same thing, for doubt[1] is invariably[2] the result of want or weakness of faith. 'Lord, give me faith' is, therefore, my prayer day and night.

Soon after I began taking goat's milk, Dr. Dalal performed on me a successful operation for fissures. As I recuperated[3], my desire to live revived, especially because God had kept work in store for me.

I had hardly begun to feel my way towards recovery, when I happened casually to read in the papers the Rowlatt Committee's report which had just been published. Its recommendations startled me. Shankarlal Banker and Umar Sobani approached me with the suggestion that I should take some prompt action in the matter. In about a month I went to Ahmedabad. I mentioned my apprehensions[4] to Vallabhbhai, who used to come to see me almost daily. 'Something must be done,' said

1. *doubt: a feeling of uncertainty or lack of conviction*
2. *invariably: never changing*
3. *recuperated: recover from illness or exertion*
4. *apprehensions: anxious or fearful anticipation*

I to him. 'But what can we do in the circumstances?' he asked in reply. I answered, 'If even a handful of men can be found to sign the pledge of resistance, and the proposed measure is passed into law in defiance of it, we ought to offer Satyagraha at once. If I was not laid up like this, I should give battle against it all alone, and expect others to follow suit. But in my present helpless condition I feel myself to be altogether unequal[1] to the task.'

As a result of this talk, it was decided to call a small meeting of such persons as were in touch with me. The recommendations of the Rowlatt Committee seemed to me to be altogether unwarranted by the evidence published in its report, and were, I felt, such that no self-respecting people could submit to them.

The proposed conference was at last held at the Ashram. Hardly a score of persons had been invited to it. So far as I remember, among those who attended were, besides Vallabhbhai, Shrimati Sarojini Naidu, Mr. Horniman, the late Mr. Umar Sobani, Sjt. Shankarlal Banker and Shrimati Anasuyabehn. The Satyagraha pledge was drafted at this meeting, and, as far as I recollect, was signed by all present. I was not editing any journal at that time, but I used occasionally to ventilate my views through the daily press. I followed the practice on this occasion. Shankarlal Banker took up the agitation in right earnest, and for the first time I got an idea of his wonderful capacity for organization and sustained[2] work.

As all hope of any of the existing institutions adopting a novel weapon like Satyagraha seemed to me to be in vain, a separate body called the Satyagraha Sabha was established at my instance. Its principal members were drawn from Bombay where, therefore, its headquarters were fixed. The intending covenanters began to sign the Satyagraha pledge in large numbers, bulletins[3] were issued, and popular meetings began to be held everywhere recalling[4] all the familiar features of the Kheda campaign.

I became the president of the Satyagraha Sabha. I soon found that there was not likely to be much chance of agreement between myself and the intelligentsia composing this Sabha. My insistence on the use of Gujarati in the Sabha, as also some of my other methods of work that would appear to be peculiar, caused them no small worry and

1. *unequal: not having the ability or resources to meet a challenge*
2. *sustained: keep going over time or continuously*
3. *bulletins: a short official statement or summary of news; a regular newsletter or report*
4. *recalling: remember; cause one to remember or think of; bring back the memory of someone or something to*

embarrassment. I must say to their credit, however, that most of them generously put up with my idiosyncrasies[1].

But from the very beginning it seemed clear to me that the Sabha was not likely to live long. I could see that already my emphasis on truth and Ahimsa had begun to be disliked by some of its members. Nevertheless in its early stages our new activity went on at full blast, and the movement gathered head rapidly.

1. *idiosyncrasies: a mode of behaviour or way of thought peculiar to an individual*

CHAPTER 154

THAT WONDERFUL SPECTACLE!

Thus, while on the one hand the agitation against the Rowlatt Committee's report gathered volume and intensity, on the other the Government grew more and more determined to give effect to its recommendations, and the Rowlatt Bill was published. I have attended the proceeding of India's legislative chamber only once in my life, and that was on the occasion of the debate on this Bill. Shastriji delivered an impassioned speech, in which he uttered a solemn note of warning to the Government. The Viceroy seemed to be listening spell-bound, his eyes riveted on Shastriji as the latter poured forth the hot stream of his eloquence[1]. For the moment it seemed to me as if the Viceroy could not but be deeply moved by it, it was so true and so full of feeling.

But you can wake a man only if he is really asleep; no effort that you may make will produce any effect upon him if he is merely pretending sleep. That was precisely the Government's position. It was anxious only to go through the farce[2] of legal formality. Its decision had already been made. Shastriji's solemn warning was, therefore, entirely lost upon the Government.

In these circumstances mine could only be a cry in the wilderness. I earnestly pleaded with the Viceroy. I addressed him private letters as also public letters, in the course of which I clearly told him that the Government's action left me no other course except to resort to Sayagraha. But it was all in vain.

The Bill had not yet been gazetted as an Act. I was in a very weak condition, but when I received an invitation from Madras I decided to take the risk of the long journey. I could not at that time sufficiently raise my voice at meetings. The incapacity to address meetings standing still abides[3]. My entire frame would shake, and heavy throbbing[4] would start on an attempt to speak standing for any length of time.

I have ever felt at home in the south. Thanks to my South African work I felt I had some sort of special right over the Tamils and Telugus

1. *eloquence: fluent or persuasive speaking or writing*
2. *farce: a comic dramatic work or genre using buffoonery and horseplay and typically including ludicrously improbable situations, the debate turned into a drunken farce*
3. *abides: endure*
4. *throbbing: beat or sound with a strong, regular rhythm; pulsate*

and the good people of the south have never belied my belief. The invitation had come over the signature of the late Sjt. Kasturi Ranga Iyengar. But the man behind the invitation, as I subsequently learnt on my way to Madras, was Rajagopalachari. This might be said to be my first acquaintance with him; at any rate this was the first time that we came to know each other personally.

Rajagopalachari had then only recently left Salem to settle down for legal practice in Madras at the pressing invitation of friends like the late Sjt. Kasturi Ranga Iyengar, and that with a view to taking a more active part in public life. It was with him that we had put up in Madras. This discovery I made only after we had stayed with him for a couple of days. For, since the bungalow that we were staying in belonged to Sjt. Kasturi Ranga Iyengar. I was under the impression that we were his guests. Mahadev Desai, however, corrected me. He very soon formed a close acquaintance with Rajagopalachari, who, from his innate shyness, kept himself constantly in the background. But Mahadev put me on my guard. 'You should cultivate this man' he said to me one day.

And so I did. We daily discussed together plans of the fight, but beyond the holding of public meetings I could not then think of any other programme[1]. I felt myself at a loss to discover how to offer civil disobedience against the Rowlatt Bill if it was finally passed into law. One could disobey it only if the Government gave one the opportunity for it. Failing that, could we civilly disobey other laws? And if so, where was the line to be drawn? These and a host of similar questions formed the theme[2] of these discussions of ours.

Sjt. Kasturi Ranga Iyengar called together a small conference of leaders to thrash out the matter. Among those who took a conspicuous[3] part in it was Sjt. Vijayaraghavachari. He suggested that I should draw up a comprehensive manual of the science of Satyagraha, embodying even minute details. I felt the task to be beyond my capacity, and I confessed as much to him.While these cogitations were still going on, news was received that the Rowlatt Bill had been published as an Act. That night I fell asleep while thinking over the question. Towards the small hours of the morning I woke up somewhat earlier than usual. I was still in that twilight[4] condition between sleep and consciousness when suddenly the idea broke upon me—it was as if in a dream. Early in the morning I related the whole story to Rajagopalachari.

1. *programme: a planned series of events; a set of related measures or activities with a long-term aim*
2. *theme: a subject or topic on which a person speaks, writes, or thinks; the first major constituent of a clause, indicating the subject matter; contrasted with rheme*
3. *conspicuous: clearly visible; attracting notice or attention*
4. *twilight: the soft glowing light from the sky when the sun is below the horizon, caused by the reflection of the sun's rays from the atmosphere*

'The idea came to me last night in a dream that we should call upon the country to observe a general hartal. Satyagraha is a process of self-purification[1], and ours is a sacred fight, and it seems to me to be in the fitness[2] of things that it should be commenced with an act of self-purification. Let all the people of India, therefore, suspend their business on that day and observe the day as one of fasting and prayer. The Musalmans may not fast for more than one day; so the duration of the fast should be twenty-four hours. It is very difficult to say whether all the provinces would respond to this appeal of ours or not, but I feel fairly sure of Bombay, Madras, Bihar and Sindh. I think we should have every reason to feel satisfied even if all these places observe the hartal fittingly.'

Rajagopalachari was at once taken up with my suggestion. Other friends too welcomed it when it was communicated to them later. I drafted a brief appeal. The date of the hartal was first fixed on the 30th March 1919, but was subsequently changed to 6th April. The people thus had only a short notice of the hartal. As the work had to be started at once, it was hardly possible to give longer notice.

But who knows how it all came about? The whole of India from one end to the other, towns as well as villages, observed a complete hartal on that day. It was a most wonderful spectacle.

1. *purification: remove contaminants from*

2. *fitness: the state of being fit*

CHAPTER 155

THAT MEMORABLE WEEK! – I

After a short tour in South India I reached Bombay, I think on the 4th April, having received a wire from Sjt. Shankarlal Banker asking me to be present there for the 6th of April celebrations.

But in the meanwhile Delhi had already observed the *hartal* on the 30th March. The word of the late Swami Shraddhanandji and Hakim Ajmal Khan Saheb was law there. The wire about the postponement of the *hartal* till the 6th of April had reached there too late. Delhi had never witnessed a *hartal* like that before. Hindus and Musalmans seemed united like one man. Swami Shraddhanandji was invited to deliver a speech in the Jumma Masjid which he did. All this was more than the authorities could bear. The police checked the *hartal* procession as it was proceeding towards the railway[1] station, and opened fire, causing a number of casualties, and the reign of repression commenced in Delhi. Shraddhanandji urgently[2] summoned me to Delhi. I wired back, saying I would start for Delhi immediately after the 6th of April celebrations were over in Bombay.

The story of happenings in Delhi was repeated with variations in Lahore and Amritsar. From Amritsar Drs. Satyapal and Kitchlu had sent me a pressing invitation to go there. I was altogether unacquainted with them at at that time, but I communicated to them my intention[3] to visit Amritsar after Delhi.

On the morning of the 6th the citizens of Bombay flocked to the Chowpati for a bath in the sea, after which they moved on in a procession to Thakurdvar. The procession included a fair sprinkling of women and children, while the Musalmans joined it in large numbers. From Thakurdvar some of us who were in the procession were taken by the Musalman friends to a mosque[4] near by, where Mrs. Naidu and myself were persuaded to deliver speeches. Sjt. Vithaldas Jerajani proposed that we should then and there administer the Swadeshi and Hindu-Muslim

1. *railway: a system of such tracks with the trains, organization, and personnel required for its working*
2. *urgently: requiring immediate action or attention*
3. *intention: an aim or plan; the action or fact of intending; a person's, especially a man's designs in respect to marriage*
4. *mosque: a muslim place of worship*

unity pledges to the people, but I resisted the proposal on the ground that pledges should not be administered or taken in precipitate hurry, and that we should be satisfied with what was already being done by the people. A pledge once taken, I argued, must not be broken afterwards; therefore it was necessary that the implications[1] of the Swadeshi pledge should be clearly understood, and the grave responsibility entailed by the pledge regarding Hindu-Muslim unity fully realized by all concerned. In the end I suggested that those who wanted to take the pledges should again assemble on the following morning for the purpose.

Needless to say the *hartal* in Bombay was a complete success. Full preparation had been made for starting civil disobedience. Two or three things had been discussed in this connection. It was decided that civil disobedience might be offered in respect of such laws only as easily lent themselves to being disobeyed by the masses. The salt tax was extremely unpopular[2] and a powerful movement had been for some time past going on to secure its repeal. I therefore suggested that the people might prepare salt from sea-water in their own houses in disregard of the salt laws. My other suggestion was about the sale of proscribed literature. Two of my books, *viz.*, *Hind Swaraj* and *Sarvodaya* (Gujarati adaptation of Ruskin's *Unto This Last*), which had been already proscribed, came handy for this purpose. To print and sell them openly seemed to be the easiest way of offering civil disobedience. A sufficient number of copies of the books was therefore printed, and it was arranged to sell them at the end of the monster meeting that was to be held that evening after the breaking of the fast.

On the evening of the 6th an army of volunteers issued forth accordingly with this prohibited literature to sell it among the people. Both Shrimati Sarojini Devi and I went out in cars. All the copies were soon sold out. The proceeds of the sale were to be utilized for furthering the civil disobedience campaign. Both these books were priced at four annas per copy, but I hardly remember anybody having purchased them from me at their face value merely. Quite a large number of people simply poured out all the cash that was in their pockets[3] to purchase their copy. Five and ten rupee notes just flew out to cover the price of a single copy, while in one case I remember having sold a copy for fifty rupees! It was duly explained to the people that they were liable to be arrested and

1. *implications: the implicit conclusion that can be drawn from something; a likely consequence*
2. *unpopular: not liked or popular*
3. *pockets: a small bag sewn into or on clothing so as to form part of it, used for carrying small articles; a pouch like compartment providing separate storage space; [informal] one's financial resources*

imprisoned for purchasing the proscribed literature. But for the moment they had shed all fear of jail-going.

It was subsequently learnt that the Government had conveniently taken the view that the books that had been proscribed by it had not in fact been sold, and that what we had sold was not held as coming under the definition of proscribed literature. The reprint was held by the Government to be a new edition of the books that had been proscribed, and to sell them did not constitute an offence under the law. This news caused general disappointment.

The next morning another meeting was held for the administration of the pledges with regard to Swadeshi and Hindu-Muslim unity. Vithaldas Jerajani for the first time realized that all is not gold that glitters. Only a handful of persons came. I distinctly remember some of the sisters who were present on that occasion. The men who attended were also very few. I had already drafted the pledge and brought it with me. I thoroughly explained its meaning to those present before I administered it to them. The paucity of the attendance neither pained nor surprised me, for I have noticed this characteristic difference in the popular attitude partiality for exciting work, dislike for quiet constructive effort. The difference has persisted to this day.

But I shall have to devote to this subject a chapter by itself. To return to the story. On the night of the 7th I started for Delhi and Amritsar. On reaching Mathura on the 8th I first heard rumours about my probable arrest. At the next stoppage after Mathura, Acharya Gidvani came to meet me, and gave me definite news that I was to be arrested, and offered his services to me if I should need them. I thanked him for the offer, assuring him that I would not fail to avail myself of it, if and when I felt it necessary.

Before the train had reached Palwal railway station, I was served with a written order to the effect that I was prohibited from entering the boundary[1] of the Punjab, as my presence there was likely to result in a disturbance of the peace. I was asked by the police to get down from the train. I refused to do so saying, 'I want to go to the Punjab in response to a pressing invitation not to foment unrest[2], but to allay it. I am therefore sorry that it is not possible for me to comply[3] with this order.'

At last the train reached Palwal. Mahadev was with me. I asked him to proceed to Delhi to convey[4] to Swami Shraddhanandji the news

1. *boundary: a line marking the limits of an area*
2. *unrest: a state of rebellious dissatisfaction and agitation in a group of people: civil unrest; a state of uneasiness or disturbance*
3. *comply: act in accordance with a wish or command*
4. *convey: transport or carry to a place*

about what had happened and to ask the people to remain clam. He was to explain why I had decided to disobey the order served upon me and suffer the penalty for disobeying it, and also why it would spell victory for our side if we could maintain perfect peace in spite of any punishment that might be inflicted upon me.

At Palwal railway station I was taken out of the train and put under police custody. A train from Delhi came in a short time. I was made to enter a third class carriage, the police party accompanying. On reaching Mathura, I was taken to the police barracks, but no police official could tell me as to what they proposed to do with me or where I was to be taken next. Early at 4 o'clock the next morning I was awoken up and put in a goods train that was going towards Bombay. At noon I was again made to get down at Sawai Madhopur. Mr. Bowring, Inspector of Police, who arrived by the mail train from Lahore, now took charge of me. I was put in a first class compartment with him. And from an ordinary prisoner I became a 'gentleman[1]' prisoner. The officer commenced a long panegyric of Sir Michael O'Dwyr. Sir Michael had nothing against me personally, he went on, only he apprehended a disturbance of the peace if I entered the Punjab and so on. In the end he requested me to return to Bombay of my own accord and agree not to cross the frontier of the Punjab. I replied that I could not possibly comply with the order, and that I was not prepared of my own accord to go back. Whereupon the officer, seeing no other course, told me that he would have to enforce law against me. 'But what do you want to do with me?' I asked him. He replied that he himself did not know, but was awaiting further orders. 'For the present,' he said, I am taking you to Bombay.'

We reached Surat. Here I was made over to the charge of another police officer. 'You are now free,' the officer told me when we had reached Bombay. 'It would however be better,' he added, 'if you get down near the Marine Lines where I shall get the train stopped for you. At Colaba there is likely to be a big crowd.' I told him that I would be glad to follow his wish. He was pleased and thanked me for it. Accordingly I alighted[2] at the Marine[3] Lines. The carriage of a friend just happened to be passing by. It took me and left me at Revashankar Jhaveri's place. The friend told me that the news of my arrest had incensed the people and roused them to a pitch of mad frenzy. 'An outbreak is apprehended[4] every minute near Pydhuni, the Magistrate and the police have already arrived there,' he added.

1. *gentleman: a courteous or honourable man*
2. *alighted: descend form public transport*
3. *marine: of, relating to, or produced by the sea*
4. *apprehended: intercept in the course of harmful or illicit action; seize or arrest*

Scarcely had I reached my destination, when Umar Sobani and Anasuyabehn arrived and asked me to motor to Pydhuni at once. 'The people have become impatient, and are very much excited,' they said, 'we cannot pacify them. Your presence alone can do it.'

I got into the car. Near Pydhuni I saw that a huge crowd had gathered. On seeing me the people went mad with joy. A procession was immediately formed, and the sky was rent with the shouts of *Vande mataram* and *Allaho akbar*. At Pydhuni we sighted a body of mounted police. Brickbats were raining down from above. I besought the crowd to be calm, but it seemed as if we should not be able to escape the shower of brickbats. As the procession issued out of Abdur Rahman Street and was about to proceed towards the Crawford Market, it suddenly found itself confronted by a body of the mounted police, who had arrived there to prevent it from proceeding further in the direction of the Fort. The crowd was densely packed. It had almost broken through the police cordon. There was hardly any chance of my voice being heard in that vast concourse[1]. Just then the officer in charge of the mounted police gave the order to disperse the crowd, and at once the mounted party charged upon the crowd brandishing[2] their lances as they went. For a moment I felt that I would be hurt. But my apprehension was groundless, the lances[3] just grazed the car as the lancers swiftly passed by. The ranks of the people were soon broken, and they were thrown into utter confusion, which was soon converted into a rout. Some got trampled[4] under foot, others were badly mauled and crushed. In that seething mass of humanity there was hardly any room for the horses to pass, nor was there an exit by which the people could disperse. So the lancers blindly cut their way through the crowd. I hardly imagine they could see what they were doing. The whole thing presented a most dreadful[5] spectacle. The horsemen and the people were mixed together in mad confusion.

Thus the crowd was dispersed and its progress checked. Our motor was allowed to proceed. I had it stopped before the Commissioner's office, and got down to complain to him about the conduct of the police.

1. *concourse: a large open central area inside or in front of a public building*
2. *brandishing: wave or flourish as a threat or in anger or excitement*
3. *lances: a long weapon with a wooden shaft and a pointed steel head, formerly used by a horseman in charging*
4. *trampled: tread on and crush*
5. *dreadful: anticipate with great apprehension or fear*

CHAPTER 156

THAT MEMORABLE WEEK! – II

So I went to the Commissioner Mr. Griffith's office. All about the staircase leading to the office I saw soldiers armed from top to toe, as though for military action. The verandah was all astir. When I was admitted to the office, I saw Mr. Bowring sitting with Mr. Griffith.

I described to the Commissioner the scenes I had witnessed. He replied briefly: 'I did not want the procession[1] to proceed[2] to the Fort, as a disturbance was inevitable there. And as I saw that the people would not listen to persuasion[3], I could not help ordering the mounted police to charge through the crowd.'

'But,' said I, 'you knew what the consequences must be. The horses were bound to trample on the people. I think it was quite unnecessary to send that contingent[4] of mounted men.'

'You cannot judge that,' said Mr. Griffith. 'We police officers know better than you the effect of your teaching on the people. If we did not start with drastic measures, the situation would pass out of our hands. I tell you that the people are sure to go out of your control. Disobedience of law will quickly appeal to them; it is beyond them to understand the duty of keeping peaceful. I have no doubt about your intentions, but the people will not understand them. They will follow their natural instinct.'

'It is there that I join issue with you,' I replied. 'The people are not by nature violent but peaceful.'

And thus we argued at length. Ultimately Mr. Griffith said, 'But suppose you were convinced that your teaching had been lost on the people, what would you do?'

'I should suspend civil disobedience if I were so convinced.'

'What do you mean? You told Mr. Bowring that you would proceed to the Punjab the moment you were released.'

'Yes, I wanted to do so by the next available train. But it is out of the question today.'

1. *proceed: begin a course of action go on to do something; carry on or continue*
2. *procession: a number of people or vehicles moving forward in an orderly fashion, especially as part of a ceremony; the action of moving in such a way; a relentless succession of people or things*
3. *persuasion: the action of persuading someone to do or believe in something*
4. *contingent: a group of people within a larger group; a body of troops or police sent to join a larger force*

'If you will be patient, the conviction is sure to grow on you. Do you know what is happening in Ahmedabad? And what has happened in Amritsar? People have everywhere gone nearly mad. I am not yet in possession of all the facts. The telegraph wires have been cut in some places. I put it to you that the responsibility for all these disturbances lies on you.'

'I assure you I should readily take it upon myself wherever I discovered it. But I should be deeply pained and surprised, if I found that there were disturbances in Ahmedabad. I cannot answer for Amritsar. I have never been there, no one knows me there. But even about the Punjab I am certain of this much that, had not the Punjab Government prevented my entry into the Punjab, I should have been considerably helpful in keeping the peace there. By preventing me they gave the people unnecessary provocation[1].'

And so we argued on and on. It was impossible for us to agree. I told him that I intended to address a meeting on Chowpati and to ask the people to keep the peace, and took leave of him. The meeting was held on the Chowpati sands. I spoke at length on the duty of non-violence and on the limitations of Satyagraha, and said: 'Satyagraha is essentially a weapon of the truthful. A Satyagrahi is pledged to non-violence, and, unless people observe it in thought, word and deed, I cannot offer[2] mass Satyagraha.'

Anasuyabehn, too, had received news of disturbances in Ahmedabad. Some one had spread a rumour[3] that she also had been arrested. The mill-hands had gone mad over her rumoured arrest, struck work and committed acts of violence, and a sergeant had been done to death.

I proceeded to Ahmedabad. I learnt that an attempt had been made to pull up the rails near the Nadiad railway station, that a Government officer had been murdered in Viramgam, and that Ahmedabad was under martial law. The people were terror-stricken. They had indulged in acts of violence and were being made to pay for them with interest.

A police officer was waiting at the station to escort me to Mr. Pratt, the Commissioner. I found him in a state of rage[4]. I spoke to him gently, and expressed my regret for the disturbances. I suggested that martial law was unnecessary, and declared my readiness to co-operate in all efforts to restore peace. I asked for permission to hold a public meeting on the grounds of the Sabarmati Ashram. The proposal appealed to him, and

1. *provocation: the action of provoking; action or speech that provokes; an action or speech held to be likely to prompt physical retaliation*
2. *offer: present or proffer*
3. *rumour: a currently circulating story or report of unverified or doubtful truth*
4. *rage: violent uncontrollable anger; violent anger associated with conflict arising form a particular context: air rage; the violent action of a natural agency*

the meeting was held, I think, on Sunday, the 13th of April, and martial law was withdrawn the same day or the day after. Addressing the meeting, I tried to bring home to the people the sense of their wrong, declared a penitential fast of three days for myself, appealed to the people to go on a similar fast for a day, and suggested to those who had been guilty of acts of violence to confess their guilt.

I saw my duty as clear as daylight. It was unbearable for me to find that the labourers, amongst whom I had spent a good deal of my time, whom I had served, and from whom I had expected better things, had taken part in the riots[1], and I felt I was a sharer in their guilt[2].

Just as I suggested to the people to confess their guilt, I suggested to the Government to condone the crimes. Neither accepted my suggestion.

The late Sir Ramanbhai and other citizens of Ahmedabad came to me with an appeal to suspend Satyagraha. The appeal was needless, for I had already made up my mind to suspend Satyagraha so long as people had not learnt the lesson of peace. The friends went away happy.

There were, however, others who were unhappy over the decision. They felt that, if I expected peace everywhere and regarded it as a condition precedent[3] to launching Satyagraha, mass Satyagraha would be an impossibility. I was sorry to disagree with them. If those amongst whom I worked, and whom I expected to be prepared for non-violence and self-suffering, could not be non-violent, Satyagraha was certainly impossible. I was firmly of opinion that those who wanted to lead the people to Satyagraha ought to be able to keep the people within the limited non-violence expected of them. I hold the same opinion even today.

1. *riots: a violent disturbance of the peace by a crowd; rowdy behavior*
2. *guilt: the fact of having committed an offence or crime*
3. *precedent: an earlier event or action serving as an example or guide; law a previous case or legal decision that may be or must be followed in subsequent similar cases*

CHAPTER 157

'A HIMALAYAN MISCALCULATION'

Almost immediately after the Ahmedabad meeting I went to Nadiad. It was here that I first used the expression 'Himalayan miscalculation' which obtained such a wide currency afterwards. Even at Ahmedabad I had begun to have a dim perception of my mistake. But when I reached Nadiad and saw the actual state of things there and heard reports about a large number of people from Kheda district having been arrested, it suddenly dawned upon me that I had committed a grave error in calling upon the people in the Kheda district and elsewhere to launch upon civil disobedience prematurely, as it now seemed to me. I was addressing a public meeting. My confession brought down upon me no small amount of ridicule. But I have never regretted having made that confession. For I have always held that it is only when one sees one's own mistakes with a convex[1] lens, and does just the reverse in the case of others, that one is able to arrive at a just relative estimate of the two. I further believe that a scrupulous and conscientious observance of this rule is necessary for one who wants to be a Satyagrahi.

Let us now see what that Himalayan miscalculation was. Before one can be fit for the practice of civil disobedience one must have rendered[2] a willing and respectful obedience to the state laws. For the most part we obey such laws out of fear of the penalty[3] for their breach, and this holds good particularly in respect of such laws as do not involve a moral principle. For instance, an honest, respectable man will not suddenly take to stealing, whether there is a law against stealing or not, but this very man will not feel any remorse[4] for failure to observe the rule about carrying head-lights on bicycles after dark. Indeed it is doubtful whether he would even accept advice kindly about being more careful in this respect. But he would observe any obligatory rule of this kind, if only to escape the inconvenience of facing a prosecution for a breach of the rule. Such compliance is not, however, the willing and spontaneous

1. *convex: having an outline or surface curved like the exterior of a circle or sphere, compare with concave*
2. *rendered: provide or give a service, help, etc. submit for inspection, consideration, or payment; poetic hand over; surrender*
3. *penalty: a punishment imposed for breaking a law, rule, or contract*
4. *remorse: deep regret or guilt for a wrong committed*

obedience that is required of a Satyagrahi. A Satyagrahi obeys the laws of society intelligently and of his own free will, because he considers it to be his sacred duty to do so. It is only when a person has thus obeyed the laws of society scrupulously that he is in a position to judge as to which particular rules are good and just and which are injust and iniquitous. Only then does the right accrue to him of the civil disobedience of certain laws in well-defined circumstances. My error lay in my failure to observe this necessary limitation. I had called on the people to launch upon civil disobedience before they had thus qualified themselves for it, and this mistake seemed to me of Himalayan magnitude. As soon as I entered the Kheda district, all the old recollections of the Kheda Satyagraha struggle came back to me, and I wondered how I could have failed to perceive what was so obvious. I realized that before a people could could be fit for offering civil disobedience, they should thoroughly understand its deeper implications. That being so, before restarting civil disobedience on a mass scale, it would be necessary to create a band of well-tried, pure-hearted volunteers who thoroughly understood the strict conditions of Satyagraha. They could explain these to the people, and by sleepless vigilance keep them on the right path.

With these thoughts filling my mind I reached Bombay, raised a corps of Satyagrahi volunteers through the Satyagraha Sabha there, and with their help commenced[1] the work of educating the people with regard to the meaning and inner significance[2] of Satyagraha. This was principally done by issuing leaflets of an educative character bearing on the subject.

But whilst this work was going on, I could see that it was a difficult task to interest the people in the peaceful side of Satyagraha. The volunteers too failed to enlist themselves in large numbers. Nor did all those who actually enlisted take anything like a regular systematic training, and as the days passed by, the number of fresh recruits began gradually to dwindle[3] instead of to grow. I realized that the progress of the training in civil disobedience was not going to be as rapid[4] as I had at first expected.

1. *commenced: begin*
2. *significance: the quality of being significant; importance*
3. *dwindle: diminish gradually*
4. *rapid: happening in a short time or at great speed*

CHAPTER 158

'NAVAJIVAN' AND 'YOUNG INDIA'

Thus, whilst this movement for the preservation of non-violence was making steady though slow progress on the one hand, Government's policy of lawless repression was in full career on the other, and was manifesting itself in the Punjab in all its nakedness. Leaders were put under arrest, martial law, which in other words meant no law, was proclaimed, special tribunals were set up. These tribunals were not courts of justice but instruments for carrying out the arbitrary will of an autocrat. Sentences were passed unwarranted by evidence and in flagrant violation of justice. In Amritsar innocent men and women were made to crawl like worms on their bellies. Before this outrage the Jalianwala Bagh tragedy paled into insignificance in my eyes, though it was this massacre principally that attracted the attention of the people of India and of the world.

I was pressed to proceed to the Punjab immediately in disregard[1] of consequences. I wrote and also telegraphed to the Viceroy asking for permission to go there, but in vain. If I proceeded without the necessary permission, I should not be allowed to cross the boundary of the Punjab, but left to find what satisfaction I could from civil disobedience. I was thus confronted by a serious dilemma. As things stood, to break the order against my entry into the Punjab could, it seemed to me, hardly be classed as civil disobedience, for I did not see around me the kind of peaceful atmosphere that I wanted, and the unbridled repression[2] in the Punjab had further served to aggravate and deepen the feelings of resentment[3]. For me, therefore, to offer civil disobedience at such a time, even if it were possible, would have been like fanning the flame. I therefore decided not to proceed to the Punjab in spite of the suggestion of friends. It was a bitter[4] pill for me to swallow. Tales of rank injustice and oppression came pouring in daily from the Punjab, but all I could do was to sit helplessly by and gnash my teeth.

1. *disregard: pay no attention to*
2. *repression: subdue by force*
3. *resentment: bitterness; indignation*
4. *bitter: causing pain or unhappiness; feeling or showing angry hurt or resentment*

Just then Mr. Horniman, in whose hands The Bombay Chronicle had became a formidable force, was suddenly spirited away by the authorities. This act of the Government seemed to me to be surrounded by a foulness which still stinks in my nostrils. I know that Mr. Horniman never desired lawlessness. He had not liked my breaking the prohibitory order of the Punjab Government without the permission of the Satyagraha Committee, and had fully endorsed the decision to suspend[1] civil disobedience. I had even received from him a letter advising suspension before I had announced my decision to that effect. Only owing to the distance between Bombay and Ahmedabad I got the letter after the announcement. His sudden deportation therefore caused me as much pain as surprise.

As a result of these developments I was asked by the directors of The Bombay Chronicle to take up the responsibility of conducting that paper. Mr. Brelvi was already there on the staff, so not much remained to be done by me, but as usual with my nature, the responsibility would have become an additional tax.

But the Government came as it were to my rescue, for by its order the publication of The Chronicle had to be suspended.

The friends who were directing[2] the management of *The Chronicle, viz.*, Messrs. Umar Sobani and Shankarlal Banker, were at this also controlling[3] Young India. They suggested that, in view of the suppression of The Chronicle, I should now take up the editorship of Young India, and that, in order to fill the gap left by the former, Young India should be converted from a weekly into a bi-weekly organ. This was what I felt also. I was anxious to expound[4] the inner meaning of Satyagraha to the public, and also hoped that through this effort I should at least be able to do justice to the Punjab situation. For, behind all I wrote, there was potential Satyagraha, and the Government knew as much. I therefore readily accepted the suggestion made by these friends.

But how could the general public be trained in Satyagraha through the medium of English? My principal field of work lay in Gujarat. Sjt. Indulal Yajnik was at that time associated with the group of Messrs. Sobani and Banker. He was conducting the Gujarati monthly Navajivan which had the financial backing of these friends. They placed the monthly at my disposal, and further Sjt. Indulal offered to work on it. This monthly was converted into a weekly.

1. *suspend: halt temporarily*
2. *directing: instructions on how to reach a destination or about how to do something*
3. *controlling: the power to influence people's behavior or the course of events*
4. *expound: present and explain (a theory of idea) systematically*

In the meantime The Chronicle was resuscitated. Young India was therefore restored to its original weekly form. To have published the two weeklies from two different places would have been very inconvenient to me and involved more expenditure. As Navajivan was already being published from Ahmedabad Young India was also removed there at my suggestion[1].

There were other reasons besides for this change. I had already learnt from my experience of Indian Opinion that such journals needed a press of their own. Moreover the press laws in force in India at that time were such that, if I wanted to express my views untrammelled, the existing printing presses, which were naturally run for business, would have hesitated to publish them. The need for setting up a press of our own, therefore, became all the more imperative, and since this could be conveniently done only at Ahmedabad, Young India too had to be taken there.

Through these journals I now commenced to the best of my ability the work of educating the reading public in Satyagraha. Both of them had reached a very wide circulation, which at one time rose to the neighbourhood of forty thousand each. But while the circulation[2] of Navajivan went up at a bound, that of Young India increased only by slow degrees. After my incarceration the circulation of both these journals fell to a low ebb, and today stands below eight thousand.

From the very start I set my face against taking advertisements in these journals. I do not think that they have lost anything thereby. On the contrary, it is my belief that it has in no small measure helped them to maintain their independence.

Incidentally these journals helped me also to some extent to remain at peace with myself for, whilst immediate resort to civil[3] disobedience[4] was out of the question, they enabled me freely to ventilate my views and to put heart into the people. Thus I feel that both the journals rendered good service to the people in this hour of trial, and did their humble bit towards lightening the tyranny of the martial law.

1. *suggestion: an idea or plan put forward for consideration; the action of suggesting*
2. *circulation: the number of copies sold of a newspaper or magazine*
3. *civil: of or relating to ordinary citizens, as distinct from military or ecclesiastical matters*
4. *disobedience: non-compliance*

CHAPTER 159

IN THE PUNJAB

Sir Michael O'Dwyer held me responsible for all that had happened in the Punjab, and some irate young Punjabis held me responsible for the martial law. They asserted that, if only I had not suspended civil disobedience, there would have been no Jalianwala Bagh massacre. Some of them even went the length of threatening me with assassination if I went to the Punjab.

But I felt that my position was so correct and above question that no intelligent person could misunderstand it.

I was impatient to go to the Punjab. I had never been there before, and that made me all the more anxious to see things for myself. Dr. Satyapal, Dr. Kitchlu and Pandit Rambhaj Dutt Chowdhari, who had invited me to the Punjab, were at this time in jail. But I felt sure that the Government could not dare to keep them and the other prisoners in prison for long. A large number of Punjabis used to come and see me whenever I was in Bombay. I ministered to them a word of cheer on these occasions, and that would comfort them. My self-confidence of that time was infectious[1].

But my going to the Punjab had to be postponed[2] again and again. The Viceroy would say, 'not yet,' every time I asked for permission to go there, and so the thing dragged on.

In the meantime the Hunter Committee was announced to hold an inquiry in connection with the Punjab Government's doings under the martial law. Mr. C. F. Andrews had now reached the Punjab. His letters gave a heart-rending description of the state of things there, and I formed the impression that the martial law atrocities were in fact even worse than the press reports had showed. He pressed me urgently to come and join him. At the same time Malaviyaji sent telegrams[3] asking me to proceed to the Punjab at once. I once more telegraphed to the Viceroy asking whether I could now go to the Punjab. He wired[4] back in reply that

1. *infectious: likely to spread to or influence others*
2. *postponed: arrange for to take place at a time later than that first scheduled*
3. *telegrams: a message sent by telegraph and delivered in written or printed form, used in the UK only for international messages since 1981*
4. *wired: send a telegram or cablegram to*

I could go there after a certain date. I cannot exactly recollect now, but I think it was 17th of October.

The scene that I witnessed on my arrival at Lahore can never be effaced from my memory. The railway station was from end to end one seething mass of humanity. The entire populace had turned out of doors in eager expectation, as if to meet a dear relation after a long separation, and was delirious with joy. I was put up at the late Pandit Rambhaj Dutt's bungalow, and the burden of entertaining me fell on the shoulders of Shrimati Sarala Devi. A burden it truly was, for even then, as now, the place where I was accommodated became a veritable caravanserai.

Owing to the principal Punjab leaders being in jail, their place, I found, had been properly taken up by Pandit Malaviyaji, Pandit Motilalji and the late Swami Sharddhanandji. Malaviyaji and Shraddhanandji I had known intimately before, but this was the first occasion on which I came in close personal contact with Motilalji. All these leaders, as also such local leaders as had escaped the privilege of going to jail[1], at once made me feel perfectly at home amongst them, so that I never felt like a stranger in their midst.

How we unanimously decided not to lead evidence before the Hunter Committee is now a matter of history. The reasons for that decision were published[2] at that time, and need not be recapitulated[3] here. Suffice[4] it to say that, looking back upon these events from this distance of time, I still feel that our decision to boycott the Committee was absolutely correct and proper.

As a logical consequence of the boycott of the Hunter Committee, it was decided to appoint a non-official Inquiry Committee, to hold almost a parallel inquiry on behalf of the Congress. Pandit Motilal Nehru, the late Deshbandhu C. R. Das, Sjt. Abbas Tyebji, Sjt. M.R. Jayakar and myself were appointed to this Committee, virtually by Pandit Malaviyaji. We distributed ourselves over various places for purposes of inquiry. The responsibility for organizing the work of the Committee devolved on me, and as the privilege of conducting the inquiry in the largest number of places fell to my lot, I got a rare opportunity of observing at close quarters the people of the Punjab and the Punjab villages.

In the course of my inquiry I made acquaintance with the women of the Punjab also. It was as if we had known one another for ages. Wherever

1. *jail: a place for the confinement of people accused or convicted of a crime*
2. *published: prepare and issue for public sale; print in a book or journal so as to make generally known*
3. *recapitulated: summarize and state again the main points of*
4. *suffice: be enough or adequate; meet the needs of*

I went they came flocking, and laid before me their heaps of yarn. My work in connection with the inquiry brought home to me the fact that the Punjab could become a great field for *khadi* work.

As I proceeded further and further with my inquiry into the atrocities that had been committed on the people, I came across tales of Government's tyranny[1] and the arbitrary despotism of its officers such as I was hardly prepared for, and they filled me with deep pain. What surprised me then, and what still continues to fill me with surprise, was the fact that a province that had furnished the largest number of soldiers to the British Government during the war, should have taken all these brutal[2] excesses lying down.

The task of drafting the report of this Committee was also entrusted[3] to me. I would recommend a perusal of this report to anyone who wants to have an idea of the kind of atrocities that were perpetrated on[4] the Punjab people. All that I wish to say here about it is that there is not a single conscious exaggeration in it anywhere, and every statement made in it is substantiated by evidence. Moreover, the evidence published was only a fraction of what was in the Committee's possession. Not a single statement, regarding the validity of which there was the slightest room for doubt, was permitted to appear in the report. This report, prepared as it was solely with a view to bringing out the truth and nothing but the truth, will enable the reader to see to what lengths the British Government is capable of going, and what inhumanities and barbarities it is capable of perpetrating in order to maintain its power. So far as I am aware, not a single statement made in this report has ever been disproved.

1. *tyranny: cruel and oppressive government or rule; a state under such rule*
2. *brutal: savagely violent*
3. *entrusted: assign a responsibility to; put into someone's care*
4. *perpetrated on: carry out or commit*

CHAPTER 160

THE KHILAFAT AGAINST COW PROTECTION?

We must now leave, for the time being these dark happenings in the Punjab.

The Congress inquiry into Dyerism in the Punjab had just commenced, when I received a letter of invitation to be present at a joint conference of Hindus and Musalmans that was to meet at Delhi to deliberate[1] on the Khilafat question. Among the signatories to it were the late Hakim Ajmal Khan Sahab and Mr. Asaf Ali. The late Swami Shraddhanandji, it was stated, would be attending and, if I remember aright, he was to be the vice-president of the conference, which, so far as I can recollect, was to be held in the November of that year. The Conference was to deliberate on the situation arising out of the Khilafat betrayal, and on the question as to whether the Hindus and Musalmans should take any part in the peace[2] celebrations. The letter of invitation went on to say, among other things, that not only the Khilafat question but the question of cow protection as well would be discussed at the conference, and it would, therefore, afford a golden opportunity for a settlement of the cow question. I did not like this reference to the cow question. In my letter in reply to the invitation[3], therefore, whilst promising to do my best to attend, I suggested that the two questions should not be mixed up together or considered in the spirit of a bargain, but should be decided on their own merits and treated separately.

With these thoughts filling my mind, I went to the conference. It was a very well attended gathering, though it did not present the spectacle of later gatherings that were attended by tens of thousands. I discussed the question referred to above with the late Swami Shraddhanandji, who was present at the conference. He appreciated my argument and left it to me to place it before the conference. I likewise discussed it with the late Hakim Saheb. Before the conference I contended that, if the Khilafat question had a just and legitimate basis, as I believe it had, and if the Government had really committed a gross injustice[4], the Hindus

1. *deliberate: long and careful consideration*
2. *peace: freedom from or the cessation of war*
3. *invitation: a written or verbal request inviting someone to go somewhere or to do something; the action of inviting*
4. *injustice: an unjust act or occurrence*

were bound to stand by the Musalmans in their demand for the redress of the Khilafat wrong. It would ill become them to bring in the cow question in this connection, or to use the occasion to make terms with the Musalmans, just as it would ill become the Musalmans to offer to stop cow slaughter as a price for the Hindus' support on the Khilafat question. But it would be another matter and quite graceful, and reflect great credit on them, if the Musalmans of their own free will stopped cow slaughter out of regard for the religious sentiments of the Hindus, and from a sense of duty towards them as neighbours and children of the same soil. To take up such an independent attitude was, I contended, their duty, and would enhance the dignity of their conduct. But if the Musalmans considered it as their neighbourly duty[1] to stop cow slaughter, they should do so regardless of whether the Hindus helped them in the Khilafat or not. 'That being so,' I argued, 'the two questions should be discussed independently of each other, and the deliberations of the conference should be confined to the question of the Khilafat only.' My argument appealed to those present and, as a result, the question of cow protection was not discussed at this conference.

But in spite of my warning Maulana Abdul Bari Saheb said: 'No matter whether the Hindus help us or not, the Musalmans ought, as the countrymen of the Hindus, out of regard for the latter's susceptibilities, to give up cow slaughter.' And at one time it almost looked as if they would really put an end to it.

There was a suggestion from some quarters that the Punjab question should be tacked on to that of the Khilafat wrong. I opposed the proposal. The Punjab question, I said, was a local affair and could not therefore weigh with us in our decision to participate or not in the peace celebrations. If we mixed up the local question with the Khilafat question, which arose directly out of the peace terms, we should be guilty of a serious indiscretion[2]. My argument easily carried conviction.

Maulana Hasrat Mohani was present in this meeting. I had known him even before, but it was only here that I discovered what a fighter he was. We differed from each other almost from the very beginning, and in several matters the differences have persisted[3].

Among the numerous resolutions that were passed at this conference, one called upon both Hindus and Musalmans to take the Swadeshi

1. *duty: a general duty that individuals must take reasonable care in their actions or omissions, so as not to cause harm to others proximate to them*
2. *indiscretion: behavior showing lack of good judgment*
3. *persisted: continue firmly or obstinately in an opinion or a course of action in spite of difficulty or opposition*

vow, and as a natural corollary[1] to it, to boycott foreign goods. Khadi had not as yet found its proper place. This was not a resolution that Hasrat Saheb would accept. His object was to wreak vengeance[2] on the British Empire, in case justice was denied in the matter of the Khilafat. Accordingly, he brought in a counter proposal for the boycott purely of British goods so far as practicable. I opposed it on the score of principle, as also of practicability, adducing for it those arguments that have now become pretty familiar. I also put before the conference my viewpoint of non-violence. I noticed that my arguments made a deep impression on the audience. Before me, Hasrat Mohani's speech had been received with such loud acclamations[3] that I was afraid that mine would only be a cry in the wilderness. I had made bold to speak only because I felt it would be a dereliction[4] of duty not to lay my views before the conference. But, to my agreeable surprise, my speech was followed with the closest attention by those present, and evoked a full measure of support among those on the platform, and speaker after speaker rose to deliver speeches in support of my views. The leaders were able to see that not only would the boycott of British goods fail of its purpose, but would, if adopted, make of them a laughing stock. There was hardly a man present in that assembly but had some article of British manufacture on his person. Many of the audience therefore realized that nothing but harm could result from adopting a resolution that even those who voted for it were unable to carry out.

'Mere boycott of foreign cloth cannot satisfy us, for who knows long it will be, before we shall be able to manufacture Swadeshi cloth in sufficient quantity for our needs, and before we can bring about effective boycott of foreign cloth? We want something that will produce an immediate effect on the British. Let your boycott of foreign cloth stand, we do not mind it, but give us something quicker, and speedier in addition' - so spoke in effect Maulana Hasrat Mohani. Even as I was listening to him, I felt that something new, over and above boycott of foreign cloth, would be necessary. An immediate boycott of foreign cloth seemed to me also to be a clear impossibility at that time. I did not then know that we could, if we liked, produce enough *khadi* for all our clothing requirements; this was only a later discovery. On the other hand, I knew even then that, if we depended on the mills alone

1. *corollary: a direct consequence or result*
2. *vengeance: punishment inflicted or retribution exacted for an injury or wrong*
3. *acclamations: enthusiastic approval*
4. *dereliction: in a very poor condition as a result of disuse and neglect*

for effecting the boycott of foreign cloth, we should be betrayed. I was still in the middle of this dilemma when the Maulana concluded[1] his speech.

I was handicapped for want of suitable Hindi or Urdu words. This was my first occasion for delivering an argumentative speech before an audience especially composed of Musalmans of the North. I had spoken in Urdu at the Muslim League at Calcutta, but it was only for a few minutes, and the speech was intended only to be a feeling appeal to the audience. Here, on the contrary, I was faced with a critical, if not hostile[2], audience, to whom I had to explain and bring home my viewpoint. But I had cast aside all shyness. I was not there to deliver an address in the faultless[3], polished Urdu of the Delhi Muslims, but to place before the gathering my views in such broken Hindi as I could command. And in this I was successful. This meeting afforded me a direct proof of the fact that Hindi-Urdu alone could become the *lingua franca* of India. Had I spoken in English, I could not have produced the impression that I did on the audience, and the Maulana might not have felt called upon to deliver his challenge. Nor, if he had delivered it, could I have taken it up effectively.

I could not hit upon a suitable Hindi or Urdu word for the new idea, and that put me out somewhat. At last I described it by the word 'non-co-operation,' an expression that I used for the first time at this meeting. As the Maulana was delivering his speech, it seemed to me that it was vain for him to talk about effective[4] resistance to a Government with which he was co-operating in more than one thing, if resort to arms was impossible or undesirable[5]. The only true resistance to the Government, it therefore seemed to me, was to cease to co-operate with it. Thus I arrived at the word non-co-operation. I had not then a clear idea of all its manifold implications. I therefore did not enter into details. I simply said:

'The Musalmans have adopted a very important resolution. If the peace terms are unfavourable to them - which may God forbid - they will stop all co-operation with Government. It is an inalienable right of the people thus to withhold co-operation. We are not bound to retain Government titles and honours, or to continue in Government service. If Government should betray us in a great cause like the Khilafat, we

1. *concluded: bring or come to an end; formally settle or arrange a treaty or agreement*
2. *hostile: antagonistic; opposed; of or belonging to a military enemy; opposed by the company to be bought*
3. *faultless: without any fault or defect; perfect production a desired or intended result*
4. *effective: production a desired or intended result*
5. *undesirable: not wanted or desirable because harmful, objectionable, or unpleasant*

could not do otherwise than non-co-operate. We are therefore entitled[1] to non-co-operate with Government in case of a betrayal.'

But months elapsed before the word non-co-operation became current coin. For the time being it was lost in the proceedings of the conference. Indeed when I supported the co-operation resolution at the Congress which met at Amritsar a month later, I did so in the hope that the betrayal would never come.

1. *entitled: believing oneself to be inherently deserving of privileges or special treatment*

CHAPTER 161

THE AMRITSAR CONGRESS

The Punjab Government could not keep in confinement the hundreds of Punjabis who, under the martial law regime, had been clapped into jail on the strength of the most meagre[1] evidence by tribunals[2] that were courts only in name. There was such an outcry all round against this flagrant piece of injustice that their further incarceration became impossible. Most of the prisoners were released before the Congress opened. Lala Harkishanlal and the other leaders were all released, while the session of the Congress was still in progress. The Ali Brothers too arrived there straight from jail. The people's joy knew no bounds. Pandit Motilal Nehru, who, at the sacrifice of his splendid practice, had made the Punjab his headquarters and had done great service, was the President of the Congress; the late Swami Shraddhanandji was the Chairman of the Reception Committee.

Up to this time my share in the annual proceedings of the Congress was confined only to the constructive advocacy of Hindi by making my speech in the national language, and to presenting in that speech the case of the Indians overseas. Nor did I expect to be called upon to do anything more this year. But, as had happened on many a previous occasion, responsible work came to me all of a sudden.

The King's announcement on the new reforms had just been issued. It was not wholly satisfactory even to me, and was unsatisfactory to everyone else. But I felt at that time that the reforms, though defective, could still be accepted. I felt in the King's announcement and its language the hand of Lord Sinha, and it lent a ray of hope. But experienced stalwarts like the late Lokamanya and Deshabandhu Chittaranjan Das shook their heads. Pandit Malaviyaji was neutral[3].

Pandit Malaviyaji had harboured me in his own room. I had a glimpse of the simplicity of his life on the occasion of the foundation ceremony of the Hindu University; but on this occasion, being in the same room with him, I was able to observe his daily routine[4] in the closest detail,

1. *meagre: lacking in quantity or quality*
2. *tribunals: a body established to settle certain types of dispute*
3. *neutral: impartial, belonging to an impartial state or group, unbiased*
4. *routine: a sequence of actions regularly followed; a fixed unvarying programme*

and what I saw filled me with joyful surprise. His room presented the appearance of a free inn for all the poor. You could hardly cross from one end to the other. It was so crowded. It was accessible at all odd hours to chance visitors who had the licence to take as much of his time as they liked. In a corner of this crib lay my *charpai*[1] in all its dignity.

But I may not occupy this chapter with a description of Malaviyaji's mode of living, and must return to my subject. I was thus enabled to hold daily discussions with Malaviyaji, who used lovingly to explain to me, like an elder brother, the various viewpoints of the different parties. I saw that my participation in the deliberations on the resolution on the reforms was inevitable. Having had my share of responsibility in the drawing up of the Congress report on the Punjab wrongs, I felt that all that still remained to be done in that connection must claim my attention. There had to be dealings with Government in that matter. Then similarly there was the Khilafat question. I further believed at that time that Mr. Montagu would not betray or allow India's cause to be betrayed. The release of the Ali Brothers and other prisoners too seemed to me to be an auspicious sign. In these circumstances I felt that a resolution not rejecting but accepting the reforms was the correct thing. Deshabandhu Chittaranjan Das, on the other hand, held firmly to the view that the reforms ought to be rejected as wholly inadequate and unsatisfactory. The late Lokamanya was more or less neutral, but had decided to throw in his weight on the side of any resolution that the Deshabandhu might approve.

The idea of having to differ from such seasoned, well tried and universally revered leaders was unbearable to me. But on the other hand the voice of conscience[2] was clear. I tried to run away from the Congress and suggested to Pandit Malaviyaji and Motilalji that it would be in the general interest if I absented myself from the Congress for the rest of the session. It would save me from having to make an exhibition of my difference with such esteemed leaders.

But my suggestion found no favour with these two seniors. The news of my proposal was somehow[3] whispered[4] to Lala Harkishanlal. 'This will never do. It will very much hurt the feelings of the Punjabis,' he said. I discussed the matter with Lokamanya, Deshabandhu and Mr. Jinnah, but no way out could be found. Finally I laid bare my distress to Malaviyaji. 'I see no prospect of a compromise,' I told him, 'and if I am to move my resolution, a division will have to be called and votes taken.

1. *charpai: a light Indian bedstead*
2. *conscience: a person's moral sense of right and wrong*
3. *somehow: in some way; for an unknown or unspecified reason*
4. *whispered: speak very softly using one's breath rather than one's throat*

But I do not find here any arrangements for it. The practice in the open session of the Congress so far has been to take votes by a show of hands with the result that all distinction between visitors and delegates is lost, while, as for taking a count of votes in such vast assemblies, we have no means at all. So it comes to this that, even if I want to call a division, there will be no facility for it, nor meaning in it.' But Lala Harkishanlal came to the rescue and undertook to make the necessary arrangements. 'We will not,' he said, 'permit visitors in the Congress pandal on the day on which voting is to take place. And as for taking the count, well, I shall see to that. But you must not absent yourself from the Congress.' I capitulated; I framed my resolution, and in heart trembling undertook to move it. Pandit Malaviyaji and Mr. Jinnah were to support it. I could notice that, although our difference of opinion was free from any trace of bitterness, and although our speeches too contained nothing but cold reasoning, the people could not stand the very fact of a difference; it pained them. They wanted unanimity.

Even while speeches were being delivered, efforts to settle the difference were being made on the platform, and notes were being freely exchanged among the leaders for that purpose. Malaviyaji was leaving no stone unturned to bridge[1] the gulf. Just then Jeramdas handed over his amendment to me and pleaded in his own sweet manner to save the delegates from the dilemma of a division. His amendment appealed to me. Malaviyaji's eye was already scanning every quarter for a ray of hope. I told him that Jeramdas's amendment seemed to me to be likely to be acceptable to both the parties. The Lokamanya, to whom it was next shown, said, "If C.R. Das approves, I will have no objection.' Deshabandhu at last thawed, and cast a look towards Sjt. Bepin Chandra Pal for endorsement[2]. Malaviyaji was filled with hope. He snatched away the slip of paper containing the amendment, and before Deshabandhu had even pronounced a definite 'yes', shouted out, 'Brother delegates, you will be glad to learn that a compromise had been reached.' What followed beggars description. The pandal was rent with the clapping of hands, and the erstwhile[3] gloomy[4] faces of the audience lit up with joy.

It is hardly necessary to deal with the text of the amendment. My object here is only to describe how this resolution was undertaken as part of my experiments with which these chapters deal.

The compromise further increased my responsibility.

1. *bridge: a structure that allows people or vehicles to cross on obstacle such as a river or and or railway etc.*
2. *endorsement: declare one's public approval of*
3. *erstwhile: long ago; formerly*
4. *gloomy: causing or feeling depression or despondency*

CHAPTER 162

CONGRESS INITIATION

I must regard my participation in Congress proceedings at Amritsar as my real entrance into the Congress politics. My attendance at the previous Congress was nothing more perhaps than an annual renewal of allegiance[1] to the Congress. I never felt on these occasions that I had any other work cut out for me except that of a mere private, nor did I desire more.

My experience of Amritsar had shown that there were one or two things for which perhaps I had some aptitude and which could be useful to the Congress. I could already see that the late Lokamanya, the Deshabandhu, Pandit Motilalji and other leaders were pleased with my work in connection with the Punjab inquiry. They used to invite me to their informal gatherings where, as I found resolutions for the Subjects Committee were conceived. At these gatherings only those persons were invited who enjoyed the special confidence of the leaders and whose services were needed by them. Interlopers also sometimes found their way to these meetings.

There were, for the coming year, two things which interested me, as I had some aptitude for them. One of these was the memorial of the Jalianwala Bagh Massacre. The Congress had passed a resolution for it amid great enthusiasm. A fund of about five lakhs had to be collected for it. I was appointed one of the trustees. Pandit Malaviyaji enjoyed the reputation of being the prince among beggars for the public cause. But I knew that I was not far behind him in that respect. It was whilst I was in South Africa that I discovered my capacity in this direction. I had not the unrivalled magic of Malaviyaji for commanding princely donations[2] from the potentates of India. But I knew that there was no question of approaching the Rajas and Maharajas for donations for the Jalianwala Bagh memorial. The main responsibility for the collection thus fell, as I had expected, on my shoulders. The generous citizens of Bombay subscribed most liberally, and the memorial trust[3] has at present a handsome[4] credit balance in the bank. But the problem that

1. *allegiance: steadfast in devotion*
2. *donations: something that is given to a charity, especially a sum of money*
3. *handsome: of obvious quality, substantial*
4. *trust: an arrangement whereby a person is made the nominal owner of property to be held or used for the benefit of one or more others*

faces the country today is what kind of memorial to erect on the ground, to sanctify which, Hindus, Musalmans and Sikhs mingled their blood. The three communities, instead of being bound in a bond of amity and love, are, to all appearance, at war with one another, and the nation is at a loss as to how to utilize the memorial fund.

My other aptitude which the Congress could utilize was as a draftsman. The Congress leaders had found that I had a faculty for condensed expression, which I had acquired by long practice. The then existing constitution of the Congress was Gokhale's legacy. He had framed a few rules which served as a basis for running the Congress machinery. The interesting history of the framing of these rules I had learnt form Gokhale's own lips. But everybody had now come to feel that these rules were no longer adequate[1] for the ever increasing business of the Congress. The question had been coming up year after year. The Congress at that time had practically no machinery functioning during the interval between session and session, or for dealing with fresh contingencies that might arise in the course of the year. The existing rules provided for three secretaries, but as a matter of fact only one of them was a functioning secretary, and even he was not a whole-timer. How was he, single-handed, to run the Congress office, to think of the future, or to discharge during the current year the obligations contracted by the Congress in the past? During that year, therefore, everybody felt that this question would assume all the more importance. The Congress was too unwieldy a body for the discussion of public affairs. There was no limit set to the number of delegates[2] in the Congress or to the number of delegates that each province could return, Some improvement upon the existing chaotic condition was thus felt by everybody to be an imperative[3] necessity. I undertook the responsibility of framing a constitution on one condition. I saw that there were two leaders, *viz.*, the Lokamanya and the Deshabandhu who had the greatest hold on the public. I requested that they, as the representatives of the people, should be associated with me on the Committee for framing the constitution. But since it was obvious that they would not have the time personally to participate in the constitution-making work, I suggested that two persons enjoying their confidence should be a appointed[4] along with me on the Constitution Committee, and that the number of its

1. *adequate: satisfactory or acceptable*
2. *delegates: a person sent or authorized to represent others, in particular a representative sent to a conference; a member of a committee*
3. *imperative: of vital importance*
4. *appointed: assign a job or role to*

personnel should be limited to three. This suggestion was accepted by the late Lokmanya and the late Deshabandhu, who suggested the names of Sjts. Kelkar and I.B. Sen respectively as their proxies[1]. The Constitution Committee could not even once come together, but we were able to consult with each other by correspondence, and in the end presented a unanimous[2] report. I regard this constitution with a certain measure of pride. I hold that, if we could fully work out this constitution, the mere fact of working it out would bring us Swaraj. With the assumption of this responsibility I may be said to have made my real entrance into the Congress politics.

1. *proxies: the authority to represent someone else, especially in voting; a person authorized to act on behalf of another*
2. *unanimous: of an opinion, decision, or vote held or carried by everyone involved*

CHAPTER 163

THE BIRTH OF KHADI

I do not remember to have seen a handloom or a spinning wheel when in 1908 I described it in *Hind Swaraj* as the panacea for the growing pauperism of India. In that book I took it as understood that anything that helped India to get rid of the grinding poverty of her masses would in the same process also establish Swaraj. Even in 1915, when I returned to India from South Africa, I had not actually seen a spinning[1] wheel. When the Satyagraha Ashram was founded at Sabarmati, we introduced a few handlooms there. But no sooner had we done this than we found ourselves up against a difficulty. All of us belonged either to the liberal professions or to business; not one of us was an artisan[2]. We needed a weaving expert to teach us to weave before we could work the looms. One was at last procured from Palanpur, but he did not communicate to us the whole of his art. But Maganlal Gandhi was not to be easily baffled. Possessed of a natural talent for mechanics, he was able fully to master the art before long, and one after another several new weavers were trained up in the Ashram.

The object that we set before ourselves was to be able to clothe ourselves entirely in cloth manufactured[3] by our own hands. We therefore forthwith discarded the use of mill-woven cloth, and all the members of the Ashram resolved to wear hand-woven cloth made from Indian yarn only. The adoption of this practice brought us a world of experience. It enabled us to know, from direct contact, the conditions of life among the weavers, the extent of their production, the handicaps in the way of their obtaining[4] their yarn supply, the way in which they were being made victims of fraud, and, lastly, their ever growing indebtedness. We were not in a position immediately to manufacture all the cloth for our needs. The alternative therefore was to get our cloth supply from handloom weavers. But ready-made cloth from Indian mill-yarn was not easily obtainable either from the cloth-dealers or from the weavers themselves. All the fine cloth woven by the weavers was from foreign yarn,

1. *spinning: turn or cause to turn round quickly*
2. *artisan: a skilled worker who makes things by hand*
3. *manufactured: make on a large scale using machinery*
4. *obtaining: acquire or secure*

since Indian mills did not spin fine counts. Even today the out-turn of higher counts by Indian mills is very limited, whilst highest counts they cannot spin at all. It was after the greatest effort that we were at last able to find some weavers who condescended to weave Swadeshi yarn for us, and only on condition that the Ashram would take up all the cloth that they might produce. By thus adopting cloth woven from mill-yarn as our wear, and propagating it among our friends, we made ourselves voluntary agents of the Indian spinning mills. This in its turn brought us into contact with the mills, and enabled us to know something about their management and their handicaps. We saw that the aim of the mills was more and more to weave the yarn spun by them: their co-operation with the handloom weaver was not willing, but unavoidable and temporary[1]. We became impatient to be able to spin our own yarn. It was clear that, until we could do this ourselves, dependence on the mills would remain. We did not feel that we could render any service to the country by continuing as agents of Indian spinning mills.

No end of difficulties again faced us. We could get neither spinning wheels nor a spinner to teach us how to spin. We were employing some wheel for filling pearns and bobbins for weaving in the Ashram. But we had no idea that these could be used as spinning wheels. Once Kalidas Jhaveri discovered a woman who, he said, would demonstrate to us how spinning was done. We sent to her a member of the Ashram who was known for his great versatility in learning new things. But even he returned without wresting[2] the secret of the art.

So the time passed on, and my impatience grew with the time. I plied every chance visitor to the Ashram who was likely to possess some information about hand spinning with questions about the art. But the art being confined to women and having been all but exterminated, if there was some stray[3] spinner still surviving in some obscure corner, only a member of that sex was likely to find out her whereabouts.

In the year 1917 I was taken by my Gujarati friends to preside[4] at the Broach Educational Conference. It was here that I discovered that remarkable lady Gangabehn Majmundar. She was a widow, but her enterprising spirit knew no bounds. Her education, in the accepted sense of the term, was not much. But in courage and commonsense she easily surpassed the general run of our educated women. She had already got

1. *temporary: lasting for only a limited period*
2. *wresting: forcibly pull from a person's grasp*
3. *stray: not in the right place; separated from a group*
4. *preside: be in a position of authority in a meeting, court, etc. be in charge of a situation*

rid of the curse of untouchability, and fearlessly moved among and served the suppressed[1] classes. She had means of her own, and her needs were few. She had a well seasoned constitution, and went about everywhere without an escort. She felt quite at home on horseback. I came to know her more intimately at the Godhra Conference. To her I poured out my grief about the charkha, and she lightened my burden by a promise to prosecute an earnest and incessant[2] search for the spinning wheel.

1. *suppressed: prevent or inhibit*

2. *incessant: continuing without pause or interruption*

CHAPTER 164

FOUND AT LAST!

At last, after no end of wandering in Gujarat, Gangabehn found the spinning wheel in Vijapur in the Baroda State. Quite a number of people there had spinning wheels in their homes, but had long since consigned[1] them to the lofts as useless lumber. They expressed to Gangabehn their readiness to resume spinning, if someone promised to provide them with a regular supply of slivers, and to buy the yarn spun by them. Gangabehn communicated the joyful news to me. The providing of slivers was found to be a difficult task. On my mentioning the thing to the late Umar Sobani, he solved the difficulty by immediately undertaking to send a sufficient supply of slivers from his mill. I sent to Gangabehn the slivers received from Umar Sobani, and soon yarn began to pour[2] in at such a rate that it became quite a problem how to cope with it.

Mr. Umar Sobani's generosity was great, but still one could not go on taking advantage of it for ever. I felt ill at ease, continuously receiving slivers from him. Moreover, it seemed to me to be fundamentally wrong to use mill-slivers. If one could use mill-slivers, why not use mill-yarn as well? Surely no mills supplied slivers to the ancients[3]? How did they make their slivers then? With these thoughts in my mind I suggested to Gangabehn to find carders who could supply slivers. She confidently undertook the task. She engaged a carder who was prepared to card cotton. He demanded thirty-five rupees, if not much more, per month. I considered no price too high at the time. She trained a few youngsters to make slivers out of the carded cotton. I begged for cotton in Bombay. Sjt. Yashvantprasad Desai at once responded. Gangabehn's enterprise thus prospered beyond expectations. She found out weavers to weave the yarn that was spun in Vijapur, and soon Vijapur *khadi* gained a name for itself.

While these developments were taking place in Vijapur, the spinning wheel gained a rapid footing in the Ashram. Maganlal Gandhi, by bringing to bear all his splendid mechanical talent on the wheel, made

1. *consigned: deliver to someone's custody; send by a public carrier; put someone or something in order to be rid of them*
2. *pour: flow or cause to flow in a steady stream; fall heavily; prepare and serve*
3. *ancient: very old*

many improvements in it, and wheels and their accessories began to be manufactured at the Ashram. The first piece of *khadi* manufactured in the Ashram cost 17 annas per yard. I did not hesitate to commend this very coarse *khadi* at that rate to friends, who willingly paid the price.

I was laid up in bed at Bombay. But I was fit enough to make searches for the wheel there. At last I chanced upon two spinners. They charged one rupee for a seer of yarn, i.e., 28 *tolas* or nearly three quarters of a pound. I was then ignorant of the economics of *khadi*. I considered no price too high for securing handspun yarn. On comparing the rates paid by me with those paid in Vijapur I found that I was being cheated. The spinners refused to agree to any reduction in their rates. So I had to dispense with their service. But they served their purpose. They taught spinning to Shrimatis Avantikabai, Ramibai Kamdar, the widowed mother of Sjt. Shankarlal Banker and Shrimati Vasumatibehn. The wheel began merrily to hum in my room, and I may say without exaggeration that its hum had no small share in restoring me to my health. I am prepared to admit that its effect was more psychological[1] than physical. But then it only shows how powerfully the physical in man reacts to the psychological. I too set my hand to the wheel, but did not do much with it at the time.

In Bombay, again, the same old problem of obtaining a supply of hand-made slivers presented itself. A carder twanging his bow used to pass daily by Sjt. Revashankar's residence. I sent for him and learnt that he carded cotton for stuffing mattresses. He agreed to card cotton for slivers, but demanded a stiff price for it, which, however, I paid. The yarn thus prepared I disposed of to some Vaishnava friends for making from it the garlands for the *pavitra ekadashi*. Sjt. Shivji started a spinning class in Bombay. All these experiments involved considerable expenditure. But it was willingly defrayed by patriotic friends, lovers of the motherland, who had faith in *khadi*. The money thus spent, in my humble opinion, was not wasted. It brought us a rich store of experience, and revealed to us the possibilities of the spinning wheel.

I now grew impatient for the exclusive adoption of *khadi* for my dress. Mt *dhoti* was still of Indian mill cloth. The coarse *khadi* manufactured in the Ashram and at Vijapur was only thirty inches in width[2]. I gave notice to Gangabehn that, unless she provided me with a *khadi dhoti* of forty-five inches with within a month. I would do with coarse[3], short *khadi dhoti*.

1. *psychological: the mental characteristics or attitude of a person; the mental factors governing a situation or activity*
2. *width: the measurement or extent of something from side to side; the lesser of two or the least of three dimensions of a body; a piece of something at its full extent from side to side*
3. *coarse: rough or harsh in texture; unrefined; consisting of large grains or particles*

The ultimatum[1] came upon her as a shock. But she proved equal to the demand made upon her. Well within the month she sent me a pair of *khadi dhotis* of forty-five inches width, and thus relieved me from what would then have been a difficult situation for me.

At about the same time Sjt. Lakshmidas brought Sjt. Ramji, the weaver, with his wife Gangabehn from Lathi to the Ashram and got *khadi dhotis* woven at the Ashram. The part played by this couple in the spread of *khadi* was by no means insignificant. They initiated a host of persons in Gujarat and also outside into the art of weaving hand-spun yarn. To see Gangabehn at her loom is a stirring[2] sight. When this unlettered but self-possessed sister plies at her loom, she becomes so lost in it that it is difficult to distract her attention, and much more difficult to draw her eyes off her beloved loom.

1. *ultimatum: a final demand or statement of terms, the rejection of which will result in retaliation or breakdown in relations*
2. *stirring: a commotion*

CHAPTER 165

AN INSTRUCTIVE DIALOGUE

From its very inception the *khadi* movement, Swadeshi movement as it was then called, evoked much criticism from the mill-owners. The late Umar Sobani, a capable mill-owner himself, not only gave me the benefit of his own knowledge and experience, but kept me in touch with the opinion of the other mill-owners as well. The argument advanced by one of these deeply impressed him. He pressed me to meet him. I agreed. Mr. Sobani arranged the interview. The mill-owner opened the conversation.

'You know that there has been Swadeshi agitation before now?'

'Yes, I do,' I replied.

'You are also aware that in the days of the Partition we, the mill-owners, fully exploited the Swadeshi movement. When it was at its height, we raised the prices of cloth, and did even worse things.'

'You, I have heard something about it, and it has grieved me.'

'I can understand your grief, but I can see no ground for it. We are not conducting our business out of philanthropy. We do it for profit, we have got to satisfy the shareholders. The price of an article is governed by the demand for it. Who can check the law of demand and supply? The Bengalis should have known that their agitation[1] was bound to send up the price of Swadeshi cloth by stimulating the demand for it.'

I interrupted: 'The Bengalis like me were trustful in their nature. They believed, in the fullness of their faith, that the mill-owners would not be so utterly[2] selfish and unpatriotic as to betray their country in the hour of its need, and even to go the length, as they did, of fraudulently passing off foreign[3] cloth as Swadeshi.'

'I knew your believing nature,' he rejoined; 'that is why I put you to the trouble of coming to me, so that I might warn you against falling into the same error as these simple-hearted Bengalis.'

1. *agitation: a state of turbulent change or development*
2. *utterly: complete; absolute*
3. *foreign: of, from, in, or characteristic of a country or language other than one's own; dealing with or relating to other countries*

With these words the mill-owner beckoned to his clerk who was standing by to produce samples of the stuff that was being manufactured in his mill. Pointing to it he said: 'Look at this stuff. This is the latest variety turned out by our mill. It is meeting with a widespread demand. We manufacture it from the waste. Naturally, therefore, it is cheap. We send it as far North as the valleys of the Himalayas. We have agencies all over the country, even in places where your voice or your agents can never reach. You can thus see that we do not stand in need of more agents. Besides, you ought to know that India's production of cloth falls far short of its requirements. The question of Swadeshi, therefore, largely resolves itself into one of production. The moment we can increase our production sufficiently, and improve its quality to the necessary extent, the import of foreign cloth will automatically cease. My advice to you, therefore, is not to carry on your agitation on its present lines, but to turn your attention to the erection of fresh mills. What we need is not propaganda to inflate demand for our goods, but greater production.'

'Then, surely, you will bless my effort, if I am already engaged in that very thing,' I asked.

'How can that be?' he exclaimed, a bit puzzled, 'but may be, you are thinking of promoting the establishment of new mills, in which case you certainly deserve to be congratulated[1].'

' I am not doing exactly that,' I explained, 'but I am engaged in the revival of the spinning wheel.'

'What is that?' he asked, feeling still more at sea. I told him all about the spinning wheel, and the story of my long quest[2] after it, and added, 'I am entirely of your opinion; it is no use my becoming virtually an agent for the mills. That would do more harm than good to the country. Our mills will not be in want of custom[3] for a long time to come. My work should be, and therefore is, to organize the production of handspun cloth, and to find means for the disposal of the *khadi* thus produced. I am, therefore, concentrating my attention on the production of *khadi*. I swear by this form of Swadeshi, because through it I can provide work to the semi-starved, semi-employed women of India. My idea is to get these women to spin yarn[4], and to clothe the people of India with *khadi* woven out of it. I do not know how far this movement is going to succeed, at present it is only in the incipient stage. But I have full faith in it. At any

1. *congratulated: express pleasure at the happiness or good fortune of; praise for an achievement; feel pride or satisfaction*
2. *quest: a long or arduous search*
3. *custom: a traditional and widely accepted way of behaving or doing something that is specific to a particular society, place, or time; law established usage having the force of law or right*
4. *yarn: spun thread used for knitting, weaving, or sewing*

rate it can do no harm. On the contrary to the extent that it can add to the cloth production of the country, be it ever so small, it will represent so much solid gain. You will thus perceive that my movement is free from the evils mentioned by you.'

He replied, 'If you have additional production in view in organizing your movement, I have nothing to say against it. Whether the spinning wheel can make headway in this age of power machinery[1] is another question. But I for one wish you every success.

1. *machinery: machines collectively, or the components of a machine*

CHAPTER 166

ITS RISING TIDE

I must not devote any more chapters here to a description of the further progress of *khadi*. It would be outside the scope of these chapters to give a history of my various activities after they came before the public eye, and I must not attempt it, if only because to do so would require a treatise on the subject. My object in writing these chapters is simply to describe how certain things, as it were spontaneously, presented themselves to me in the course of my experiments with truth.

To resume, then, the story of the non-co-operation movement. Whilst the powerful Khilafat agitation set up by the Ali Brothers was in full progress, I had long discussions on the subject with the late Maulana Abdul Bari and the other *Ulema*, especially, with regard to the extent to which a Musalman could observe the rule of non-violence. In the end they all agreed that Islam did not forbid its followers from following non-violence as a policy, and further, that, while they were pledged to that policy, they were bound faithfully to carry it out. At last the non-co-operation resolution was moved in the Khilafat conference, and carried after prolonged deliberations[1]. I have a vivid recollection how once at Allahabad a committee sat all night deliberating upon the subject. In the beginning the late Hakim Saheb was skeptical as to the practicability of non-violent non-co-operation. But after his scepticism was overcome he threw himself into it heart and soul, and his help proved invaluable[2] to the movement.

Next, the non-co-operation resolution was moved by me at the Gujarat political conference that was held shortly afterwards. The preliminary contention raised by the opposition was that it was not competent to a provincial conference to adopt a resolution in advance of the Congress. As against this, I suggested that the restriction could apply only to a backward movement; but as for going forward, the subordinate[3] organizations were not only fully competent[4], but were in duty bound to do so, if they had in them the necessary girt and confidence.

1. *deliberations: long and careful consideration*
2. *invaluable: extremely useful*
3. *subordinate: lower in rank or position; of less or secondary importance*
4. *competent: having the necessary ability or knowledge to do something successfully; efficient and capable; having legal authority to deal with a particular matter*

No permission, I argued was needed to try to enhance the prestige of the parent institution, provided one did it at one's own risk. The proposition was then discussed on its merits, the debate being marked by its keenness no less than the atmosphere of 'sweet reasonableness' in which it was conducted. On the ballot being taken the resolution was declared carried by an overwhelming majority. The successful passage of the resolution was due not a little to the personality[1] of Sjt. Vallabhbhai and Abbas Tyabji. The latter was the president, and his leanings were all in favour of the non-co-operation resolution.

The All-India Congress Committss resolved to hold a special session of the Congress in September 1920 at Calcutta to deliberate on this question Preparations were made for it on a large scale. Lala Lajpat Rai was elected President. Congress and Khilafat specials were run to Calcutta from Bombay. At Calcutta there was a mammoth gathering of delegates and visitors.

At the request of Maulana Shaukat Ali I prepared a draft of the non-co-operation resolution in the train. Up to this time I had more or less avoided the use of the word non-violent in my drafts. I invariably made use of this word in my speeches. My vocabulary on the subject was still in process of formation. I found that I could not bring home my meaning to purely Moslem audiences with the help of the Samskrit equivalent for non-violent. I therefore asked Maulana Abdul Kalam Azad to give me some other equivalent for it. He suggested the word *ba-aman*; similarly for non-co-operation he suggested the phrase *tark-i-mavalat*.

Thus, while I was still busy devising suitable Hindi, Gujarati and Urdu phraseology for non-co-operation, I was called upon to frame the non-co-operation resolution for that eventful Congress. In the original draft the word 'non-violent' had been left out by me. I had handed over the draft to Maulana Shaukat Ali who was travelling in the same compartment, without noticing the omission[2]. During the night I discovered the error. In the morning I sent Mahadev with the message that the omission should be made good before the draft was sent to the press. But I have an impression that the draft was printed before the insertion could be made. The Subjects Committee was to have met the same evening. I had therefore to make the necessary correction in the printed[3] copies of the draft[4]. I afterwards saw that there would have been great difficulty, had I not been ready with my draft.

1. *personality: the combination of characteristics or qualities that from an individual's distinctive character*
2. *omission: someone or something that has been left out*
3. *printed: produce by a mechanical process involving the transfer of text or designs to paper; produce in such a way; publish; produce a paper copy of information stored on a computer*
4. *draft: a preliminary version of a piece of writing; a plan or sketch*

None the less my plight was pitiable indeed. I was absolutely at sea as to who would support the resolution and who would oppose it. Nor had I any idea as to the attitude that Lalaji would adopt. I only saw an imposing phalanx of veteran warriors assembled for the fray at Calcutta, Dr. Besant, Pandit Malaviyaji, Sjt. Vijayaraghavachari, Pandit Motilalji and the Deshabandhu being some of them.

In my resolution non-co-operation was postulated only with a view to obtaining redress of the Punjab and the Khilafat wrongs. That, however, did not appeal to Sjt. Vijayaraghavachari. 'If non-co-operation was to be declared, why should it be with reference to particular wrongs? The absence of Swaraj was the biggest wrong that the country was labouring under; it should be against that that non-co-operation should be directed,' he argued. Pandit Motilalji also wanted the demand for Swaraj to be included in the resolution. I readily accepted the suggestion and incorporated the demand for Swaraj in my resolution, which was passed after an exhaustive, serious and somewhat stormy[1] discussion.

Motilalji was the first to join the movement. I still remember the sweet discussion that I had with him on the resolution. He suggested some changes in its phraseology which I adopted. He undertook to win the Deshabandhu for the movement. The Deshbandhu's heart was inclined towards it, but he felt sceptical as to the capacity of the people to carry out the programme. It was only at the Nagpur Congress that he and Lalaji accepted it whole heartedly.

I felt the loss of the late Lokamanya very deeply at the special session. It has been my firm faith to this day that, had the Lokamanya been then alive, he would have given his benedictions to me on that occasion. But even if it had been otherwise, and he had opposed the movement, I should still have esteemed his opposition as a privilege and an education for myself. We had our differences of opinion always, but they never led to bitterness. He always allowed me to believe that the ties between us were of the closest. Even as I write these lines, the circumstances of his death stand forth vividly before my mind's eye. It was about the hour of midnight, when Patwardhan, who was then working with me, conveyed over the telephone the news of his death. I was at that time surrounded by my companions. Spontaneously the exclamation escaped my lips, 'My strongest bulwark is gone.' The non-co-operation movement was

1. *stormy: a sudden violent display of strong feeling*

then in full swing[1], and I was eagerly looking forward to encouragement and inspiration[2] from him. What his attitude would have been with regard to the final phase of non-cooperation will always be a matter of speculation[3], and an idle[4] one at that. But this much is certain that the deep void left by his death weighed heavily upon everyone present at Calcutta. Everyone felt the absence of his counsels in that hour of crisis in the nation's history.

1. *swing: move or cause to move in a smooth, curving line; attempt to hit or punch, especially with a wide curving movement; throw with such a movement*
2. *inspiration: a feeling of enthusiasm driving someone to do something*
3. *speculation: theory or conjecture without firm evidence*
4. *idle: laziness; indolence*

CHAPTER 167

AT NAGPUR

The resolutions adopted at the Calcutta special session of the Congress were to be confirmed at its annual session at Nagpur. Here again, as at Calcutta there was a great rush of visitors and delegates. The number of delegates in the Congress had not been limited yet. As a result, so far as I can remember, the figure on this occasion reached about fourteen thousand. Lalaji pressed for a slight amendment to the clause about the boycott of schools, which I accepted. Similarly some amendments were made at the instance of the Deshabandhu, after which the non-co-operation resolution was passed unanimously.

The resolution regarding the revision of the Congress constitution too was to be taken up at this session of the Congress. The sub-committee's draft was presented at the Calcutta special session. The matter had therefore been thoroughly ventilated and thrashed out. At the Nagpur session, where it came up for final disposal, Sjt. C. Vijayaraghavacharia was the President. The Subjects Committee passed the draft with only one important change. In my draft the number of delegates had been fixed, I think, at 1,500; the Subjects Committee substituted in its place the figure 6,000. In my opinion this increase was the result of hasty[1] judgment, and experience of all these years has only confirmed me in my view. I hold it to be an utter delusion to believe that a large number of delegates is in any way a help to the better conduct of the business, or that it safeguards the principle of democracy. Fifteen hundred delegates, jealous of the interests of the people, broad-minded and truthful, would any day be a better safeguard for democracy than six thousand irresponsible men chosen anyhow. To safeguard democracy the people must have a keen[2] sense of independence, self-respect and their oneness, and should insist upon choosing as their representatives only such persons as are good and true. But obsessed with the idea of numbers as the Subjects Committee was, it would have liked to go even beyond the figure of six thousand. The limit[3] of six thousand was therefore in the nature of a compromise.

1. *hasty: something done in a hurry*
2. *keen: showing eagerness or enthusiasm*
3. *limit: a restriction*

The question of the goal of the Congress formed a subject for keen discussion. In the constitution that I had presented, the goal of the Congress was the attainment of Swaraj within the British Empire if possible and without if necessary. A party in the Congress wanted to limit the goal to Swaraj within the British Empire only. Its viewpoint was put forth by Pandit Malaviyaji and Mr. Jinnah. But they were not able to get many votes. Again the draft constitution provided that the means for the attainment were to be peaceful and legitimate[1]. This condition too came in for opposition, it being contended that there should be no restriction upon the means to be adopted. But the Congress adopted the original draft after an instructive and frank discussion. I am of opinion that, if this constitution had been worked out by the people honestly, intelligently and zealously, it would have become a potent[2] instrument of mass education, and the very process of working it out would have brought us Swaraj. But a discussion of the theme would be irrelevant here.

Resolutions about Hindu-Muslim unity, the removal of untouchability and *khadi* too were passed in this Congress, and since then the Hindu members of the Congress have taken upon themselves the responsibility of ridding Hinduism of the curse of untouchability, and the Congress has established a living bond of relationship with the 'skeletons[3]' of India through *khadi*. The adoption of non-co-operation for the sake of the Khilafat was itself a great practical attempt made by the Congress to bring about Hindu-Muslim unity.

1. *legitimate: permitted by law*
2. *potent: having great power; influence, or effect*
3. *skeletons: framework of bone cartilage supports the body or other structure*

CHAPTER 168

FAREWELL

The time has now come to bring these chapters to a close.

My life from this point onward has been so public that there is hardly anything about it that people do not know. Moreover, since 1921 I have worked in such close association with the Congress leaders that I can hardly describe any episode in my life since then without referring to my relations with them. For though Shraddhanandji, the Deshabandhu, Hakim Saheb and Lalaji are no more with us today, we have the good luck to have a host of other veteran[1] Congress leaders still living and working in our midst. The history of the Congress, since the great changes in it that I have described above, is still in the making. And my principal experiments during the past seven years have all been made through the Congress. A reference to my relations with the leaders would therefore be unavoidable[2], if I set about describing my experiments further. And this I may not do, at any rate for the present, if only from a sense of propriety. Lastly, my conclusions from my current experiments can hardly as yet be regarded as decisive. It therefore seems to me to be my plain[3] duty to close this narrative here. In fact my pen instinctively refuses to proceed further.

It is not without a wrench that I have to take leave of the reader. I set a high value on my experiments. I do not know whether I have been able to do justice to them. I can only say that I have spared no pains to give a faithful narrative. To describe truth, as it has appeared to me, and in the exact manner in which I have arrived at it, has been my ceaseless effort. The exercise has given me ineffable mental peace, because, it has been my fond hope that it might bring faith in Truth and Ahimsa to waverers.

My uniform experience has convinced me that there is no other God than Truth. And if every page of these chapters does not proclaim[4] to the reader that the only means for the realization of Truth is Ahimsa, I shall deem all my labour in writing these chapters to have been in vain.

1. *veteran: a person who has had long experience in a particular field*
2. *unavoidable: not able to be avoided or prevented; inevitable*
3. *plain: easy to perceive or understand; clear*
4. *proclaim: announce officially or publicly; declare to be; indicate clearly*

And, even though my efforts in this behalf may prove fruitless, let the readers know that the vehicle, not the great principle, is at fault. After all, however sincere my strivings after Ahimsa may have been, they have still been imperfect and inadequate. The little fleeting glimpses, therefore, that I have been able to have of Truth can hardly convey an idea of the indescribable lustre of Truth, a million times more intense than that of the sun we daily see with our eyes. In fact what I have caught is only the faintest glimmer of that mighty effulgence. But this much I can say with assurance, as a result of all my experiments, that a perfect vision of Truth can only follow a complete realization of Ahimsa.

To see the universal and all-pervading Spirit of Truth face to face one must be able to love the meanest of creation[1] as oneself. And a man who aspires after that cannot afford to keep out of any field of life. That is why my devotion to Truth has drawn me into the field of politics; and I can say without the slightest hesitation, and yet in all humility, that those who say that religion has nothing to do with politics do not know what religion means.

Identification with everything that lives is impossible without self-purification; without self-purification the observance of the law of Ahimsa must remain an empty dream; God can never be realized by one who is not pure of heart. Self-purification therefore must mean purification in all the walks of life. And purification being highly infectious, purification of oneself necessarily leads to the purification of one's surroundings.

But the path of self-purification is hard and steep. To attain to perfect purity one has to become absolutely passion-free in thought, speech and action; to rise above the opposing currents of love and hatred, attachment and repulsion. I know that I have not in me as yet that triple purity, in spite of constant ceaseless striving for it. That is why the world's praise fails to move me, indeed it very often stings me. To conquer the subtle passions seems to me to be harder far than the physical conquest of the world by the force of arms. Ever since my return to India I have had experience of the dormant[2] passions lying hidden within me. The knowledge of them has made me feel humiliated though not defeated. The experiences and experiments have sustained me and given me great joy. But I know that I have still before me a difficult path to traverse[3].

1. *creation: the action or process of creating; a thing which has been made or invented, especially something showing artistic talent*
2. *dormant: temporarily inactive*
3. *traverse: travel or extend across or through; cross a rock face by means of a series of sideways movements from one practicable line of ascent or descent to another*

I must reduce myself to zero. So long as a man does not of his own free will put himself last among his fellow creatures, there is no salvation[1] for him. Ahimsa is the farthest limit of humility.

In bidding farewell to the reader, for the time being at any rate, I ask him to join with me in prayer to the God of Truth that He may grant me the boon of Ahimsa in mind, word and deed.

1. *salvation: preservation or deliverance from harm, ruin, or loss; a source or means of being saved in this way*